Memories of Home

Food, Family, and Friends

Beta Sigma Phi

EDITORIAL STAFF

Managing Editor	Mary Cummings
Executive Editor	Anita McKay
Editorial Manager	Georgia Brazil
Editor	Anne Lacy Boswell
Associate Editor	Linda Bennie
Project Coordinator	Tanis Westbrook
Award Selection Judge	Charlene Sproles
Art Director	Steve Newman
Production Design	Jessie Anglin, Sara Anglin
Test Kitchen	Charlene Sproles

Line Art ©2002 Barbara Ball

Cover Photograph: California Strawberry Commission

© Favorite Recipes® Press, A Division of Heritage House, Inc. 2002
  P.O. Box 305141, Nashville, Tennessee 37230

ISBN: 0-87197-485-1

Manufactured in the United States of America
First Printing 2002

Recipe for cover photograph is on page 190.

Contents

Some memories may have been edited for clarity and/or length.

Beta Sigma Phi Fact Sheet

Description International women's social, cultural, and service organization.

International Headquarters Beta Sigma Phi International
1800 West 91st Place
Kansas City, Missouri 64114-0500

Founded 1931, by Walter W. Ross in Abilene, Kansas, with seven members.

Purpose To provide women with a social outlet, a cultural forum, and service opportunities.

Membership More than 165,000 active members. Chapters are located in more than 20 countries, with chapters in all states of the United States and all provinces of Canada.

Service Chapters donate between two and three hundred thousand hours of time each year to charitable causes and raise more than $2 million annually. Internationally, chapters contribute to several special funds. These include:
- International Endowment Fund donating to health research groups and charitable organizations
- Disaster Relief Fund aiding members who are victims of natural disasters
- Breast Cancer Research Endowment Fund supporting research organizations
- Scholarship Fund awarding scholarships to members, as well as to their children and grandchildren

Other Facts Beta Sigma Phi is the largest Greek-letter women's association in the world. It is not a secret group, not affiliated with any school or university, and is nonpolitical and nonsectarian. Members have included: Hillary Rodham Clinton, Barbara Bush, Ginger Rogers, Eleanor Roosevelt, and many other outstanding women.

When It All Started . . .

*I*n 1931, during the Great Depression, there was a need for an organization that could bring women together and expose them to a social, cultural, and educational climate that was not available in those difficult times. Most important, there was a need for friendship and support from other women. Beta Sigma Phi was created out of this need. It did not take long before Beta Sigma Phis were helping others. Members worked together to raise $22 million in war bonds during World War II.

The 1950s brought peace and prosperity to the world, and Beta Sigma Phi membership doubled. This era was filled with grand balls, elegant teas, and the growing strength of sisterhood as thousands of women joined Beta Sigma Phi. As the times have changed, so has Beta Sigma Phi.

The 1960s and 1970s found our organization less formal, but the ideals were the same. Now in the 21st century, our 200,000 members find that the more we grow, the more valuable we become to our sisters and our communities.

Typical chapters enjoy socials that range from informal gatherings to gala affairs that often include friends and family. Fascinating cultural programs offer insight into subjects that range from the arts and gardening to in-home businesses. Membership provides opportunities to contribute to community, develop lifelong friends, and polish leadership skills.

Our members raise more than $3 million for local charities and donate over two hundred thousand volunteer hours in an average year. Each chapter determines its own service projects and participation is always voluntary. The chapters have created International Funds that donate millions of dollars to health research groups, hunger projects, and other worthwhile causes. Members and their families can receive assistance through international loan, scholarship, and disaster funds.

What makes us unique? Unlike a college sorority, our organization has members of all ages and educational backgrounds. Our sisterhood constantly redefines itself through the diversity and vitality of members who share their ideas, talents, and enthusiasm. That is why we are known as "The Friendship Organization."

Find out more about Beta Sigma Phi. We are dedicated to helping women fulfill their lives. Whether your fulfillment lies in making new friends, helping your community, or just finding time for you, the choice is yours.

To learn more about how you can join Beta Sigma Phi in your area, or to start a chapter, contact Beta Sigma Phi International. We will be happy to share the benefits of "The Friendship Organization."

Beta Sigma Phi

This cookbook is lovingly dedicated to the members of Beta Sigma Phi, their chapters, and their councils, for they have created this cookbook.

Using the cookbook is the members' way to raise money for worthy causes which has enabled the Beta Sigma Phis to contribute $7,153,709.11 to The International Endowment Fund, The Disaster Fund, The Loan Fund, The Exemplar Fund, The Scholarship Fund, and The Breast Cancer Fund.

Congratulations to all the members, chapters, and councils of Beta Sigma Phi for making this great gift to life possible.

From Your Friends at Beta Sigma Phi International

A Note from the Editors

The 2002 Beta Sigma Phi cookbook is more than just a cookbook. The editors have included some of the history and personality of this outstanding organization. Each member was invited to submit her best recipes as well as favorite memories of food, family, and friends. Some of those memories appear as chapter openers or scattered throughout the book.

Notice that in addition to the ususal symbol ✤ indicating the recipe prize winners, we have included (in parentheses) when a member has belonged to Beta Sigma Phi for 25 years or longer. Amazingly, some contributors have been members for more than 50 years. Those golden members have been designated by 🌹 representing the Beta Sigma Phi yellow rose.

We know that this book will be cherished for years to come and passed through future generations of Beta Sigma Phi members.

Snacks and Beverages

The first year my husband and I were married, money was very tight. Since we were spending Christmas Day with our families, we decided to make punch to celebrate our first Christmas Eve together. That tradition has made it through two grown children and two grandchildren. We have our Christmas toast with our punch before we open our presents. We haven't missed a Christmas yet.

Loise Evelyn Shell (25 years)
Xi Alpha Alpha Lambda
Richmond, Texas

DEVILED PEANUTS

3 cups shelled raw peanuts	1½ teaspoons onion salt
2 tablespoons butter or margarine	⅛ teaspoon cayenne or red pepper
½ teaspoon garlic powder	2 teaspoons chili powder
	1 teaspoon celery salt

Remove the hulls from the peanuts by rubbing between hands and set aside. Combine the margarine, garlic powder, onion salt, cayenne pepper, chili powder and celery salt in a mixing bowl. Add the peanuts and stir to coat well. Spread on a baking pan. Bake at 350 degrees for several minutes or until lightly browned, stirring frequently. Yield: 3 cups.

Pat Duncan
Durant, Oklahoma

MEMORIES

Back in the '50s, I met a woman while we were both patients in the hospital. She invited me over to her house and we became good friends, and then she invited me to join Beta Sigma Phi. I've always been thankful to her. We traveled and moved a lot, including Nebraska, New Mexico, San Antonio, Houston, and now Waco, Texas; no matter where we went, I had sisters. Beta Sigma Phi is a wonderful organization. I would give up any of my other clubs, but never BSP.

G. Juliana Swanson (43 years), Preceptor Eta Eta
Waco, Texas

SUPER BOWL SNACK

This is a family favorite. When everyone arrives at my house, they look for the snacks, and when I visit, they look for the filled container that I bring with me.

10 cups Crispix	2 tablespoons Worcestershire sauce
2 cups Cheddar cheese crackers	2 tablespoons liquid smoke
2 cups small twisted pretzels	¼ teaspoon garlic salt
2 cups mixed nuts	¼ teaspoon onion salt
1 cup small bagel chips	
½ cup (1 stick) butter or margarine	

Combine the Crispix, crackers, pretzels, nuts and bagel chips in a large sealable bag. Heat the butter, Worcestershire sauce and liquid smoke in a small saucepan over medium-low heat; heat until the butter has melted. Pour over the cereal mixture, gently shaking to coat well. Pour the mixture into a 10×15-inch baking pan. Sprinkle with the garlic and onion salts and mix well. Bake at 250 degrees for 1 hour, stirring every 20 minutes. Let stand until cool. Yield: 3 quarts.

Marilyn Gillham (44 years), Omicron Master
Redmond, Oregon

GIGGLE MIX

½ cup honey	1¼ cups small twisted pretzels
1 cup packed brown sugar	1 (12-ounce) can mixed nuts
1½ cups (3 sticks) butter or margarine	1 (12-ounce) can peanuts
1 (12-ounce) box Crispix	

Combine the honey, brown sugar and butter in a small saucepan over medium-low heat. Bring to a boil and cook until thickened and clear, stirring constantly. Place the Crispix, pretzels, mixed nuts and peanuts in a 9×13-inch baking dish. Pour the brown sugar mixture over the cereal mixture, stirring gently to coat well. Bake at 250 degrees for 40 minutes, stirring after 20 minutes. Spread over waxed paper and let stand until cool. Yield: 1 quart.

Trudy Ruch (26 years), Xi Eta
Omaha, Nebraska

BIKER'S BUDDIES

1 cup (2 sticks) butter or margarine, softened	½ teaspoon maple extract
2 pounds peanut butter	4 teaspoons baking soda
6 eggs	1 pound "M&M's" chocolate candies (optional)
9 cups rolled oats	
1 pound packed brown sugar	1 pound butterscotch chips (optional)
1½ teaspoons honey or corn syrup	1½ pounds chopped dried fruit (optional)
1½ teaspoons vanilla extract	

Cream the butter and peanut butter in a mixing bowl. Mix in the eggs, oats, brown sugar, honey, vanilla, maple extract and baking soda. Stir in the remaining ingredients. Scoop onto a 9×13-inch baking sheet using an ice cream scoop. Bake at 350 degrees for 15 minutes. Yield: 4 to 5 dozen.

Connie Swain (25 years), Preceptor Beta Iota
Garner, North Carolina

MEMORIES

Growing up on our Kansas farm during the Great Depression and the Dust Bowl Days we didn't have much money and we seldom went anywhere except to our country school. There were eight children in our family; four girls and four boys. We had no electricity or gas. We cooked mostly with a wood fire and heated our home with wood. We used kerosene lamps during the cold, dark winter evenings. Making popcorn balls was a pleasant way to relax and have fun.

Lois O. Tucker, Laureate Alpha Omega
Wichita, Kansas

I have made popcorn balls for Halloween treats for 40 years and I still have three generations coming for them.

Betty Beith (39 years), Laureate Alpha Omicron
La Grande, Oregan

Our chapter hired a horse-drawn sleigh to take us Christmas caroling. As we sang carols in a Senior Citizens park, we gave out soft popcorn balls to the seniors.

Joyce L. Dole, Preceptor Nu Xi
Redding, California

MARSHMALLOW POPCORN BALLS

These popcorn balls are the best because they are soft and chewy. My son (age 30) and my daughter (age 27) both look forward to this treat at Thanksgiving and Christmas.

1 (1-pound) package miniature marshmallows	**1/2 cup sugar**
1/2 cup (1 stick) butter or margarine	**1 teaspoon vanilla extract**
	4 quarts popped popcorn

Combine the marshmallows, butter, sugar and vanilla in a saucepan and cook over medium-low heat stirring constantly until melted. Place popcorn in a roasting pan and pour the marshmallow mixture over the popcorn, mixing lightly. Shape into balls. Yield: 15 balls.

Mary Rector, Epsilon
Watertown, South Dakota

ANNA MARIE'S CARAMEL CORN

I grew up as an only child and married a man who was one of eleven. His sister, Anna Marie, would make anything your heart desired and her caramel corn was wonderful!

2 cups packed brown sugar	**1 teaspoon salt**
1 cup (2 sticks) butter or margarine	**1 teaspoon vanilla extract**
1/2 cup light corn syrup	**1 teaspoon baking soda**
	7 quarts popped popcorn

Combine the brown sugar, butter, corn syrup and salt in a saucepan and mix well. Bring to a boil. Boil for 5 minutes, stirring constantly. Remove from the heat and stir in the vanilla and baking soda. Pour the brown sugar mixture over the popcorn in a large bowl and mix lightly to coat. Spread the mixture in 2 shallow baking pans and bake at 200 degrees for 60 minutes, stirring every 15 minutes. Cool completely; break into bite-sized pieces. Store in airtight containers or sealable bags. Yield: 7 quarts.

Carol H. Goll, Xi Alpha Epsilon Xi
Mabank, Texas

WALKING TACO

This is a unique snack that can be made for your sorority ways and means fundraiser.

1 pound ground beef	**Shredded lettuce**
1 envelope taco seasoning mix	**Sliced black olives**
3/4 cup water	**Sliced green onions**
6 (1-ounce) bags corn chips	**Taco sauce**
Shredded Cheddar cheese	**Sour cream**

Brown the ground beef in a skillet, stirring until crumbly; drain. Stir in the taco seasoning mix and water. Bring to a boil; reduce the heat. Simmer for 5 minutes, stirring occasionally. Cut a small hole in the top of each corn chip bag to release air. Crush the corn chips slightly. Cut off the top of the bag. Spoon layers of the ground beef, cheese, lettuce, olives, green onions, taco sauce and sour cream over the corn chips. Mix and eat right out of the bag. Yield: 6 servings.

Loween Clayberg (28 years), Preceptor Delta Beta
Webster City, Iowa

MEMORIES

I had surgery on my nose and was at home feeling down; my face was black and blue and there was a wad of cotton under my nose. The doorbell rang, I went to the door, and to my surprise, there was a person with a paper sack over her head with a gift from my secret sister. I shut the door and had a good laugh, which was something I really needed. I still laugh after all these years when I think about it.

Sue Music, Alpha Pi Rho
Amarillo, Texas

ARTICHOKE PIZZA APPETIZER

2 (8-count) cans crescent rolls	1 (14-ounce) can artichoke hearts, drained, chopped
3/4 cup mayonnaise	
1/4 cup grated Parmesan cheese	1 1/2 cups shredded Cheddar cheese
1 envelope Italian dressing mix	Paprika to taste

Separate the dough into 4 rectangles. Place crosswise in a lightly greased 10×15-inch jelly roll pan and press onto the bottom and up the sides of the pan to form a crust, pressing to seal perforations and seams. Bake at 375 degrees for 10 minutes or until golden brown. Cool completely. Combine the mayonnaise, Parmesan cheese and salad dressing mix in a medium bowl. Stir in the artichokes and 1 cup of the Cheddar cheese. Spread the mixture over the cooled crust; sprinkle with the remaining 1/2 cup Cheddar cheese and paprika. Bake for 10 minutes longer. Cut into 1-inch squares and serve warm.
Yield: 60 servings.

Amy Shugart, Kappa Kappa
Baytown, Texas

MEMORIES

*M*y mother and mother-in-law taught me to cook for my family and friends as an expression of love, not a drudgery that has to be performed.

Willie Sloan (44 years), Laureate Alpha Beta
La Mesa, New Mexico

CHEESE PUFFS

Every time that I make these, I am reminded of when my grandmother, Gram, would come to visit for a month every summer. She didn't cook much, but she would make these for cocktail hour. I couldn't wait until the Cheese Puffs were served. I would watch as Gram would pick up her puff with her long finger-nails and delicately take a bite of it. She would then compliment my mom on a job well done. Unfortunately, she did not live long enough to see me serve the cheese puffs, but making them gives me great pleasure because I feel the glamorous Gram!

1/2 cup (1 stick) butter or margarine, softened	1/4 cup mayonnaise
1 (5-ounce) jar Old English cheese spread	1 loaf unsliced white bread, crusts trimmed

Combine the butter, cheese and mayonnaise in a medium bowl and blend well. Set aside. Cut the bread loaf into 1-inch cubes. Spread the cheese mixture onto five sides of each cube and arrange with the uncoated side down on a lightly greased 10x15-inch baking sheet. Bake at 350 degrees for 5 to 10 minutes or until light brown. Yield: 10 servings.

Maureen Trentadue, Zeta Iota
Fort Wayne, Indiana

PARTY SANDWICH

My mother, my sisters, and I have started taking four- to five-day trips without our husbands or children. We spend the days sharing family memories as well as making new memories. We like to find special eating places, craft and antique shops, and other historical settings. Our destination is not as important as the fun and laughter we share in getting there. My sisters and our mother (who turned 81 years young this spring) look forward to these special days together. This sandwich recipe was served to us as we stopped to visit relatives in the Kansas City area.

1 (10- to 12-inch) round loaf unsliced pumpernickle bread	3 tomatoes, thinly sliced
	1 pound sliced deli roast pork, ham or corned beef
8 ounces cream cheese, softened	
1 bunch green onions, thinly sliced	8 to 12 ounces sliced bacon, crisp-cooked, crumbled
1 teaspoon Italian seasoning	Mayonnaise
1 pound sliced deli roast beef	

Cut a 1-inch slice off the top of the bread and set aside. Hollow out the loaf to resemble a bowl. Reserve the scooped-out bread for another purpose. Mix cream cheese, green onions and Italian seasoning in a medium bowl. Spread over the bottom and up the side of the bowl. Layer roast beef, half the tomato slices, roast pork, the remaining tomato slices, and bacon in the bread bowl. The bread bowl should be full to the top. Spread mayonnaise on the inside of the bread cap and place on the top. Wrap in plastic wrap and refrigerate for 8 to 10 hours or until ready to serve. Slice into pie-shaped pieces. Yield: 8 to 10 servings.

Gretchen Hild (25 years), Alpha Nu
Norfolk, Nebraska.

❖ SAUSAGE STARS

I've used this recipe for several sorority parties over the years and each time it seems to be well liked.

1 (12-ounce) package won ton wrappers	1¹/₂ cups shredded Monterey Jack cheese
¹/₄ cup vegetable oil	1 cup ranch salad dressing
1 pound bulk sausage	
1¹/₂ cups shredded Cheddar cheese	1 (4-ounce) can sliced black olives

Separate the won ton wrappers. Brush each lightly with the oil. Press each wrapper into a miniature muffin cup, arranging edges to form a star. Bake at 350 degrees for 8 to 10 minutes or until golden. Remove from muffin cups and to a baking sheet. Brown the sausage in a skillet, stirring until crumbly; drain. Combine the sausage, Cheddar cheese, Monterey Jack cheese, ranch dressing and olives in a medium bowl; mix well. Fill the won ton shells with the sausage mixture. Bake for 10 minutes or until the cheese is bubbly. Yield: 24 to 36 servings.

Janet Walker, Xi Beta Epsilon
Woodward, Oklahoma

SHRIMP PINEAPPLE DELIGHT

Christmas is special at my home on Christmas Eve. In addition to eggnog and all the other yummy munchies that I serve, the Shrimp Pineapple is always a big hit and very festive looking. Even the kiddies dive in.

1 whole pineapple	1 pound small shrimp, cooked, shelled, deveined
1 (12-ounce) bottle of cocktail sauce	

Cut off the top of the pineapple and set aside. Scoop out the center of the pineapple, leaving ¹/₂-inch-thick sides to form a bowl. Cut out and discard the pineapple core and place the pineapple pulp in a blender (or food processor). Add the cocktail sauce and blend on high for 30 seconds or until well blended. Cover the outside of the pineapple with the shrimp using wooden picks. Pour the pineapple pulp mixture into the pineapple shell and serve. Yield: 12 servings.

Karen Bouvier, Xi Phi Iota
Hesperia, California

VEGGIE TORTILLA PINWHEELS

8 ounces cream cheese, softened	¹/₂ cup chopped cauliflower
4 teaspoons ranch salad dressing mix	¹/₄ cup chopped green onions
1 (3-ounce) package dried beef, chopped	¹/₄ cup chopped stuffed olives
¹/₂ cup chopped broccoli	5 (8-inch) flour tortillas Salsa

Combine cream cheese and salad dressing mix in a medium bowl and mix well. Stir in the dried beef, broccoli, cauliflower, green onions and olives. Spread the cream cheese mixture over the tortillas. Roll tightly and wrap in plastic wrap. Refrigerate for 2 hours or longer. Cut the tortillas into ¹/₂-inch slices and serve with salsa. Yield: 60 servings.

Laura Mikiska, Theta
Vincennes, Indiana

SCOTCH EGGS

My mother made these "surprise bundles" for me when I was a child.

1 pound bulk pork sausage	4 cups Italian seasoned bread crumbs
6 hard-cooked eggs	Vegetable oil for deep-frying
4 eggs, beaten	

Divide the sausage into 6 portions. Press the sausage around the eggs, sealing completely. Dip the sausage-enclosed eggs in the beaten eggs; roll in the bread crumbs to coat. Fry in hot deep oil for 5 minutes or until brown; drain. Serve hot or cold. Yield: 6 servings.

Sandra Sweeney, Xi Beta Beta
Port Alberni, British Columbia, Canada

MEMORIES

My friend Jean Wolford and I spent 27 years in the sorority, planning many theme parties and special events. Jean passed away six years ago, and as for me, my brain is often willing to put forth 100% effort, but my body sometimes isn't. It's a comfort to know my younger sorority sisters are carrying the torch on to plan memorable events.

Joyce Horvath (33 years), Preceptor Epsilon Lambda
Wellington, Ohio

BAGEL DIP

This dip is easy to make but tastes great. It has been enjoyed at a number of parties.

2 cups sour cream	1 tablespoon onion
1½ cups mayonnaise	flakes
8 ounces dried beef,	2 teaspoons MSG
snipped	1 teaspoon dillweed
1 tablespoon parsley	
flakes	

Combine the sour cream, mayonnaise, dried beef, parsley flakes, onion flakes, MSG and dillweed in a bowl and mix well. Spoon into a serving dish. Chill, covered, until serving time. Cut assorted bagels into wedges and serve with the dip. Yield: 4½ cups.

Susan Dugger, Pi Gamma
Decorah, Iowa

HOT ARTICHOKE DIP

All the ladies in my family are terrific cooks. We all try to please one another. This was the winning recipe in 2001. Our niece who is just learning to cook won the honor.

1 (14-ounce) can	½ cup grated Parmesan
artichoke hearts,	cheese
drained, chopped	8 ounces mozzarella
1 cup mayonnaise	cheese, shredded
½ cup cottage cheese	½ cup salsa

Combine the ingredients in a bowl and mix well. Spoon into a 2-quart baking dish. Bake at 350 degrees for 30 minutes or until hot and bubbly. Serve with tortilla chips or corn chips. Yield: 4½ cups.

Patricia A. Siron, Laureate Gamma Nu
Mexico, Missouri

GO-GO'S CRAB MEAT DIP

My sister, Joan, was the only one in our family who could make this dip perfectly. We nicknamed her Go-Go because of her zest for life and endless energy. In March of 2001 she lost her battle with cancer and she is sadly missed, but she left all of us with wonderful memories of her in the kitchen. It did not matter who was coming to visit; she always had a dish ready for them when they arrived. Without fail their faces would light up with extreme pleasure when they sat down at the dinner table.

8 ounces cream cheese,	2 tablespoons milk
softened	¼ teaspoon salt
2 tablespoons	¼ teaspoon
mayonnaise	Worcestershire sauce
2 tablespoons finely	8 ounces fresh crab meat
chopped onion	or 2 (6-ounce) cans,
2 tablespoons ketchup	drained, flaked

Combine the cream cheese, mayonnaise, onion, ketchup, milk, salt and Worcestershire sauce in a mixing bowl. Beat with an electric mixer until well mixed. Fold in the crab meat. Chill, covered, for 3 to 4 hours before serving. Serve with crackers or French bread. Yield: 2½ cups.

Janie Gagnon, Omicron Zeta
Ocala, Florida

SHRIMP DUNK

We began having a family Christmas party when our sons were in junior high. It has allowed us to get to know our children's friends and their parents. Our boys are in college now and we held our eighth annual party this past year with many of the same people that attended the first year.

32 ounces Velveeta	3 (4-ounce) cans shrimp,
cheese	drained
2 (11-ounce) cans cream	
of shrimp soup	

Cut the cheese into cubes and place in a slow cooker. Heat on Low until the cheese melts. Add the soups and mix well. Stir in the shrimp. Serve from the slow cooker to keep warm. Serve with assorted crackers, toasted bread strips and sturdy chips for dunking. Yield: 7 cups.

Alice Wright, Xi Gamma
Pierre, South Dakota

SHRIMP DIP

I can picture my mom's smile as people would plead for this recipe. She served it for years before revealing that it had been printed on the cream of shrimp soup can! Thank you Campbell's for the great recipe and the great memories.

8 ounces cream cheese, softened	1 (4-ounce) can shrimp, drained
1 cup mayonnaise	1 cup chopped onion
1 (11-ounce) can cream of shrimp soup	1 tablespoon lemon juice

Combine the cream cheese and mayonnaise in a medium bowl and mix until well blended. Add the soup, shrimp, onion and lemon juice and stir until completely mixed. Chill until ready to serve. Yield: 4 cups.

Sharon Wilson, Zeta Nu
Cheney, Washington

CATTLEMAN'S DIP

1 cup chopped pecans	1/2 teaspoon garlic powder
2 tablespoons butter	
16 ounces cream cheese, softened	2 (4-ounce) packages dried beef, chopped
1 cup sour cream	1/4 cup chopped onion

Sauté the pecans in butter in a skillet until toasted; set aside. Combine the cream cheese, sour cream and garlic powder in a mixing bowl. Beat with an electric mixer until smooth. Stir in the dried beef and onion. Spoon into a greased 9x13-inch baking dish. Sprinkle the toasted pecans on top and bake at 350 degrees for 30 minutes. Serve with corn chips or favorite crackers. May substitute fat-free cream cheese for the cream cheese and fat-free sour cream for the sour cream. Yield: 20 servings.

Cris Sparks, Xi Alpha Theta
Frankfort, Kentucky

MEMORIES

The importance of family was instilled in my siblings and me. I'm very fortunate to have a husband with the same values. We hope that by sharing family vacations, our children will someday pass these values on to their own families.

Al Briggs, Xi Kappa Upsilon
Cameron, Missouri

DEVILED HAM DIP

Back during our early days of marriage, money, of course, was scarce. But we loved to get together. This recipe was inexpensive to serve but made us feel we were offering a great treat to our guests. It's not the money we spend to treat guests but the love we share with them.

1 (5-ounce) jar pimento cheese spread	1 teaspoon instant minced onions
1 (4-ounce) can deviled ham	4 drops of hot pepper sauce
1/4 cup mayonnaise	
1 tablespoon parsley flakes	

Combine the pimento cheese spread, deviled ham, mayonnaise, parsley flakes, instant minced onions and hot pepper sauce in a bowl. Beat with an electric mixer until well blended. Chill, covered, until serving time. Serve with corn chips and raw vegetables such as carrots, green bell peppers, celery and cucumbers. Yield: 1 1/4 cups.

Jayne Hornsby, Xi Alpha Xi
Hueytown, Alabama

SPICY CHEESE DIP

This has been a tradition on Christmas Eve since our children were small. They are grown now and still look forward to the dip when they come home on Christmas Eve.

1 pound ground beef	2 pounds Velveeta cheese
8 ounces bulk pork sausage	1 can tomatoes with green chiles, mashed
1 small onion, chopped	

Brown the ground beef and sausage with the onion in a skillet, stirring until ground beef and sausage are crumbly; drain. Combine cheese and tomatoes with green chiles in a large saucepan. Cook over low heat until cheese is melted, stirring continually. Add ground beef mixture and mix well. Spoon into a serving dish. Serve immediately with tortilla chips. Yield: 7 cups.

Linda Paulsen, Eta Delta
Ponca City, Oklahoma

Lana Lukes, Xi Beta Epsilon, Woodward, Oklahoma, makes **Baked Mushrooms** by cutting off button mushroom stems, sprinkling generously with steak seasoning and baking at 350 degrees for 15 minutes. Serve with melted Mexican Velveeta cheese or ranch dressing for dipping.

DAVE'S FAMOUS KILLER DIP

Everyone loves his dip so much that not a special occasion goes by that Dave isn't asked to bring it. It is also a favorite requested Christmas gift.

1 (28-ounce) can diced tomatoes
1 (14-ounce) can tomato sauce
1 (6-ounce) can tomato paste
1/4 cup seedless raspberry jam
4 garlic cloves, minced

2 to 4 banana peppers, thinly sliced
2 to 4 jalapeños, thinly sliced
2 bunches green onions, chopped
2 tablespoons chopped fresh cilantro

Combine the tomatoes, tomato sauce, tomato paste, raspberry jam, garlic, jalapeños, green onions and cilantro in a large bowl and mix well. Chill, covered, for 24 hours or longer. Yield: 7 cups.

Kathy Rand, Xi Alpha Pi
Madison, Wisconsin

❖ FRUIT SALSA WITH CINNAMON TORTILLA CHIPS

I always remember the excitement of being pregnant with our first child, because I was given this recipe and first tried it at a Lamaze class.

1 cup sugar
1/4 cup cinnamon
1/2 cup lemon-lime soda
1/2 cup water
1 package flour tortillas
3 or 4 large Granny Smith apples, cored

2 kiwifruit, peeled
1 quart fresh strawberries, hulls removed
Juice of 2 oranges
1/4 cup packed brown sugar

For the cinnamon tortilla chips, combine the sugar and cinnamon in a bowl and mix well. Combine the lemon-lime soda and water in a bowl and stir to mix. Cut the tortillas into triangles. Brush the lemon-lime soda mixture on one side of each tortilla. Coat the tortillas with the cinnamon mixture. Arrange on a foil-lined baking sheet. Bake at 475 degrees for 5 to 7 minutes or until bubbly. Remove tortillas to a wire rack to cool. For the salsa, combine the apples, kiwifruit and strawberries in a food processor. Process until coarsely chopped. Combine the chopped fruit, orange juice and brown sugar in a medium bowl and mix well. Chill, covered, for 8 to 10 hours before serving. May substitute 1 quart frozen strawberries, thawed and drained, for the fresh strawberries. Serve with the cinnamon tortilla chips. Yield: 12 to 16 servings.

Julie Hill, Upsilon Beta
Newark, Ohio

TEXAS CAVIAR

1 (15-ounce) can black beans, drained
1 (16-ounce) can Shoe Peg corn, drained
1 (10-ounce) can tomatoes with green chiles, drained
1 (2-ounce) can sliced black olives, drained
1 (15-ounce) can black-eyed peas, drained

1 hot pepper, chopped
1 red bell pepper, chopped
1 green bell pepper, chopped
1 small onion, chopped (optional)
1 small bottle zesty Italian salad dressing

Combine all the ingredients except the salad dressing in a bowl and mix well. Add the salad dressing and mix well. Chill, covered, for 8 to 10 hours. Serve with corn chips. Yield: 6 cups.

Leatrice Cole, Epsilon Master
Huntsville, Alabama

❖ VIDALIA ONION APPETIZER

5 Vidalia onions, thinly sliced
1 cup water
1 cup sugar
1/2 cup cider vinegar

1 cup mayonnaise
16 ounces cream cheese, softened
1 teaspoon celery seed

Place the onions in a large bowl. Combine the water, sugar and vinegar in a small saucepan. Bring to a boil, stirring constantly. Pour over the onions. Chill, tightly covered, for 8 to 10 hours. Drain the onions. Add the remaining ingredients and mix well. Serve with Wheat Thins or Triscuits. Yield: 8 cups.

Margaret (Peggy) N. Camp, Xi Beta Lambda
Leesville, South Carolina

MEMORIES

When my oldest daughter got married, my sister had all her friends, family and co-workers contribute a favorite recipe to make a cookbook my daughter could treasure for the rest of her life. Now she has memories of her friends, co-workers and family (especially her grandparents, who are no longer living). A cookbook of special recipes from family and friends is a treasured gift you can have for life.

Cindy Theriot (25 years), Xi Delta Pi
Breaux Bridge, Louisiana

MEXICAN FUDGE

A childhood friend gave this recipe to me. Our parents were friends before we were born and as a child and young adult we were close friends. Every time I make this I remember all our past experiences.

2 cups shredded Cheddar cheese	3 eggs, beaten
2 cups shredded Monterey Jack cheese	1/2 cup mild green taco sauce

Combine the Cheddar cheese and Monterey Jack cheese in a bowl and mix well. Combine the eggs and taco sauce in a small bowl and mix well. Spoon half the cheese into an 8×8-inch baking dish. Pour the egg mixture evenly over the cheese. Top with the remaining cheese. Bake at 350 degrees for 30 minutes. Yield: 16 servings.

Nancy Burkhardt, Xi Gamma Gamma
Richmond, Indiana

SAUSAGE AND CHUTNEY

1 pound pork, beef or turkey sausage	1 pint sour cream
	1 (8-ounce) jar chutney

Combine the sausage and enough water to cover in a saucepan. Bring to a boil over high heat. Boil until cooked through. Let stand to cool. Cut into bite-size pieces. Combine the sour cream and chutney in a saucepan. Cook over low heat until heated through, stirring constantly. Add the sausage. Cook for 5 minutes. Spoon into a serving dish. Serve warm with crackers. Yield: 5 cups.

Diana Attaway Reed (32 years), Alpha Upsilon
Ville Platte, Louisiana

SALMON MOUSSE

2 envelopes unflavored gelatin	1 cup chopped celery
1/2 cup water	1 teaspoon chopped onion
1 cup mayonnaise	1/4 cup chopped green pepper
1/3 cup lemon juice	
1 (15-ounce) can salmon	

Sprinkle the gelatin over water in a small saucepan; let stand for 5 minutes to soften. Heat over medium-low heat until the gelatin is dissolved completely, stirring constantly. Let stand until cool. Mix the mayonnaise and lemon juice together in a large bowl. Add the cooled gelatin slowly to the mayonnaise mixture, mixing well. Chill until partially set. Fold the salmon, celery, onion and green pepper into the chilled gelatin mixture. Pour the mixture into a 1-quart mold. Chill, covered, for 8 to 10 hours or longer. Unmold the mousse onto a serving plate. Serve with crackers. Yield: 12 to 16 servings.

Carolyn Lancaster, Xi Alpha Omega
North Charleston, South Carolina

OLIVE AND PIMENTO SPREAD

8 ounces nonfat cream cheese, softened	10 black olives, chopped
1/2 teaspoon dried basil	10 to 15 stuffed green olives, chopped
1/4 teaspoon garlic powder	1 tablespoon chopped fresh chives

Combine the cream cheese, basil and garlic in a medium bowl and mix well. Add the black olives, green olives and chives and stir until completely mixed. Chill, covered, until ready to serve. Yield: 1 1/2 cups.

Julie Thompson, Psi Eta
Metropolis, Illinois

PORCUPINE CHEESE BALL

8 ounces cream cheese, softened	1 (3-ounce) package slivered almonds, toasted
1/4 cup amaretto	

Beat the cream cheese and liqueur in a bowl until creamy. Shape into a ball. Place on a serving plate. Press the ends of the almonds into the cheese ball to resemble a porcupine. Chill, covered, until serving time. May add honey to cream cheese mixture if using an inexpensive amaretto. May freeze cheese ball. Serve with grapes, apple wedges, pear wedges and crackers. Yield: 8 servings.

Rita K. Bradshaw (50 years)
Newton, Kansas

HOLIDAY CHEESE BALL

This recipe is a favorite at my workplace.

24 ounces cream cheese, softened	1 bunch green onions, chopped
1 (3-ounce) package dried beef, chopped	Dash of garlic powder
1 (2-ounce) jar pimento, drained	1 cup chopped pecans or walnuts

Combine the cream cheese, dried beef, pimento, green onions and garlic powder in a bowl and mix well. Shape into a ball. Coat with the pecans. Chill, covered, until serving time. Serve with crackers. Yield: 24 servings.

Kathleen McKenna, Gamma Theta
Steubenville, Ohio

HAM CHEESE BALL

This cheese ball is a favorite of many of my friends.

16 ounces cream cheese,
  softened
12 ounces boiled ham,
  chopped

1 medium onion,
  chopped
Chives or green onion
  tops, chopped

Combine the cream cheese, ham and onion in a bowl and mix well. Shape into 1 large ball or 2 small balls. Coat with the chives. Chill, covered, until serving time. Serve with crackers. Yield: 16 servings.

Marie Ann LeBas, Alpha Upsilon
Ville Platte, Louisiana

SHRIMP CHEESE BALL

1 (1-pound) bag frozen
  shrimp, thawed, tails
  removed
16 ounces cream cheese,
  softened
1 tablespoon lemon juice

1/2 cup chopped green
  onions
1 (12-ounce) bottle of
  chili sauce
1 to 2 tablespoons
  horseradish sauce

Combine the shrimp, cream cheese, lemon juice and green onions in a large bowl and mix well. Shape into a ball and place on a serving plate. Chill, covered, until ready to serve. Mix the chili sauce and horseradish sauce together in a small bowl just before serving. Pour the chili sauce mixture over the cheese ball and serve with crackers. Yield: 15 to 20 servings.

Kim Stinson, Zeta Upsilon
Palmetto, Florida

CHOCOLATE CHIP CHEESE BALLS

This is a requested dish at the yearly Christmas Parade Party our friends have been attending for 22 years. Surprise! It is a sweet cheese ball!

8 ounces cream cheese,
  softened
1/2 cup (1 stick) butter
  or margarine,
  softened
1 teaspoon vanilla
  extract

3/4 cup confectioners'
  sugar
2 tablespoons brown
  sugar
3/4 cup miniature
  chocolate chips
3/4 cup chopped pecans

Combine the cream cheese and butter in a large mixing bowl and mix well. Add the vanilla, confectioners' sugar, brown sugar and chocolate chips and stir until completely mixed. Shape into a ball. Roll the cheese ball in the pecans to coat. Chill, covered, until ready to serve. Serve with graham crackers. Yield: 12 servings.

Becky Watson, Xi Lambda
Columbus, Mississippi

MEMORIES

My mother and dad always entertained family and friends for Christmas Day breakfast. One year they invited my boyfriend (who later became my husband) and his parents. He sure didn't score any points with my very traditional mother when she was serving beverages. When she asked him if he would like coffee, tea, or orange juice, he asked, "Do you have any Dr. Pepper?" Mother thought he was awfully strange wanting soda pop for breakfast!

Cindy Foreman (25 years), Xi Zeta Pi
Pryor, Oklahoma

FRIENDSHIP COFFEE

This drink is especially good around the holidays, but can be enjoyed all year round.

3/4 cup instant coffee
  granules
2 cups chocolate drink
  mix
2 tablespoons cinnamon

1 (16-ounce) jar
  nondairy creamer
1 tablespoon salt
8 cups sugar

Mix the ingredients in an airtight storage container. Add one or two heaping teaspoons of mix to one cup of boiling water to serve. Yield: Variable.

Veronica Fox, Xi Gamma Kappa
Havelock, North Carolina

KAHLUA

3 tablespoons instant
  coffee granules
2 cups boiling water
6 cups sugar

51/4 cups water
1 liter 190 proof vodka
1/4 cup vanilla extract

Mix the coffee and the boiling water in a saucepan. Steep, covered, for 5 minutes. Set aside and let cool. Combine the sugar and the 51/4 cups water in a saucepan. Bring to a boil and boil for 10 minutes or until the sugar is completely dissolved, stirring frequently. Set aside and let cool completely. Pour in the vodka, coffee mixture and vanilla. Mix well and pour into a 3-quart container. Add cold water to the rim. Close tightly and store in a cool dark place. Serve with coffee. Yield: 3 quarts.

Dorothy Dickman (49 years), Preceptor Beta Alpha
Sioux City, Iowa

HOMEMADE BAILEY'S IRISH CREAM

4 eggs
1 (14-ounce) can
    evaporated milk
1³/4 cups brandy
1 cup whipping cream
2 tablespoons chocolate
    syrup

2 teaspoons instant
    coffee granules
1 teaspoon vanilla
    extract
¹/2 teaspoon almond
    extract

Combine the ingredients in a blender container and process until smooth. Pour into a tightly sealed container and refrigerate overnight. Shake well before serving. Store in the refrigerator for up to 2 months. Yield: 4 cups.

Riki Mazurkiewicz, Xi Tau
Havre, Montana

MEMORIES

Harvest season was always enjoyable. The day began at sunrise and ended at sunset. Horse-drawn wagons would bring grain bundles to the threshing machine that Dad tended. Many people in the community always helped out. Food was the chore of Mother. Breakfast always included coffee and doughnuts. In the afternoon for lunch we would have sandwiches, cakes or cookies and plenty of coffee. For dinner we usually were fed fried chicken, corn on the cob and pie.

Ann J. Cazer, Xi Alpha Iota
Custer, South Dakota

HOT BUTTERED RUM MIX

We make this every year to share with friends and family at our annual Christmas party. It was especially good on cold days after chopping wood with our friends in Montana.

1 quart vanilla ice
    cream, softened
2 cups (4 sticks) butter,
    softened
1 (1-pound) package
    brown sugar

1 (1-pound) package
    confectioners' sugar
Dark rum
Nutmeg to taste
Cinnamon to taste

Combine the ice cream and butter in a mixing bowl; blend well. Add the brown sugar and confectioners' sugar. Beat at high speed for 10 minutes or until light.

Freeze in a covered container until firm. Spoon 1 to 2 heaping tablespoons of mixture into a mug. Add 1¹/2 ounces of dark rum; fill with boiling water. Sprinkle with nutmeg and cinnamon. Yield: Variable.

Carrie Christiansen, Xi Beta Phi
Bend, Oregon

HAYMAKER SWITCHEL OR GINGER WATER

I remember this beverage being served to my grandpa and the hired hands some 60 years ago during the summer when the men were "putting up" the hay.

2 cups sugar
1 cup apple cider
    vinegar

2 teaspoons ground
    ginger
1 gallon water

Combine the sugar and vinegar in a 1-gallon container stirring until the sugar is dissolved completely. Stir in the ginger and mix well. Add the water and crushed ice. Yield: 1 gallon.

Betty Doubravsky, Xi Delta Tau
Dove Creek, Colorado

ICE CREAM PUNCH

3 (46-ounce) cans red
    Hawaiian punch
2 (2-liter) bottles
    ginger ale

1 gallon vanilla ice
    cream, softened

Pour the punch and ginger ale into a large punch bowl. Spoon the ice cream into the liquid. Stir gently and serve immediately. Yield: 40 servings.

Melody Cook (25 years), Preceptor Chi
Rockview, West Virginia

MEMORIES

I have four grandchildren and love each one so very much. I was in the room during the births of two of them, and it was so wonderful to witness these miracles. I am lucky enough to keep these children while their parents work. It is a joy to see them grow and I hope I live to see each of them married and happy.

Patricia Hall, Xi Delta Omega
Bartow, Florida

MEMORIES

I believe that the food we prepare has a language all its own. As you recreate a tasty shared family recipe for friends and family, ask yourself what the cook was communicating. In my view, this offers a fun way to keep family close together and to bridge the miles and events that tend to separate us.

Billy Jane Gabel (30 years), Xi Master
South Bend, Indiana

APRICOT BRANDY SLUSH

2 cups boiling water	1 (12-ounce) can frozen
4 tea bags	lemonade
2 cups sugar	concentrate, thawed
7 cups boiling water	4 (10-ounce) bottles
2 cups apricot brandy	ginger ale
1 (12-ounce) can frozen	
orange juice	
concentrate, thawed	

Pour 2 cups boiling water over the tea bags in a pitcher; cover. Let steep for 5 minutes. Remove tea bags, squeezing gently. Dissolve the sugar in 7 cups boiling water. Stir in the brewed tea, brandy, orange juice and lemonade. Divide the mixture between two gallon-size sealable plastic freezer bags; freeze. Place contents of 1 plastic bag in a serving container. Break the mixture into chunks. Add 2 bottles ginger ale and stir until mixture is slushy. Yield: 19 servings each.

Carolyn Harper, Xi Beta Sigma
Hutchinson, Kansas

STRAWBERRY SLUSHES

2 cups sugar	1 (2-quart) packet
9 cups water	unsweetened
2 cups vodka	strawberry-flavored
1 (12-ounce) can frozen	drink mix
orange juice	1 (2-liter) bottle lemon-
1 (20-ounce) bag frozen	lime soda
strawberries	

Combine the sugar and water in a large saucepan over medium heat and bring to a boil. Boil until the mixture is a thin syrup consistency, stirring frequently. Remove from heat. Add the vodka, orange juice, strawberries and drink mix to the sugar mixture and mix well. Pour into freezer containers and freeze overnight. Let stand at room temperature for 3 to 4 hours before serving. Spoon the thawed mixture into a glass and fill to the rim with lemon-lime soda. Yield: Variable.

Susan Hummel, Preceptor Alpha Upsilon
Tamaqua, Pennsylvania

MEMORIES

My grandmother was a very small, short woman who was married to a very tall, bony man. They had fourteen children. She always did as he told her except the day that she got tired of the still that he kept in the barn. One day when he was out haying, she took an axe and chopped down the still. Knowing that she would be in deep trouble, she went into the house, took out her rosary beads, knelt down and prayed the Rosary over and over. Grandfather came in and just looked at her. There was never any mention of her dastardly deed.

Noella LaCouvee, Laureate Omicron
Port Alberni, British Columbia, Canada

PINA COLADA

This is always in my freezer ready to be served when unexpected company drops by for a visit.

1 (14-ounce) can cream	1 (46-ounce) can
of coconut	pineapple juice
2 (12-ounce) cans	1 fifth vodka or light
frozen lemonade	rum
concentrate, thawed	Diet lemon-lime soda

Combine the cream of coconut, lemonade, pineapple juice and vodka in a freezer-safe container. Freeze, covered, for 24 hours. Fill glasses one-forth to one-half full of mixture. Fill with diet lemon-lime soda. Garnish with a pineapple chunk, cherry or lime wedge. May substitute rum extract for the vodka. Yield: 32 servings.

Marilyn Bieber, Eta Sigma
New Port Richey, Florida

Soups and Salads

Marilyn Kelley asked me to join Beta Sigma Phi
in 1956 after I met her at work. She became my best
friend both in and out of sorority. When she
passed away, our chapter had a dinner for her family
after the funeral. I know that she was looking down on
us laughing. One of us tripped over the step into her
kitchen, causing the salad, as well as a pecan pie,
to turn upside down. Both were okay, though,
due to good lids. Baked beans in the oven spilled over
and set off the smoke alarm. When her son arrived, he said,
"Mom must be here; the smoke alarm is going off!"
Five years have passed, and I still find myself wanting
to call her about a sorority event. It is hard to
let go of a forty-year friendship.

Naomi Golden (46 years), Alpha Nu Master
Van Buren, Ohio

CHERYL'S TURKEY CHILI

This delicious low-fat recipe was not handed down for generations—in fact, it was given to me by my daughter—but it has become a family favorite!

1½ to 2 pounds ground turkey	1 bottle of beer
1 to 3 teaspoons minced garlic	2 cups water
1 teaspoon oregano	2 to 3 tablespoons cumin
2 (14-ounce) cans diced tomatoes	5 to 7 tablespoons chili powder
2 (15-ounce) cans hot chili beans	1 tablespoon sugar
	1 teaspoon (heaping) salt

Brown the ground turkey with the garlic and oregano in a skillet, stirring until crumbly; drain. Combine the undrained tomatoes, undrained beans, beer and water in a kettle over medium heat. Stir in the cumin, chili powder, sugar, salt and turkey mixture. Bring to a simmer. Cook for 25 minutes, adding more water if necessary. Yield: 6 to 8 servings.

Frances Rambacher (35 years), Laureate Delta Sigma
Ironton, Ohio

MEMORIES

I've been a member for 38 years, and every Christmas Dinner that we sisters share includes a group picture. From 17 and single to 56 and a grandmother of five, it's fun to look back on these photos; especially dear are the friends who joined at the same time (1964) and the dear friends who have passed on. These are cherished Beta Sigma Phi memories.

Candace R. M. Promowicz (38 years), Laureate Alpha Iota
Niagara Falls, New York

Gayle West (27 years), Laureate Delta Epsilon, Independence, Missouri, prepares **Cheesy Cauliflower Soup** by simmering 4 cups chopped cauliflower in two 14-ounce cans chicken broth for 10 minutes or until tender. Add two 16-ounce cans potato soup, 2 cups milk, one 16-ounce jar of Cheez Whiz and 1 to 2 cups chopped ham. Heat over low heat until the Cheez Whiz melts and the soup is heated to serving temperature, stirring frequently.

CALIFORNIA BEEF CHILI

My husband and I developed this recipe as our four sons were growing up. Every Saturday night we had a large pot of chili simmering on the stove to be eaten at any time.

¼ cup (½ stick) butter	1 (46-ounce) can vegetable juice cocktail
2 pounds ground beef	
1 large onion, chopped	1 (15-ounce) can tomato purée
1 cup ketchup	
Salt to taste	2 (or more) tablespoons (heaping) sugar
3 (or more) tablespoons (heaping) chili powder	
2 (16-ounce) cans kidney beans	Salt and pepper to taste

Melt the butter in a skillet over medium heat. Brown the ground beef with ¾ of the onion in the butter, stirring until crumbly; drain. Stir in the ketchup, salt and chili powder. Simmer, uncovered, for 20 minutes, stirring occasionally. Combine the undrained beans, the remaining onion, vegetable juice cocktail, tomato purée, sugar, salt and pepper in a large kettle. Add the beef mixture and bring to a boil. Reduce heat and simmer for 1 hour or longer. Yield: 8 to 12 servings.

Mary Kohorst, Preceptor Beta Nu
Fullerton, California

CAJUN POTATO SOUP

5 red Irish potatoes, peeled, chopped	2 to 2½ cups water
2 onions, chopped	1 (26-ounce) can cream of mushroom soup
3 large cloves garlic, minced	1 (8-ounce) can mushroom stems and pieces
1 green bell pepper, chopped	1 (12-ounce) can evaporated milk
1 large rib celery, chopped	1 bunch green onions
1 pound smoked sausage, ham or shrimp	½ bunch parsley
	6 to 8 broccoli stalks

Combine the potatoes, onions, garlic, green pepper, celery, sausage and water in a large kettle and bring to a boil. Reduce heat and simmer for 20 minutes or until potatoes are tender. Stir in the soup, mushrooms and evaporated milk. Remove and discard the green onion bulbs. Finely chop the green onion tops, parsley and broccoli and add to the soup mixture. Simmer for about 15 minutes, adding milk to thin if necessary. Add salt and pepper to taste. Serve with saltines. Yield: 8 to 10 servings.

Becky A. Buller, Alpha Upsilon
Ville Platte, Louisiana

MEMORIES

When I was a child, every Christmas Eve, my mother would make Oyster Stew which we would eat before opening our gifts. When I became a wife and mother I wanted to start a Christmas Eve tradition of my own. I decided to make Potato Soup. Every Christmas Eve we would make the soup, go to church, and drive around and look at the pretty Christmas lights. When we returned home, we would enjoy the soup and open our gifts. Our sons are now grown, but the Potato Soup recipe has gone with them as far away as Puerto Rico where my son was serving in the Navy. That same son told me when he was a young boy that he wanted to marry a girl in Beta Sigma Phi "because they go to nice places and have so much fun!"

Sheila Hartl (25 years), Xi Alpha Beta
Sidney, Montana

VICHYSSOISE

Chicken bouillon cubes or granules dissolved in water may be substituted for the chicken stock.

6 leeks
1/4 cup (1/2 stick) butter
4 cups chicken stock
4 potatoes, sliced
3 ribs celery, chopped
White pepper, cayenne pepper and salt to taste
2 cups crème fraîche or heavy cream
1 or 2 garlic cloves, minced (optional)
1/4 cup chopped parsley

Mince the white parts of the leeks and sauté in the butter in a large saucepan for 5 to 10 minutes or until limp; do not brown. Add the stock, potatoes and celery. Simmer, covered, over low heat for 20 minutes or until vegetables are tender. Place the leek mixture in a blender and blend until smooth. Return the leek mixture to the saucepan. Stir in the white pepper, cayenne pepper and salt. Stir in the crème fraîche, garlic and parsley just before serving. Garnish with chopped chives. Serve hot or cold; if cold, season generously. Yield: 6 to 8 servings.

Judy Sharp (28 years), Preceptor Gamma Epsilon
Rochelle, Illinois

BAKED POTATO CHEDDAR SOUP

4 large baking potatoes
2/3 cup butter or margarine
2/3 cup flour
6 cups milk, regular or 2%
1/2 teaspoon white pepper
Salt to taste
4 green onions, chopped
12 slices bacon, crisp-cooked, crumbled
1 1/4 cups shredded sharp Cheddar cheese
8 ounces sour cream
2 tablespoons cream sherry (optional)

Wash and pierce potatoes; bake at 400 degrees for 1 hour or until tender. Let cool. Cut in half lengthwise. Scoop out the pulp; discard the skins. Melt the butter in a heavy saucepan over low heat. Add the flour and whisk until smooth. Cook for 1 minute over medium heat, whisking in the milk. Cook for 20 minutes longer or until thick and bubbly, stirring constantly. Stir in the potato pulp, white pepper, salt, half the green onions, half the bacon and 1 cup of the Cheddar cheese. Cook until heated through, stirring frequently. Stir in the sour cream and cream sherry, adding milk if necessary to achieve desired thickness. Garnish with the remaining green onions, bacon and cheese and serve. Yield: 6 to 8 servings.

Jan Sjodin (32 years), Preceptor Iota Mu
Fountain Valley, California

SLOW COOKER POTATO CHOWDER

8 cups diced peeled potatoes
1/3 cup chopped onion
3 (14-ounce) cans chicken broth
1 (10-ounce) can cream of chicken soup
1/4 teaspoon pepper
8 ounces cream cheese, diced

Combine the potatoes, onion, chicken broth, soup and pepper in a slow cooker. Cook on Low for 8 to 10 hours or until potatoes are tender. Add the cream cheese and heat until melted, stirring until smooth. Garnish with crumbled bacon and snipped chives if desired. Yield: 12 servings.

Nancy Hamilton, Xi Tau
Havre, Montana

Nancy L. Barclay (25 years), Laureate Epsilon Phi, Pittsburgh, Pennsylvania, serves **Spinach Egg Soup** with fresh garlic bread as a first course. She cooks a 10-ounce package of frozen chopped spinach in two 14-ounce cans chicken broth, adds 2 tablespoons pastina and simmers, covered, for 5 minutes. Stir in a well-beaten egg and 2 tablespoons grated Parmesan cheese.

❖ CHICKEN VEGETABLE SOUP

This soup does not take as long to prepare as did my mother's all-day soup, but it is so tasty it brings back fond memories of my childhood—and it takes only thirty minutes or so!

12 ounces celery, chopped	1 (15-ounce) can diced tomatoes with celery and onions
16 ounces baby carrots, chopped	1 (15-ounce) can early peas or green beans, drained
12 ounces cauliflower, chopped	
Lemon pepper and dill to taste	1 (15-ounce) can whole kernel corn, drained
1 (16-ounce) package frozen chicken stir-fry meal, thawed	1 (15-ounce) can black-eyed peas, drained
1 (26-ounce) roasted garlic and Romano spaghetti sauce	1 (4-ounce) can sliced mushrooms, drained
	Cayenne pepper to taste (optional)

Place a vegetable steamer in a large stockpot. Add 1 inch of water. Bring to a boil. Add the celery, carrots and cauliflower. Season with lemon pepper and dill. Steam, covered, until the vegetables are tender-crisp. Add the chicken stir-fry meal to the vegetables and steam, covered, for 5 minutes. (If a sauce comes with the meal, save for another use). Remove the steamer from the stockpot. Combine the spaghetti sauce, undrained tomatoes and 3 cups water in the stockpot over medium heat. Stir in the peas, corn, black-eyed peas, mushrooms, steamed vegetables and chicken. Simmer for about 10 minutes. Season with cayenne pepper. Yield: 6 to 8 servings.

Anita Jemison, Xi
Ridgeland, Mississippi

AFRICAN PEANUT CHICKEN SOUP

1 tablespoon vegetable oil	1/4 teaspoon black pepper
1 tablespoon sesame oil	Pinch of cayenne pepper
1 large onion, chopped	1/2 teaspoon salt
1 large red bell pepper, chopped	1/4 cup uncooked white rice
2 garlic cloves, mashed	1 cup (or more) chopped cooked chicken
1 (15-ounce) can diced tomatoes	1/4 cup smooth or chunky peanut butter
4 cups chicken broth	
1 teaspoon curry powder	

Heat the vegetable oil and sesame oil in a large saucepan. Sauté the onion, red pepper and garlic in the oil for 5 to 10 minutes or until onion is tender. Stir in the undrained tomatoes, chicken broth, curry powder, black pepper, cayenne pepper, salt and rice.

Simmer, covered, for about 20 minutes or until rice is tender. Whisk in the peanut butter and stir in the chicken. Bring to a simmer, stirring frequently. Serve hot with a sprinkling of chopped peanuts.
Yield: 6 to 8 servings.

Barbara T. Coates (45 years), Preceptor Beta Alpha
Portland, Oregon

BEEF AND NOODLE SOUP

During World War II I married a U.S. Air Force man of Hungarian descent, and I soon learned to prepare some of his favorite foods, including this savory soup. The egg noodle flakes are small chips of noodles; I use the Mrs. Weiss' brand.

1 (1½- to 2-pound) rump roast	3 ribs celery with leaves
1 soup bone	1 large onion
2½ tablespoons salt	3 carrots
1/2 teaspoon pepper	1/4 head cabbage
1/2 teaspoon paprika	2 kohlrabi halves (optional)
Pinch of saffron	3 potatoes
1 cup canned tomatoes	Egg noodle flakes
3 bunches parsley	

Rinse the roast and the soup bone; place in a large kettle and cover with cold water. Bring to a boil. Reduce heat and simmer gently for 1 hour, skimming several times. Add the salt, pepper, paprika, saffron, tomatoes, parsley and celery and simmer for 1 hour longer. Clean and peel the onion, carrots, cabbage, kohlrabi and potatoes; add the whole and halved vegetables to the soup. Simmer for about 30 minutes or until beef is done to taste and vegetables are tender. Remove the beef and vegetables and keep warm. Strain the broth and bring to a boil; cook noodles in the boiling broth. Serve meat and vegetables as side dishes with the noodle soup. Yield: 6 to 8 servings.

Dee Balough (42 years), Laureate Gamma Upsilon
Columbus, Ohio

MEMORIES

*A*fter raising our kids, Beta Sigma Phi was the thing I joined just for me. No more leading Boy Scouts, Girl Scouts, Candy Stripers, 4-H or Sunday school!

Emilie A. Graham (42 years), Xi Omicron Lambda
Blythe, California

TACO SOUP

This recipe is special because the friend who gave it to me is special. After meeting at work conferences we became lifelong friends, even though she is my daughter's age. We have traveled to each other's homes for special functions and regular visits for thirty years. In some ways she has filled the void my daughter left when she married and moved to another state.

2 pounds lean ground
  beef
1 onion, finely chopped
4 (16-ounce) cans whole
  tomatoes
1 (16-ounce) can pinto
  beans
1 (16-ounce) can kidney
  beans

1 (16-ounce) can whole
  kernel corn
1 (4-ounce) can chopped
  mild or hot green
  chiles
2 envelopes taco
  seasoning mix
1 envelope original ranch
  salad dressing mix

Brown the ground beef with the onion in a skillet, stirring until crumbly; drain. Combine the remaining ingredients in a large kettle; bring to a boil. Stir in the beef mixture. Reduce heat and simmer for 35 to 40 minutes. Serve with tortilla chips. May garnish with shredded Cheddar cheese and sour cream.
Yield: 16 to 20 servings.

Mary Creekmore (29 years), Beta Chi
Ocala, Florida

MOM'S HAMBURGER SOUP

It was a joke in our family that my two sisters and I couldn't marry until we found husbands who loved this soup as much as we did. When one of my brothers-in-law and his wife moved to Ohio, he said he could always tell when my sister was homesick, for he would come home to a pot of Hamburger Soup.

1 pound ground beef
3 cups water
1 small onion, chopped
4 potatoes, peeled, diced
1 (10-ounce) package
  frozen corn kernels,
  thawed

1 (16-ounce) can kidney
  beans, drained
1 (10-ounce) can tomato
  soup
1/4 teaspoon salt
Dash of chili powder
  (optional)

Brown the ground beef in a skillet, stirring until crumbly; drain. Combine the beef, water and onion in a kettle; simmer, covered, for about 30 minutes. Add the potatoes, corn, kidney beans, soup and salt; simmer, uncovered, for 1 1/2 to 2 hours or until slightly thickened. Add chili powder during the last 10 minutes of cooking. Yield: 10 to 12 servings.

Jolene Oden, Xi Beta Rho
Exline, Iowa

VENISON VEGETABLE SOUP

Neighbors and family all clamor for this soup. My husband always prepares it in a 20-quart stockpot so we will have plenty for freezing in individual quantities.

7 (15-ounce) cans mixed
  vegetables, drained
2 (10-ounce) cans
  original tomatoes
  with green chiles
1 (14-ounce) can beef
  broth
3 (15-ounce) cans cream-
  style corn
2 (46-ounce) cans
  vegetable juice
  cocktail
2 teaspoons freshly
  ground black pepper

1 teaspoon garlic
  powder
2 large yellow onions,
  coarsely chopped
2 (15-ounce) cans black-
  eyed peas, drained
  (optional)
6 pounds lean ground
  venison
6 tablespoons olive oil
2 teaspoons seasoned
  salt
16 ounces fresh or frozen
  okra, chopped

Combine the mixed vegetables, tomatoes with green chiles, beef broth, cream-style corn, vegetable juice cocktail, pepper, garlic powder, onions and peas in a 20-quart stockpot that has been sprayed with non-stick cooking spray. Heat over medium heat while browning the venison. Brown the ground venison 1/3 at a time in the olive oil with the seasoned salt in a skillet, stirring until crumbly. Add the undrained browned venison to the vegetable mixture and bring to a boil. Reduce heat and simmer, uncovered, for 30 minutes, stirring frequently. Add the okra and simmer for 15 minutes longer. Yield: 80 (1-cup) servings.

Mary Williams, Preceptor Alpha Omega
Conway, Arkansas

LETTUCE SOUP

When the lettuce looks too bad to use in a salad but too good to throw away, we use it to make this delicious soup. Use any kind of lettuce, and serve with French bread or croutons.

2 onions, coarsely
  chopped
2 tablespoons butter or
  margarine
1 head lettuce, cut in
  large pieces

6 cups chicken or
  vegetable stock
Salt and pepper to taste
1/4 cup chopped parsley

Sauté the onions in the butter for 5 minutes. Add the lettuce and sauté for 5 minutes; lettuce will shrink. Add the stock and bring to a boil; reduce heat and simmer for 5 minutes. Add salt and pepper. Sprinkle with parsley and serve. Yield: 6 servings.

Betty Willems, Omicron Mu
Carl Junction, Missouri

MOM'S THROW-OUT-THE-BEET BORSCHT

Making borscht with my mom was an all-day affair for me and my four sisters. We all had our jobs to do, but the time passed quickly as we talked, told jokes, and sang. Mom usually started a song and we all joined in. Today I usually cook alone, but sometimes you can still catch me singing.

1 small beet (for color)	1 (29-ounce) can
4 potatoes, peeled,	tomatoes
2 quartered, 1 diced	1/2 cup evaporated milk
1 small onion, chopped	or cream
1/2 cup diced celery	1 small carrot, diced
1/2 green bell pepper,	1 tablespoon fresh dill,
chopped	or 1 teaspoon dried
6 tablespoons butter	1/2 cup fresh or frozen
4 cups shredded green	peas
cabbage	Salt and pepper to taste

Bring 6 cups of water to a boil in a large kettle. Add the beet and quartered potatoes. Simmer for 20 minutea or until potatoes are tender. Sauté the onion, celery and green pepper in 1 tablespoon butter in a large skillet until slightly browned. Remove from skillet and set aside. Melt 2 tablespoons of the butter in the skillet over medium-low heat and sauté half the cabbage until wilted. Drain the tomatoes, reserving the liquid. Add the tomatoes to the cabbage and cook until almost dry, stirring frequently. Break up the tomatoes. Remove the potatoes from the potato water with a slotted spoon; mash with the remaining 3 tablespoons butter and evaporated milk. Add the remaining 2 cups cabbage, carrot, potatoes, reserved tomato liquid and onion mixture. Simmer for 3 minutes. Remove from heat. Discard the beet. Stir in the mashed potatoes, dill, peas, salt and pepper. Yield: 8 servings.

Jo-Anne Watalla, Xi Gamma Upsilon
Richmond, British Columbia, Canada

MEMORIES

My family has always been very close. We always enjoyed getting together at special times, such as the holidays. Since I am the last of my family and 80 years old, I have turned to the wonderful Beta sisters for those close get-togethers, and we have super times all during the year.

Griff Jappé (42 years), Laureate Delta Xi
Lehigh Acres, Florida

BLACK BEAN SOUP

1 onion, chopped	1/3 to 1 (10-ounce) can
1/2 cup chopped celery	tomatoes with green
1/2 cup shredded carrot	chiles
1/2 cup chopped green	1/2 cup beef or vegetable
bell pepper	broth
1 to 2 tablespoons olive	1 cup water
oil	1/4 teaspoon garlic
2 (15-ounce) cans black	powder
beans, rinsed, drained	1/2 teaspoon cumin
1 (14-ounce) can diced	1/2 teaspoon pepper
tomatoes	

Sauté the onion, celery, carrot and green pepper in the olive oil in a Dutch oven for 5 to 10 minutes. Add the remaining ingredients and mix well. Bring to the boiling point. Remove from heat and serve with corn bread. Yield: 8 to 12 servings.

Marcia Bridgford, Xi Beta Omicron
Decatur, Alabama

CREAM OF CABBAGE SOUP

4 cups water	1 garlic clove, minced
2 tablespoons chicken	1 teaspoon salt
bouillon granules	1 teaspoon dillweed
3 cups diced peeled	1 cup (2 sticks) butter or
potatoes	margarine
1 cup finely chopped	1 cup flour
onion	2 cups milk
1 cup diced rutabaga	2 cups chicken broth
1/2 cup diced carrots	8 ounces American
6 cups chopped cabbage	cheese, cubed
1 cup chopped celery	1/2 teaspoon thyme
1/2 cup chopped green	Pepper to taste
bell pepper	

Combine the water and bouillon granules in a kettle and bring to a boil. Stir in the potatoes, onion, rutabaga and carrots. Reduce heat and simmer, covered, for 5 minutes. Stir in the cabbage, celery and green pepper; simmer, uncovered, for 5 minutes. Stir in the garlic, salt and dill. Melt the butter in a heavy saucepan over medium heat and whisk in the flour. Cook until golden brown, stirring frequently. Gradually stir in the milk and chicken broth; stir until smooth. Reduce heat to low and stir in the American cheese, thyme and pepper. Cook until cheese melts. Stir the cheese mixture into the vegetable mixture and simmer for 5 minutes. Serve with French bread and a salad. Yield: 8 servings.

Marian J. Papin (32 years), Laureate Omega
Warren, Michigan

MINORCAN CLAM CHOWDER

At Christmastime our family gathers for a soup supper and gift exchange. Each family brings a different soup, and this clam chowder is always a tremendous hit.

1 or 2 slices bacon	1 tablespoon oregano
2 cups thinly sliced	flakes
peeled carrots	3 tablespoons chopped
1/2 cup chopped onion	fresh parsley
2 cups chopped celery	2 bay leaves, crushed
3 cups minced clams,	4 cups whole canned
fresh or canned	tomatoes, crushed
2 teaspoons salt	2 cups chopped peeled
1 teaspoon pepper	potatoes
2 tablespoons seafood	
seasoning	

Crisp-cook the bacon in a large skillet. Remove bacon from skillet and add the carrots, onion and celery to the bacon drippings. Sauté for 5 to 10 minutes or until tender. Stir in the undrained clams, salt, pepper, seafood seasoning, oregano, parsley, bay leaves and undrained tomatoes. Simmer for 30 minutes. Add the potatoes and simmer for about 20 minutes or until potatoes are tender. Yield: 8 to 10 servings.

Nancy F. Durrant, Xi Iota Tau
Satsuma, Florida

MEMORIES

I am an only child. My husband's job kept us moving around a lot, and everywhere we moved, Beta sisters were waiting, because the office had sent them a notice that I was moving to their city. It was like I had lots of sisters. It has been so rewarding. Thanks for all of my 43 years.

Darlene Buchacker (43 years), Pi Master
Melbourne, Florida

CRAB AND CORN CHOWDER

This simple, delicious recipe may be served in bread bowls. Shrimp may be substituted for the crab.

1/2 cup (1 stick) butter	2 (10-ounce) cans cream
1 onion, chopped	of celery soup
1 rib celery, chopped	2 cups milk
1 green bell pepper,	2 cups half-and-half
chopped	1 pound crab meat
1 (15-ounce) can cream-	
style corn	

Melt the butter in a large heavy skillet over medium-low heat and sauté the onion, celery and green pepper until tender. Add the corn, soup, milk and half-and-half. Bring to a boil. Stir in the crab meat. Season to taste. Garnish with chopped parsley and green onions if desired. Yield: 8 to 10 servings.

Susan Dardar, Kappa Zeta
Abbeville, Louisiana

SWISS BACON OPEN-FACE SANDWICHES

4 slices bacon, crisp-	6 olives, chopped
cooked, crumbled	Mayonnaise
4 strips red or green bell	Salt and pepper to taste
pepper, diced	4 bread slices, toasted
1 slice onion, diced or	6 ounces Swiss cheese,
shredded	sliced

Combine the bacon, bell pepper, onion and olives in a bowl and mix well. Mix in 1 heaping tablespoon mayonnaise; add additional mayonnaise to make of desired consistency. Sprinkle with salt and pepper. Spread the bacon mixture over the toasted bread. Top with Swiss cheese. Broil until brown and cheese is melted. Yield: 2 servings.

Lana Moore, Alpha Upsilon
Ironton, Ohio

PARTY HAM SANDWICHES

These sandwiches are good as snacks or a main dish. Great leftovers, the sandwiches can be reheated.

24 dinner rolls	1 tablespoon poppy
8 ounces shaved ham	seeds
8 ounces Swiss cheese,	1 1/2 tablespoons
sliced	Worcestershire sauce
1/2 cup (1 stick) butter or	1 1/2 tablespoons
margarine, melted	prepared mustard
1 tablespoon onion	
flakes	

Slice the dinner rolls in half and layer ham and cheese over the bottom halves. Replace tops and arrange in a 9×13-inch baking dish. Combine the butter, onion flakes, poppy seeds, Worcestershire sauce and mustard in a small saucepan over medium-low heat. Cook until heated through. Drizzle the butter mixture evenly over the sandwiches. Chill, covered with foil, for 1 hour or longer. Bake at 350 degrees for 20 minutes. Serve hot. Yield: 12 servings.

Kay Simpson (40 years), Xi Theta Nu
Stanton, Texas

CHICKEN SALAD SANDWICHES

A dear co-worker shared this recipe with me over thirty years ago, and it is still my "most-requested" recipe. Serve with potato salad or fresh fruit. For a completely different flavor, serve on raisin bread.

4 to 8 boneless skinless chicken breasts	1/4 teaspoon pepper
4 ribs celery, chopped	Garlic powder to taste
1 carrot, peeled, sliced	Salt, pepper and paprika to taste
1 small onion, coarsely chopped	Celery, thinly sliced
2 teaspoons salt	Mayonnaise
	6 dozen slices bread

Arrange the chicken in a Dutch oven or large kettle with enough water to cover. Add the celery, carrot, onion, the 2 teaspoons salt, the 1/4 teaspoon pepper and garlic powder. Bring to a boil. Reduce heat and simmer, covered, for 1 hour or until chicken is cooked through. Remove the chicken and let it cool in a large bowl. Shred the chicken meat and add the salt, pepper and paprika to taste. Stir in the celery and enough mayonnaise to moisten. Make sandwiches and serve. Yield: 3 dozen.

JoAnn Schaefer Lofton
Oxnard, California

CRANBERRY TURKEY CROISSANT

This tempting sandwich was wonderful when served with chips, pickles, hot cocoa, and chocolate chip cookies to warm us after spending time outside in the cold. One of our family traditions was to decorate for Christmas the day after Thanksgiving, breaking at lunchtime to enjoy this tasty meal.

8 ounces cream cheese, softened	6 croissants
1/4 cup orange marmalade	6 romaine leaves
1/2 cup chopped toasted pecans	6 slices leftover turkey
	1/4 cup cranberry sauce

Combine the cream cheese, orange marmalade and pecans in a bowl and mix well. Slice each croissant in half horizontally, and toast the halves. Spread the cream cheese mixture on both halves of each croissant. Place a leaf of romaine and a slice of turkey over the cream cheese mixture on 1 half of each croissant. Spread cranberry sauce over the turkey. Top with remaining croissant half and serve. Yield: 6 servings.

Shelly Allison, Nu Kappa
Guthrie, Oklahoma

MEMORIES

My mom, a Beta member for over forty years, requested that I make her special vegetable salad as one of the dishes for her fiftieth wedding anniversary. As I began preparing it, I had to stop several times to put it in a larger bowl. When I ran out of large bowls, I had to run to the store to buy one. Not finding a large enough bowl, God finally spoke to me saying, "Kaye, how about a 'large' dishpan?" That was just the right size! Mom said that the salad serves 10 to 12 people. Well, let me tell you it served at least 20 to 25. She passed away two years later and I still remember this incident every time I make the salad.

Kaye Clay (26 years), Preceptor Beta Chi
Guthrie, Oklahoma

MOTHER'S SUMMER VEGETABLE SALAD

My mother prepared this salad only once or twice a year, and only for a special occasion such as a picnic with family or friends, a rare wonderful treat for us in the late forties and early fifties.

4 tomatoes, chopped	1 rib celery, chopped
1 cucumber, chopped	1/2 onion, finely chopped
1 green bell pepper, choppped	1/4 head cabbage, shredded
3 radishes, chopped	1/2 cup mayonnaise
	Salt and pepper to taste

Combine the first 5 ingredients a large bowl and mix well. Add the onion and cabbage and toss well. Add the mayonnaise, salt and pepper and toss. Chill, covered, until serving time. Yield: 6 to 8 servings.

Sharon Nelson, Preceptor Eta Gamma
West Chester, Ohio

Kim Healy, Preceptor Gamma Xi, Lebanon, Oregon, prepares delicious **Super Bowl Sandwiches** by slicing French bread lengthwise and saturating the cut sides with Italian salad dressing. She layers the bottom half with 4 ounces sliced provolone cheese, 12 ounces deli-sliced Black Forest ham, thinly shredded onion and additional 4 ounces provolone cheese. After placing the top of the loaf on the layers, she wraps the loaf in foil and bakes at 350 degrees until the cheese melts. Cut into 1-inch slices to serve.

EGGS AND GREENS PARTY SALAD

1 head lettuce	2 cups real mayonnaise
1 cup chopped celery	1 teaspoon sugar
1/2 cup chopped green bell pepper	6 hard-cooked eggs, finely chopped
1/2 cup sliced green onions	4 ounces Cheddar cheese, shredded
1 (10-ounce) package frozen green peas	4 ounces bacon, crisp-cooked, crumbled

Tear the lettuce into a large glass bowl. Layer the celery, green pepper, green onions and uncooked unthawed green peas over the lettuce layer. Blend the mayonnaise and sugar together. Spread the mayonnaise mixture over the top, sealing to the edge. Chill, tightly covered, for 8 to 12 hours. Sprinkle with the hard-cooked eggs, Cheddar cheese and bacon just before serving. Spoon through all the layers when serving. Yield: 10-plus servings.

Sharon E. Anderson, Xi Omicron Sigma
Lakehead, California

TOSSED SALAD CHOW MEIN

1/2 cup vegetable oil	1/3 cup sliced almonds, toasted
1/4 cup sugar	1/4 cup sesame seeds, toasted
2 tablespoons vinegar	
1 teaspoon salt	4 green onions, sliced
1/4 teaspoon pepper	3/4 cup chow mein noodles
1 large head iceberg lettuce, torn	
6 slices bacon, crisp-cooked, crumbled	

Combine the vegetable oil, sugar, vinegar, salt and pepper in a covered jar and shake until well blended; chill, covered, for 1 hour. Combine lettuce, bacon, almonds, sesame seeds and green onions in a large glass bowl. Pour the vinegar dressing over the salad and toss to combine. Yield: 6 servings.

Valerie Rankin (40 years), Preceptor Epsilon Theta
Pinellas Park, Florida

SEVEN-LAYER SALAD

2 cups chopped lettuce	1 (16-ounce) package frozen green peas, slightly thawed
2 cups chopped celery	
2 cups chopped green onions	
1 (4-ounce) can sliced water chestnuts, drained	1 1/2 cups mayonnaise
	2 cups shredded Colby or Monterey Jack cheese

Layer the lettuce, celery, green onions, water chestnuts, green peas, mayonnaise and cheese in a large glass bowl in the order listed. Chill, covered, for 1 hour or longer before serving. Spoon through all the layers when serving. Yield: 10 to 20 servings.

Linda Clark, Alpha Alpha
Ruidoso, New Mexico

TACO SALAD

A family tradition at family gatherings, this is the salad that everyone wants to bring.

1 pound lean ground beef	2 tomatoes, chopped
1 envelope taco seasoning mix	1 cup shredded Cheddar cheese
1 (10-ounce) package tortilla chips	1 (16-ounce) bottle Thousand Island salad dressing
1 head lettuce	

Brown the ground beef with the taco seasoning mix in a skillet, using the package directions. Crush the tortilla chips into bite-size pieces. Tear the lettuce into bite-size pieces and place in a large bowl. Add the tomatoes, Cheddar cheese, seasoned ground beef and tortilla chips; toss to combine. Chill, covered, until serving time. Add the salad dressing and serve with tortilla chips. Yield: 12 to 15 servings.

Jeannette Davis, Xi Zeta Rho
LeMars, Iowa

WON TON SALAD

1 cup sugar	6 chicken breasts
1 1/2 teaspoons pepper	1 (10-ounce) package won tons
1 teaspoon salt	
1 1/2 teaspoons MSG	2 heads red leaf or iceberg lettuce
1/2 cup white vinegar	
1/2 cup vegetable oil	1 bunch green onions, chopped
1 tablespoon sesame seeds	

Combine the sugar, pepper, salt, MSG, vinegar, vegetable oil and sesame seeds in a jar and shake vigorously. Chill, covered, for 8 to 10 hours. Boil or bake the chicken until cooked through; let cool and cut into bite-size pieces. Chill, covered, until ready to use. Cut the won tons into strips and fry in hot oil until brown and crispy. Tear the lettuce into bite-size pieces and place in a large bowl. Add the green onions and cooked chicken and toss to combine. Add fried won tons just before serving. Shake the dressing and add to the salad. Toss and serve.
Yield: 12 servings.

Linda K. Martin (27 years), Laureate Epsilon Delta
Camarillo, California

MEMORIES

There was once a little girl named Molly who was born with a group of birth defects, some of which affected her heart and lungs. This limited Molly physically, but she always kept a positive outlook on life: "Cheer up, things could always be worse, you know." She had an absolute zest for life, and taught all of us the gifts of friendship and caring for one another.

Carol Twining (37 years), Beta Master
Ludlow, Massachusetts

❖ CATHY'S FRUIT CASHEW SALAD

This salad was instantly embraced as a traditional Christmas dish the very first time it was served to my family, and the same thing happened when it was served at my chapter's annual potluck Christmas dinner. To reduce the fat, substitute 1/3 cup oil and 1/3 cup water for the 2/3 cup vegetable oil. To save time, you may use about 1 3/4 bags of the washed and torn romaine that can be found in the vegetable section of the grocery store.

1/2 cup sugar	1 large head romaine
1/3 cup fresh lemon juice	1 cup cashews
2 teaspoons finely chopped onion	1/4 cup sweetened dried cranberries
1 teaspoon Dijon mustard	1 cup chopped peeled Gala apple
1/2 teaspoon salt	1 pear, peeled, chopped
2/3 cup vegetable oil	3/4 cup shredded Swiss cheese
1 tablespoon poppy seeds	

Combine the sugar, lemon juice, onion, mustard, salt, vegetable oil and poppy seeds in a jar and shake vigorously; chill, covered, for 8 to 10 hours if possible. Tear the lettuce to make about 10 cups of bite-size pieces. Combine the cashews, cranberries, apple, pear and a small amount of the dressing in a bowl; chill, covered, until ready to serve. At serving time, combine the lettuce, cashew mixture, Swiss cheese and remaining dressing in a large bowl. Toss and serve. Yield: 12 to 15 servings.

Sandy Ayres, Xi Gamma Pi
Lenexa, Kansas

GARDEN-FRESH WILTED LETTUCE

This salad always reminds me of late spring–early summer suppers at my grandmother's farm. She served it with new red potatoes and baked chicken with fresh carrots.

6 medium mushrooms	2 tablespoons red wine vinegar
1 bunch leaf lettuce	
6 radishes, thinly sliced	1 tablespoon lemon juice
6 green onions, thinly sliced	1 teaspoon sugar
5 slices bacon	Cracked pepper to taste

Slice the mushrooms. Tear the lettuce into bite-size pieces and place in a large salad bowl with the radishes, green onions and mushrooms; toss to combine. Cook the bacon in a skillet over medium heat until crisp. Remove bacon and drain on paper towels. Add the vinegar, lemon juice, sugar and pepper to the hot bacon drippings; stir to combine. Pour the vinegar mixture over the salad; toss to combine. Crumble the bacon and sprinkle over the salad. Serve immediately. Yield: 6 to 8 servings.

Mickey Leubner, Xi Mu Rho
Springfield, Missouri

BROCCOLI CAULIFLOWER SALAD

I find I am signed up to bring this salad to council potlucks before the signup sheet even gets to me! It is especially good with grilled chicken.

1 bunch broccoli	1 cup mayonnaise
1 head cauliflower	1 cup sour cream
5 or 6 green onions, chopped	1 tablespoon lemon juice
1/4 cup chopped green bell pepper	1/2 cup sugar
8 ounces fresh mushrooms, sliced	1 pound bacon, crisp-cooked, crumbled
1/2 to 3/4 cup shredded Cheddar cheese	

Wash and trim broccoli and cauliflower; break into florets. Place the broccoli, cauliflower, green onions, green pepper, mushrooms and Cheddar cheese in a large bowl; toss to combine. Chill, covered, until serving time. Combine the mayonnaise, sour cream, lemon juice and sugar in a bowl and whisk until smooth. Toss with the salad. Sprinkle with bacon and serve. Yield: 12 to 15 servings.

Debra Paulsen (25 years), Laureate Gamma Mu
Victorville, California

CORN BREAD SALAD

My Southern family often comes up with new, different ways to eat corn bread, and this salad has always been a favorite at family get-togethers.

2 (6-ounce) packages
   corn bread mix
1 cup chopped celery
1 cup chopped green bell
   pepper
1 bunch green onions,
   chopped
3 or 4 tomatoes, diced

6 to 8 slices bacon,
   crisp-cooked,
   crumbled
2 (16-ounce) cans whole
   kernel corn, drained
2 to 2¹/₂ cups
   mayonnaise

Prepare and bake the corn bread using the package directions; cool completely. Crumble the corn bread into a large bowl. Add the celery, green pepper, green onions, tomatoes, bacon and corn and mix well. Stir in the mayonnaise. Chill, covered, until ready to serve; it will keep for several days.
Yield: 12 to 15 servings.

Janet Berry, Alpha Kappa
Hot Springs, Arkansas

MARINATED VEGETABLES

1¹/₃ cups vinegar
²/₃ cup vegetable oil
3 tablespoons fresh
   lemon juice
¹/₂ cup sugar
2 teaspoons oregano
1 teaspoon salt
¹/₂ teaspoon pepper
Dash of Tabasco sauce
2 red onions, thinly
   sliced

1 (6-ounce) can large
   pitted black olives,
   drained
1 large head broccoli,
   cut into florets
1 head cauliflower, cut
   into florets
1 pound fresh mushroom
   caps, cleaned

Combine the vinegar, vegetable oil, lemon juice, sugar, oregano, salt, pepper and Tabasco sauce in a large bowl; stir until sugar is dissolved. Add the onions, olives, broccoli, cauliflower and mushrooms and stir gently to coat. Chill, covered, for 3 to 10 hours, stirring occasionally. Drain just before serving. Arrange on a serving platter with the broccoli forming a wreath around the other vegetables. May be served as a salad or side dish. Yield: 6 servings.

Sharlene Heinselman (44 years), Laureate Mu
Mineral Wells, West Virginia

CORN TOMATO SALAD

2 (16-ounce) cans whole
   kernel corn, drained
³/₄ cup chopped green
   bell pepper
¹/₄ cup finely chopped
   red onion
2 tomatoes, chopped

¹/₂ cup sour cream
¹/₄ cup mayonnaise
2 tablespoons vinegar
2 teaspoons salt
¹/₂ teaspoon dry mustard
1 teaspoon celery seed
Black pepper to taste

Combine the corn, green pepper, onion and tomatoes in a large bowl; chill, covered, until a little over an hour before serving time. Blend the remaining ingredients in a bowl. Add the mayonnaise mixture to the corn mixture and toss to combine. Chill, covered, for 1 hour. Yield: 6 to 8 servings.

Kimberly Sobley, Beta Lambda
Macon, Mississippi

BLACK BEAN SALAD

2 (15-ounce) cans black
   beans, rinsed, drained
3 tablespoons chopped
   jalapeño peppers
2 teaspoons minced
   garlic
1 teaspoon seasoning
   powder
1 (10-ounce) package
   frozen white corn,
   thawed, drained

1 cup diced onion
¹/₂ cup diced red bell
   pepper
1 large tomato, chopped
3 tablespoons minced
   cilantro
3 tablespoons lime juice
1 tablespoon chili
   powder
2 teaspoons cumin

Mix all the ingredients in a large bowl. Chill, covered, until ready to serve. Serve over a bed of lettuce with chips. Yield: 8 to 10 servings.

Betty Erickson, Preceptor Psi
Walnut, California

FABULOUS FIESTA ONION SALAD

6 Spanish onions, sliced
¹/₂ cup water
¹/₂ cup vinegar
³/₄ cup sugar
2 teaspoons salt

3 tablespoons celery
   seed
1¹/₂ cups mayonnaise
Salt and pepper to taste

Place the onions in a deep bowl. Pour a mixture of the water, vinegar, sugar and salt over the onions. Let stand, covered, for 3 hours. Drain well. Mix the celery seed and mayonnaise together and add to the onions; mix well. Yield: 6 to 8 servings.

Dorothy K. Giles, Laureate Alpha Phi
Delta, British Columbia, Canada

CRUNCHY PEA AND CASHEW SALAD

1 (10-ounce) package frozen peas, thawed, drained	1/2 cup bottled fat-free ranch salad dressing
1 cup cauliflower florets	1/4 cup light sour cream
1 cup sliced celery	1/2 teaspoon dillweed
1/4 cup sliced green onions	Salt and pepper to taste
	1/3 cup broken cashews

Combine the peas, cauliflower, celery and green onions in a large bowl and mix well. Combine the salad dressing, sour cream and dillweed in a small bowl and mix well. Add the sour cream mixture to the vegetables; toss to coat. Season to taste. Chill, covered, for 1 to 24 hours. Sprinkle with cashews just before serving. Yield: 8 servings.

Janet R. Hughes, Xi Gamma Iota
Winter Springs, Florida

SPINACH SALAD

This visually arresting salad keeps well in the refrigerator.

1 onion, chopped	3 tablespoons poppy seeds
1 1/2 cups sugar	
2 teaspoons dry mustard	10 ounces baby spinach
2 teaspoons salt	6 to 8 strawberries, sliced
2/3 cup red wine vinegar	
2 cups vegetable oil	Slivered almonds

Combine the onion, sugar, mustard, salt, vinegar, vegetable oil and poppy seeds in a large jar. Shake vigorously to blend. Layer the spinach and strawberries on salad plates; sprinkle with almonds. Drizzle with the dressing and serve. Yield: 3 or 4 servings.

Margaret Simms (34 years), Preceptor Alpha Omega
Conway, Arkansas

MEMORIES

I had two sisters and a brother. When we were growing up, we would gather with the neighbors and rehearse all day to put on a play that we performed for our parents. We would make up our own plays and lines or act out well-known stories with our own twists. I hope, despite all the computer games and TV shows, that kids today enjoy using their imaginations as we did.

Linda Neer, Xi Psi
Chariton, Iowa

"SUCH AS" BEEF SALAD

I always came home for the noon meal during my grade-school days—there were no school lunchroom facilities back then. A sandwich, fruit, and hot soup were often on the menu, along with lots of love and laughter. It was my very favorite time of day. Through Depression years and the rationing problems of WWII, my mother magically created wholesome, healthy, and delicious meals. I don't know why she called this salad "Such As"—perhaps that was the brand name of the canned beans.

1 (16-ounce) can cut green beans	1/2 cup minced onion
1 (16-ounce) can yellow wax beans	1/2 cup extra-virgin olive oil
1 (16-ounce) can kidney beans	1/2 cup white vinegar
	3/4 cup sugar
1/2 cup finely chopped green bell pepper	1 teaspoon salt
	1/2 teaspoon black pepper

Drain all beans well, and place in a large bowl. Add the green pepper and onion. Combine the olive oil, vinegar, sugar, salt and pepper in a small bowl and whisk to blend. Pour the dressing over the bean mixture and toss to combine. Chill, covered, for 1 hour or longer before serving; a longer chilling time will enhance the flavors. Yield: 6 to 8 servings.

Doris "Pat" Whiston (57 years), Xi Master
South Bend, Indiana

NAPA CABBAGE SALAD

You may discard the ramen noodle flavor packet or add it to the dressing.

1 large head napa cabbage	1 (3-ounce) package ramen noodles
4 green onions, sliced	1 (2-ounce) package sliced almonds
1/2 cup vegetable oil	
1/2 cup sugar	2 tablespoons butter
1/4 cup cider vinegar	Sunflower seeds
1 tablespoon soy sauce	

Discard the tough stems of the cabbage. Shred the cabbage and toss with the green onions in a large bowl. Combine the vegetable oil, sugar, cider vinegar and soy sauce in a lidded jar and shake vigorously. Sauté the ramen noodles and almonds in the butter for several minutes or until fragrant and brown. Shake the dressing just before serving. Combine the dressing, cabbage mixture and ramen noodle mixture and toss. Top with sunflower seeds and serve. Yield: 4 to 6 servings.

Linda Dick, Kappa Eta
Woodstock, Virginia

MEMORIES

My fondest memories are family gatherings at our farm, where the children had the freedom to roam the countryside. They especially loved the annual Easter egg hunt and seeing who found the egg in the cow chip. Meals for 28 were challenging to begin with, but they soon became old hat. Now that we're in our twilight years, we have moved into town. Our children are married with children of their own, but memories live on!

Kathleen Gibson, Laureate Alpha Zeta
Drumright, Oklahoma

ORIENTAL BROCCOLI SLAW

Every time I prepare this slaw I get swamped with requests for the recipe, which was given to me by a good friend.

1 (12-ounce) bag broccoli slaw	1/2 cup sugar
1 bunch green onions, chopped	2 (3-ounce) packages beef-flavored ramen noodles
3/4 cup vegetable oil	1 cup sunflower seeds
1/3 cup apple cider vinegar	1 cup salted soy nuts

Combine the broccoli slaw and green onions in a large salad bowl. Place the vegetable oil, vinegar and sugar in a jar and shake vigorously to combine. Pour over the slaw mixture and toss. Chill, covered, until ready to serve. Break up the ramen noodles and reserve the flavor packets. At serving time, add the broken noodles, flavor packets, sunflower seeds and soy nuts to the broccoli mixture. Toss and serve. Yield: 6 to 8 servings.

Barbara Bonner (32 years), Xi Zeta Psi
York, Pennsylvania

SAUERKRAUT SLAW

Excellent for summer picnics, this savory slaw complements any meat dish.

1 (28-ounce) can sauerkraut	1/2 cup red wine vinegar
1 cup chopped celery	1/3 cup vegetable oil
1 cup sugar	1/3 cup chopped green bell pepper

Drain the sauerkraut well and squeeze out moisture. Combine the sauerkraut, celery, sugar, vinegar, vegetable oil and green pepper in a large bowl and mix well. Chill, covered, for 8 to 10 hours to enhance flavors. Yield: 10 to 12 servings.

Carolyn T. Carson (41 years), Laureate Theta
Waynesboro, Pennsylvania

GINGERED MELON WITH HONEY LIME SAUCE

Our guests at our Bed and Breakfast love this as a breakfast dish or served as a low-calorie dessert.

2 cups cantaloupe balls	2 teaspoons honey
1 teaspoon grated fresh gingerroot	1 teaspoon lime juice

Place the cantaloupe, gingerroot, honey and lime juice in a medium bowl; toss to combine. Chill, covered, for 8 to 10 hours. Stir gently and spoon into individual serving bowls at serving time. Drizzle with the remaining juice. Garnish with sprigs of mint and serve. Yield: 4 servings.

Frances Goss, Delta Nu Iota
Mariposa, California

POMEGRANATE SALAD

This salad is unusual, but it's quite good, especially with turkey or ham. I liked it the first time I tasted it, although others find the taste is acquired.

1 (10-ounce) package Italian-style lettuce greens	1 1/2 cups dried cranberries
1 (5-ounce) package spring mix	1 cup pomegranate seeds
2 to 3 cups chopped lettuce	1 cup chopped walnuts or pecans
2 (11-ounce) cans mandarin oranges, drained	1/3 cup shredded Cheddar cheese
	1 (8-ounce) bottle raspberry vinaigrette dressing

Place the greens, spring mix, chopped lettuce, mandarin oranges, dried cranberries, pomegranate seeds, walnuts and Cheddar cheese in a salad bowl; toss to combine. Add the salad dressing; toss and serve. Yield: 12 to 15 servings.

Mildred Sharp (30 years), Kappa Master
McClave, Colorado

DEVILED EGG JELLIED SALAD

As survivors of the Depression on the prairies of Saskatchewan, my family members grew to like eggs in any recipe or cooked any way. This is a delicious and rather unusual egg salad.

1 envelope unflavored gelatin	2 teaspoons lemon juice
1/2 cup cold water	2 tablespoons chopped green onion
3/4 cup mayonnaise	1/2 cup chopped celery
1 teaspoon salt	1/4 cup chopped pimentos
1/8 teaspoon cayenne pepper	6 hard-cooked eggs, chopped

Sprinkle the gelatin over the cold water in a saucepan. Cook over low heat, stirring to dissolve. Remove from heat; let cool. Add the mayonnaise gradually, beating with an electric mixer or wire whisk until smooth. Beat in the salt, cayenne pepper and lemon juice. Fold in the green onion, celery, pimentos and eggs. Spoon into a 4-cup mold and chill until firm. Unmold on a bed of lettuce leaves on a serving platter. Yield: 4 to 6 servings.

Arlene Forsythe (50 years), Laureate Alpha Phi
Surrey, British Columbia, Canada

❖ GREEK PASTA SALAD

3 cups thinly sliced fresh spinach	1/2 cup chopped drained sun-dried tomatoes
12 ounces feta cheese, crumbled	1 garlic clove, crushed
1 pound spinach fusilli, cooked al dente	3 tablespoons red wine vinegar
1 cup pitted kalamata olives	1/2 cup extra-virgin olive oil
1/4 cup chopped red onion	1/2 teaspoon salt
	Pepper to taste

Place the spinach, feta cheese, fusilli, kalamata olives, red onion and sun-dried tomatoes in a large bowl and toss to combine. Place the garlic, vinegar, olive oil, salt and pepper in a jar and shake vigorously to combine. Add the dressing to the salad and toss well. Chill, covered, for 1 hour before serving to enhance flavor. Yield: 8 servings.

Breean Schwab, Sigma Zeta
Overland Park, Kansas

RICE PRIMAVERA SALAD

This fantastic side dish can be served with almost any kind of meat entrée.

2 zucchini	1/3 cup buttermilk
2 yellow squash	2 tablespoons Dijon mustard
1 large red bell pepper, chopped	2 tablespoons white vinegar
1 purple onion, chopped	1/2 teaspoon black pepper
5 cups cooked long grain rice	
1/4 cup mayonnaise	

Cut the zucchini and yellow squash in half lengthwise; cut into 1/4-inch slices. Place the zucchini, yellow squash, red pepper, onion and rice in a large bowl; toss to combine. Place the mayonnaise, buttermilk, mustard, vinegar and black pepper in a jar and shake vigorously to combine. Add the buttermilk mixture to the zucchini mixture and toss well. Chill, covered, for 8 to 10 hours. Yield: 8 cups.

Carol Zeiss, Preceptor Zeta Phi
St. Peters, Missouri

VEGETABLE PEPPERONI SALAD

My sorority sisters always request this dish for our salad dinners.

24 ounces vegetable rotini	8 ounces Monterey Jack cheese, diced
1 cucumber, thinly sliced	3/4 cup vegetable oil
2 to 3 (10-ounce) cans tomatoes with green chiles, drained	1 cup vinegar
	1 1/2 cups sugar
1 large red onion, thinly sliced	1 tablespoon MSG
1 large green bell pepper, thinly sliced	1 tablespoon garlic salt
2 (3-ounce) packages sliced pepperoni	1 tablespoon parsley flakes
	1 teaspoon salt
8 ounces Cheddar cheese, diced	1 1/2 teaspoons black pepper
	2 tablespoons Dijon mustard

Cook the rotini al dente; drain. Rinse in cool water and drain again. Place in a very large bowl. Add the cucumber, tomatoes with green chiles, red onion, green pepper, pepperoni and cheeses; mix well. Place the vegetable oil, vinegar, sugar, MSG, garlic salt, parsley flakes, salt, black pepper and mustard in a jar and shake vigorously to combine. Pour over the rotini mixture and mix well. Chill, covered, for 3 to 10 hours, stirring occasionally. Yield: 15 to 20 servings.

Dee Friel, Xi Eta Epsilon
Sweet Springs, Missouri

Meat and Meatless Dishes

For our second wedding anniversary, my husband and
I decided to keep our celebration costs to a minimum.
I was pregnant with our first child and planned to
quit my job a few weeks before the baby was due,
so money was going to be tight. For dinner I called our
favorite pizza parlor and ordered a large pepperoni
pizza with the pepperoni arranged in the shape of
the number "2." I made a salad and set the table.

The phone rang. It was the pizza parlor calling to ask if it would be okay
NOT to slice the pizza because "it will ruin the '2'." I said it was fine and waited
for it to be delivered. When the pizza came, the delivery man refused my check.
"This one is on us," he said, insisting he was later than the 30-minute promised
delivery time. He was well within the time frame, but he just walked away smiling
and saying, "Happy Anniversary." We have enjoyed some lovely anniversary
dinners since, but the memory of our second will always be a favorite.

Cheryl Alexander, Zeta Nu
Westover, West Virginia

STUFFED ROUND STEAK

This yummy main dish was one of my grandmother's favorite recipes.

1 (2-pound) round steak
1 teaspoon salt
1¼ cups water
1 beef bouillon cube
2 tablespoons lemon
   juice
2 pinches of garlic
   powder
½ cup vegetable oil
1 teaspoon thyme
1 teaspoon rosemary
1 tablespoon brown
   sugar
1 tablespoon
   Worcestershire sauce
2 teaspoons prepared
   mustard

¼ cup ketchup
1½ tablespoons onion
   powder
⅓ cup red wine vinegar
1 pound bulk pork
   sausage
1 cup sliced mushrooms
1 pound mozzarella
   cheese, shredded
1 egg, well beaten
1 cup tomato paste
1 teaspoon basil
1 teaspoon oregano
1½ teaspoons parsley
   flakes
1 bay leaf

Pound the round steak to flatten. Combine the salt, water, bouillon cube, lemon juice, half the garlic powder, vegetable oil, thyme, rosemary, brown sugar, Worcestershire sauce, mustard, ketchup, onion powder and vinegar in a large glass dish and whisk well. Add the round steak and marinate, covered, in the refrigerator for 3 hours. Drain steak and pound again. Brown the sausage in a skillet, stirring until crumbly; drain. Combine the sausage, mushrooms, mozzarella cheese and egg in a bowl and mix well. Spread ⅔ of the sausage mixture evenly over the round steak; roll to enclose the filling and secure with wooden picks. Place in a baking dish. Bake at 250 degrees for 3½ to 4 hours, basting occasionally. Combine the tomato paste, basil, oregano, parsley, bay leaf, remaining sausage mixture and remaining pinch of garlic powder in a saucepan over medium heat. Simmer, covered, for 1½ hours. Serve with steak and rice. Yield: 6 servings.

Miranda Barcelona, Lambda Alpha
Denham Springs, Louisiana

Norma Albright, Preceptor Phi, Madison, Wisconsin, makes **Fast "Roasted" Ribeye** by browning a 2-pound ribeye roast in 2 tablespoons oil in a Dutch oven, adding 4 cups water, a 10-ounce can of beef broth, 1 cup red wine, 2 minced garlic cloves, 1 teaspoon marjoram, 4 peppercorns and 3 whole cloves. Simmer, covered, for 30 minutes or until done to taste.

MARINATED STEAK WITH VEGETABLES

My mother served this dish to our family at least once a month. I always looked forward to the delicious taste, and the tender steak was so easy to cut with a fork.

1 (2-pound) round steak
1 (8-ounce) can tomato
   sauce
1 (4-ounce) can sliced
   mushrooms, drained
¾ cup chopped onions
½ cup chopped green
   bell pepper

2 tablespoons vegetable
   oil
1 teaspoon prepared
   mustard
¼ teaspoon black
   pepper

Place the round steak on a large sheet of heavy-duty foil. Combine the tomato sauce, mushrooms, onions, green pepper, vegetable oil, mustard and black pepper in a small bowl and mix well. Drizzle the tomato sauce mixture evenly over the steak. Enclose the steak in the foil, sealing the ends tightly to prevent liquid from leaking. Place the foil package in a 10×14-inch baking dish. Chill for 2 to 10 hours. Bake at 350 degrees for 1½ to 2 hours or until meat is fork-tender. Yield: 6 servings.

Carol Tomko, Delta Delta Pi
Elk Grove, California

MARINATED FLANK STEAK

This recipe was given to me by my best friend of fifty years.

1 (1½-pound) flank
   steak
½ cup prepared mustard
Pepper to taste
2 teaspoons onion salt

2 tablespoons butter,
   melted
1 tablespoon minced
   parsley
2 teaspoons lemon juice

Use a sharp knife to score both sides of the steak with light diagonal strokes. Apply a mixture of the mustard, pepper and onion salt to both sides. Chill, covered, for 1 to 2 hours. Grill over hot coals to desired doneness. Cut steak diagonally into slices no more than ¼ inch thick. Pour a mixture of the butter, parsley and lemon juice over the steak.
Yield: 4 servings.

Susie Mosier (30 years), Preceptor Alpha Kappa
Fort Collins, Colorado

BARBECUED BRISKET

1 (7-pound) beef brisket	1 cup apple cider or
1 cup sugar	cherry apple cider
1/2 cup salt	Hickory-Smoke
1 tablespoon Monterey-	barbecue sauce
Style Spice Blend	

Rub both sides of the brisket with a mixture of the sugar, salt and spice blend. Place in a glass dish. Drizzle with the cider. Chill, covered, for 8 to 10 hours. Place the brisket fat side up with the marinade in a baking pan; cover loosely with foil. Bake at 250 degrees for 7 hours, or 1 hour per pound. Pull or shred the brisket and mix with desired amount of barbecue sauce. Yield: 15 servings.

Tomi Baldridge (26 years), Preceptor Delta
Walnut Hill, Illinois

MEMORIES

"Eat your liver!" I can remember the ongoing issue my parents had with me when I was a child and refused to eat liver when it was served. I simply could not stand the taste! My parents would try to make me stay at the dinner table until I would finish eating the liver, which never happened. My mom would always give in and say, "Okay, get up from the table." I would ask them if not eating my liver meant that I would never grow up to be an adult. Apparently not, since I am 55 years old now. We still laugh about this!

Darlene Major (29 years), Xi Alpha Eta
Williamston, South Carolina

MOM MALONE'S BASQUE PICKLED TONGUE

My grandmother has American Indian and Spanish heritages. Whenever her ten children got together, we were offered a variety of foods—and everyone in her family loves to cook, including the men!

1 beef tongue	2/3 cup extra-virgin
Salt and pepper to taste	olive oil
1 white onion, sliced	3 tablespoons chopped
4 garlic cloves, minced	parsley
1 bay leaf	3 tablespoons chopped
1/2 cup rice vinegar	chives

Rinse the tongue and pat dry. Season with salt and pepper. Place in a Dutch oven with the onion, 1 of the garlic cloves and bay leaf. Add enough water to cover. Simmer, covered, over low heat for 3 to 3 1/2 hours or until cooked through. Chill, covered, until cool. Peel off the skin. Slice the tongue very thin and arrange in a shallow glass dish. Add a mixture of the rice vinegar, olive oil, remaining 3 garlic cloves, parsley and chives; marinate until serving time, turning occasionally. Arrange on a platter and serve. Yield: 6 to 8 servings.

Cheryl Kramer, Preceptor Lambda Mu
Ridgecrest, California

GLAZED CORNED BEEF AND CABBAGE

The men in my family rejoice when I prepare this hearty, flavorful dish. I love all the compliments and happy grins I receive when I serve it. Serve with hot biscuits and fruit salad.

1 (3- to 4-pound) brisket	1 tablespoon prepared
or flat round corned	mustard
beef	1/2 cup ketchup
6 peppercorns	2 tablespoons butter
4 whole cloves	3 or 4 potatoes, peeled,
1 rib celery	quartered
1 onion, sliced	3 or 4 carrots, peeled,
1/3 cup brown sugar	cut in 3-inch pieces
1 teaspoon prepared	1 cabbage, quartered
horseradish	
3 tablespoons apple	
cider vinegar	

Place the corned beef, peppercorns, cloves, celery and onion with enough water to cover in a Dutch oven. Simmer for about 4 hours. Remove the corned beef to an ovenproof platter. Combine the brown sugar, horseradish, cider vinegar, mustard, ketchup and butter in a saucepan and bring to a simmer; cook for about 5 minutes. Pour half the brown sugar glaze over the corned beef and keep warm in a 325-degree oven for 30 minutes. Add the potatoes and carrots to the corned beef water in the Dutch oven over medium heat; simmer for about 15 minutes. Add the cabbage and simmer for 15 minutes longer or until vegetables are tender; drain. Remove corned beef from oven. Arrange the cooked vegetables around the meat on the platter. Serve with the remaining glaze as a sauce. Yield: 4 to 6 servings.

Ruth E. Hull, Beta Nu
Enterprise, Oregon

MEMORIES

The Renner family was expected for dinner every Sunday at Mom and Dad Renner's house. My husband and his four siblings along with their children and grand-children ate Mom's great cooking and shared the past week's happenings. When the five children's families multiplied beyond the available seating around the big dining room table, Papa cried as the children moved to the kitchen table. By then, daughters and daughters-in-law would prepare their favorite dish. There was no thought given to calories or balanced meals. Papa's favorite was roast beef and homemade noodles. We also enjoyed baked beans, maca-roni and cheese, canned tomatoes heated over buttered bread cubes, tossed salad and pickles or cucumbers, depending on the season. For dessert we ate pie, which was a specialty of the eldest daughter, and Mom Kenner's favorite Sour Cream Chocolate Cake. With our tum-mies full and our emotional needs satisfied, we all left happy and ready for farm chores and the following week's work.

Dorathea Renner (40 years), Xi Alpha Beta
Smith, Nevada

OLD WORLD SUNDAY BEEF DINNER

I was raised on a farm in a family of Czechoslovakian descent, and this meal was served every Sunday. Homemade noodles and bread were made on Saturday. Mom put the meat on to simmer early Sunday morning, adding the potatoes and carrots as we left for church. When we returned home from church Mom cooked the noodles, the table was set, and dinner was ready. For dessert we had a mile-high chiffon cake made with farm-fresh eggs and iced with fluffy seven-minute frosting.

1 large chuck roast with bone, or 1 large stewing chicken	Peeled carrots and potatoes
2 large onions	Fresh parsley with root
2 ribs celery	Paprika
Salt and pepper to taste	12 to 16 ounces extra-fine noodles

Combine the beef, onions, celery, salt, pepper and water to cover in a 12- to 15-quart stockpot. Bring to a boil. Reduce heat and simmer until almost tender. Add carrots, potatoes and parsley; simmer until meat and vegetables are tender. Cook the noodles in boiling water for 5 minutes or until tender; drain. Arrange the meat and vegetables on a platter. Sprinkle with paprika. Place the noodles in a soup tureen and pour the beef broth over the noodles. Serve with homemade bread, pickled beets, tomato gravy and cucumbers in vinegar. Yield: Varies.

Judith Roberts, Theta Beta
Panama, New York

EASY POT ROAST

This recipe has been a family favorite for more than thirty years, and I have yet to find anyone who does not like it. Serve with mashed potatoes, rice, or noodles.

1 (4-pound) boneless chuck roast	2¹/₂ cups water
¹/₄ cup flour	¹/₂ cup chopped green bell pepper
¹/₂ cup soy sauce	¹/₂ cup chopped onion
¹/₂ cup burgundy	¹/₂ cup chopped celery

Coat the beef with the flour, and brown slowly in hot oil in a Dutch oven or large skillet. Combine the soy sauce, burgundy and water in a bowl and whisk to blend. Add the soy sauce mixture, green pepper, onion and celery to the browned beef. Simmer, covered, for about 2 hours or until beef is tender. Remove beef to a serving platter. Whisk together the remaining flour with enough water to make a smooth paste; stir into the pan drippings and cook until thickened, stirring constantly. Serve the beef with the gravy. Yield: 12 to 16 servings.

Sally Hall (43 years), Laureate Beta Zeta
Surprise, Arizona

SLOW-COOKER BEEF STEW

2 pounds (1-inch) beef cubes	1 cup coarsely sliced celery
1 envelope sloppy Joe mix	1 (15-ounce) can whole tomatoes
1 (6-ounce) can tomato paste	¹/₂ cup water
1 green bell pepper, diced	2 tablespoons vinegar

Combine all the ingredients in a slow cooker; mix well. Cook on High for 4¹/₂ to 5 hours or on Low for 8 to 10 hours. Serve with noodles or rice.
Yield: 6 to 8 servings.

Jacquie Forbes, Xi Delta
Portage la Prairie, Manitoba, Canada

MEMORIES

Having passed my golden years and retirement age, my long-time sorority sisters and I are slowing down. The big "take along" get-togethers are in the past. We had such wonderful times. Now we have covered dish luncheons, play bridge or have dessert while we recall pleasant memories. Still, we haven't given up our Beta Sigma Phi meetings and traditions.

Elaine Sills (44 years), Beta Gamma Master
El Paso, Texas

BAKED REUBEN SALAD

Great for football parties. Try serving with baked potato wedges.

1 (16-ounce) can sauerkraut, drained	3 (3-ounce) packages sliced corned beef
1 (8-ounce) package each shredded Swiss and Cheddar cheese	1 cup mayonnaise Mini rye bread slices

Combine the sauerkraut, Swiss cheese, Cheddar cheese, corned beef and mayonnaise in a large bowl and mix well. Spread in a 9×13-inch baking dish. Bake at 325 degrees for 25 to 30 minutes. Serve on mini bread slices. Yield: 12 to 15 servings.

Beverly J. Buhler, Xi Eta Xi
Rushville, Indiana

CORNED BEEF CASSEROLE

My grandmother loved to make this for our family, served with green beans and hot rolls.

1 (10-ounce) can cream of mushroom soup	4 ounces Velveeta cheese, cubed
1¼ cups milk	8 ounces noodles,
1 (12-ounce) can corned beef	cooked, drained Crushed potato chips
½ cup chopped onion	(optional)

Whisk the soup and milk in a large bowl until blended. Add the corned beef, onion, Velveeta cheese and noodles; mix well. Spoon into a 2-quart baking dish and top with crushed potato chips. Bake at 350 degrees for 45 minutes. Yield: 4 to 6 servings.

Roxanne Saathoff (27 years), Laureate Kappa
Beatrice, Nebraska

ALICE'S MEAT LOAF

My aunt doesn't even remember who Alice was, but her recipe for meat loaf will live forever in our family. We've been making it for over fifty years, and it's the only meat loaf everyone in the family will eat.

2 pounds ground beef	1 onion, chopped
2 cups quick-cooking oats	Salt to taste 1 (8-ounce) can tomato
2 eggs	sauce
3 tablespoons Worcestershire sauce	1 tablespoon sugar 2 tablespoons vinegar
½ cup ketchup	¼ cup chopped celery

Combine the ground beef, oats, eggs, 2 tablespoons of the Worcestershire sauce, ketchup, onion and salt in a bowl and mix well. Shape into a ring in a casserole dish that has been sprayed with nonstick cooking spray. Combine the tomato sauce, sugar, vinegar, celery and the remaining 1 tablespoon Worcestershire sauce in a small bowl and mix well. Drizzle the tomato sauce mixture evenly over the meat ring. Bake, uncovered, at 350 degrees for 1 hour. Yield: 8 servings.

Karen Faires, Zeta Upsilon
Portales, New Mexico

SPICY MEAT LOAF

1 pound ground beef	¼ cup prepared
½ cup dry bread crumbs or cracker meal	horseradish 1 small onion, finely
1 egg, beaten	chopped
1 teaspoon salt	1 teaspoon
1 teaspoon prepared mustard	Worcestershire sauce ½ cup ketchup

Combine the ground beef, bread crumbs, egg, salt, mustard, horseradish, onion, Worcestershire sauce and ketchup in a large bowl and mix well. Shape into a loaf in a 9×5-inch loaf pan. Bake at 350 degrees for 1½ hours. Yield: 6 to 8 servings.

Barbara M. Dick, Preceptor Gamma Lambda
Winchester, Virginia

Lauretta Philhower, Laureate Beta Kappa, Middletown, Ohio, says that **Rump Roast in Foil** is the tenderest roast with the easiest cleanup and the most delicious gravy. Place a 3- to 4-pound rump roast on a large sheet of heavy foil. Spread a can of cream of mushroom soup over the top and sides, sprinkle with an envelope of onion soup mix and seal the foil tightly. Place in a baking pan and bake at 350 degrees for 1 hour per pound.

❖ APPLESAUCE MEAT LOAF

Serve this family favorite, a true comfort food, with potatoes, vegetables, and a baked custard or pudding.

1 cup soft bread crumbs	2 teaspoons Dijon
1 cup applesauce	mustard
2 tablespoons finely	1 egg, slightly beaten
chopped onion	1 pound ground beef
1/2 teaspoon salt	1 tablespoon brown
Dash of pepper	sugar
1 teaspoon dried celery	1 tablespoon vinegar
flakes	

Combine the bread crumbs and 1/2 cup of the applesauce in a large bowl and mix well. Add the onion, salt, pepper, celery flakes, 1 teaspoon of the Dijon mustard, egg and ground beef; mix well. Shape into a round loaf in a 9×9-inch baking dish. Make a rounded depression in the top of the loaf and fill it with a mixture of the remaining 1/2 cup applesauce, brown sugar, vinegar and the remaining 1 teaspoon Dijon mustard. Bake at 350 degrees for 1 hour. Yield: 4 to 5 servings.

Jane Rice (40 years), Preceptor Psi
Sheridan, Wyoming

TACO MEAT LOAF

2 pounds ground beef	8 ounces shaved ham
1 envelope onion soup	1 (8-ounce) package
mix	shredded Monterey
1 egg	Jack cheese
1 (8-ounce) jar taco	1 (8-ounce) package
sauce	shredded Cheddar
Salt and pepper to taste	cheese
1 (8-ounce) package	
tortilla chips	

Combine the ground beef, onion soup mix, egg, 1/4 cup of the taco sauce, salt, pepper and a few crumbled tortilla chips in a bowl and mix well. Spread half the ground beef mixture in the bottom of a loaf pan. Layer the shaved ham, 1/4 cup of the Monterey Jack cheese, 1/4 cup of the Cheddar cheese and about 1/4 cup of the taco sauce over the ground beef layer. Spread the remaining ground beef mixture over the taco sauce layer. Press to make a loaf. Top with the remaining taco sauce and cheeses. Bake at 350 degrees for 30 to 40 minutes or until brown. Yield: 6 to 10 servings.

Jeri Lou Herbert, Xi Eta Zeta
Terre Haute, Indiana

MEMORIES

When I first told my sons that we were having porcupines for dinner they yelled, "Eeww! Yuck!" It quickly became one of their favorites.

Maureen MacDonald (30 years), Laureate Gamma Rho
Oakville, Ontario, Canada

My mom made porcupine meatballs when I was a kid. It was always one of my favorites.

Stacy Smith, Xi Iota Delta
Denver City, Texas

PORCUPINE MEATBALLS

1 1/2 pounds ground beef	1/8 teaspoon pepper
3/4 cup uncooked rice	1 (8-ounce) can tomato
3/4 cup milk	sauce
3 tablespoons chopped	3 tablespoons flour
onion	Salt and pepper to taste
1 1/2 teaspoons salt	

Combine the ground beef, rice, milk, onion, the 1 1/2 teaspoons salt and the 1/8 teaspoon pepper in a large bowl and mix well. Shape into 1-inch balls. Arrange in a buttered 9×13-inch baking dish so that sides are not touching. Combine the tomato sauce, flour and the salt and pepper to taste in a small bowl and whisk to blend, adding water if sauce is too thick. Pour the sauce over the meatballs. Bake, tightly covered, at 350 degrees for 1 1/2 hours. Yield: 6 to 8 servings.

Sharon Ingram (25 years), Preceptor Epsilon Theta
St. Petersburg, Florida

APPLESAUCE MEATBALLS

We have so many good cooks in our family that we compiled a cookbook of the recipes that were brought to our family reunion. Don't be disturbed by the name of this recipe—the applesauce simply makes the meatballs moist and delicious! Serve with au gratin potatoes and a salad.

2 pounds ground round	1 1/2 teaspoons salt
1 cup uncooked instant	1/2 teaspoon pepper
rice	2 cups ketchup
1 cup chopped onion	1 1/2 cups water
1 (16-ounce) can	
applesauce	

Combine the ground round, rice, onion, applesauce, salt and pepper in a large bowl and mix well. Shape into 1½-inch balls and arrange so that sides are not touching in a 9×13-inch baking dish. Pour a mixture of the ketchup and water over the meatballs. Bake, uncovered, for 1 hour. Note: You may freeze unbaked meatballs on a baking sheet; when frozen, place in a storage bag. Remove as many as needed for a meal, cover with a mixture of ketchup and water, and bake until cooked through. Yield: 25 meatballs.

Donna McCloud, Xi Lambda Chi
Robinson, Illinois

SPICY MEATBALLS

This recipe is a family favorite. The uncooked meatballs may be frozen, then removed from the freezer to be easily made into a quick meal for unexpected guests.

3 pounds lean ground beef	1 teaspoon garlic powder, or 2 garlic
1 (12-ounce) can evaporated milk	cloves, minced
1 cup rolled oats	2 teaspoons salt
1 cup graham cracker crumbs	½ teaspoon pepper
2 eggs	2 teaspoons chili powder
¾ cup chopped Spanish onion	2 cups ketchup
	1 cup packed brown sugar

Combine the ground beef, evaporated milk, rolled oats, graham cracker crumbs, eggs, ½ cup of the chopped onion, half the garlic powder, salt, pepper and chili powder in a large bowl and mix well. Shape into 2-inch balls. Arrange so that sides are not touching in a 9×13-inch baking dish. Pour a mixture of the ketchup, brown sugar, the remaining garlic and the remaining ¼ cup chopped onion over the meatballs. Bake, covered, at 350 degrees for 1 hour. Note: To prepare in a slow cooker, combine the meatballs and ketchup mixture in the slow cooker and cook on High for 2 hours, then on Low for 4 to 6 hours longer, stirring occasionally. Yield: 8 to 10 servings.

Diana Sterenberg-van Ryswyk, Xi Gamma Omega
Guelph, Ontario, Canada

Alice Lanes (40 years), Laureate Lambda, Sherwood Park, Alberta, Canada, makes **Red Simmered Beef** by placing a 6- to 10-pound chuck roast trimmed of fat in a heavy pot, adding 1½ cups soy sauce, ¾ cup sherry or white wine, 3 tablespoons brown sugar and 6 cups water and simmering for 3 hours, turning several times. Slice the roast thinly and serve on thick bread slices with the cooking liquid for dipping.

MEATBALLS AND GRAVY

Serve with rice or mashed potatoes, green beans, and a salad.

2 pounds ground beef	2 eggs
2 teaspoons salt	2 slices fresh bread, diced
¼ teaspoon pepper	1 cup milk
¼ teaspoon celery salt	1 (10-ounce) can cream of celery soup
1 teaspoon Worcestershire sauce	
1 onion, chopped	2 soup cans milk

Combine the ground beef, salt, pepper, celery salt, Worcestershire sauce, onion and eggs in a large bowl and mix well. Combine the bread and the 1 cup milk in a small bowl and mix gently. Add to the ground beef mixture and mix well. Shape into 1-inch balls. Brown on all sides in a skillet; drain. Arrange in a 9×13-inch baking dish. Pour a mixture of the cream of celery soup and the cans of milk over the meatballs. Bake, uncovered, at 350 degrees for ½ hour. Yield: 6 servings.

Kay Havig (42 years), Laureate Alpha Nu
The Dalles, Oregon

SWEDISH MEATBALLS

I received this recipe from my mother, and we have it every Christmas with lutefisk, boiled potatoes, lettuce salad, a vegetable, and cranberry sauce.

1 small onion, finely chopped	½ cup milk, whole or 2%
1½ pounds lean ground beef	1 teaspoon salt
½ pound ground pork	½ teaspoon pepper
2 eggs	⅛ teaspoon nutmeg
1 cup soda cracker crumbs	1 envelope onion soup mix
	2½ cups water

Sauté the onion in a small amount of butter or margarine. Combine the onion, ground beef, ground pork, eggs, cracker crumbs, milk, salt, pepper and nutmeg in a large bowl and mix well. Shape into 1- to 2-inch balls. Arrange in a 9×13-inch baking dish or broiler pan. Pour a mixture of the soup mix and water over the meatballs. Cover tightly with aluminum foil. Bake at 350 degrees for 1½ hours, turning meatballs once. Uncover if more browning is desired. Remove meatballs to a serving dish and thicken the drippings with a small amount of flour to make a gravy. Yield: 8 to 10 servings.

Connie Krenz (28 years), Preceptor Theta
Virginia, Minnesota

MOM'S SAVORY MEATBALLS

My mom and dad made this dish for us during World War II, substituting beef for the lamb in the original recipe. They loved each other and worked together to make this very special meal. They were married for sixty-one years!

1 small onion, finely chopped	2 shallots, finely chopped
4 tablespoons bacon drippings	1 small green bell pepper, finely chopped
2 cups white bread crumbs	1 teaspoon flour
Milk	Pinch of thyme
1 pound ground beef	2 drops Tabasco sauce
1 egg	1 (10-ounce) can tomato soup
Salt and pepper to taste	
Pinch of ground nutmeg	1/2 soup can water

Brown the onion in 2 tablespoons of the bacon drippings in a skillet over medium heat. Soften the bread crumbs in a small amount of milk. Combine the onion, bread crumb mixture, ground beef, egg, salt, pepper and nutmeg in a large bowl and mix well. Shape into 8 balls. Brown the meatballs in the remaining 2 tablespoons bacon drippings. Add the shallots and cook over medium-low heat for 4 minutes. Add the green pepper and flour, and cook for 10 minutes longer. Arrange the meatballs in a large skillet over medium heat. Combine the thyme, Tabasco sauce, soup and water in a medium bowl and whisk to blend. Pour the soup mixture over the meatballs. Simmer, covered, for 15 minutes or until meat is cooked through. Serve with mashed potatoes, peas and carrots and green salad. Yield: 8 meatballs.

Joan D. Burkhardt (29 years), Alpha Iota Master
Springfield, Illinois

MEATBALLS AND CORN

My mother used to prepare this dish, and now it is a favorite of my children.

2 pounds ground beef	1 onion, chopped
3/4 cup bread crumbs	Salt and pepper to taste
1 egg	2 (15-ounce) cans whole
1 green bell pepper, chopped	kernel corn, drained, liquid reserved

Combine the ground beef, bread crumbs, egg, green pepper, onion, salt and pepper in a large bowl and mix well. Shape into 1-inch balls. Coat the meatballs with flour and brown in a Dutch oven in a small amount of oil. Remove the meatballs; drain. Add the corn to the beef drippings and sauté for 5 to 10 minutes or until soft. Stir in a small amount of flour and cook until lightly browned, stirring constantly. Return the meatballs to the Dutch oven; add the reserved corn liquid. Simmer, covered, over low heat for 45 minutes. Serve over cooked rice.
Yield: 4 to 6 servings.

Sherrell C. LeBoeuf
Ville Platte, Louisiana

QUICK SALISBURY STEAK

This wonderful dish can be ready in 30 minutes or less, or it can be made ahead and frozen. Serve with mashed potatoes and other vegetables.

1/2 cup soft bread crumbs	1 (15-ounce) can beef broth
1/2 cup chopped onion	1/4 cup ketchup
2 teaspoons Worcestershire sauce	1 tablespoon Worcestershire sauce
1/2 teaspoon garlic powder	1/4 teaspoon basil
1 egg	1 (4-ounce) can sliced mushrooms, drained
1 pound ground beef	
2 tablespoons flour	

Combine the bread crumbs, onion, Worcestershire sauce, garlic powder and egg in a large bowl and mix well. Add the ground beef; mix well. Shape into 4 patties and place them in a shallow 2-quart microwave-safe dish. Microwave, covered, on Medium-High for 6 minutes, turning once; drain. Combine the flour and broth in a small bowl and whisk until smooth. Stir in the ketchup, Worcestershire sauce, basil and mushrooms. Pour the broth mixture evenly over the patties. Microwave, covered, on Medium-High for 6 to 8 minutes. Stir the liquid gently. Let stand, covered, for 5 minutes.
Yield: 4 servings.

June Parrish (25 years)
Barrie, Ontario, Canada

BROWN DERBY WITH SAUCE DIABLO

2 pounds lean ground beef	1 teaspoon pepper
2 eggs	1 large onion, chopped
2 cups chicken broth	4 tablespoons Worcestershire sauce
1/2 teaspoon prepared mustard	2 cups canned beef gravy
1 teaspoon salt	1/2 cup ketchup
	1 tablespoon butter

Combine the ground beef, eggs, chicken broth, mustard, salt, pepper, onion and 2 tablespoons of the Worcestershire sauce in a large bowl and mix well. Shape into 6 to 8 patties. Place in a heavy skillet over medium heat and brown both sides. Arrange the patties in a large baking dish. Combine the canned beef gravy, the 2 tablespoons Worcestershire sauce, ketchup and butter in a saucepan over medium-low heat and cook until butter is melted, stirring constantly. Pour the gravy mixture over the patties. Bake at 350 degrees for 30 minutes. Yield: 8 servings.

Clara M. Badger, Laureate Alpha Zeta
Drumright, Oklahoma

MEMORIES

Every Christmas my father, uncles, six brothers and one sister got together. After we had eaten our big meal and rested awhile, my uncles got out their instruments and started playing. They would play the guitar, harmonica, piano, saxophone, violin, Hawaiian guitar, steel guitar and accordion, and we would sing for hours. I'm 54 and my uncles are still alive and still play when we get together. I love it and feel that I have a special family.

Linda M. Helmuth, Xi Beta Epsilon
Mooreland, Oklahoma

YOUNG HOMEMAKERS BEEF AND BEANS

For many years the town of Hughson put on a tractor rodeo in the spring, accompanied by a "bean feed" put on by the Young Farmers and Homemakers club.

2 pounds uncooked pinto beans	3 tablespoons sugar
1 pound ground beef, crumbled	1¾ teaspoons salt
6 ounces white onions, chopped	2 tablespoons chili powder
½ cup olive oil	2 tablespoons paprika
2 (8-ounce) cans tomato sauce	1 tablespoon cumin
	1 tablespoon garlic powder

Combine the pinto beans, ground beef, onions, olive oil, tomato sauce, sugar, salt, chili powder, paprika, cumin, garlic powder and enough water to cover in a 6-quart kettle over low heat. Simmer, covered, for 8 hours, adding water when necessary. Yield: 4 quarts.

Janis Starn, Preceptor Delta Phi
Modesto, California

BEEF AND VEGETABLE STIR-FRY

1 pound ground beef	1½ teaspoons garlic powder
1 onion, finely chopped	1 teaspoon MSG
¼ cup vegetable oil	2 to 3 tablespoons curry powder
1 green bell pepper, thinly sliced	½ teaspoon black pepper
3 carrots, thinly sliced	8 ounces spaghetti, cooked, drained
1 small cabbage, shredded	¼ cup soy sauce
1½ teaspoons onion powder	

Brown the ground beef with the onion in a skillet, stirring until crumbly; drain. Add the vegetable oil, green pepper, carrots, cabbage, onion powder, garlic powder, MSG, curry powder and black pepper; stir-fry until vegetables are tender. Add the spaghetti and soy sauce. Toss and serve. Yield: 6 to 8 servings.

Brenda Hansen, Xi Alpha Nu
Baker, Montana

PIGS IN BLANKETS

3 pounds lean ground beef	1 large head cabbage
¾ cup uncooked rice	1½ cups vinegar
4 teaspoons salt	1 (14-ounce) can sauerkraut
Pepper to taste	

Combine the ground beef, rice, 3 teaspoons of the salt and the pepper in a large bowl; mix well. Shape into 16 large balls. Steam cabbage until limp. Drain, and separate into individual leaves. Place each meatball on a leaf, roll to enclose, and secure with a wooden pick. Place the wrapped meatballs in a large stockpot. Add the vinegar and enough water to cover. Add the undrained sauerkraut and the remaining 1 teaspoon salt. Place the stockpot over medium to low heat and bring to a simmer. Cook, covered, for 2 hours. Yield: 16 servings.

Barbara Beran, Xi Beta Omicron
Hays, Kansas

Edna H. Cornell-Moyer, Laureate Alpha Nu, Anacortes, Washington, says this **Kentucky Delight** recipe is 145 years old. Cook 1 pound ground beef until brown and crumbly. Drain and cool. Stir in a can of cream-style corn, 2 beaten eggs, a cup of milk, salt and pepper and mix well. Sprinkle a layer of bread crumbs into a baking dish and spoon in the ground beef mixture. Slice ½ green bell pepper thinly and press the slices over the top. Bake at 350 degrees for 1 hour or until firm.

BEEF NOODLE ONE-DISH MEAL

½ pound ground beef
1 small onion, chopped
1 large green bell pepper,
   chopped
1 (15-ounce) can diced
   tomatoes
1 (14-ounce) can sliced
   carrots, drained
1 (12-ounce) can sliced
   mushrooms, drained
½ teaspoon garlic
   powder
¼ teaspoon oregano
Salt and pepper to taste
1 (8-ounce) package
   shredded mozzarella
   or Cheddar cheese
8 ounces noodles,
   cooked, drained

Brown the ground beef in a skillet, stirring until crumbly; drain. Add the onion and green pepper; cook for 10 minutes, stirring frequently. Add the tomatoes, carrots, mushrooms, garlic powder, oregano, salt and pepper; cook for 15 minutes, stirring frequently. Stir in half the mozzarella cheese and the noodles. Sprinkle with the remaining cheese. Yield: 4 servings.

Mary Jean Scheller, Preceptor Epsilon Nu
Nokomis, Illinois

BEEF AND BEAN STEW

When I serve this to my children, the taste takes me back to my own childhood.

1½ pounds ground beef
¼ pound bacon, crisp-
   cooked
2 large Spanish onions,
   chopped
2 large green bell
   peppers, chopped
1 (4-ounce) can sliced
   mushrooms, drained
1 (16-ounce) can kidney
   beans, drained
2 cups cooked egg
   noodles, rice or
   spaghetti
3 large tomatoes, thinly
   sliced
Salt and pepper to taste

Brown the ground beef in a skillet, stirring until crumbly; drain. Add the bacon, onions and green peppers; cook over medium-low heat for 10 minutes, stirring frequently. Add the mushrooms, kidney beans, noodles and tomatoes and mix well. Season and simmer, covered, for 20 minutes, adding water if necessary. Note: If desired, the cooked ingredients may be placed in a casserole, topped with shredded cheese, bread crumbs and bacon slices, and browned in the oven. Yield: 6 to 8 servings.

Lynn Schwehr (26 years), Preceptor Beta Iota
Quesnel, British Columbia, Canada

CREAMY TACOS

When I ask for a dinner suggestion, I often hear: "Let's have Creamy Tacos!"

1 pound ground beef
1 (15-ounce) can chili
   with no beans
1 pound Velveeta cheese,
   melted
1 cup heavy cream
¼ cup taco or picante
   sauce

Brown the ground beef in a skillet, stirring until crumbly; drain. Stir in the chili. Gradually beat the cream into the melted Velveeta cheese in a large bowl; stir in the taco sauce. Add the ground beef mixture to the Velveeta cheese mixture and mix well. Serve over round taco chips. Top with lettuce, tomato and shredded Cheddar cheese. Yield: 6 to 8 servings.

Louise Long (36 years), Alpha Epsilon Master
Bethany, Missouri

WINEBURGERS

This recipe brings to memory those times our family spent holidays and weekends at our cabin in Blue Lake Springs. The fire would be going full blast and we would have just come in from spending time outdoors, our stomachs ready for something warm and quick. This easy, tasty dish was the perfect answer. Whether served with a salad or just pickles and chips, it is a satisfying meal.

1 large onion, chopped
1 tablespoon butter
1 pound lean ground
   beef
2 tablespoons flour
1 (8-ounce) can tomato
   soup
⅓ cup dry red wine
1 beef bouillon cube
½ teaspoon
   Worcestershire sauce
1 tablespoon chili
   powder
Salt and pepper to taste

Sauté the onion in butter in a large skillet over medium-low heat for 5 minutes or until browned. Add the ground beef and brown, stirring until crumbly; drain. Sprinkle the flour over the ground beef mixture and mix well. Add the soup, wine, bouillon cube, Worcestershire sauce, chili powder, salt and pepper. Simmer, covered, for 15 minutes, adding more wine if too thick. Serve over toasted hamburger buns. Yield: 6 servings.

Nancy Ulrich, Preceptor Nu Tau
Davis, California

❖ ASPARAGUS SHEPHERD'S PIE

This recipe makes a great one-dish meal. My son doesn't especially like asparagus by itself, but he loves it prepared this way. Serve with a tossed salad and roll, and your meal is complete.

6 potatoes, peeled	1 cup milk
1 pound ground beef	1 pound fresh asparagus
1 large onion, chopped	1/4 cup (1/2 stick) butter
2 garlic cloves, minced	or margarine
1/4 teaspoon pepper	3/4 teaspoon salt
1 (10-ounce) can cream	1/2 cup shredded
of asparagus soup	mozzarella cheese

Combine the potatoes with enough water to cover in a saucepan. Bring to a boil. Boil until tender; drain. Brown the ground beef in a large skillet, stirring until crumbly; drain. Stir in the onion and garlic and cook until onion is tender; remove from heat. Stir in the pepper and a mixture of the soup and 1/2 cup of the milk. Spoon the ground beef mixture into a buttered 2-quart baking dish. Trim the asparagus and boil for 3 or 4 minutes or until tender-crisp; drain. Arrange the asparagus over the beef mixture. Mash the potatoes with the remaining 1/2 cup milk, butter and salt; spread over the asparagus layer. Sprinkle with the mozzarella cheese. Bake, uncovered, at 350 degrees for 30 minutes. Yield: 6 to 8 servings.

Jonnie L. Stahl (25 years), Xi Eta Tau
Muncy, Pennsylvania

MEMORIES

*B*eta Sigma Phi is a group I have belonged to for 45 years now. My truest friends have been with me all this time. Raising my children, having a very successful government career and being active in church and community kept me busy, but there was always time for the sorority. Fundraisers, socials, meetings and conventions have made us close sisters. My husband always enjoyed the couples socials. Retirement gives me more time for the Beta Sigma Phi sisters and this has been good for my life.*

Margaret I. Green (45 years), Laureate Lambda
Pendleton, Oregon

UNDER-THE-STAIRS SHEPHERD'S PIE

I grew up in wartime England and once the doodle-bugs and rockets started dropping on London we spent most nights under the stairs, which was considered the safest place in case there was a direct hit. Shepherd's Pie was always a treat, given that rationing was in effect and there was very little of anything. When my mother was able to scrape the ingredients together with the help of our small garden, this meal served to us under the stairs was gourmet dining at its best! Life was never all bad. In addition to the gourmet meal, we had lots of laughs, and my family was always optimistic and knew things would get better eventually—which, of course, they did.

2 tablespoons vegetable oil	1 teaspoon mixed herbs of choice
1 onion, finely chopped	1 tablespoon chopped
1 pound ground beef	parsley
1 cup beef stock	1 1/2 pounds potatoes,
1 tablespoon tomato	peeled
sauce	1 tablespoon butter or
Salt and pepper to taste	margarine
2 teaspoons	1/2 cup milk
Worcestershire sauce	

Heat the vegetable oil in a large skillet over medium-low heat. Sauté the onion in the hot oil for 5 minutes or until soft. Add the ground beef and cook until brown, stirring until crumbly; drain. Add the next 6 ingredients. Simmer, covered, for 45 minutes to 1 hour. Combine the potatoes with enough salted water to cover in a saucepan. Bring to a boil. Boil until tender; drain and mash well. Add the butter and milk; beat until smooth. Spoon the beef mixture into a 5-cup pie pan. Spread the creamed potatoes over the beef mixture with a fork, sealing to the edge. Decorate the potato layer with the fork, swirling or pressing. Place on a baking sheet. Bake, uncovered, at 375 degrees for 30 minutes or until golden brown. Serve hot with a green vegetable. Yield: 4 servings.

Rita M. Coe (30 years), Preceptor Kappa Mu
San Rafael, California

Terri English (46 years), Alpha Omicron Master, Mountlake Terrace, Washington, says this treasured recipe for **Texas Hash** was found in her late mother's recipe box. Brown 1 1/2 pounds ground round with 2 chopped large onions. Mix in a chopped green bell pepper, 2 cups tomato sauce, 1/2 cup uncooked rice and 1 teaspoon each chili powder, salt and ground cumin. Bake at 350 degrees for 45 to 60 minutes.

TACO PIE

This dish was one of the many excellent recipes that belonged to my husband's mother, who died over ten years ago. We have many good stories and great recipes such as this one to remember her by.

1 pound ground beef	Mild jalapeño peppers,
2 (8-ounce) cans tomato	chopped
sauce	1 small onion, sliced
1 (3-ounce) package taco	1 cup shredded lettuce
seasoning mix	½ cup chopped tomato
1 (8-count) can crescent	1 (6-ounce) can black
rolls	olives, drained
8 ounces Mexican	
Velveeta cheese, diced	

Brown the ground beef in a skillet, stirring until crumbly; drain. Stir in the tomato sauce and taco seasoning mix; simmer, uncovered, for 5 minutes. Unroll the dough. Separate into a large rectangle, pressing the perforations to seal. Line an ungreased 8×11-inch baking dish with the dough, pressing into the bottom and up the sides of the dish. Prick the dough all over with a fork. Bake at 370 degrees for 10 to 12 minutes or until golden brown. Spoon the ground beef mixture into the dough-lined baking dish. Layer the Velveeta cheese evenly over the ground beef mixture. Bake for 5 minutes longer or until the cheese begins to melt. Remove from oven. Layer the jalapeño peppers, onion, lettuce, tomato and olives over the cheese. Serve with chips and salsa.
Yield: 4 to 8 servings.

Katherine A. Gose (28 years), Xi Delta Kappa
Littleton, Colorado

BEEF AND CHEESE QUICHE

This recipe was given to me by a very special aunt.

½ pound ground beef	⅓ cup chopped green
½ cup mayonnaise	onion
2 eggs, beaten	½ cup milk
1 tablespoon cornstarch	Salt and pepper to taste
1½ cups shredded	1 unbaked (9-inch) pie
Cheddar cheese	shell

Brown the ground beef in a skillet, stirring until crumbly; drain. Combine the ground beef, mayonnaise, eggs, cornstarch, Cheddar cheese, green onion, milk, salt and pepper in a bowl and mix well. Spoon into the pie shell. Bake at 350 degrees for 35 minutes. Yield: 4 to 6 servings.

Suzanne Bartlett (25 years), Xi Upsilon
Lincoln, Nebraska

MEMORIES

Some of my favorite memories are of time spent with family. The reunions were times to catch up on everyone and everything: who died, who had babies, who had married and who had divorced. And the stories that were told—I sure miss them—especially when Grandpa Brandol talked about Italy.

Jane A. Edmonson, Laureate Beta Iota
Harrisonville, Missouri

BEEF AND BISCUIT PIE

When I was a young girl, in the early 1940s, I prepared this new recipe for my family and was so pleased that they all liked it.

¼ cup vegetable oil	¼ cup flour
3 tablespoons chopped	2 cups milk
onion	½ cup chopped cooked
2 tablespoons diced	carrots
green bell pepper	Baking mix to make 6 to
½ cup diced celery	8 biscuits
1 cup diced cooked beef	

Heat the vegetable oil in a large skillet. Sauté the onion, green pepper, celery and beef in the hot oil for 5 to 10 minutes or until just beginning to brown. Sprinkle the flour over the beef mixture and cook until browned, stirring constantly. Add the milk and carrots and bring to a boil, stirring constantly. Spoon into a buttered 9×11-inch baking dish. Prepare the biscuit dough using the package directions and cut into rounds. Arrange over the beef mixture. Bake at 425 degrees for 12 minutes or until biscuits are golden brown. Yield: 4 to 6 servings.

Patricia Sienko (47 years), Delta Master
Raymond, Washington

Nancy McDaniel, Epsilon Tau Alpha, Marion, Ohio, shares her grandmother's **Baked Spaghetti**. Combine a can of tomato soup with a small jar of pitted green olives and their juice, a cup of milk, a can of drained mushrooms, 2 cups shredded Cheddar cheese, 2 tablespoons butter, 1 teaspoon salt and ¼ teaspoon pepper in a saucepan and heat until the cheese melts, stirring frequently. Cook 8 ounces spaghetti, drain and mix with the sauce. Pour into a 9×13-inch baking pan and bake at 350 degrees for 30 minutes.

STUFFED ARTICHOKES

To eat a stuffed artichoke, first remove a single stuffed leaf. Hold the tip of the leaf and gently scrape it with your teeth, removing the stuffing and a thin layer of artichoke skin.

1¹/₂ pounds ground sirloin	¹/₂ teaspoon oregano
¹/₃ cup Italian seasoned bread crumbs	1 large artichoke
2 garlic cloves, crushed	¹/₂ lemon
¹/₂ small onion, grated	1 bay leaf
1 tablespoon grated Romano cheese	³/₄ teaspoon sugar
¹/₂ teaspoon parsley flakes	1 (12-ounce) can tomato paste
	1 (6-ounce) can tomato sauce

Combine the ground sirloin, bread crumbs, 1 of the garlic cloves, half the onion, Romano cheese, half the parsley flakes and half the oregano in a large bowl; mix well with the hands. Chill, covered, until ready to use. Place the artichoke and lemon in a kettle. Add 5 cups of water and bring to a boil. Turn off the heat. Let stand, covered, for 30 minutes. Chill, covered, until ready to use. Place 4 cups water, bay leaf, sugar and the remaining garlic clove, onion, parsley flakes and oregano in a large saucepan over medium heat. Bring to a simmer. Add the tomato paste and tomato sauce, stirring until well blended. The consistency should be like that of a thin tomato soup; add more water if necessary. Remove from heat. Remove the artichoke from the refrigerator. Slice ¹/₂ to ³/₄ inch off the top of the artichoke; cut the stem to enable the artichoke to stand flat on a dinner plate. Remove the ground sirloin mixture from the refrigerator. Stuff each artichoke leaf individually with the mixture, starting with the outermost leaves and moving around the artichoke until the center is reached. Place the stuffed artichoke in a small roasting pan. Pour the tomato sauce mixture over the stuffed artichoke; only the very tips of the artichoke should break the surface. Bake, uncovered, at 325 degrees for 3 hours or until one stuffed leaf can be removed without offering any resistance, basting every 30 minutes as if for a turkey. Place the stuffed artichoke on a serving platter and sprinkle with the Romano cheese. Serve with an Italian salad and Italian bread. Yield: 3 servings.

Mary Puntureri, Preceptor Xi Epsilon
Harlingen, Texas

DONNA'S BAKED CHOP SUEY

1 pound ground beef	1 (10-ounce) can cream of mushroom soup
¹/₂ cup chopped onion	
1 cup chopped celery	1 (14-ounce) can bean sprouts, drained
¹/₂ cup water	
1 (10-ounce) can cream of chicken soup	¹/₄ cup soy sauce
	¹/₂ cup uncooked rice

Brown the ground beef with the onion in a skillet, stirring until crumbly; drain. Combine the ground beef mixture, celery, water, soups, bean sprouts, soy sauce and rice in a large bowl and mix well. Spoon into a large casserole. Bake, covered, at 375 degrees for 1¹/₂ hours. Serve hot. Yield: 6 to 8 servings.

Lucy Brushaber (25 years), Preceptor Epsilon Theta
St. Petersburg, Florida

HEARTY BEEF HODGEPODGE

1¹/₂ pounds ground beef	1 (28-ounce) can pork and beans
³/₄ cup chopped onion	
1 garlic clove, minced	1¹/₂ cups chopped celery
3 cups water	1 tablespoon Worcestershire sauce
3 (10-ounce) cans condensed minestrone soup	
	1 teaspoon oregano
1 (10-ounce) can tomato soup	1 envelope taco mix

Brown the ground beef with the onion and garlic in a skillet, stirring until crumbly; drain. Combine the ground beef mixture, water, soups, pork and beans, celery, Worcestershire sauce, oregano and taco mix in a large kettle; bring to a boil. Reduce heat and simmer for 30 minutes. Yield: 10 to 12 servings.

Kathleen Jenkins (51 years), Iota Master
Columbus, Ohio

BEEF BEAN GOULASH

1 pound ground beef	¹/₂ cup shredded sharp Cheddar cheese
2 onions, sliced	
1 pound navy beans, soaked, cooked, drained	6 to 8 bacon slices
	¹/₄ cup packed brown sugar
1 quart canned tomatoes	

Brown the ground beef with the onions in a skillet, stirring until crumbly; drain. Layer the navy beans, beef mixture, tomatoes and cheese in a 9×13-inch baking dish. Lay bacon slices over the cheese layer and sprinkle with brown sugar. Bake, covered, at 350 degrees for 1¹/₂ hours. Yield: 6 to 10 servings.

Joyce Dosch (35 years), Xi Master
Kennewick, Washington

BEAN AND BISCUIT CASSEROLE

1 pound ground beef
1 onion, chopped
1 (1-pound) package
    brown sugar
1 (40-ounce) can pork
    and beans

1 (10-count) can biscuits
8 ounces Cheddar
    cheese, shredded

Brown the ground beef with the onion in a skillet, stirring until crumbly; drain. Stir in the brown sugar and pork and beans. Spoon the beef mixture into a 9×13-inch baking dish. Bake, uncovered, at 350 degrees for 45 minutes. Remove from oven. Separate each biscuit into 2 layers and arrange the biscuits over the beef mixture, sides touching. Bake for about 10 minutes longer or until biscuits are golden brown. Yield: 6 to 8 servings.

Dee Taylor, Laureate Omega
Temple Terrace, Florida

STUFFED CABBAGE ROLLS

My Polish grandmother and mother prepared this special dish, which they called Golabki, for special days such as Easter, Christmas, and many Sundays when I was a little girl. Now I am married, and I use the same recipe.

1 whole cabbage (about
    4 pounds), cored
1 onion, chopped
2 tablespoons vegetable
    oil
1½ pounds ground beef
½ pound ground pork

1 cup cooked rice
1 teaspoon salt
¼ teaspoon pepper
1 (10-ounce) can tomato
    soup
1 (32-ounce) can tomato
    juice

Place the cabbage in enough boiling water to cover in a large kettle. Cook, covered, for 3 minutes or until cabbage is soft enough that individual leaves may be easily removed; pull off the loosened individual leaves. Cook, covered, for 3 minutes longer and pull off more individual leaves. Repeat process until all large leaves (about 25) have been removed. Cut and discard the thick center stem from each leaf. Chop the remaining, smaller cabbage leaves. Sauté the onion in the vegetable oil in a large skillet for about 5 minutes. Brown the ground beef with the ground pork in a skillet, stirring until crumbly; drain. Combine the ground beef mixture, rice, salt and pepper in a large bowl and mix well. Place about 2 heaping tablespoons of the ground beef filling in the center of each large cabbage leaf. Tuck the sides of the leaf over the filling, then roll to enclose. Spread half the chopped cabbage in a Dutch oven or large casserole. Layer the cabbage rolls over the chopped cabbage. Cover with the remaining chopped cabbage. Combine the tomato soup, tomato juice and 1½ cups water in a bowl and whisk until smooth; pour over the cabbage rolls. Bake, covered, at 350 degrees for 1½ hours. Yield: About 15 servings.

Martha Jean Shipco (52 years), Theta Master
Fairmont, West Virginia

CABBAGE ROLLS

My grandmother taught us how to make these cabbage rolls, which she called Kraut Birrock. It was always a special treat to go to her house in the winter, where she would have fresh cabbage rolls hot from the oven. When I grew up, I made them for my sons to take to school in their lunches. Each would always take two or three rolls, but they were growing, active boys, after all, so I didn't mind. Years later I found out they were selling their homemade lunches to their friends and would then buy hamburgers, hot dogs, or nachos for themselves!

1 cup chopped onion
2 tablespoons butter
1 large head cabbage,
    chopped
1 pound ground beef or
    other ground meat

Salt and pepper to taste
Bread dough, white or
    rye (I frequently use
    frozen dough)

Sauté the onion in the butter in a large heavy saucepan until tender. Add the cabbage and enough water to steam the cabbage; steam until tender. Brown the ground beef in a skillet, stirring until crumbly; drain. Add the ground beef, salt and pepper to the cabbage mixture; mix well. Allow to cool. Roll the bread dough into a large rectangle on a lightly floured surface. Cut into 4-inch squares. Place a large spoonful of cabbage filling in the center of each square. Pull up the edges and pinch together securely to enclose the filling. Arrange in a buttered 9×13-inch baking dish. Let rise for 45 minutes to 1 hour or until doubled in bulk. Bake at 375 degrees for 20 minutes or until golden brown. Yield: 12 to 16 servings.

Doris E. Arntz, Delta Mu Mu
Pioneer, California

Betty Herring, Preceptor Xi Epsilon, Lyford, Texas, shares **Spaghetti with Herbed Tomatoes and Cheese.** Cook 8 ounces spaghetti, drain and mix in 2 tablespoons olive oil, a minced garlic clove, 3 diced tomatoes, 2 teaspoons basil and 1 cup shredded mozzarella cheese. Pour into a buttered baking pan, bake at 350 degrees until heated through and top with Parmesan cheese.

BEEF AND CARROT CASSEROLE

This recipe was given to me by my sister many years ago. Serve with marinated tomato wedges, and baked apples for dessert. The dish freezes well; remove from the freezer and bake, covered, at 350 degrees for 1 hour.

1 tablespoon butter or margarine	1 cup cream-style cottage cheese
1 pound ground beef	1 cup sliced cooked carrots
1/2 cup minced onion	1/4 cup chopped parsley
1 garlic clove, minced (optional)	8 ounces medium noodles, cooked, drained
2 (8-ounce) cans tomato sauce	1 cup shredded Cheddar cheese
1 teaspoon salt	
1/4 teaspoon pepper	
1 cup sour cream	

Melt the butter in a skillet. Cook the ground beef in the butter. When ground beef begins to brown, stir in the onion and garlic. Finish browning the ground beef with the onion and garlic, stirring until crumbly; drain. Stir in the tomato sauce, salt and pepper. Simmer, uncovered, for 5 minutes. Combine the sour cream, cottage cheese, carrots and parsley in a bowl and mix well. Add the noodles and mix well. Layer the noodle mixture and beef mixture alternately in a buttered 3-quart baking dish until all the ingredients are used, beginning and ending with noodle mixture. Top with Cheddar cheese. Bake, uncovered, at 350 degrees for 30 minutes or until bubbly. Yield: 6 to 8 servings.

Alice Brewer (27 years), Laureate Pi
Independence, Missouri

BEEF AND CORN BAKE

My mother made this when we were kids in the fifties, and now it is a favorite of my own children. Chill, covered, for 8 or more hours before serving to enhance the flavor. It also freezes well.

1 1/2 pounds ground beef	1 (10-ounce) can tomato soup
1 onion, chopped	8 ounces noodles, cooked, drained
1/2 cup chopped green bell pepper	1 to 2 tablespoons Worcestershire sauce
1 (4-ounce) can mushrooms, drained	Salt and pepper to taste
1 (15-ounce) can cream-style corn	Sliced or shredded Colby or other cheese
1 (15-ounce) can diced tomatoes	

Brown the ground beef with the onion and green pepper in a skillet, stirring until crumbly; drain.

Add the mushrooms, corn, undrained tomatoes, soup, noodles, Worcestershire sauce, salt and pepper; mix well. Simmer, covered, for 1 hour. Bake, uncovered, at 350 degrees for 30 to 40 minutes or until hot and bubbly; sprinkle with cheese for the last 5 minutes of cooking time. Yield: 6 to 8 servings.

Linda Humphrey, Xi Beta Epsilon
Woodward, Oklahoma

MEMORIES

My first memories of Beta Sigma Phi are from the '60s. I remember my mother hosting meetings and socials. My sister and I would peek around the corner of the door to see what all the fun was about. I know that growing up with BSP is what helped shape my life today. I feel truly blessed to be part of this incredible organization.

Deanna Wilson, Xi Rho Chi
Orangevale, California

AFRICAN CHOW MEIN

This delicious dish is so easy and economical. When I prepare it for our chapter potlucks, I never come home with leftovers.

1 pound ground beef or ground chicken	1 (10-ounce) can cream of mushroom soup
1 onion, chopped	1 (10-ounce) can cream of chicken soup
1 cup chopped celery	1/4 cup soy sauce
1 (10-ounce) can mushroom slices or pieces	1 cup uncooked rice

Brown the ground beef with the onion and celery in a skillet, stirring until crumbly; drain. Drain the mushrooms, reserving the liquid. Combine the mushrooms, soups, soy sauce and ground beef mixture in a large bowl and mix well. Layer half the beef mixture in a buttered 2-quart baking dish. Sprinkle the rice evenly over the layer. Layer the remaining beef mixture evenly over the rice. Bake, uncovered, at 350 degrees, for 1 1/4 hours, adding some of the mushroom liquid during baking if mixture appears too dry. Yield: 6 to 8 servings.

Therese Hawkins, Epsilon Epsilon
Surrey, British Columbia, Canada

MEMORIES

*O*ne of my favorite cooking memories is the first time I really cooked for my grandmother, Nana. Nana was very particular when it came to cooking and her kitchen. Everything had to be done just so. Being trusted to dry the dishes was an honor, let alone cooking something. While Nana was recovering from surgery I was in charge of caring for her and her house. I decided it was too difficult to keep bringing food over and knew that I must enter her sanctuary and do the cooking at her house. While I was making roast beef with all the fixings, I could see the nervous looks Nana would shoot me from her bedroom. She would call to me from her room and remind me of the "Nana way" to do things. In the end, the meal was fantastic, but not nearly as fantastic as the look of approval and thanks I received for my first meal cooked in Nana's kitchen.

Mary Bravo, Rho
Ely, Nevada

BEEF AND POTATOES HOT DISH

Serve this easy, hearty, tasty, economical dish with crusty bread and a salad of assorted greens.

1 pound ground beef	1/4 cup milk or water
1 onion, chopped	4 or 5 potatoes, peeled
1 (10-ounce) can cream of mushroom soup	

Brown the ground beef with the onion in a skillet, stirring until crumbly; drain. Combine the cream of mushroom soup and milk in a bowl; add the ground beef mixture and mix well. Cut the potatoes into 1/4-inch slices. Layer the potatoes and beef mixture 1/2 at a time in a buttered 2-quart baking dish, ending with a beef layer. Bake, covered, at 375 degrees for 1 hour; cover may be removed for the last 10 minutes of baking time. Yield: 4 to 6 servings.

Ardyce Cibuzar (41 years), Beta Master
Golden Valley, Minnesota

BEEF AND POTATO CASSEROLE

4 cups thinly sliced potatoes	1 teaspoon parsley flakes
5 tablespoons minced onion	1 pound ground beef
2 teaspoons salt	3/4 cup evaporated milk
1/2 teaspoon pepper	1/2 cup rolled oats
	1/4 cup chili sauce

Layer the potatoes and 1 tablespoon of the minced onion in a buttered 8×12-inch or 2-quart baking dish. Sprinkle with half the salt, half the pepper and the parsley flakes. Combine the ground beef, evaporated milk, rolled oats, chili sauce, the remaining 4 tablespoons minced onion, 1 teaspoon salt and 1/4 teaspoon pepper in a large bowl; mix well. Spread the ground beef mixture evenly over the potatoes. Decorate the top with a little ketchup. Bake, uncovered, at 350 degrees for 1 hour. Yield: 6 servings.

Nadine Hitt, Theta Master
Rogers, Arkansas

BEEF AND POTATO HASH

1 pound ground beef	1 (13-ounce) can evaporated milk
1 (24-ounce) package frozen shredded potatoes, thawed	1 (10-ounce) can cream of celery soup
1/2 cup chopped onion	1/3 cup crushed cornflakes
1 teaspoon salt	1 tablespoon butter, melted
Pepper to taste	
2 tablespoons Worcestershire sauce	

Brown the ground beef in a skillet, stirring until crumbly; drain. Combine the next 7 ingredients in a large bowl and mix gently. Stir in the ground beef. Spoon into a buttered 2-quart baking dish. Sprinkle with the cornflakes and drizzle with the butter. Bake, uncovered, at 350 degrees for 30 to 45 minutes or until hot and bubbly; or microwave on High for 10 to 15 minutes. Yield: 6 to 8 servings.

Shirley Hanna, Omicron Master
Maryville, Missouri

Delores Kopec (44 years), Kappa Master, Bay City, Michigan, shares her *Sausage Spaghetti Sauce*. Remove the casings from 5 links Italian sausage and cook in olive oil until brown and crumbly; drain. Sauté the desired amount of crushed garlic in olive oil. Add 2 large cans of Italian tomatoes, 1 tablespoon each oregano, basil and parsley and the sausage. Simmer for 30 minutes.

MEXICAN BEEF CASSEROLE

The original recipe came from my grandmother. It was the first thing I cooked for my future husband when we were dating, and he ate three helpings! We made a few additions, such as the sausage, and a few other changes to perfect it.

1 pound lean ground beef	1 (10-ounce) can golden mushroom soup
1 onion, chopped	1 (10-ounce) can Cheddar cheese or nacho cheese soup
1 green bell pepper, chopped	
Garlic powder, cumin, chili powder to taste	1 (10-ounce) can tomatoes with green chiles
1 pound sage (or regular) bulk pork sausage	Tortillas, quartered

Brown the ground beef with the onion, green pepper and seasonings such as garlic powder, cumin and chili powder in a skillet, stirring until crumbly; drain. Brown the sausage in a separate skillet, stirring until crumbly; drain. Combine the ground beef mixture and sausage in a large bowl; mix well. Combine the soups and tomatoes with green chiles in a saucepan; bring to the boiling point. Remove from heat. Layer the tortilla quarters, sausage mixture and soup mixture alternately in a greased baking dish until all the ingredients are used, ending with the soup mixture. The deeper the dish, the better, as you can make 3 to 4 layers in a small, deep dish; a 9×13-inch baking dish will allow for only 2 layers. Place a final layer of tortillas over the soups layer and sprinkle with shredded Cheddar or mozzarella cheese. Bake at 350 degrees for 30 to 40 minutes or until hot and bubbly. Serve with sour cream, salsa and chips. Yield: 4 to 6 servings.

Teri Hodges, Xi Zeta Pi
Pryor, Oklahoma

BURRITO CASSEROLE

Serve with salsa, sour cream, and avocado.

1 (16-ounce) can refried beans	1 (8-ounce) can tomato sauce
8 tortilla shells	1½ cups water
½ cup chopped onion	⅔ cup shredded Monterey Jack cheese
½ pound ground beef	
1 envelope enchilada sauce mix	

Place about 3 tablespoons refried beans in a strip across each tortilla. Sprinkle the onion over the beans. Fold the sides to overlap at the center; arrange seam side down in a buttered 6×9-inch baking dish.

Brown the ground beef in a skillet, stirring until crumbly; drain. Add the enchilada sauce mix, tomato sauce and water to the beef in the skillet and cook over medium-low heat for about 10 minutes, stirring frequently. Pour the beef mixture evenly over the tortillas and sprinkle with the Monterey Jack cheese. Bake at 350 degrees for 20 minutes or until hot and bubbly. Yield: 4 to 6 servings.

Mary Lou Markley, Laureate Pi
Glendora, California

ANN'S BAKED BURRITOS

This meal is easy, tasty, and not too spicy. Serve with taco toppings, refried beans, and flan for dessert.

1 pound ground beef	1 (10-ounce) can cream of chicken soup
¼ cup chopped onion	
1 envelope taco seasoning mix	8 (burrito-size) flour tortillas
1 (15-ounce) can diced tomatoes, drained	8 ounces Colby cheese, shredded

Brown the ground beef with the onion in a skillet, stirring until crumbly; drain. Add the taco seasoning mix. Remove from heat. Combine the tomatoes and cream of chicken soup in a bowl and mix well. Place ¼ cup ground beef mixture in the center of each tortilla. Fold up one end of the tortilla, roll to enclose the filling and tuck under the other end of the tortilla. Place seam side down in a 9×13-inch baking dish. Pour the soup mixture evenly over the burritos. Sprinkle with Colby cheese. Bake at 350 degrees for 30 minutes. Yield: 8 servings.

Denise Gorham, Alpha Epsilon
Minneapolis, Minnesota

GROUND ROUND ONE-DISH MEAL

2 large potatoes, peeled	1 pound ground round
⅛ teaspoon pepper	1 onion, sliced
1½ teaspoons salt	2 carrots, sliced
⅓ cup uncooked rice	2 cups tomato juice

Slice the potatoes into a buttered 8×11×2-inch baking dish. Sprinkle with the pepper and ½ teaspoon of the salt. Layer the rice and ground round over the potato layer. Sprinkle with the remaining 1 teaspoon salt. Layer the onion and carrots over the round steak layer. Pour the tomato juice evenly over the carrot layer. Bake, covered, at 350 degrees for 1½ hours. Yield: 8 servings.

Marilyn Crawford (41 years), Laureate Eta
Salina, Kansas

CREAMY OVERNIGHT LASAGNA

Serve with a tossed green salad and garlic bread.

1 pound ground beef	1 (10-ounce) can tomato
1/2 cup chopped onion	soup
1 garlic clove, minced	1 (6-ounce) can tomato
3/4 teaspoon basil	paste
1 tablespoon sugar	2 1/2 cups water
3/4 tablespoon parsley	10 uncooked lasagna
flakes	noodles
1 teaspoon seasoned	1 pound mozzarella
salt	cheese, shredded
1 (15-ounce) can	1/4 cup grated Parmesan
tomatoes, drained	cheese

Brown the ground beef with the onion and garlic in a skillet, stirring until crumbly; drain. Stir in the basil, sugar, parsley flakes, seasoned salt, tomatoes, tomato soup, tomato paste and water; bring to a boil. Reduce heat and simmer, uncovered, for 20 minutes, stirring occasionally. Spread 2 cups of the tomato mixture in a 9×13-inch baking dish. Layer half the noodles over the tomato layer and sprinkle with 1/3 of a mixture of the mozzarella cheese and Parmesan cheese. Layer 2 cups of the tomato mixture, the remaining noodles, 1/3 of the cheese mixture and the remaining tomato mixture over the cheese layer. Chill, covered, for 8 to 12 hours. Bake, covered, at 350 degrees for 30 minutes. Uncover and sprinkle with remaining cheese mixture. Bake, uncovered, for 30 to 40 minutes. Let stand at room temperature for 15 minutes before cutting into squares. Yield: 12 servings.

Janet Clatney (29 years), Laureate Delta
Saskatoon, Saskatchewan, Canada

LASAGNA

2 tablespoons olive or	2 (6-ounce) cans tomato
vegetable oil	paste
1 garlic clove, minced	3 cups hot water
1 onion, chopped	8 ounces lasagna
1 pound lean ground	noodles, cooked,
beef	drained
2 teaspoons salt	8 ounces ricotta or
1/4 teaspoon pepper	cottage cheese
1/2 teaspoon Italian	8 ounces mozzarella
seasoning	cheese, thinly sliced

Heat the olive oil in a large heavy skillet; add the garlic and onion and sauté until soft. Brown the ground beef with the garlic and onion, stirring until crumbly; drain. Combine the salt, pepper, Italian seasoning, tomato paste and hot water in a bowl; whisk to blend. Stir the tomato paste mixture into the ground beef mixture. Simmer, uncovered, for 30 minutes.

Spread a thin layer of the meat sauce in a shallow 9×13-inch baking dish. Layer the noodles, ricotta cheese, mozzarella cheese and remaining meat sauce 1/2 at a time over the thin sauce layer. Sprinkle with grated Parmesan cheese and shredded mozzarella cheese to taste. Bake, covered, at 350 degrees for 30 minutes. Let stand at room temperature for 15 minutes before cutting into squares. Yield: 12 servings.

Lois Bradstreet (25 years), Preceptor Zeta Tau
Bloomington, Illinois

CHILI LASAGNA

8 ounces lasagna	10 ounces Cheddar
noodles, cooked,	cheese, shredded
drained	1/2 cup grated Parmesan
3 (15-ounce) cans chili	cheese
without beans	

Layer the lasagna noodles, chili, Cheddar cheese and Parmesan cheese in a 9×13-inch baking dish, 1/3 at a time. Bake at 350 degrees for 35 minutes or until hot and bubbly. Serve with garlic bread.
Yield: 4 to 6 servings.

Margie F. Shanafelt (54 years)
Centralia, Illinois

4-H MACARONI BAKE

I participated in five years of sewing and cooking activities in 4-H when I was a child, and this is one of the recipes we prepared. It is a hearty "make you feel good" dish. Serve with muffins.

1 1/2 teaspoons salt	Pepper to taste
1 tablespoon butter	1/4 cup milk
1 cup uncooked	1 (10-ounce) can tomato
macaroni	soup
1 pound ground beef	1 cup cooked green peas
1/4 cup chopped onion	

Pour 3 cups of water into a kettle and bring to a boil. Add 1/2 teaspoon of the salt, butter and macaroni. Boil gently for 2 minutes, stirring constantly. Cover and remove from heat. Let stand for 15 minutes; drain. Brown the ground beef with the onion, the remaining 1 teaspoon salt and pepper in a skillet, stirring until crumbly; drain. Combine the milk and tomato soup in a bowl and whisk to blend. Add the soup mixture to the ground beef mixture and cook over medium-low heat until hot, stirring frequently. Layer the macaroni, peas and ground beef mixture in a buttered 2-quart baking dish. Bake at 350 degrees for 20 minutes or until hot and bubbly. Yield: 4 to 6 servings.

Julianne Desmond, Alpha Lambda
Phoenix, Arizona

MEMORIES

I remember my dad reading bedtime stories to my sister and me. He read us the original fairy tales from Hans Christian Andersen, the Grimm fairy tales and nursery rhymes. This is something I will carry on with my children.

Signe Cook, Xi Delta Pi
Horton, Kansas

BAKED SPAGHETTI

The flavor is enhanced if you prepare this dish the day before serving and let it stand, covered, in the refrigerator before baking.

1 (28-ounce) can
  tomatoes
1 pound ground beef
1 tablespoon butter or
  margarine
1 cup chopped onion
2 or 3 garlic cloves,
  minced
1 cup chopped green bell
  pepper
1 (4-ounce) can
  mushroom pieces,
  drained
1 (2-ounce) can sliced
  black olives, drained

2 teaspoons oregano
Salt and pepper to taste
12 ounces spaghetti,
  cooked, drained
2 cups shredded medium
  or sharp Cheddar
  cheese
1 (10-ounce) can cream
  of mushroom soup
1/4 cup water
1/4 cup grated Parmesan
  cheese

Cut up the undrained tomatoes. Brown the ground beef in a skillet, stirring until crumbly; drain. Remove beef from skillet and heat the butter in the same skillet. Sauté the onion, garlic and green pepper in the butter until tender. Stir in the tomatoes, mushrooms, olives, oregano, salt, pepper and ground beef. Simmer, uncovered, for 10 minutes. Spread half the spaghetti in a buttered 9×13-inch baking dish. Layer half the ground beef mixture over the spaghetti layer. Sprinkle with half the Cheddar cheese. Repeat the layers. Combine the soup and water in a bowl and whisk to blend. Drizzle the soup mixture over the cheese layer. Sprinkle with Parmesan cheese. Bake, uncovered, at 350 degrees for 30 to 35 minutes or until heated through. Yield: 12 servings.

Billie Holaday (31 years), Preceptor Gamma Theta
Parker, Colorado

CHURCH SUPPER BAKED SPAGHETTI

1 pound ground beef
1 large onion, chopped
1 green bell pepper,
  chopped
1 (15-ounce) can diced
  tomatoes
1 cup water
2 tablespoons chili
  powder
1 (10-ounce) package
  frozen corn, thawed,
  drained

1 (10-ounce) package
  frozen peas, thawed,
  drained
1 (4-ounce) can
  mushroom pieces,
  drained
Salt and pepper to taste
12 ounces spaghetti,
  cooked, drained
2 cups shredded Cheddar
  cheese

Brown the ground beef with the onion and green pepper in a large skillet, stirring until crumbly; drain. Stir in the undrained tomatoes, water and chili powder. Simmer, covered, for 30 minutes. Stir in the corn, peas, mushrooms, salt, pepper and spaghetti. Spread half the beef mixture in a buttered 4-quart baking dish. Sprinkle with half the Cheddar cheese. Repeat the layers. Bake, uncovered, at 350 degrees for 20 minutes or until heated through. Yield: 12 servings.

Joyce Seger, Xi Epsilon Lambda
Coffeyville, Kansas

SNOWY, COLD OR RAINY DAY SPAGHETTI

My mom often prepared this dish to warm up our home and cheer our bodies and souls. The inviting smell when we opened the door after a long day made everything right with the world.

3 pounds ground beef
2 (15-ounce) cans whole
  tomatoes
2 (6-ounce) cans tomato
  paste
1 (4-ounce) can chopped
  mushrooms, drained
2 ribs celery, diced

1 green bell pepper, diced
1 large onion, diced
2 garlic cloves, minced
Salt and pepper to taste
Pinch of sugar
Chili powder
3 pounds spaghetti,
  cooked, drained

Brown the ground beef in a skillet, stirring until crumbly; drain. Place the undrained tomatoes in a large kettle and press to crush. Stir in the tomato paste, mushrooms, celery, green pepper, onion and garlic. Stir in the ground beef, salt, pepper and sugar. Sprinkle the chili powder sparingly over the beef mixture, as it gets stronger as it cooks. Cook over low heat for no less than 6 hours, stirring occasionally. Serve over spaghetti and sprinkle with Parmesan cheese. Yield: 10 to 12 servings.

Linda L. Buchanan (29 years), Xi Alpha Eta
Spartanburg, South Carolina

SPAGHETTI AND MEATBALLS

This is a very easy, very filling meal.

2 pounds ground beef	12 ounces spaghetti,
3 eggs	cooked, drained
24 saltines, crushed	
2 (15-ounce) jars	
traditional pasta	
sauce	

Combine the ground beef, eggs and saltines in a large bowl and mix well. Shape into 1- to 1½-inch balls. Place in a 9×13-inch baking dish. Bake, uncovered, at 400 degrees for 45 minutes. Combine the meatballs and pasta sauce in a kettle over medium-low heat and cook until heated through. Serve over spaghetti. Yield: 6 servings.

Patty Veeder, Alpha Phi
Watertown, South Dakota

SPAGHETTI PIZZA PIE

This dish was first served at my mother's ninetieth birthday party. It was such a hit that we now have it for other special occasions.

8 ounces spaghetti,	1 pound ground beef
cooked, drained	2 cups pasta sauce
½ cup grated Parmesan	8 ounces mozzarella
cheese	cheese, shredded
1 egg, lightly beaten	

Place the warm spaghetti, Parmesan cheese and egg in a bowl and toss to combine. Spread in a 9-inch pie plate, pressing up the side to form a shell. Brown the ground beef in a skillet, stirring until crumbly; drain. Combine the ground beef and pasta sauce in a bowl and mix well. Spread the meat mixture evenly in the spaghetti shell. Sprinkle with the mozzarella cheese. Bake at 350 degrees for 30 minutes or until heated through. Let stand at room temperature for 5 minutes before cutting into wedges. Yield: 8 servings.

Eloise Kisicki, Laureate Alpha Xi
Richmond, Virginia

❖ RIO GRANDE PORK ROAST

Serve with creamed potatoes.

1 (4- to 5-pound)	1 teaspoon chili powder
boneless rolled pork	½ cup apple jelly
roast	½ cup ketchup
½ teaspoon salt	1 tablespoon vinegar
½ teaspoon garlic salt	1 cup crushed corn chips

Place the roast fat side up on a rack in a shallow roasting pan. Rub the roast with a mixture of the salt, garlic salt and half the chili powder. Roast in a 325-degree oven for 2 to 2½ hours or to 165 degrees on a meat thermometer. Combine the apple jelly, ketchup, vinegar and the remaining chili powder in a small saucepan over medium-high heat; bring to a boil. Reduce heat and simmer, uncovered, for 2 minutes. Brush the roast with the apple jelly mixture. Sprinkle corn chips over the top. Roast for 10 to 15 minutes longer or until meat thermometer registers 170 degrees. Remove from oven. Let stand for 10 minutes. Remove the drippings, including any corn chips, to a measuring cup; add enough water to make 1 cup liquid. Heat to boiling and serve with the pork. Yield: 15 to 20 servings.

Lynne Colvin
Danville, California

PORK MEDALLIONS

2 pounds pork	1 cup milk
tenderloin, cut in ¾-	½ cup chicken broth
inch slices	1 tablespoon finely
Salt and freshly ground	chopped onion
pepper to taste	10 mushrooms, sliced
¼ cup (½ stick) butter	2 teaspoons lemon juice
or margarine	2 teaspoons tarragon
2 tablespoons flour	

Sprinkle the pork slices with salt and pepper. Brown the pork in the butter in a skillet over medium heat. Remove to a casserole, leaving the drippings in the skillet. Whisk the flour into the drippings over medium heat. Gradually whisk in the milk and chicken broth. Stir in the onion and mushrooms and bring to a boil. Remove from heat. Stir in the lemon juice and tarragon and pour evenly over the pork slices. Bake, covered, at 350 degrees for 30 to 45 minutes or until pork is cooked through and tender. Yield: 6 to 8 servings.

Bette Ann Bray (35 years), Laureate Lambda
Sherwood Park, Alberta, Canada

CRANBERRY PORK MEDALLIONS

1 (1- to 1½-pound) pork	½ cup cranberry juice
tenderloin	½ cup fresh or frozen
3 tablespoons vegetable	cranberries
oil	2 teaspoons Dijon
1 onion, finely chopped	mustard
2 garlic cloves, minced	½ teaspoon minced
3 tablespoons sugar	fresh rosemary
¾ cup apple juice	

Cut the tenderloin into ½-inch slices. Heat the vegetable oil in a nonstick skillet over medium heat. Cook the pork in the hot oil for 3 to 4 minutes on each side or until golden and cooked through. Remove the pork from the skillet. Sauté the onion, garlic and sugar in the drippings in the skillet for 10 minutes or until caramelized and tender. Stir in the apple juice, cranberry juice, cranberries, mustard and rosemary; bring to a boil. Reduce heat and simmer, uncovered, for 5 to 6 minutes or until sauce is reduced by half. Return the pork to the skillet and cook until heated through. Add more cranberries and rosemary if desired. Yield: 3 or 4 servings.

Donna Luus (30 years), Laureate Alpha Omega
Sault Ste. Marie, Ontario, Canada

MEMORIES

From the time that I can remember until I left for college at seventeen, our entire family would attend Sunday school and church together. After church, we would all go to Grandma and Grandpa's farm and have "Sunday Dinner." This would take place at about 2:30 or 3:00 in the afternoon since the cooking never started until after church. Of course all of the grandkids would be starving by then! The food seemed endless: three or four different meats, bowls and bowls of home-grown vegetables, mounds of mashed potatoes, homemade rolls, pickles and relishes, pies and cakes, and always home-canned fruit, which was Grandpa's favorite. This was all more than forty years ago, but I can still remember the smells and tastes like it was yesterday!

Barbara Caldwell, Laureate Alpha Lambda
Manhattan, Kansas

PORK POTATO CASSEROLE

My mother always prepared this delicious dish for me when I came home from college. She served it with salad and pecan pie.

2 large pork steaks	2 (27-ounce) cans cream
5 potatoes, peeled,	of mushroom soup
cut up	

Layer the pork steaks, potatoes and soup in a 9×13-inch baking dish. Bake, covered, at 350 degrees for 1 hour. Yield: 2 servings.

Mary E. Walter
Hope, Arkansas

ORIENTAL PORK HASH

This recipe was given to me when I first married. I prepared it for my children when they were young, and it was a favorite through my 57 years of marriage.

2 tablespoons vegetable oil	2 cups cooked rice
1 garlic clove, minced	3 tablespoons soy sauce
1 cup chopped cooked pork, ham or chicken	2 eggs, well beaten
	2 cups shredded lettuce

Heat the vegetable oil with the garlic in a skillet. Sauté the pork in the garlic oil for 5 minutes or until meat is light brown. Stir in the rice and soy sauce and cook, stirring, for 10 minutes. Stir in the eggs. Cook for 1 minute longer, stirring constantly. Stir in the lettuce. Serve immediately while lettuce is still crunchy. Yield: 6 servings.

Nadine M. Smith, Kappa Iota
Vallejo, California

SWEET-AND-SOUR PORK

You can make this dish ahead of serving time. Simply reheat, and it's delicious!

1½ pounds pork	3 tablespoons
2 tablespoons vegetable oil	cornstarch
1 cup water	1 cup small whole carrots, partially cooked
½ cup vinegar	
½ cup sugar	1 small green bell pepper, slivered
1 tablespoon soy sauce	
Dash of pepper	½ small onion, sliced into rings
1 (14-ounce) can pineapple tidbits	

Cut the pork into ½-inch cubes. Heat the vegetable oil in a skillet over medium heat. Brown the pork in the hot oil, stirring constantly; drain. Stir in the water; simmer for 10 minutes. Combine the vinegar, sugar, soy sauce and pepper in a bowl and stir until sugar is dissolved. Add the vinegar mixture to the pork. Simmer for 10 to 15 minutes or until pork is fork-tender. Drain the pineapple, reserving the juice. Combine ½ to ⅔ cup pineapple juice and cornstarch in a small bowl and blend. Add to the meat mixture. Cook until thickened, stirring constantly. Stir in the carrots, green pepper and onion; cook until vegetables are tender-crisp. Stir in the pineapple. Serve with rice and snow peas. Yield: 4 to 6 servings.

Vera Teasdale (48 years), Kappa Master
Guelph, Ontario, Canada

BEST OVEN-BARBECUED SPARERIBS

The kitchen smells so good while these ribs are baking! Serve with scalloped potatoes, applesauce, and your favorite vegetable.

3 to 4 pounds "country" spareribs	1 cup packed brown sugar
Salt and pepper to taste	1 tablespoon dry mustard
1 (14-ounce) bottle ketchup	2 tablespoons liquid smoke
1/2 cup strong coffee	

Place ribs in a single layer in an 11×13-inch baking pan and sprinkle with salt and pepper. Bake, lightly covered with foil, at 350 degrees for 1 hour. Drain off all grease. Mix the ketchup, coffee, brown sugar, mustard and liquid smoke in a bowl. Pour the ketchup mixture over the ribs to coat. Return to oven and bake, lightly covered, for 1/2 hour. Bake, uncovered, for 1/2 hour longer. Yield: 6 servings.

Priscilla Dunlap, Laureate Zeta Omicron
Livermore, California

HAWAIIAN SPARERIBS

I had an "adopted grandmother" who was raised in Hawaii and who was given this recipe by her mother. When I stayed with her, she always prepared this dish for me, served with a salad and Hawaiian bread.

1 (8-ounce) can crushed pineapple	1/2 cup packed brown sugar
1 to 2 inches fresh gingerroot, grated	1 teaspoon salt
1/2 cup soy sauce	3 pounds beef or pork spareribs
2 garlic cloves, crushed	

Combine the undrained pineapple, gingerroot, soy sauce, garlic, brown sugar and salt in a 5- to 6-quart kettle. Cut the ribs into 2- or 3-rib pieces and stir into the pineapple mixture. Bring to a boil. Reduce heat and simmer, covered, for 2 to 2 1/2 hours.
Yield: 4 to 6 servings.

Anne Stager, Xi Beta Sigma
Lake Havasu City, Arizona

Patricia Greenleaf (38 years), Laureate Beta Eta, Lorain, Ohio, prepares her **Pork Chop Meal** in a slow cooker by placing 6 boned pork chops that have been salted and peppered in a slow cooker. Add 1/2 cup water and cook on High for 2 to 3 hours. Add two 5-ounce packages scalloped potatoes following instructions for oven preparation. Cook for 2 to 2 1/2 hours. Add a package of frozen corn or other vegetables and cook for 30 minutes longer.

MEMORIES

I remember on Christmas Eve, my late Uncle Earl used to take all the young kids to see Christmas lights around town so Santa could conveniently come while we were gone. Darn—we always missed him, but we were so excited to see the mess of presents under the tree that we never thought too much about Santa's timing.

Susan Speer (34 years), Beta Epsilon
Arkansas City, Kansas

SWEET-AND-SOUR PORK CHOPS

This is my original recipe, and my family loves the kraut's sweetness with the savory pork chops.

8 to 10 (1-inch) pork chops	12 ounces honey
1 (16-ounce) can sauerkraut	1/4 cup prepared mustard
	1 tablespoon Worcestershire sauce

Brown the pork chops, without oil, in a skillet over medium heat. Layer the chops in a 9×13-inch non-metallic baking dish. Spread the sauerkraut over the chops. Combine the honey and mustard in a bowl, adjusting amounts to taste. Pour the honey mixture over the contents of the baking dish. Bake, covered, at 350 degrees for 45 to 50 minutes or until juices run clear. Yield: 8 to 10 servings.

Louise H. Stone, Preceptor Alpha Iota
Troy, Alabama

TACO PORK CHOPS

I created this recipe for my kids since they love both pork chops and tacos. I now serve it for sorority dinner, with rice or au gratin potatoes.

6 to 8 pork chops or steaks	1 teaspoon chili powder
1/2 cup flour	1 cup crumbled tortilla chips
1 onion, sliced	
1 (28-ounce) can diced tomatoes	

Coat the chops with the flour and brown in hot oil in a skillet. Place the chops in a 9×13-inch baking dish. Spread the onion slices over the chops. Mix the undrained tomatoes and chili powder together and pour evenly over the onion layer. Sprinkle with the tortilla crumbs and smooth the top with a wooden spoon. Bake, covered with foil, at 350 degrees for 1 hour. Serve over a bed of shredded lettuce or cooked rice. Yield: 6 to 8 servings.

Cheryl Kiger, Laureate Gamma Epsilon
Holland, Ohio

HOMESTYLE DOUBLE-BREADED PORK CHOPS

My husband's mother prepared these pork chops whenever we returned to Pennsylvania for Sunday visits. Her special ingredient was the cinnamon, and she served the chops with mashed potatoes, lima beans, and lemon gelatin with fruit.

6 (1/2- to 3/4-inch-thick) loin pork chops	4 cups Italian seasoned bread crumbs
1/4 cup milk	2 teaspoons cinnamon
4 eggs, beaten	1 cup vegetable oil

Rinse the pork chops and pat dry. Beat the milk into the eggs and pour into a shallow plate. Combine the bread crumbs and cinnamon in a deep dish. Dip each chop in the egg mixture, let egg mixture drip off the chop, then roll in the bread crumb mixture to coat. Repeat. Brown both sides in hot oil in a large skillet. Place in a greased 9×13-inch baking dish. Bake, covered with foil, at 325 degrees for 45 to 60 minutes or until fork-tender. Yield: 6 servings.

Claire M. Evangelista (37 years), Xi Kappa Psi
Westlake, Ohio

BAKED STUFFED PORK CHOPS

1 cup coarse bread crumbs	1/8 teaspoon paprika
1/4 cup chopped celery	1/4 cup milk
1/4 cup chopped onion	4 pork chops
2 tablespoons chopped parsley	1 (10-ounce) can cream of mushroom soup
1/4 teaspoon salt	1/3 soup can milk

Combine the bread crumbs, celery, onion, parsley, salt and paprika in a bowl and mix well. Moisten with the 1/4 cup milk. Make a horizontal cut into each pork chop to the bone. Fill each cavity with the bread crumb mixture and secure the edges with wooden picks. Heat a small amount of vegetable oil in a skillet and brown the chops slightly on both sides. Place the chops in an 8×12-inch baking dish. Blend the cream of mushroom soup and the 1/3 soup can milk and drizzle over the chops. Bake, covered, for 1 hour. Yield: 4 servings.

Marybeth Syfert, Eta Beta
Gainesville, Florida

AUNT THELMA'S BAKED PORK CHOPS

A visit to Aunt Thelma's always meant we would have these delicious pork chops.

8 (1-inch-thick) pork chops	8 teaspoons brown sugar
8 large onion slices	2 cups ketchup
8 lemon slices	2 cups water

Salt and pepper the chops lightly. Arrange the chops in a large oblong baking dish. Top each chop with 1 onion slice, 1 lemon slice and a teaspoon of brown sugar. Blend the ketchup and water; pour in the dish around the chops, not over the chops. Bake, covered, at 350 degrees for 1 to 1 1/2 hours or until cooked through. Yield: 8 servings.

Irene G. Berghoff (49 years), Pi Master
Bethalto, Illinois

BREADED PORK CHOPS

1/4 cup (1/2 stick) butter	1 teaspoon salt
20 square crackers, crumbled	1 egg, beaten
	1/2 cup milk
1 tablespoon grated Parmesan cheese	4 pork chops

Melt the butter in the bottom of a 9×13-inch baking dish. Mix the cracker crumbs, Parmesan cheese and salt in a bowl. Beat the egg and milk in another bowl. Coat each pork chop with the crumb mixture, then dip in the milk mixture. Coat with crumbs again and arrange the breaded chops in the buttered baking dish. Bake, uncovered, at 350 degrees for 30 minutes. Turn and bake for 20 to 30 minutes longer or until cooked through. Yield: 4 servings.

Linda Kirby Ball, Zi Xeta Pi
Pryor, Oklahoma

SLOW-COOKER PORK CHOPS

6 to 8 lean pork chops	2 tablespoons vegetable oil
1/2 cup flour	
1 teaspoon salt	1 (10-ounce) can chicken with rice soup
1 1/2 teaspoons dry mustard	
1/2 teaspoon garlic powder	

Coat the pork chops with a mixture of the flour, salt, mustard and garlic powder. Heat the vegetable oil in a large skillet. Brown the chops in the hot oil, and place in a slow cooker. Pour the soup over the chops. Cook on Low for 6 to 8 hours. Yield: 6 to 8 servings.

Judy Rounkles (40 years), Preceptor Sigma
Excelsior Springs, Missouri

MEMORIES

*W*hen I was a little girl, about three years old, my grandpa would take me to the small rural town near our home. We would meet up with other grandfathers who also had their grandchildren with them. Each would boast that he had the smartest grandchild. One time, I remember embarrassing my grandpa by raising my dress, pointing to my bellybutton and declaring to all that "this is where the Indian shot me." Of course, everyone laughed, including grandpa. You see, being a curious child, I had asked my parents and grandparents just what my bellybutton was and how it got there. They informed me that it was where the Indian shot me. Of course, being a child, I really did believe them.

Betty West (34 years), Laureate Omicron
Pahrump, Nevada

ASPARAGUS AND HAM MORNAY

You may substitute a package of frozen asparagus for the fresh asparagus spears if you like.

3 tablespoons butter or margarine	1/8 teaspoon nutmeg
1/4 cup flour	Black pepper to taste
1 1/2 cups milk	Pinch of cayenne pepper
1 cup shredded Swiss cheese	24 thin slices cooked ham
1 egg yolk	24 asparagus spears, cooked

Melt the butter in a saucepan over medium heat. Whisk in the flour. Add the milk gradually, whisking constantly. Cook for about 5 minutes or until thickened, stirring constantly. Remove from heat. Add 3/4 cup of the Swiss cheese while stirring rapidly with the whisk. Blend in the egg yolk, nutmeg, black pepper and cayenne pepper. Wrap a ham slice tightly around each asparagus spear. Arrange wrapped asparagus in a glass baking dish large enough to hold all spears in one layer. Spoon the milk mixture over the asparagus. Sprinkle with the remaining 1/4 cup Swiss cheese. Broil six inches from a heat source until bubbly and lightly browned. Serve immediately. Yield: 6 to 8 servings.

Lillie Dittfurth (30 years), Xi Rho Alpha
Athens, Texas

HAM AND CHEESE BAKE

Serve with fruit for a brunch or a Sunday evening meal. It can be prepared the night before baking.

6 slices English muffin bread	8 eggs
8 ounces Swiss cheese, shredded	3 cups milk
8 ounces Cheddar cheese, shredded	1 1/2 teaspoons dry mustard
1/4 to 1/2 pound chopped cooked ham	1 1/2 cups crushed cornflakes
	1/4 cup melted butter

Butter both sides of each slice of bread. Layer the bread in a buttered 9×13-inch baking dish. Layer the Swiss cheese, Cheddar cheese and ham over the bread layer, 1/2 at a time. Combine the eggs, milk and mustard in a bowl and beat well. Pour the egg mixture evenly over the top. Sprinkle with a mixture of the cornflakes and butter. Bake, uncovered, at 350 degrees for 1 hour. Let stand for 10 minutes and serve. Yield: 8 to 10 servings.

Bonnie Sauve (40 years)
Bismarck, North Dakota

GREEN EGGS AND HAM

My children like this dish so much, and they gave it its name. The original recipe was given to me by a neighbor long ago, and I have served it at sorority brunches over the years. Serve with fruit, coffee, and tea.

12 slices bread	6 eggs, beaten
1 (10-ounce) package frozen chopped broccoli, cooked, drained	3 cups milk
	2 teaspoons dry mustard
	1 teaspoon salt
2 cups chopped cooked ham	1/8 teaspoon pepper
	1 cup shredded sharp Cheddar cheese

Cut the bread pieces into rounds with a glass. Line the bottom of a 9×13-inch baking dish with the bread rounds. Layer the broccoli and ham over the bread. Combine the eggs, milk, mustard, salt and pepper in a large bowl and beat well. Pour the egg mixture evenly over the ham layer. Sprinkle the Cheddar cheese evenly over the top. Bake at 350 degrees for 1 hour or until set and lightly browned.
Yield: 12 servings.

Mary Lou Gleeson (44 years), Laureate Epsilon Tau
Punta Gorda, Florida

BREAD AND CHEESE BAKE

We often serve this dish for brunch on holidays and special occasions. It should really serve more than six, but it is too well liked to stretch it that far!

16 slices white bread, cubed

3/4 cup diced green or red bell pepper

3/4 cup chopped onion

1 pound cooked ham, cubed

8 ounces American cheese, shredded

6 large eggs, well beaten

2 cups milk

1 teaspoon salt

1/2 cup (1 stick) butter, melted

Layer the bread, bell pepper, onion, ham and American cheese 1/2 at a time in a 9×13-inch baking dish that has been sprayed with nonstick cooking spray. Beat the eggs, milk and salt in a bowl. Pour the egg mixture over the cheese layer. Drizzle with the butter. Chill, covered, for 8 to 10 hours. Place the baking dish in a larger baking pan. Add water to the larger pan to a depth of 1 inch. Bake, covered, at 450 degrees for 45 minutes. Uncover and bake for 10 minutes longer. Yield: 6 servings.

Ella Sears, Xi Alpha Mu
Bozeman, Montana

HAM AND POTATO DUMPLINGS

My mother prepared this delicious meal after the holidays or whenever our family had a leftover ham bone. When dropping the dumplings into the boiling broth, be sure to drop them—do not push them off a spoon.

Leftover ham bone

5 or 6 potatoes, thinly sliced

2 cups self-rising flour

1 cup milk

Cut pieces of ham off the bone. Place the bone and ham pieces in a large kettle with enough water to cover and bring to a boil. Add the potatoes. Reduce heat and simmer, covered, for 10 minutes. Uncover the kettle and bring to a boil. Combine the flour and milk in a bowl and mix into a smooth paste. Drop the flour mixture by teaspoons into the boiling broth. Reduce heat and simmer, covered, for 20 minutes. Yield: Varies.

Mary Wright Powell (32 years), Laureate Alpha Delta
Roanoke, Virginia

Nela Manning (48 years), Washington, Pennsylvania, makes **Chipped Ham Barbecue** by mixing a pound of chipped ham with 1 cup ketchup, 1/4 cup cider vinegar, a chopped onion, 1/3 cup sugar, 4 teaspoons each mustard and Worcestershire sauce and 1/8 teaspoon pepper. Simmer for 30 minutes.

BREAKFAST SAUSAGE BAKE

This recipe brings back memories of Christmas mornings with all my children and their families. Serve with muffins or biscuits.

1 pound hot bulk pork sausage

2 pounds mild bulk pork sausage

10 to 12 slices white bread, cubed

3 cups shredded Cheddar cheese

12 eggs

2 cups milk

1 teaspoon salt

1 teaspoon pepper

2 teaspoons dry mustard

Cook each of the sausages in a skillet until brown and crumbly; drain and set aside. Layer the bread, Cheddar cheese, hot sausage and mild sausage in a buttered 9×13-inch glass baking dish, 1/2 at a time. Combine the eggs, milk, salt, pepper and mustard in a large bowl and beat well. Pour the egg mixture evenly over the top sausage layer. Bake at 350 degrees for 1 1/2 hours or until light golden brown. Yield: 12 servings.

Maxine Hardin (27 years), Xi Alpha Eta
Greenville, South Carolina

LAYERED SAUSAGE AND POTATO BAKE

12 ounces sweet Italian sausage, casings removed

1/4 cup vegetable oil

1 1/2 cup thinly sliced peeled potatoes

1/2 cup chopped green bell pepper

1/3 cup chopped onion

6 eggs

1/2 cup milk

3/4 teaspoon baking powder

1/4 cup grated Parmesan cheese

Salt and pepper

1/2 cup canned tomato sauce

4 ounces mozzarella cheese, shredded

Cut the sausage into bite-size pieces. Spread the vegetable oil in a 9×13-inch baking dish. Layer the sausage, potatoes, green pepper and onion in the baking dish. Bake at 375 degrees for 35 minutes. Combine the eggs, milk, baking powder and Parmesan cheese in a medium bowl and beat until smooth. Add a little salt and pepper. Pour egg mixture evenly over the contents of the baking dish. Bake at 325 degrees for 30 minutes. Drizzle with tomato sauce and sprinkle with mozzarella cheese. Bake for 10 minutes longer. Yield: 6 to 9 servings.

Elizabeth S. Czysz, Eta Tau
Fredonia, New York

SAUSAGE SALSA SPAGHETTI

I created this recipe to enter a cooking contest in the Nevada State Fair . . . and won first prize!

Olive oil	3 pounds hot or medium
3 large sweet white	Italian sausage,
onions	casings removed
2 to 4 garlic cloves,	2 pounds spaghetti
pressed	Garlic salt
3 bunches parsley, stems	2¹/₂ pounds mozzarella
removed, chopped	cheese, shredded
14 sliced unpeeled	1 (7-ounce) can pitted
zucchini	olives, halved
3 (7-ounce) cans green	1 (8-ounce) can button
chile salsa	mushrooms, drained

Cover the bottom of an electric skillet with ¹/₈ to ¹/₄ inch olive oil. Cut the onions into thin slices and separate into rings. Sauté the onion rings in the hot oil for 2 minutes. Add the garlic, parsley, zucchini and salsa. Stir gently and bring to a simmer. Simmer for 8 minutes or until zucchini is tender. Brown the sausage in a separate skillet; drain. Boil the spaghetti in salted water for 8 minutes. Rinse with cool water; drain. Oil 6 (8×10×2-inch) baking pans with olive oil. Cover bottom of pans with a ³/₄-inch layer of spaghetti; sprinkle with garlic salt. Layer the sausage, zucchini mixture and mozzarella cheese evenly over the spaghetti. Garnish with the olives and button mushrooms. Bake at 350 degrees for 30 minutes. Yield: 20 to 22 servings.

Kathie Preston (34 years), Preceptor Chi
Reno, Nevada

POLYNESIAN SAUSAGES

This dish can be prepared in advance and refrigerated until mealtime. Reheat in the oven and make rice. Moose sausages may be substituted for the pork sausages.

1 pound sausage links	2 tablespoons
1 green bell pepper,	cornstarch
sliced	¹/₄ cup packed brown
2 ribs celery, sliced	sugar
1 onion, sliced	¹/₄ cup vinegar
1 (14-ounce) can	1 tablespoon soy sauce
pineapple chunks	

Brown the sausages lightly in a skillet; remove from skillet and keep warm. Add the green pepper, celery and onion to the drippings in the skillet; brown slightly. Drain the pineapple, reserving juice. Add the pineapple to the onion mixture. Combine the cornstarch and brown sugar in a small bowl and mix well. Add the pineapple juice, vinegar and soy sauce; beat until smooth. Add the cornstarch mixture gradually to the pineapple mixture and cook until thickened, stirring constantly. Return the sausages to the skillet and reheat. Serve with rice. Yield: 4 servings.

Judy Parsons, Xi Beta
Corner Brook, Newfoundland, Canada

CABBAGE AND ONION WITH SAUSAGE

A great one-dish meal. A pound of bacon, chopped, may be substituted for the pork sausage.

1 pound bulk pork	2 teaspoons parsley
sausage	flakes
1 large onion, chopped	1 tablespoon Italian
1 head cabbage, coarsely	seasoning
shredded	Salt and pepper to taste
1 teaspoon sage	

Brown the sausage in a skillet over medium heat, stirring until crumbly; drain, leaving 2 tablespoons of the drippings in the skillet with the sausage. Stir in the onion, cabbage, sage, parsley flakes, Italian seasoning, salt and pepper. Simmer, covered, for 10 minutes or until onion and cabbage are limp. Yield: 6 servings.

April L. Johnston, Alpha Phi Kappa
Flint, Texas

CRESCENT LASAGNA

2 (8-count) cans crescent	1 (6-ounce) can tomato
rolls	paste
¹/₂ pound bulk pork	1 cup creamed cottage
sausage	cheese
¹/₂ pound ground beef	1 egg
³/₄ cup chopped onion	¹/₄ cup grated Parmesan
1 garlic clove, minced	cheese
1 tablespoon parsley	2 (4×7-inch) slices
flakes	mozzarella cheese
¹/₂ teaspoon oregano	1 tablespoon milk
¹/₂ teaspoon basil	1 tablespoon sesame
¹/₂ teaspoon salt	seeds
Dash of pepper	

Unroll the dough. Separate into 2 rectangles, pressing perforations to seal. Place on an ungreased baking sheet, pressing the edges to seal and make a 13×15-inch rectangle. Brown the sausage and ground beef in a skillet, stirring until crumbly; drain. Return the sausage mixture to the skillet. Stir in the onion, garlic, parsley, oregano, basil, salt, pepper and tomato paste. Bring to a simmer. Simmer, uncovered, for 10 minutes. Combine the cottage cheese, egg and Parmesan cheese in a small bowl; mix well. Spread half the meat mixture down the center of the dough.

Spread to within 1 inch of each short end. Spread the cottage cheese filling over the meat mixture. Spoon the remaining meat mixture over the top. Place the mozzarella cheese over the meat layer. Pull up long ends to meet and pinch to seal. Brush with milk and sprinkle with sesame seeds. Bake at 375 degrees for 30 minutes or until golden brown.
Yield: 4 to 6 servings.

Cheryl Northern, Xi Delta Kappa
Littleton, Colorado

MEMORIES

For many years, our Beta chapter has gathered at a member's home about 1½ weeks before Thanksgiving Day for a traditional Thanksgiving meal. Each member brings a dish. The tables are set with candles, good china, etc. We enjoy sharing recipes and the fellowship. Every year we are thankful for our blessings.

Gwynn Stastny (28 years), Laureate Alpha Xi
Richmond, VA

SAUSAGE NOODLE ONE-DISH MEAL

1 pound bulk pork	**Salt and pepper to taste**
sausage	**16 ounces egg noodles,**
1 cup (or more) milk	**cooked, drained**
1 pound American	
cheese, chopped	

Brown the sausage in a skillet, stirring until crumbly; drain. Return the sausage to the skillet over low heat. Add the milk and American cheese and heat until cheese melts, stirring frequently. Stir in the salt, pepper and noodles. Yield: 4 servings.

Helen Sidebottom, Upsilon Nu
Versailles, Missouri

Mary Ann Haley (31 years), Xi Kappa Pi, Fairfield, California, ate **Monterey Jack Soufflé** at a catered party. The caterers agreed to share the recipe after much entreaty. Beat 6 eggs with 1 cup milk and ½ cup flour until smooth. Beat in 1 teaspoon baking powder and 6 tablespoons melted butter. Spread 4 cups small curd cottage cheese in a buttered 9×13-inch baking dish. Pour in the egg mixture evenly, add a layer of 4 cups shredded Monterey Jack cheese and dot with 3 ounces cream cheese. Bake at 350 degrees for 1 hour or until light brown.

MOCK CHICKEN ALMOND

This dish was served at one of the first socials I attended as a pledge to Nu chapter, Albuquerque, New Mexico.

2 pounds mild bulk pork	**4 (10-ounce) cans**
sausage	**chicken soup**
2 onions, chopped	**2 cups uncooked long**
2 green bell peppers,	**grain rice**
diced	**9 cups boiling water**
4 ribs celery,	**6 ounces slivered**
chopped	**almonds**

Brown the sausage in a skillet, stirring to prevent lumps. Remove the sausage from the skillet, leaving the drippings. Sauté the onions, green peppers and celery in the drippings; drain on a paper towel. Place the sausage, onion mixture, soup and rice in 1 or 2 large baking dishes. Stir in the boiling water. Bake at 375 degrees for 50 minutes. Remove from oven and stir. Add the almonds and stir again. Return to oven. Bake for 10 minutes longer. Yield: 25 servings.

Frances Parks (39 years), Laureate Beta Sigma
St. Charles, Missouri

SWISS CHEESE AND MUSHROOM STRATA

My husband and I had a bed-and-breakfast inn, Shari's Garden Home, in our 1905 Mission Oak–style house for 7½ years. We made many friends from as far away as Norway, Washington, D.C. (a congressman), many different states, and our own hometown. We held fundraisers for children in need with tours of the B&B, and we held an Artist's Christmas Sale twice. Many wonderful people passed through our front door. We never once regretted our decision or the work involved.

1½ cups pork-and-	**16 slices white bread,**
bacon sausage	**crusts trimmed**
8 eggs, beaten	**1 (4-ounce) can sliced**
1 teaspoon dry mustard	**mushrooms, drained**
3 cups milk	**8 slices Swiss cheese**

Brown the sausage in a skillet, stirring until crumbly; drain. Combine the eggs, mustard and milk in a large bowl and beat until smooth. Line a 9×13-inch baking dish with 8 slices of bread. Layer the sausage, mushrooms, Swiss cheese and remaining bread slices over the bread. Pour the egg mixture evenly over the top. Chill, covered, for 12 to 24 hours. Bake, uncovered, at 350 degrees for 1 hour. Yield: 8 to 12 servings.

Shari Oleson, Alpha Lambda
Carroll, Iowa

OVERNIGHT SALAMI OMELET

5 cups small torn pieces of French bread	1 1/2 cups milk
3 tablespoons melted butter or margarine	1/4 cup dry white wine
1 1/2 cups shredded Swiss cheese	1/4 cup chopped green onion
2 cups shredded Colby cheese	2 teaspoons Dijon mustard
6 thin slices salami, or 1/2 cup chopped	1/4 teaspoon pepper
8 eggs	1/4 teaspoon paprika
	3/4 cup sour cream
	1/2 cup freshly grated Parmesan cheese

Spread the bread in a buttered 9×13-inch baking dish. Drizzle with the melted butter. Layer the Swiss cheese, Colby cheese and salami over the bread. Combine the eggs, milk, wine, green onion, mustard, pepper and paprika in a large bowl and beat well. Pour evenly over the salami layer. Chill, covered tightly with foil, for 8 to 24 hours. Remove from refrigerator 30 minutes before baking. Bake, covered, at 325 degrees for 1 hour. Uncover. Spread sour cream over the top and sprinkle with Parmesan cheese. Bake, uncovered, for 10 minutes longer or until lightly browned. Serve immediately. Yield: 8 to 12 servings.

Shirley T. Wall, Preceptor Epsilon
Grand Falls-Windsor, Newfoundland, Canada

VEGETABLE HAM OMELET

1 dozen eggs, beaten	1 pound smoked ham, diced
2 green bell peppers, diced	1 cup sour cream
1 (15-ounce) can diced stewed tomatoes, drained	1/4 cup (1/2 stick) margarine
1 pound Velveeta cheese, diced	1 teaspoon chopped parsley
	Salt and pepper to taste

Combine the eggs, green peppers, tomatoes, Velveeta cheese, ham, sour cream, margarine, parsley, salt and pepper in a large bowl and mix well. Pour into a 3-quart baking dish. Bake, covered, at 350 degrees for 1 hour or until set. Yield: 8 servings.

Madeline Watson (30 years), Xi Alpha Beta Omega
Jasper, Texas

RED HOT POTATO SCALLOP

Red Hot Potato Scallop, served with cabbage salad, was (and is) always a family favorite on a cold night. My three children love this dish and they always request it when they visit. The leftovers always leave when they do!

2 onions, sliced	1 tablespoon brown sugar
8 hot dogs, cut in bite-size pieces	1 teaspoon dry mustard
1/2 cup diced celery	1/2 teaspoon salt
3 carrots, sliced	1 (10-ounce) can tomato soup
3 cups diced peeled potatoes	1 cup water

Combine the onions, hot dogs, celery, carrots and potatoes in a large casserole and mix gently. Sprinkle with brown sugar. Combine the mustard, salt, soup and water in a bowl and whisk to blend. Pour evenly over the hot dog mixture. Bake, covered, at 350 degrees for 1 1/2 hours. Yield: 6 to 8 servings.

Kaaren Dunford (36 years), Laureate Beta Pi
Cavan, Ontario, Canada

FRIED DOGS

1 cup milk	1 tablespoon prepared mustard
1 egg	1 (12- or 16-ounce) package hot dogs
1 cup flour	Vegetable oil for deep-frying
1/8 teaspoon salt	
1 teaspoon baking powder	

Whisk the milk, egg, flour, salt, baking powder and mustard in a bowl. Drain and completely dry the hot dogs with paper towels so the batter will cling tightly. Insert a fork into the end of each dried-off hot dog and dip into the batter to coat. Place the coated hot dogs carefully in the hot oil and deep-fry until brown on all sides. Serve hot with mustard or ketchup or both. Yield: 8 to 10 servings.

Evalene Marie Howell (27 years), Alpha Delta Beta
Glen Rose, Texas

Deb Daniels, Xi Zeta Rho, LeMars, Iowa, prepares **Country Club Ham and Eggs**. Layer 7 slices cubed bread, 2 cups shredded Colby cheese, 1 pound cubed ham and drained, canned, sliced mushrooms in a greased 9×13-inch baking dish. Beat 4 eggs, 2 1/2 cups milk and a pinch each of salt and dry mustard. Pour over the layers. Drizzle with 1/2 cup melted butter and pat 2 slices cubed bread on top. Chill, covered, for 8 to 10 hours. Bake, uncovered, at 325 degrees for 1 hour.

LAMB STEW WITH ARTICHOKE HEARTS

1 tablespoon olive oil
2 garlic cloves, minced
1 red onion, chopped
2 ribs celery, chopped
1 pound (1-inch) lamb
  cubes
1/2 cup chicken broth or
  bouillon
1/2 cup white sherry
1 (15-ounce) can diced
  tomatoes with basil,
  garlic and oregano
1 teaspoon crushed
  fennel seed
1 (10-ounce) package
  frozen artichoke
  hearts, thawed
4 large potatoes, peeled,
  quartered
1 tablespoon fresh
  lemon juice
Salt and pepper to taste

Combine the olive oil, garlic, onion and celery in a 4-quart saucepan over medium heat. Cook for 10 minutes or until mixture is browned, stirring frequently. Stir in the lamb cubes and chicken broth. Boil gently, covered, until juices evaporate and meat is lightly browned. Add the sherry, undrained tomatoes and fennel seed, stirring and scraping to free browned bits. Bring to a boil. Reduce heat and simmer, covered, for 40 minutes. Stir in the artichokes and potatoes. Simmer, covered, for 30 minutes or until potatoes are tender and lamb is fork-tender, stirring occasionally. Stir in the lemon juice. Season with salt and pepper. Sprinkle with chopped parsley and serve. Yield: 6 servings.

 Rose Gaspari (53 years), Beta Chi Master
Santa Rosa, California

VEGETABLE HOT POTPIE

This dish brings back memories of cold winter nights in England, sitting by the fire in my parents' house. They served the potpie with love and a nice dish of pickled beets.

2 cups flour
Pinch of salt
2 tablespoons baking
  powder
1/2 cup (1 stick) cold
  margarine
2 or 3 vegetable bouillon
  cubes
1 large onion, chopped
1 (12-ounce) package
  tofu chunks
1 carrot, chopped
2 pounds potatoes,
  peeled, chopped
1 to 2 tablespoons
  cornstarch
Vegetable oil for frying

Combine the flour, salt and baking powder in a bowl. Cut in the margarine until the mixture resembles coarse crumbs. Add cold water 1 tablespoon at a time, mixing with a fork until the mixture forms a ball. Chill, wrapped in plastic wrap, for 30 minutes or longer. Dissolve the vegetable bouillon cubes in 2 to 3 cups water. Sauté the onion in hot oil for 5 to 10 minutes or until tender. Add the tofu chunks and sauté for 5 minutes. Add the carrot and sauté a few minutes longer. Add the vegetable bouillon and potatoes; bring to a boil. Reduce heat and simmer for 20 to 30 minutes or until potatoes are tender. Thicken the liquid with cornstarch. Spoon potato mixture into a 2-quart baking dish. Roll the chilled pastry into a 12-inch circle or square on a lightly floured surface. Fit over the potato mixture. Bake at 375 degrees for 25 to 30 minutes or until hot and golden brown. Yield: 6 to 8 servings.

Jan L. Wainwright, Preceptor Sigma
Ottawa, Ontario, Canada

SOUTHWESTERN TWO-BEAN CHILI AND RICE

1 1/2 cups uncooked rice
1 tablespoon vegetable
  oil
1 cup chopped onion
1 cup chopped green or
  red bell pepper
2 garlic cloves, minced
1 (15-ounce) can chili
  beans in spicy or
  mild sauce
1 (15-ounce) can black
  or pinto beans,
  drained
1 (10-ounce) can diced
  tomatoes with green
  chiles
1 tablespoon chili
  powder
2 teaspoons cumin

Cook the rice using package directions. Heat the oil in a large saucepan over medium-high heat. Add the onion, bell pepper and garlic and cook for 5 minutes, stirring occasionally. Stir in the undrained chili beans, black beans, undrained tomatoes with green chiles, chili powder and cumin. Cover and bring to a boil over high heat. Reduce heat to medium-low and simmer for 10 minutes. Serve over hot cooked rice. Yield: 6 to 8 servings.

Gayle Schlotfeldt, Xi Tau
Havre, Montana

Sue Jenkins, Xi Epsilon Nu, Monument, Colorado, shares this favorite after-Easter ritual to use up all those eggs. Bake a package of patty shells and keep warm. Sauté 1/3 cup finely chopped onion and 8 ounces sliced mushrooms in 1/4 cup butter for 5 minutes. Stir in a can of cream of mushroom soup, 1/4 cup chopped parsley and 1/4 teaspoon white pepper and bring to a simmer, stirring frequently. Add 6 chopped hard-cooked eggs and heat to serving temperature. Ladle into patty shells and presto!—***Mushrooms and Eggs in Patty Shells***. Also good on hot toast or toasted English muffins.

BAKED MEATLESS STUFFED PEPPERS

My Granny Arthula prepared this dish on "hay baling day" or "threshing day," when fifteen or so neighboring farmers would go from farm to farm, working until the crops of the entire community were "put up." It was the responsibility of a farmer's wife to cook the meal for all the neighboring farmhands when her farm was being worked. Granny always had plenty of meatless dishes as well as lots of fried chicken to serve. I had the privilege of washing and drying all the dishes that week! All the food came from Granny's garden or chicken house or pig pen or milk barn, as she went to the grocery store very seldom. The Stuffed Green Peppers were served with roast corn, sliced tomatoes, and hot rolls.

6 large green bell peppers	1/2 teaspoon oregano
4 cups cooked brown rice	1/2 teaspoon basil
6 ounces Swiss cheese, finely diced	2 eggs, well beaten
1/2 cup chopped parsley	1/2 cup half-and-half
1/2 cup chopped celery	1 tablespoon prepared mustard
1 small onion, chopped	Salt and pepper to taste
	1/2 cup grated Parmesan cheese

Slice the tops from the green peppers and remove the seeds. Cook in boiling water for 5 minutes. Drain; cool. Combine the rice, Swiss cheese, parsley, celery, onion, oregano, basil, eggs, half-and-half and mustard in a large bowl and mix well. Season with salt and pepper. Spoon the rice mixture into the green peppers. Arrange the stuffed peppers in a shallow baking pan. Add water to the pan to a depth of 1/4 inch. Sprinkle tops of peppers with Parmesan cheese. Bake at 350 degrees for 30 to 40 minutes or until hot and browned. Yield: 6 servings.

Joycee Davis, Laureate Alpha Epsilon
Lowell, Arkansas

Mary McBride Johnson (57 years), Laureate Zeta Sigma, Lubbock, Texas, shares **Nancy's Twenty-Four-Hour Cheese Omelet**. Butter 8 slices white or wheat bread, cut into cubes and spread in a buttered 9×13-inch baking dish. Add layers of 4 cups shredded Cheddar cheese and any combination and amounts of sliced green onions, fresh mushrooms, black or green olives, cooked bacon or sausage, green peppers, etc. Beat 8 eggs with 3/4 teaspoon each salt and dry mustard, 3 cups milk and cayenne pepper to taste. Pour over the layers and chill, covered, for 6 to 10 hours. Bake, covered, at 350 degrees for 1 hour and uncovered for 5 to 10 minutes longer or until set.

MEMORIES

Funerals are sad occasions for families to have to go through, but they offer the chance to reconnect with family and friends. It is unfortunate that it takes a sad occasion to get people together. My fondest childhood memories regarding my extended family are of my grandparents' funerals, where I had the chance to play with cousins and eat some of the best food I have ever had. It's a great place to pick up new recipes.

Cathy Baber, Xi Theta Chi
Chesapeake, Virginia

CREAMY SCRAMBLED EGGS

This is an excellent breakfast entrée for a weekend party. The eggs stay creamy and warm as each person comes down for breakfast. Choose from a variety of condiments to embellish the eggs: caviar, shrimp, bleu cheese, green onion slices, chopped green pepper, sliced black or green olives, salsa, bacon bits, chopped ham, sliced sausage, and jellies or jams.

4 tablespoons butter	3/4 teaspoon salt
2 tablespoons flour	1/8 teaspoon white pepper
1 cup sour cream	
2 dozen eggs	

Melt half the butter in a small saucepan over medium heat. Whisk in the flour and cook until bubbly, stirring constantly. Remove from heat. Blend in the sour cream. Return to heat and cook until smooth and bubbly, stirring constantly. Remove from heat. Combine the eggs, salt and white pepper in a large bowl and beat well. Melt the remaining 2 tablespoons butter in a large skillet over medium-low heat. Pour in the egg mixture and cook until eggs are softly set, gently lifting cooked portions to allow uncooked portions to flow underneath. Remove from heat and gently stir in the sour cream mixture. Spoon into a serving dish and garnish with parsley, or keep warm for as long as 1 hour in a slow cooker or on an electric warming tray. Serve with condiments in individual bowls. Yield: 12 servings.

Merline McCoy (43 years), Alpha Psi Master
Village Mills, Texas

Poultry and Seafood

One Thanksgiving I bought a large frozen turkey,
and put it in a seldom-used refrigerator to thaw.
My husband saw that the refrigerator was plugged in
and, to save on power, unplugged it without asking
why it was plugged in. On Thanksgiving Day, I went to
get the turkey out of the refrigerator. When I
opened the door, I recoiled at the aroma.
My husband made a quick trip to the store to buy
another turkey which the butcher quartered for
faster cooking. I got it cooked, and no one was any wiser.
In fact, they thought that it was a good idea to have the
butcher cut the turkey. They just didn't know why!

Marion Buchanan, Xi Eta Kappa
Cloyne, Ontario, Canada

❖ CHICKEN AND PEPPERS OVER PASTA

This recipe came to me by way of San Diego and Switzerland—from my son, who received it from his mother-in-law. It is also delicious served over rice.

8 large red bell peppers	2 pounds boneless
1 large onion, chopped	skinless chicken
5 tablespoons olive oil	breasts
2 garlic cloves, pressed	1/2 cup white wine
1/2 teaspoon salt	16 ounces uncooked
1/4 teaspoon black	spaghetti or linguini
pepper	1/2 cup (1 stick) butter,
1/2 teaspoon sugar	melted
1 teaspoon oregano	1/4 cup grated Parmesan
1 (28-ounce) can whole	cheese
tomatoes	

Roast the red peppers over the stove or grill until blackened. Peel, remove seeds and cut roasted peppers into 1-inch pieces. Sauté the onion in 3 tablespoons of the olive oil in a large skillet until onion is translucent. Add the garlic, roasted peppers, salt, black pepper, sugar and oregano. Slice the canned tomatoes into the onion mixture; add the liquid from the can. Cut the chicken breasts into 3/4-inch cubes and brown lightly in a separate skillet in a small amount of olive oil. Add the chicken to the onion mixture. Deglaze the chicken skillet with the white wine and add the wine mixture to the chicken mixture. Simmer, covered, for 45 minutes to 1 hour or until chicken is cooked through and tender. Cook the pasta al dente in boiling water in a saucepan; drain well. Place the pasta in a large warm bowl. Add the melted butter and Parmesan cheese; toss to combine. Serve the chicken mixture over the prepared pasta. Yield: 6 servings.

Marilyn K. Higbee, Xi Sigma Upsilon
North Fork, California

❖ CHUNKY CHICKEN SPAGHETTI

4 chicken breasts,	1/2 to 1 cup sliced fresh
cooked, boned,	mushrooms
chopped	1 (32-ounce) jar
2 tablespoons vegetable	spaghetti sauce
oil	2 cups shredded
1 red bell pepper,	mozzarella cheese
chopped	8 ounces spaghetti,
1 green bell pepper,	cooked, drained
chopped	2 tablespoons chopped
1 onion, chopped	parsley (optional)
1 garlic clove, minced	

Brown the cooked chicken in hot vegetable oil in a 12-inch-or-larger skillet over medium heat. Add the bell peppers, onion, garlic and mushrooms and sauté for 5 to 10 minutes or until vegetables are tender. Stir in the spaghetti sauce and half the mozzarella cheese. Serve over the spaghetti. Sprinkle with the parsley and remaining cheese. A 4-ounce can of drained sliced mushrooms may be substituted for the fresh ones. A cup of shredded Cheddar cheese plus a cup of shredded mozzarella may be substituted for the 2 cups mozzarella cheese. Yield: 4 to 6 servings.

Jacque L. Martin, Xi Upsilon
Wichita, Kansas

CHICKEN LASAGNA

My family loves this lasagna for our Christmas Eve dinner.

1/2 cup (1 stick) butter	8 ounces lasagna
2 garlic cloves, minced	noodles, cooked,
1/2 cup flour	drained
1 teaspoon salt	2 cups ricotta cheese
2 cups half-and-half	2 cups chopped cooked
2 cups chicken stock	chicken
2 cups shredded	2 (10-ounce) packages
mozzarella cheese	frozen chopped
1 cup grated Parmesan	spinach, thawed,
cheese	drained
1 onion, finely chopped	

Melt the butter in a large saucepan. Add the garlic, flour and salt; cook until bubbly, stirring constantly. Remove from heat. Stir in the half-and-half and chicken stock. Return to heat and bring to a boil. Boil for 1 minute, stirring constantly. Add the mozzarella cheese, half the Parmesan cheese and the onion. Reduce heat to low and cook until cheeses melt, stirring constantly. Remove from heat. Spread 1/4 of the cheese mixture in a 9×13-inch baking dish. Layer 3 or 4 noodles, half the ricotta cheese, 1/4 of the cheese mixture, another 3 or 4 noodles and the remaining ricotta cheese over the first cheese layer. Layer the chicken, spinach, another 1/4 of the cheese mixture, another 3 or 4 noodles and the remaining cheese mixture over the second cheese layer. Top with the remaining 1/2 cup Parmesan cheese. Bake, covered tightly with foil, at 350 degrees for 35 to 40 minutes. Turn off oven heat. Let stand in the hot oven without opening the oven door for 15 minutes. Remove from oven and let stand for 5 minutes before serving. Yield: 6 to 8 servings.

Fran Bogar (25 years), Preceptor Zeta Phi
St. Charles, Missouri

CHICKEN PENNE FLORENTINE

This recipe offers a quick, easy, tasty way to get spinach into a finicky eater.

1 whole boneless
    skinless chicken
    breast, cut into thin
    strips
2 tablespoons olive oil
2 or 3 garlic cloves,
    minced
8 ounces mushrooms,
    sliced

10 ounces spinach,
    washed, trimmed
1 (26-ounce) jar
    spaghetti sauce
16 ounces penne, cooked
    al dente, drained

Sauté the chicken strips in half the olive oil in a large skillet until slightly browned; remove from heat. Sauté the garlic and mushrooms in the remaining olive oil in a separate skillet over medium heat for 5 minutes. Stir in the spinach and heat until wilted, stirring constantly. Stir in the chicken and spaghetti sauce; cook until heated through. Serve over penne with freshly grated Romano cheese. Yield: 6 servings.

Pam Augustine (25 years), Preceptor Psi
Budd Lake, New Jersey

CHICKEN AND NOODLES

My grandmother made noodles for us every Christmas, and now I do so for my daughters.

1 whole chicken, cut in
    pieces
3 drops yellow food
    coloring
3 cups flour

1/2 teaspoon salt
2 eggs
1 cup cold water
1 (10-ounce) can cream
    of chicken soup

Place the chicken in a kettle with enough water to cover; bring to a boil. Reduce heat and simmer for 30 minutes to an hour or until tender. Remove from heat. Remove the chicken from the broth; add the food coloring to the broth. Chop the cooled chicken, discarding the skin and bones. Combine the flour, salt and eggs in a bowl. Add the water a little at a time, mixing with a fork until the mixture forms a ball. Roll 1/8 inch thick on a floured board and cut into 1/2-inch-wide noodles; let dry. Bring the chicken broth to a boil. Add the cream of chicken soup and mix well. Stir in the chicken and noodles. Simmer for 20 minutes or until noodles are tender.
Yield: 8 to 10 servings.

Jean Caldwell, Laureate Delta Epsilon
Independence, Missouri

CHEDDAR TURKEY TETRAZZINI

Substitute tuna, ground beef, or leftover cooked turkey for the ground turkey if you like.

7 ounces spaghetti,
    broken into 2-inch
    pieces
1 pound ground turkey
1 onion, chopped
1/4 cup chopped green
    bell pepper
1 (10-ounce) can cream
    of mushroom soup
1/2 cup milk

2 (4-ounce) cans sliced
    mushrooms, drained
1 (2-ounce) jar chopped
    pimentos, drained
1 cup shredded Cheddar
    cheese
1/4 teaspoon salt
Pinch of pepper
Pinch of oregano

Cook the spaghetti using the package directions; drain. Brown the ground turkey in a skillet, stirring until crumbly. Add the onion and green pepper; sauté for a few minutes. Stir in the soup, milk, mushrooms, pimentos, Cheddar cheese, salt, pepper and oregano. Stir in the drained spaghetti and spoon into a greased 2 1/2-quart baking dish. Sprinkle with additional shredded cheese if desired. Bake, uncovered, at 350 degrees for 30 to 45 minutes or until hot and bubbly. Yield: 6 to 8 servings.

Betty Fielding (45 years), Preceptor Lambda
Ely, Nevada

MEMORIES

My grandmother is 85 years young, and her name is Mary Helen Snyder. My grandfather is 90 years young, and his name is Harry Snyder. They live in Columbus Junction, Iowa. I try to visit my grandparents every year or two; I enjoy their company. My grandparents have been married for almost 68 years, and they have lived there all their lives. My father and mother, Farrel and Pat Snyder, have lived in Iowa all their lives too. This past year I took my two-year-old son, Adam, to visit his grandparents and great-grandparents, as well as other relatives. We took fourth-generation pictures and had a wonderful time, and my grandmother made wonderful dishes for the family gatherings.

Pamella Carlson, Preceptor Xi Zeta
West Sacramento, California

CHICKEN POTPIE

As I have gotten older and become a mother of two, I certainly appreciate the extra time my mom spent in the kitchen. I, however, have cheated with this recipe and used prepared pie dough!

2 cups plus 1/3 cup flour	1/2 teaspoon salt
2 teaspoons celery seed	1/4 teaspoon pepper
1 teaspoon salt	1 3/4 cups chicken broth
2/3 cup plus 2 tablespoons shortening	2/3 cup milk
	2 cups chopped cooked chicken
4 to 5 tablespoons water	1 (10-ounce) package frozen peas and carrots, thawed
1/3 cup butter	
1/3 cup chopped onion	

Combine the 2 cups flour, celery seed and salt in a bowl. Cut in the shortening until crumbs are the size of peas. Sprinkle 1 tablespoon cold water over part of the mixture; toss gently with a fork and push to the side of the bowl. Repeat until all the flour mixture is moistened. Roll into 2 balls. Flatten each ball with the hands on a lightly floured surface. Roll each from the center outward into a 12-inch circle. Wrap 1 pastry around a rolling pin and unroll into a 9-inch pie plate. Fit into the pie plate, being careful not to stretch the pastry. Trim to 1/2 inch beyond the plate edges; fold under the extra pastry. Melt the butter in a saucepan over medium heat. Stir in the 1/3 cup flour, onion, salt and pepper; cook until bubbly, stirring constantly. Remove from heat. Stir in the chicken broth and milk. Return to heat and bring to a boil, stirring constantly. Stir in the chicken and peas and carrots. Pour the chicken mixture into the pastry-lined pie plate. Top with the remaining pastry, fluting edge and cutting vents. Bake at 425 degrees for 30 to 35 minutes or until hot and golden brown. Yield: 6 servings.

*Susan D. Job
Canton, Missouri*

CRUNCHY CHICKEN PIE

Serve with fruit and miniature muffins.

2 cups chopped cooked chicken	1 tablespoon lemon juice
3 green onions, chopped	1/4 teaspoon salt
1/2 cup chopped pecans	1/2 teaspoon pepper
1 1/2 cups chopped celery	1 baked (9-inch) pie shell
1/2 cup shredded Cheddar or Swiss cheese	1 cup crushed potato chips
1 1/2 cups mayonnaise	

Combine the chicken, green onions, pecans, celery and cheese in a bowl and mix well. Add a mixture of the mayonnaise, lemon juice, salt and pepper and mix well. Spread the chicken mixture in the pie shell and top with the potato chips. Bake at 350 degrees for 25 minutes. Let cool slightly before serving. Yield: 6 servings.

*Nancy Reichart
Houston, Texas*

TURKEY VEGETABLE PIE

I had leftover turkey, and this recipe was a "spur of the moment" idea. My family loved it. Serve with fruit and tossed salad or coleslaw.

1 cup chopped cooked turkey or chicken	2 cups diced peeled potatoes
1 (10-ounce) can cream of celery soup	1 cup flour
1/2 soup can water	1 tablespoon sugar
1 cup sliced green beans	1 tablespoon vegetable oil
1 cup sliced carrots	1/4 cup milk

Combine the turkey, soup, water, green beans, carrots and potatoes in a 1 1/2-quart casserole and mix well. Combine the flour, sugar, vegetable oil and milk in a bowl and mix until a ball is formed. Roll the dough on a floured surface until it is large enough to cover the top of the casserole. Fit the pastry over the top of the casserole. Bake at 350 degrees for 1 hour. Yield: 4 servings.

*JoAnn Gruber, Laureate Theta
Hagerstown, Maryland*

MEMORIES

I would never use my mother's Chicken and Dumplings recipe because I didn't want to ruin a chicken that I had to buy. My cousin raised fighting chickens. He didn't use the pullets so he would either give them away or bury them. My husband and I decided we would dress and freeze several of them. I wouldn't feel so bad if they didn't turn out well since I didn't have to buy the chickens.

*Charlotte Wood (30 years), Preceptor Delta Epsilon
Lindale, Texas*

"Practice makes perfect" is an expression that relates to my Chicken and Dumplings recipe. My mother-in-law showed me how to make these without a recipe. Needless to say, it took several tries before they tasted like hers. My

granddaughter, Morgan, says that they are her favorite.

George Anne Bedford (32 years), Laureate Zeta Gamma
Deer Park, Texas

I got my Chicken and Dumplings recipe from a community cookbook from my hometown. Originally it came from my high school English teacher. My family loves it and my kids request it when they come home!

Judy Moore, Xi Kappa Chi
Refugio, Texas

My Chicken and Dumplings recipe is special to me because it was my mother's. My mother passed away three years ago after a battle with Alzheimer's disease. This was one of the last dishes that she could remember how to make.

Edith Oates, Zeta Alpha
Sheridan, Arkansas

My grandma, Callie Coe, always made her Chicken and Dumplings for family reunions. She used to roll out the dough with a jelly glass.

Marilyn Meyers (26 years), Preceptor Gamma Epsilon
Orange City, Florida

My grandmother, Edith Armstrong, was the first cook at a little one-room school through the WPA Program in the 1940s. When the school consolidated with another school, she became the head cook. My grandmother was an excellent cook both at home and at school. One of the secrets she told me about was how she made her dumplings. She poured flour into a bowl and made a hole in the middle of the flour. Then she poured the chicken broth in the hole and used her hand to go "round and round" to mix the broth in to the flour. After they had cooked, she turned off the heat and added one-half cup of milk to the pot and let them set before serving.

Catherine "Kaye" Howell (33 years),
Laureate Gamma Alpha
Marion, Illinois

GRANDMA'S CHICKEN DUMPLINGS

3 cups flour   **1/3 cup shortening**
1 1/2 teaspoons salt   **1 cup water**

Combine the flour, salt and shortening in a bowl and mix with the hands until mixture resembles fine crumbs. Add the water and mix in with the hands; if dough is too soft, add a little more flour. Knead the dough 5 to 10 strokes on a floured surface and let stand for a few minutes. Roll to 1/8 inch thick on a well-floured surface. Cut into 1-inch-wide strips. Break each strip into 4 or 5 pieces and drop into boiling chicken broth. Simmer, uncovered, for about 20 minutes. Serve with a salad, chicken, mashed potatoes or sweet potatoes, greens, and a dessert. Yield: 6 to 10 servings.

Judy Ann Evans, Laureate Xi
Fairmont, West Virginia

CHICKEN AND DUMPLINGS

I use the Pioneer brand of country gravy mix, which makes 2 cups of gravy.

4 chicken breasts or   **1 (20-ounce) package**
** 1 (3-pound) chicken**   ** flour tortillas**
Salt and pepper
1 envelope country
** gravy mix**

Place the chicken in a large kettle. Add enough water to cover and 1/2 teaspoon salt. Simmer, covered, for 40 minutes or until chicken is tender. Remove from broth; cool. Remove and discard skin and bones. Chop the chicken and measure to make about 3 cups, packed. Measure 6 cups of broth and return to the kettle. Return the chicken to the kettle and bring the broth to a boil. Add salt and pepper to taste. Combine the gravy mix with 1/2 cup cold water and stir into the boiling chicken broth. Cut 3 or 4 tortillas at a time into 1/2-inch-wide strips. Cut across the strips once and add to the chicken mixture. Repeat until all tortillas are used. Simmer, covered, for about 10 minutes. Yield: 6 to 8 servings.

Carole Bolling (26 years), Xi Tau
Northport, Alabama

Susie Riggle (25 years), Theta, Vincennes, Indiana, tells how to make **Super Easy Chicken Pie** by lining a pie plate with a prepared pie pastry, adding a large can of drained chicken, a can of drained mixed vegetables, a can of cream of chicken soup and topping with a second pie pastry, sealing and cutting vents. Bake at 350 degrees for 1 hour.

SOUR CREAM CHICKEN PAPRIKASH

This is the family recipe I treasure most. It has been in my family for generations and was brought to America from Yugoslavia by my great-grandparents in the early 1900s. At that time it was made with spiced cream; today I use Daisy Brand Pure Sour Cream and serve with mashed potatoes or Slovakian Dumplings.

1 (2½- to 3-pound) chicken	4 to 8 cups sour cream
1 large onion, chopped	1 teaspoon paprika
Salt to taste	Slovakian Dumplings

Brown the chicken lightly in a small amount of oil until the sputtering stops. Place the chicken and onion in a kettle over medium heat. Cook, covered, for 10 minutes or until chicken is almost cooked through. Combine the sour cream and paprika in a bowl and whisk to blend. Pour the sour cream mixture evenly over the chicken before all the moisture is cooked out; turn the chicken to coat well. Reduce temperature to low. Cook, covered, for 10 minutes or until chicken is cooked through and sauce is a creamy thick texture, removing cover often to stir. Serve with Slovakian Dumplings.
Yield: 4 to 6 servings.

SLOVAKIAN DUMPLINGS

2 eggs	Flour
Salt	Salted water

Beat the eggs in a bowl; add a dash of salt. Stir in enough flour with a fork to form a stiff dough. Drop spoonfuls of the dough in boiling salted water and cook for 10 minutes or until done.

Sherry Haynes, Lambda Alpha
Denham Springs, Louisiana

HUNGARIAN CHICKEN PAPRIKASH

My mother and grandmother, of Hungarian descent, both prepared this dish many, many times. It was always delicious and now brings back many happy memories. Serve with homemade rye bread and applesauce.

1 onion, chopped	1 teaspoon salt
¼ cup shortening	1½ cups water
3 to 4 pounds chicken pieces	1 cup sour cream
	1 tablespoon flour
1 tablespoon paprika	Dumplings
1 teaspoon pepper	

Sauté the onion in the shortening in a large skillet over medium heat for about 5 minutes. Add the chicken, paprika, pepper and salt; sauté for about 10 minutes. Add the water and simmer slowly, covered, for 20 minutes or until chicken is tender. Remove chicken from the skillet. Add a mixture of the sour cream and flour to the drippings and mix well. Layer the Dumplings in the skillet and arrange the chicken pieces on top. Heat through, covered, and serve. Yield: 4 servings.

DUMPLINGS

2 eggs, beaten	1 teaspoon salt
2 cups flour	½ cup cold water

Combine the eggs, flour, salt and cold water in a bowl and beat until smooth. Drop by teaspoons into boiling salted water. Boil until dumplings rise to the top. Rinse dumplings in cold water and drain.

Vivian M. De Kar, Laureate Gamma Upsilon
Fruitland Park, Florida

THREE-CHEESE CHICKEN ENCHILADAS

These are the best enchiladas we have ever tried. Try different brands of enchilada sauce until you come up with one that has the right amount of kick for your family.

⅓ cup vegetable oil	2 cups shredded cooked chicken
8 corn tortillas	
4 ounces cream cheese, softened	2 cups shredded Monterey Jack cheese
¾ cup sour cream	1½ cups shredded Cheddar cheese
¼ teaspoon salt	
½ teaspoon cumin	1 (10-ounce) can enchilada sauce
¼ teaspoon pepper	

Heat the vegetable oil in a skillet over medium heat. Dip each tortilla in the hot oil with tongs, turning quickly to soften for about 3 to 5 seconds. Set aside. Combine the cream cheese and sour cream in a large bowl and beat until smooth. Stir in the salt, cumin and pepper. Stir in the chicken, 1 cup of the Monterey Jack cheese and 1 cup of the Cheddar cheese. Pour the enchilada sauce in a shallow bowl. Dip the tortillas in the enchilada sauce to lightly coat. Place ½ cup chicken mixture in the center of each tortilla; roll. Place filled tortillas seam side down in a lightly greased 9×13-inch baking dish. Cover with the remaining enchilada sauce. Bake, uncovered, at 350 degrees for 25 minutes. Sprinkle the remaining Monterey Jack and Cheddar cheese over the top. Bake for 3 minutes longer. Remove from oven. Top with sour cream, guacamole, onions or any other toppings of your choice. Yield: 4 servings.

Joann Keder, Xi Alpha Xi
Scottsbluff, Nebraska

LIME CHICKEN ENCHILADAS

2 whole chicken breasts, cooked	Juice and grated zest of 1 lime
2 cups sour cream	8 corn tortillas
1/2 cup half-and-half	1 cup diced onion
1/2 teaspoon salt	1 cup shredded Cheddar cheese
Pinch of cayenne pepper	

Shred the chicken with 2 forks, discarding the skin and bones. Combine the sour cream, half-and-half, salt, cayenne pepper and lime juice and zest in a medium bowl; whisk until smooth. Soften each tortilla for a few seconds in a small amount of hot oil in a large skillet over medium-high heat, turning once. Remove excess oil from tortillas by patting dry. Fill each tortilla with shredded chicken and chopped onion. Roll up and place in a lightly greased 9×13-inch baking dish. Top with the sour cream mixture and sprinkle with Cheddar cheese. Bake at 400 degrees for 20 to 25 minutes. Serve immediately. Yield: 8 servings.

Denise Ackerman, Zeta Chi
Portland, Oregon

CHICKEN VEGETABLE BAKE

This recipe is special to me because it is something my mother "cooked up" at the last minute one evening some thirty years ago when my father called to say he was bringing home unexpected out-of-town guests for dinner. I have served it many times since then, and it is always a hit.

3 large whole skinless chicken breasts, halved	1 cup sliced fresh mushrooms
1 teaspoon salt	2 tablespoons chopped green onions
1/4 teaspoon pepper	1/4 cup chopped green bell pepper
2 to 3 tablespoons vegetable oil	1 (5-ounce) can water chestnuts, drained, sliced
1 (10-ounce) can cream of chicken soup	1/4 teaspoon thyme
3/4 cup white wine	

Sprinkle the chicken with salt and pepper and brown in hot vegetable oil in a skillet. Arrange the chicken in a 9×13-inch baking dish. Whisk the soup into the drippings in the skillet. Stir in the wine gradually. Stir in the remaining ingredients. Bring to a boil. Pour carefully into the baking dish around the chicken breasts. Bake, covered, at 350 degrees for 25 to 30 minutes. Bake, uncovered, for 25 to 30 minutes longer or until chicken is cooked through and tender. Serve with hot rice or noodles. Yield: 4 to 6 servings.

Catherine McNamara, Alpha Beta Omicron
Williston, Florida

CHEESY CHICKEN AND ASPARAGUS

This dish has been a favorite in our household for many years, and my husband, daughter, and son all know how to prepare it. Both my college-age children request it when they come home from school, and now my daughter has started preparing it for her roommates. It's always a hit and there are never any leftovers. I can see this recipe will be handed down for many generations to come.

2 tablespoons lemon juice	2 tablespoons chopped onion
1 (10-ounce) can cream of asparagus soup	1 cup cooked rice
3/4 cup mayonnaise	1 cup shredded Cheddar cheese
3 cups chopped cooked chicken	2 cups crushed potato chips or bread crumbs
2 cups chopped fresh or frozen asparagus, cooked	Creole seasoning (optional)

Whisk together the lemon juice, soup and mayonnaise in a large bowl. Add the chicken, asparagus, onion, rice and Cheddar cheese and mix well. Spoon the mixture into a greased 7×11-inch 2-quart baking dish. Top with potato chips and sprinkle with Creole seasoning. Bake at 350 degrees for 25 to 30 minutes or until heated through. It may be prepared ahead of time and potato chips topping added just before baking. Yield: 6 to 8 servings.

Tami Walker, Alpha Rho
Havana, Illinois

MOM'S SPANISH CHICKEN

1 (3-pound) chicken, cut up	1 cup uncooked rice
1 cup chopped onion	1 1/2 to 2 cups chicken bouillon
1 cup chopped green bell pepper	1 1/2 teaspoons turmeric
2 garlic cloves, minced	1 teaspoon salt
1/3 cup pimentos, cut in strips	1 teaspoon pepper
	Dash of chili powder

Coat the chicken with seasoned flour and brown in hot oil in a skillet. Remove chicken from skillet. Place the onion, green pepper and garlic in the oil remaining in the skillet and sauté until onion is golden. Add pimentos and rice; stir over low heat for 2 minutes. Add the remaining ingredients; bring to a boil. Pour into a greased 2-quart baking dish. Arrange the chicken over the top. Bake, covered, at 350 degrees for 1 1/2 hours. Yield: 4 servings.

Barbara Kennedy (46 years), Laureate Lambda
Fort Pierce, Florida

SHERRIED PHEASANT CASSEROLE

This recipe was given to me by a special friend seventeen years ago when I married, to make a start on the recipes I would collect in response to my husband's love for hunting. Serve with wild rice and gravy.

1 or 2 pheasants, cut in pieces	1 (10-ounce) can cream of mushroom soup
Flour	1 soup can milk
1/4 cup vegetable oil	1/2 cup sherry or white wine
1 green bell pepper, chopped	
1 onion, sliced, separated into rings	

Coat the pheasants with flour and brown in hot vegetable oil. Place in a casserole. Sprinkle with the green pepper and onion rings. Pour a mixture of the soup and milk over the pheasant. Cover tightly with foil and the casserole lid. Bake at 350 degrees for 30 minutes. Uncover and pour the sherry over the top. Replace cover tightly and bake at 350 degrees for 1 hour longer. Yield: 4 to 6 servings.

Colette Theel, Xi Zeta
Rapid City, South Dakota

HAWAIIAN CHICKEN

I often prepare this meal ahead of time and keep it frozen for those nights I needed to have a great dinner in very little time. Serve with rice pilaf and Swiss green beans.

6 chicken breasts	2 tablespoons lemon juice
1/2 cup (1 stick) butter or margarine, melted	1 teaspoon garlic salt
1 large onion, sliced	1 teaspoon salt
1 cup brown sugar	1/2 teaspoon ground cloves
1/3 cup flour	4 teaspoons Worcestershire sauce
1 (6-ounce) can pineapple juice	
1 (8-ounce) can crushed pineapple	

Place the chicken in a greased 9×13-inch baking dish. Combine the remaining ingredients in a large saucepan and bring to a boil. Reduce heat and simmer until thickened, stirring frequently. Pour the pineapple mixture evenly over the chicken and chill, covered, for up to 24 hours. Bake, uncovered, at 300 degrees for 2 hours. Yield: 6 servings.

Bettie Coffman, Kappa Eta
Edinburg, Virginia

THE FASSIO FAMILY REUNION "BAUNA CALDA"

At some of our parties we will have four electric frying pans going at once. We will start cooking at 1:00 p.m. and have been known to keep on partying way past dark. If we run low on the Bauna Calda sauce, we add more oil and butter. At many of our reunions we have had over seventy relatives and guests, and these parties have been going on for almost forty years.

3 cups peeled whole garlic cloves	1 cup chopped carrot, parboiled
3 to 4 cups vegetable oil	1 cup chopped peeled potato, parboiled
5 (2-ounce) cans anchovy fillets	1 cup chopped cooked chicken
1 pound butter	1 cup chopped cooked beef
1 cup chopped celery	
1 cup chopped cabbage	1 cup cooked shrimp
1 cup chopped mushrooms	4 loaves French bread, sliced

Place the garlic in a 1-quart measuring cup. Add enough vegetable oil to fill to the 4-cup line. Let stand for 12 or more hours. When ready to cook, place the garlic, oil, anchovies and butter in a large electric frying pan. Simmer for 1 hour. Dip the vegetables and meats on fondue forks into the hot oil mixture and cook until desired doneness. Serve over French bread. Yield: 8 to 12 servings.

Barbara Fassio, Xi Alpha Gamma
Rock Springs, Wyoming

CHICKEN TARRAGON

4 boneless skinless chicken breasts	1 tablespoon Dijon mustard
3 tablespoons vegetable oil	1 tablespoon lemon juice
1 tablespoon finely chopped shallots	3 tablespoons chopped fresh tarragon
3 tablespoons finely chopped green onions	1/2 cup chicken stock
3 tablespoons brandy	1 tablespoon butter

Place the chicken breasts between sheets of waxed paper and pound lightly to 1/4-inch thickness. Sauté the chicken in the vegetable oil in a skillet over medium heat, 3 minutes on each side. Remove chicken to a platter and keep warm in the oven. Sauté the shallots and green onions in the skillet over medium heat for 1 minute. Stir in the brandy, mustard, lemon juice and tarragon. Add the chicken stock and whisk until smooth. Heat until the mixture starts to bubble, stirring constantly. Remove from heat.

Stir in the butter. Remove chicken from the oven and drizzle with the tarragon mixture. Serve immediately. Yield: 4 servings.

Chris Manchon, Eta Xi
Langley, British Columbia, Canada

MEMORIES

As I grew up in the country, I always found games to play with my sisters and brother, along with the neighborhood kids. We would play baseball, kickball, or hide and seek. There was always enough to keep us busy, and we didn't return to the house until dusk.

Today I have kids of my own, but it seems that most children seem to be more content in front of a TV, video game or even a computer. (No wonder we hear so much about obesity at early ages.) I guess my parents didn't realize they were really on top of things by keeping us playing outdoors, when we were actually exercising our bodies!

Debbie Vonderheide, Theta
Vincennes, Indiana

BLACKENED CHICKEN

My husband's favorite recipe . . . and he makes it himself, so I don't have to cook!

1 tablespoon salt	1/2 teaspoon oregano
1 tablespoon paprika	1/2 teaspoon cayenne
1 teaspoon black pepper	pepper
1/2 teaspoon each garlic powder, onion powder and chili powder	6 boneless skinless chicken breasts
1/2 teaspoon thyme	3 tablespoon butter or margarine, melted

Combine the first 9 ingredients in a bowl and mix well. Pound the chicken 1/4 inch thick between sheets of waxed paper. Heat a heavy skillet over medium-high heat until drops of water bounce vigorously in the skillet. Brush the chicken on both sides with melted butter and sprinkle liberally with the paprika mixture. Place 2 or 3 chicken breasts in the preheated skillet. When blackened on one side, turn to the other side; it cooks quickly. Yield: 6 servings.

Beverly Clarkson
Portage, Manitoba, Canada

EASY BAKED CHICKEN

2 to 3 pounds chicken pieces	1/2 cup ketchup
Dry bread crumbs	1 garlic clove, minced
1/4 cup prepared mustard	1/4 onion, chopped
1/4 cup frozen orange juice concentrate, thawed	11/2 tablespoons brown sugar

Coat the chicken with the bread crumbs and arrange in a 9×13-inch baking dish. Bake, uncovered, at 350 degrees for 40 minutes. Combine the mustard, orange juice concentrate, ketchup, garlic, onion and brown sugar in a bowl and mix well. Remove chicken from oven and loosen pieces stuck to bottom of the pan. Spoon mustard mixture over each piece of chicken. Return to oven and bake for 20 to 25 minutes longer. Remove from oven and carefully cover tightly with foil. Return to oven and bake, covered, for 10 to 15 minutes longer. Yield: 4 to 6 servings.

Rita Sommerfeld, Xi Gamma Upsilon
Richmond, British Columbia, Canada

ORANGE GINGER CHICKEN

My whole family loves this special dish. It's easy to prepare, so you can spend more time with guests. You may substitute 1 sliced orange with its peel and 1/4 cup water for the mandarin oranges if you like.

2 tablespoons vegetable oil	1 (11-ounce) can mandarin oranges
4 whole boneless skinless chicken breasts, halved	1 (1/2-inch) piece fresh gingerroot
1/2 cup orange marmalade	2 garlic cloves, peeled
1/3 cup soy sauce	1 tablespoon crushed chile pepper
1/2 teaspoon cinnamon	1 onion, thinly sliced
1 teaspoon black pepper	1 red or yellow bell pepper

Coat the bottom of a 9×13-inch baking dish with the vegetable oil. Add the chicken, turning once to coat. Combine the marmalade, soy sauce, cinnamon, black pepper and undrained mandarin oranges in a bowl and mix well. Place the gingerroot, garlic and chile pepper in a teaball or tie in cheesecloth. Stir into the orange mixture. Stir in the onion and bell pepper. Pour the mixture evenly over the chicken breasts. Bake, covered with foil, at 350 degrees for 40 minutes. Yield: 8 servings.

Sarah Cannon, Laureate Gamma Rho
Bellevue, Washington

OVEN-FRIED CHICKEN

1 cup sour cream	2 tablespoons lemon
2 garlic cloves, minced	juice
2 teaspoons celery salt	3 pounds chicken pieces,
2 teaspoons	or 6 chicken breasts
Worcestershire sauce	1½ cups bread crumbs,
1 teaspoon paprika	toasted
1 teaspoon salt	½ to ¾ cup butter,
Pepper to taste	melted

Combine the sour cream, garlic, celery salt, Worcestershire sauce, paprika, salt, pepper and lemon juice in a large glass dish and whisk well. Add the chicken. Marinate, covered, in the refrigerator for 8 to 10 hours. Drain the chicken and roll it in the bread crumbs. Arrange in a buttered 9×13-inch baking dish. Drizzle with half the melted butter. Bake, uncovered, at 350 degrees for 45 minutes. Drizzle with remaining melted butter. Bake for 15 minutes longer or until golden. Yield: 6 servings.

Suzanne Rhodes, Preceptor Alpha Gamma
Brookfield, Missouri

COFFEE ROASTED CHICKEN

Lining the pan with foil makes for easy cleanup.

¼ cup French dressing	4 tablespoons butter,
1 tablespoon vinegar	melted
½ teaspoon	1 (3-pound) chicken,
Worcestershire sauce	cut up
½ teaspoon instant	
coffee granules	

Combine the French dressing, vinegar, Worcestershire sauce and coffee granules in a small bowl and whisk well to blend. Line a 10×15-inch cake pan with foil and brush the foil with 1 tablespoon of the melted butter. Salt and flour the chicken pieces and arrange in the prepared cake pan. Baste with the remaining 3 tablespoons melted butter. Bake, uncovered, at 350 degrees for 50 minutes. Baste with the French dressing mixture. Bake for 50 minutes longer. Yield: 4 servings.

Norma Owen (47 years), Laureate Delta Beta
Princeton, Missouri

Mary F. Marabotto (40 years), Gamma Rho Master, Escondido, California, prepares **Mexican Baked Turkey** by stuffing a turkey with peeled canned tamalees and a large can of enchilada sauce. Bake at 350 degrees until the turkey is tender, basting frequently with additional enchilada sauce. Serve with Spanish rice, refried beans and tortillas or tortilla chips.

MEMORIES

Dorsie Oral Osburn Miles was born in Kansas on January 15, 1891. Her family traveled by covered wagon to Muleshoe, Texas. Because she was the oldest child in Muleshoe, she was the teacher in the one-room schoolhouse at the age of sixteen. She was the oldest of seven children. She married and had three boys and one girl of her own. She worked on the family farm and cleaned and washed for other people. Sometimes she walked ten miles to and from work so that her family could make ends meet. She was gracious, proper and interested in everything. After her husband's death, she lived by herself until the age of 103 when she developed a hearing problem and had to go to a care facility. While there, she broke her hip reaching for the political page of the paper; but that didn't slow her down. She enjoyed her fried chicken, onion rings and chocolates until the day that she got sick. She passed away two days later at 104. She said the secret to a long life was getting out of bed every day even when you'd rather stay there.

Ann E. Miles, Xi Zeta Pi
Meriden, Kansas

MOM'S SUNDAY FRIED CHICKEN

Memories are a wonderful way to keep one's windows open on the past. My mother prepared many wonderful meals for us, and her fried chicken was always a special one. Like so many cooks of her time, my mom didn't know what it was to use a recipe. It was always a pinch of this or a handful of that. It took me many years of watching her to learn her method of frying chicken. I'm so happy that I did . . . for Mom, now eighty-four, had a debilitating stroke ten years ago, and all those wonderful pinches and handfuls are now forever locked away.

1 (3- to 4-pound)	1 teaspoon cinnamon
chicken, cut up	1½ cups buttermilk
1½ teaspoons salt	Shortening for deep-
Garlic powder to taste	frying
2 cups self-rising flour	Buttermilk Gravy
¾ teaspoon pepper	

Rinse the chicken and pat dry. Season with salt and garlic powder. Coat the chicken with a mixture of the flour, pepper, cinnamon and additional garlic powder. Set aside to dry. Pour the buttermilk into a shallow bowl. Dip the coated chicken in the buttermilk, then again in the seasoned flour. Melt shortening 2½ to 3 inches deep in an iron skillet over high heat. Place the chicken meat side down in the hot shortening and brown on both sides, turning often. Reduce heat and cover the skillet. Cook for 15 to 20 minutes, depending on size of pieces. Remove the cover. Turn up heat and continue frying chicken until crisp. Drain on paper towels. Serve with Buttermilk Gravy. Yield: 6 to 8 servings.

BUTTERMILK GRAVY

1 tablespoon leftover seasoned flour	**Leftover buttermilk plus more if needed to make 1 cup**

Pour most of the grease from the skillet, saving the brown bits. Stir in the flour and cook over medium heat until brown, stirring constantly. Add the buttermilk and cook until thickened, stirring constantly.

Beverly Binder (29 years), Laureate Gamma Epsilon
Toledo, Ohio

CHICKEN CHIMICHANGAS

A special recipe for those who love Mexican food.

2 whole boneless skinless chicken breasts	**1 cup shredded Cheddar cheese**
½ teaspoon cumin	**2/3 cup cooked rice**
¼ teaspoon garlic powder	**2 tablespoons taco seasoning mix**
1 tablespoon olive oil	**15 (6-inch) flour tortillas**
½ onion, chopped	**2 cups vegetable oil**
1/3 cup salsa	

Cut the chicken into ¼-inch strips. Season with the cumin and garlic powder. Heat the olive oil in an 8-inch nonstick skillet over medium heat. Brown the chicken in the hot oil until no longer pink. Stir in the onion and cook until limp, stirring frequently. Remove from heat. Combine the salsa, Cheddar cheese, rice and taco seasoning mix in a bowl; mix well. Place the cooled chicken mixture in a food processor container and pulse until shredded. Combine the chicken mixture and the salsa mixture in a bowl and mix well. Place a heaping tablespoon of the chicken mixture on the bottom third of each tortilla and roll. Fold each side as you roll and secure with a wooden pick. Heat the vegetable oil in a skillet.

Brown the tortillas on each side over medium-high heat for 1 to 2 minutes or until brown. Serve with shredded lettuce and top with sour cream, guacamole and salsa. Yield: 15 servings.

Carol Mendoza, Iota Epsilon
St. Amant, Louisiana

ARTICHOKE CHICKEN

I got this recipe from a television cooking show while visiting my three-week-old granddaughter in Norfolk, Virginia. It is now a favorite with her and with my daughter and son-in-law.

1 (14-ounce) can artichoke hearts, drained	**2 tablespoons margarine**
	½ cup chicken broth
	1/3 cup white wine
8 boneless skinless chicken breasts	**Juice of 1 lemon**
Seasoned flour	**1 tablespoon crushed garlic**

Halve or quarter the artichokes. Coat the chicken breasts with seasoned flour and brown in melted margarine in a heavy skillet over medium heat. Stir in the chicken broth, wine, lemon juice and garlic. Reduce heat and cook, uncovered, until thickened, stirring frequently. Serve over buttered noodles. Yield: 6 servings.

Esther Crandall (38 years), Preceptor Alpha Alpha
North Charleston, South Carolina

RUSSIAN SAUERKRAUT CHICKEN

1 (16-ounce) can sauerkraut, rinsed, drained	**1 (8-ounce) bottle Russian salad dressing**
1 (3-pound) chicken, cut up	**9 slices Swiss cheese**

Layer the sauerkraut in a 9×13-inch baking dish. Arrange the chicken parts over the sauerkraut. Pour the salad dressing over the top and bake, uncovered, at 350 degrees for 1 hour. Layer the Swiss cheese over the top and bake for 15 minutes longer. Yield: 6 to 8 servings.

Joyce Keller, Preceptor Epsilon Theta
Pinellas Park, Florida

Cindy Wilson, Eta Tau, Brocton, New York, makes **Easy Chicken Parmigiana** by spreading about 1½ cups jarred spaghetti sauce in a 9x13-inch baking pan, fitting frozen chicken tenders in the pan, covering chicken with 4 to 5 cups additional sauce and topping with 3 cups shredded mozzarella cheese. Bake, covered with foil, at 350 degrees for 1 hour.

APRICOT CHICKEN CURRY

This is the very first recipe I got from a Beta sister, twenty-three years ago, and I have prepared it hundreds of times.

1 (3-pound) chicken, cut up, or 6 chicken breasts	1 envelope onion soup mix
1 (8-ounce) bottle Russian salad dressing	1 (4- to 6-ounce) jar apricot preserves
	1 teaspoon curry powder

Arrange the chicken skin side up in a single layer in a 9×13-inch baking dish. Combine the salad dressing, soup mix, apricot preserves and curry powder in a small bowl and mix well. Pour the apricot mixture evenly over the chicken. Bake, uncovered, at 350 degrees for 1 to 1 1/2 hours, basting every 1/2 hour. Yield: 6 servings.

Gale Smyth, Omicron
Trail, British Columbia, Canada

CHEESE-STUFFED CHICKEN

This company-impressing dish looks so fancy, but it is so easy. Serve with a medley of sautéed vegetables or a spinach salad or both.

2 tablespoons unsalted butter, softened	2 tablespoons chopped parsley
1/2 cup shredded Monterey Jack cheese	1/2 teaspoon dried tarragon, or
1/2 cup shredded Cheddar cheese	1 tablespoon chopped fresh
4 (4- to 5-ounce) boneless skinless chicken breasts	Freshly ground pepper to taste
8 sheets phyllo dough	1/4 teaspoon salt
1/4 cup (1/2 stick) butter, melted	

Combine the softened butter, Monterey Jack cheese and Cheddar cheese in a bowl; mash together with fingers or a wooden spoon until mixture is a thick paste. Divide the cheese mixture into four 3-inch-long finger-shaped logs. Pound the chicken 1/4 inch thick and 5 to 6 inches across between sheets of waxed paper. Season lightly with salt and pepper. Place a cheese log in the center of each chicken breast. Roll and fold chicken around the log to enclose it. Place 1 sheet of phyllo dough on a work surface. Top with a second sheet and brush lightly with melted butter. Place a chicken roll in the center of 1 of the narrower ends and roll the phyllo, tucking under the ends of the dough like a burrito. Repeat with remaining 3 breasts. Place the phyllo-wrapped breasts seam side down in a 9×13-inch baking dish and brush with remaining melted butter. Bake at 350 degrees for about 40 minutes or until sizzling and well browned, or to 170 degrees on a meat thermometer inserted in the center of the chicken. Yield: 4 servings.

Karen Casson, Xi Beta Delta
Encampment, Wyoming

SOUPY CHICKEN STRATA

2 (10-ounce) cans cream of mushroom soup	8 to 10 boneless skinless chicken breasts
8 ounces sour cream	1/4 cup chopped parsley
4 ounces dried beef	8 to 10 slices bacon

Combine the soup and sour cream in a bowl and mix well. Layer the dried beef, half the soup mixture, chicken breasts, the remaining soup mixture, parsley and bacon in a 9×13-inch baking dish. Bake, covered, at 275 degrees for 3 hours. Serve over flat egg noodles. Yield: 8 to 10 servings.

Carolyn B. Worthington (34 years),
Preceptor Theta Lambda
Miami Lakes, Florida

SPINACH CHICKEN SAUSAGE STRATA

8 ounces chicken apple sausage	2 1/2 cups shredded mild Cheddar cheese
1 (10-ounce) package frozen chopped spinach, thawed	2 1/2 cups shredded Monterey Jack cheese
1 yellow onion, chopped	1 (7-ounce) can roasted green chiles, drained
1 small loaf day-old white or egg bread	3 cups milk
	4 eggs

Cook the sausage until brown and crumbly; drain. Squeeze the spinach dry. Sauté the onion until tender. Cut the bread into 12 thin slices and trim the crusts. Arrange half the bread slices, slightly overlapping, in a well-greased 9×13-inch baking dish. Toss the cheeses together. Layer half the cheese mixture, all the green chiles, sausage, spinach, sautéed onion and the remaining cheese mixture. Add the remaining bread slices over the top. Whisk the milk and eggs in a medium bowl until smooth. Pour the egg mixture slowly and evenly over the bread layer. Press the bread down gently to absorb liquid. Chill, covered tightly with foil, for 8 to 10 hours. Bake, uncovered, at 350 degrees on center rack of oven for 1 hour or until center is puffed and golden and a knife inserted in the center comes out clean. Let stand for 15 minutes and serve hot. Yield: 8 large servings.

Leah Hermsen (30 years), Xi Kappa
Corvallis, Oregon

ADOBE CHICKEN LAYUG

After World War II, my father left the Philippines for the U.S. and was discharged from the Army Air Corps. He returned to the Philippines to work as an auditor at Clark Field Air Force Base in Manila, and it was there that he met Adelaida Layug, a "Filipino princess," the daughter of the mayor of a neighboring town. They married and had three children. Back in the U.S., Dwight Eisenhower was elected president, and funding for certain programs was discontinued . . . which eliminated my father's civil service job. Dad called himself "FBI"—Fired By Ike. My parents decided we should go to the United States, and my mother said good-bye to her country, her culture, and her family, which included her parents and fourteen brothers and sisters. We came to live with my American grandmother in Kansas City. My mother had led a pampered life in the Philippines, and now she found herself in the U.S., the wife of an ex-G.I. who needed a job. Talk about culture shock! I marvel at how she managed to raise four children in a culture so different from hers. Our family celebrations always included lots of delicious food. My father prepared traditional American food and my mother prepared Filipino food. My parents have passed away, and are fondly remembered. My older brother and I get together each year on our parents' birthdays to eat Adobe Chicken and Pancit and talk and laugh about our family memories.

1 whole chicken, cut up, or 4 pounds chicken pieces	*3 garlic cloves, minced*
	1 onion, sliced
	1 teaspoon minced
³/4 cup soy sauce	*peeled gingerroot*
³/4 cup apple cider vinegar	*2 bay leaves*
	¹/2 teaspoon pepper

Combine the chicken, soy sauce, vinegar, garlic, onion, gingerroot, bay leaves and pepper in a large kettle with enough water to cover; bring to a boil. Reduce heat and simmer, covered, for 30 minutes. Uncover and simmer for 20 minutes longer or until chicken is tender and sauce is reduced. Discard bay leaves. Serve chicken and sauce over rice or noodles. Yield: 5 to 6 servings.

Cora Collins (27 years), Preceptor Lambda Theta
Blue Springs, Missouri

BAKED MUSTARD CHICKEN

Serve with rice or noodles, a vegetable, a salad, and crusty bread.

4 boneless skinless chicken breasts	*¹/4 cup (¹/2 stick) butter, melted*
¹/4 cup spicy brown mustard	*2 tablespoons lemon juice*
1 tablespoon honey	*2 tablespoons white wine or water*
¹/2 cup Italian seasoned bread crumbs	

Brush the chicken with a mixture of the mustard and honey. Coat with the bread crumbs and place in a buttered 9×13-inch baking dish. Combine the butter, lemon juice and wine in a small bowl and whisk until smooth. Drizzle the wine mixture over the chicken. Bake, covered with foil, at 350 degrees for 45 minutes. Sprinkle with paprika and bake, uncovered, for 15 minutes longer. Yield: 4 to 6 servings.

Shirley M. Erickson (40 years), Delta Delta
Conway, South Carolina

MEMORIES

*M*y sorority has been my lifeline several times; it has seen me through divorce and illnesses. When I had surgery, they sat with me while I slept. When I bought my condo, they helped me move and get it ready.

Linda Wilmoth (27 years), Preceptor Gamma Xi
St. Petersburg, Florida

MAPLE MUSTARD GRILLED CHICKEN

2 tablespoons Dijon mustard	*1 teaspoon pepper*
	1 teaspoon minced fresh garlic
3 tablespoons balsamic vinegar	*6 to 8 boneless skinless chicken breasts*
¹/2 cup peanut oil	
¹/2 cup maple syrup	

Combine the mustard, vinegar, peanut oil, maple syrup, pepper and garlic in a bowl and whisk to blend. Place the chicken in a sealable plastic bag and add the mustard mixture. Chill, sealed, for 4 to 10 hours, turning bag occasionally. Grill over hot coals for 10 to 20 minutes or until cooked through, turning once. Yield: 6 servings.

Beverley Fobert, Xi Leta Phi
Tweed, Ontario, Canada

MEMORIES

For Christmas 1991, my mother presented my sister-in-law and me with three Xi Mu volume, hand-typed cookbooks. In these cookbooks were all the best recipes that she had cooked over the years, plus others that she had saved to try. They are true family treasures because she used a manual typewriter and was 75 years old when she made them for us. Mom was working on a third set when my father had a tragic accident and died.

Sylvia Labelle, Xi Mu
Edmonton, Alberta, Canada

STUFFED CHICKEN IN PHYLLO

8 boneless skinless chicken breasts	1/2 cup crumbled feta cheese
1 teaspoon salt	1/2 cup shredded Cheddar cheese
1/2 teaspoon pepper	1 egg yolk, beaten
4 cups chopped fresh spinach	1 tablespoon flour
1 onion, chopped	1/2 teaspoon nutmeg
2 tablespoons olive oil	1/2 teaspoon cumin
8 ounces cream cheese, softened	16 frozen phyllo sheets, thawed
1 cup shredded mozzarella cheese	1/2 cup (1 stick) butter, melted

Pound the chicken 1/8 inch thick between sheets of waxed paper. Sprinkle with salt and pepper. Sauté the spinach and onion in olive oil in a large skillet over medium-high heat for 3 to 4 minutes or until tender. Remove from heat. Stir the cream cheese into the hot spinach mixture. Stir in the cheeses, egg yolk, flour, nutmeg and cumin. Spoon 1/4 cup of the spinach mixture in the center of each chicken breast and roll as for a jelly roll. Unfold phyllo sheets on a lightly floured surface and keep covered with plastic wrap so they won't dry out while working. Stack 2 phyllo sheets on the floured working surface, brushing melted butter between the sheets. Place 1 chicken roll on the short side of the phyllo stack and roll up gently, folding in the long side. Repeat until all chicken breasts are rolled. Place the rolls in a shallow baking dish and brush with melted butter. Bake at 375 degrees for 40 to 60 minutes or until hot and golden. Serve over a bed of mixed greens. Yield: 8 servings.

Leah Hoffman, Xi Upsilon
Wichita, Kansas

ED'S CHICKEN STEW

Our fire department held an annual Fireman's Ball in the late sixties and early seventies. We dressed in formal attire and had a great time while raising money for the fire department. My husband had spent hours in our kitchen, preparing his famous chicken stew to be served after the ball. We would invite four or five couples for a midnight meal, and we always served Ed's stew with his homemade biscuits. These were special times and created precious memories.

5 to 6 pounds chicken drumsticks and breasts	2 ribs celery, chopped
	1/2 cup French dressing
4 cups diced peeled potatoes	3/4 cup chili sauce
	1/2 cup Durkee sauce
1 (28-ounce) can diced tomatoes, drained	1 teaspoon minced fresh garlic
	Salt and pepper to taste
1 large onion, chopped	8 ounces egg noodles

Place the chicken in a large kettle and add enough water to cover. Bring to a boil. Reduce heat and simmer until tender. Remove chicken from the broth. Add the potatoes, tomatoes, onion, celery, French dressing, chili sauce, Durkee sauce, garlic, salt and pepper to the broth and bring to a boil. Reduce heat and simmer, covered, for about 15 minutes. Add the egg noodles and simmer for 30 minutes longer, adding water or canned broth if stew becomes too thick. Chop the cooled chicken, discarding the skin and bones; add to the stew. Yield: 15 to 20 servings.

Carol Darsey, Epsilon Sigma
Hawkinsville, Georgia

CHICKEN AND RICE WITH BEAN SAUCE

My dad was in the U. S. Air Force and we lived in Puerto Rico during the fifties. Our neighbors were native to the island, and the daughters and their mother became friends with my sisters and me and our mother. Their mother shared this recipe with our mother, and we enjoy it to this day.

1 (2 1/2-pound) chicken, cut in pieces	1 green bell pepper, chopped
Salt, pepper and oregano to taste	1 large tomato, diced
	1 cilantro leaf
3 slices bacon, chopped	6 olives, pitted
1 (8-ounce) can tomato sauce	1 garlic clove, minced
	1 1/2 cups uncooked rice
1 small onion, chopped	Bean Sauce

Season the chicken with salt, pepper and oregano 1 hour before cooking. Boil the chicken giblets, back and neck to make a broth for cooking the rice.

Cook the bacon in a large heavy skillet over medium heat. Brown the chicken pieces with the bacon in the drippings. Remove 2 to 4 tablespoons from the can of tomato sauce and set aside to use in the Bean Sauce. Add the remaining tomato sauce, onion, green pepper, tomato, cilantro, olives and garlic to the chicken mixture and bring to a simmer. Cook for 20 minutes. Stir in the rice and broth made from the giblets and bring to a boil. Reduce heat and simmer, covered, for 20 minutes or until rice is tender. Serve with Bean Sauce. Yield: 10 or more servings.

BEAN SAUCE

2 slices bacon, chopped
1/3 small onion, chopped
1/3 green bell pepper, chopped
2 sweet peppers (optional)
1 garlic clove, minced
1 small potato, peeled, diced
1 teaspoon hot water
1 (16-ounce) can kidney or pinto beans
2 to 4 tablespoons tomato sauce (from Chicken and Rice recipe)
Chopped hot chile peppers to taste
1/2 cup water
Salt and pepper to taste

Sauté the bacon in a small skillet over medium heat until half-cooked. Stir in the onion, green pepper, sweet peppers and garlic; simmer, covered, until vegetables are soft. Drain off excess grease. Add the potato and hot water; simmer, covered, for 20 minutes or until potato is tender. Combine the potato mixture, undrained kidney beans, tomato sauce, chile peppers and water in a saucepan and mix well. Season with salt and pepper. Heat and serve over Chicken and Rice.

Anita Sutherland, Preceptor Alpha Beta
New Orleans, Louisiana

CREAMY POPPY SEED CHICKEN

3 medium whole chicken breasts, cooked
2 (10-ounce) cans cream of chicken soup
2 cups sour cream
1 teaspoon poppy seeds
2 tubes butter crackers, crushed
3/4 cup (1 1/2 sticks) margarine, melted

Cut the chicken into large pieces, discarding the skin and bones. Layer in a greased 9×13-inch baking dish. Combine the soup, sour cream and poppy seeds in a bowl and mix well. Spread the soup mixture over the chicken layer. Combine the butter crackers and margarine in a bowl and mix well; spread over the soup mixture. Bake at 350 degrees for about 30 minutes. Yield: 6 to 8 servings.

Louise S. Gandy, Laureate Gamma Pi
Century, Florida

THAI BARBECUED CHICKEN

This recipe will make enough marinade for three whole chickens, or seven pounds of pieces. For a spicier version, add 1/4 cup lime juice and 1 tablespoon Thai chili paste.

2/3 cup chopped cilantro
1/2 head garlic, peeled, minced
1/4 cup freshly ground pepper
1/3 cup sugar
1/2 cup shrimp sauce
1/2 cup white vinegar
3 whole chickens, cut up

Combine the cilantro, garlic, pepper, sugar, shrimp sauce and white vinegar in a large glass dish and whisk well. Add the chicken. Marinate, covered, in the refrigerator for 4 to 10 hours. Drain the chicken, reserving the marinade. Grill slowly over hot coals, basting occasionally with the marinade. Yield: 1 to 1 1/2 cups.

Donna J. Myers, Preceptor Beta Nu
La Habra, California

RASPBERRY BALSAMIC CHICKEN

1 teaspoon vegetable oil
1/2 cup chopped red onion
4 (4-ounce) boneless skinless chicken breasts
1/2 teaspoon salt
1 1/2 teaspoons minced fresh thyme
1/3 cup seedless raspberry preserves
2 tablespoons balsamic vinegar
1/4 teaspoon pepper

Heat the vegetable oil in a large nonstick skillet over medium-high heat. Sauté the onion in the hot oil for 5 minutes. Season the chicken with half the salt and the thyme, and add to the onion in the skillet. Cook for 6 minutes on each side or until cooked through. Remove chicken from skillet; keep warm. Reduce heat to medium and combine the remaining salt, raspberry preserves, vinegar and pepper in the skillet; heat until preserves melt, stirring constantly. Spoon the raspberry sauce over the chicken and serve immediately. Yield: 4 servings.

Syble A. Shoults (30 years), Xi Mu
Bessemer, Alabama

Harolyn Long, Alpha Eta, Nanton, Alberta, Canada, makes **Creamy Onion Chicken** by browning skinless chicken breasts in a small amount of hot oil in a skillet and arranging the chicken in a baking dish. Deglaze the skillet with a mixture of 1 cup sour cream and 1/2 envelope onion soup mix and mix in 8 ounces whipped topping. Pour over the chicken and sprinkle with Parmesan cheese. Bake, covered, at 350 degrees for 20 to 30 minutes.

TUNA CURRY CASSEROLE

Every year when we went to visit my grandmother, she would prepare this dish for my father (her son-in-law)—we all loved it!

3 (10-ounce) cans cream of chicken soup	1 cup chopped onion
2 (10-ounce) cans cream of mushroom soup	1/2 teaspoon thyme
	1/4 teaspoon basil
1 cup milk	1/4 teaspoon oregano
1/2 cup water	2 (12-ounce) cans tuna, drained
1/4 cup warm water	
4 to 6 teaspoons curry powder	16 ounces spaghetti, cooked, drained
1 (16-ounce) can mushrooms	

Combine the soups, milk and the 1/2 cup water in a large saucepan over medium heat and mix well. Simmer for 10 minutes, stirring frequently. Add a mixture of the 1/4 cup warm water and curry powder; mix well. Stir in the undrained mushrooms, onion, thyme, basil and oregano; simmer for 10 minutes longer. Stir in the tuna and cooked spaghetti. Spoon the tuna mixture into a greased 9×13-inch baking dish. Bake, covered, at 350 degrees for 1 hour. Yield: 10 servings.

Mary Walton, Xi Tau
Alliance, Nebraska

SPICY TUNA NOODLE BAKE

After trying many different recipes for tuna casseroles, I combined a little of each and came up with what I think is the ultimate.

4 ounces Philadelphia cream cheese, softened	2 garlic cloves, minced
	1 (4-ounce) can sliced black olives, drained
1 (10-ounce) can clam chowder or cream of mushroom soup	8 ounces mozzarella cheese, shredded
1/4 cup chopped marinated red peppers	8 to 10 ounces egg noodles, cooked al dente, drained
1 teaspoon black pepper	
1 cup diced celery	3 (6-ounce) cans tuna, drained
1 small onion, chopped	
1 (4-ounce) can chopped green chiles	1 (8-ounce) can green peas, drained
1/4 cup mayonnaise	1 (6-ounce) can French-fried onions

Combine the cream cheese, clam chowder, red peppers, black pepper, celery, onion, green chiles, mayonnaise, garlic, olives and 6 ounces of the moz-zarella cheese in a large bowl; mix well. Fold in the noodles, tuna and green peas. Spoon the tuna mixture into a greased 9×13-inch baking dish. Sprinkle with the remaining 2 ounces mozzarella cheese and French-fried onions. Bake at 350 degrees for 30 minutes. Reduce heat to 200 degrees and bake for 10 to 15 minutes longer or until hot and bubbly and beginning to brown. Let stand at room temperature for 10 minutes before serving. Yield: 8 servings.

Donna J. Myers, Preceptor Beta Nu
La Habra, California

TUNA BRAID

This was one of my mother's favorite recipes, a way to serve tuna in a dish other than the traditional tuna and noodles. She often used a can of cream of mushroom soup as a topping. You may substitute 1 1/2 cups of drained canned salmon for the tuna, and Velveeta cheese for the American.

1 (6-ounce) can tuna, drained	1 cup diced American cheese
1/4 cup chopped onion	2 teaspoons chopped pimento
1 cup cooked lima beans, green beans, peas, corn or a mixture	2 cups flour
	3 teaspoons baking powder
1 teaspoon salt	1/3 cup vegetable oil
1/4 teaspoon pepper	2/3 cup milk

Combine the tuna, onion, lima beans, half the salt, pepper, American cheese and pimento in a bowl and mix well; let stand while preparing the dough. Combine the flour, baking powder and remaining salt in a bowl and mix well. Place the vegetable oil and milk in a measuring cup; do not stir. Pour the vegetable oil and milk all at once into the flour mixture. Stir with a fork until the mixture cleans the side of the bowl and forms a ball. Knead about 10 times to smooth the dough. Roll between sheets of waxed paper into a 10×12-inch rectangle. Place on an ungreased baking sheet. Spread the tuna filling down the center. Make seven 3-inch-long cuts on each side; fold alternately over the center, braiding to enclose the filling. Bake at 425 degrees for 20 to 25 minutes or until hot and golden brown. Yield: 8 to 10 servings.

Sandi Keim (35 years), Preceptor Alpha Phi
Wooster, Ohio

JOSEPHINE'S COD CURRY

Josephine and Freddie were two dear family friends who operated a restaurant for many years. Their restaurant was "home" for them, where everyone was welcomed with a smile, a greeting, and cups of coffee. Freddie usually did the cooking, but he was not there the evening that Josephine prepared this delicious Cod Curry for me for the first time.

1 pound fresh or frozen cod fillets	1 tablespoon chopped parsley
¼ cup white wine or unsweetened pineapple juice	1 tablespoon margarine or vegetable oil
1 large onion or 4 green onions, sliced	1½ teaspoons each curry powder and sugar
¼ cup chopped celery	1½ teaspoons vinegar
½ cup diced tomatoes, fresh or canned	¼ teaspoon ginger
	1 cup milk
	1 tablespoon cornstarch

Place the cod fillets in a greased 2-quart baking dish and sprinkle lightly with salt and pepper. Pour the wine over the fillets and chill, covered, while preparing the sauce. Sauté the onion, celery, tomatoes and parsley in the margarine in a skillet over medium heat for a few minutes. Stir in the curry powder, sugar, vinegar, ginger and ¼ teaspoon each salt and pepper; simmer for a few minutes. Add ¾ cup of the milk and simmer for 1 minute longer, stirring slowly to prevent curdling. Whisk the cornstarch into the remaining ¼ cup milk; whisk into the hot curry mixture. Cook until thickened, stirring constantly. Pour over the fish and bake, covered, at 350 degrees for 30 minutes. Yield: 3 to 4 servings.

M. Elizabeth Thomey, Xi Nu
Deer Lake, Newfoundland, Canada

TUNA PATTY MELT

1 (6-ounce) can tuna, drained, flaked	¼ cup mayonnaise
½ cup rolled oats	Pinch of salt
⅓ cup shredded carrot	Dash of pepper
1 egg, beaten	2 tablespoons vegetable oil
2 tablespoons chopped onion	Sliced Cheddar or Swiss cheese

Combine the tuna, rolled oats, carrot, egg, onion, mayonnaise, salt and pepper in a bowl and mix well. Shape into patties. Brown in hot vegetable oil in a skillet over medium heat for 3 to 4 minutes on each side. Place a slice of cheese on each patty during the last 2 minutes of cooking time. Yield: 4 patties.

Jennifer Koch, Preceptor Xi
Lafayette, Indiana

SALMON CRUNCH PIE

1½ cups flour	3 eggs, beaten
1 teaspoon salt	1 cup sour cream
1 teaspoon paprika	½ cup mayonnaise
½ cup cold butter, chopped	½ cup shredded Swiss cheese
1 cup shredded medium Cheddar cheese	1 teaspoon finely chopped onion
½ cup chopped pecans	
2 (7-ounce) cans salmon, drained, chunked	

Combine the flour, salt, paprika and butter in a food processor container and pulse until mixture resembles coarse crumbs. Pulse in the Cheddar cheese and pecans. Set aside ½ cup of the flour mixture for a topping. Press the remaining mixture in the bottom and up the side of a 10-inch pie plate. Arrange the salmon in the pie shell. Combine the eggs, sour cream, mayonnaise, Swiss cheese and onion in a bowl and mix well. Spoon the egg mixture evenly over the salmon layer. Sprinkle the reserved flour mixture evenly over the top. Bake at 375 degrees for 35 minutes. Yield: 8 servings.

Florence Brendon (52 years), Alpha Zeta Master
London, Ontario, Canada

BLUE MOUNTAIN BARBECUED SALMON

I grew up in the Pacific Northwest, where there is lots of fresh salmon. This recipe always takes me home again. Serve with steamed asparagus and new potatoes.

1 whole salmon	2 garlic cloves, crushed
½ cup (1 stick) butter	¼ cup ketchup
¼ cup soy sauce	Dash of Worcestershire sauce
2 tablespoons prepared mustard	

Cut the salmon open, close to the spine, leaving the bone in. Melt the butter in a skillet over low heat. Add the soy sauce, mustard, garlic, ketchup and Worcestershire sauce; simmer over low heat for 5 to 8 minutes. Place the opened salmon meat side down on a grill over hot coals. Sear the meat, about 7 minutes for a 5- to 8-pound salmon. Loosen with a spatula and turn salmon over onto a large piece of foil. Pour ¾ of the soy sauce mixture evenly over the salmon; wrap in the foil and seal to enclose. Close the grill and finish cooking the salmon in the grill, 15 to 20 minutes for a 5- to 8-pound salmon. Just before fish is done, remove the backbone and add the remaining soy sauce mixture. Yield: 8 servings.

Darla Steiner, Xi Theta Chi
Chesapeake, Virginia

VERACRUZ FISH FILLETS

1 pound red snapper, perch or salmon fillets	1/4 teaspoon garlic powder
2 tablespoons vegetable oil	1 (15-ounce) can diced tomatoes, drained
1 cup sliced onions	1 (16-ounce) jar mild picante sauce
1/2 cup sliced green bell pepper	1/4 teaspoon lemon pepper

Rinse the fish and pat dry. Cook in hot vegetable oil in a large nonstick skillet until fish flakes easily with a fork. Remove fish from the skillet; cover and keep warm. Sauté the onions and green pepper in the remaining oil in the skillet for 5 minutes or until they begin to soften; drain on doubled paper towels to remove excess oil. Return the onions and green pepper to the skillet; add the garlic powder, tomatoes, picante sauce and lemon pepper and bring to a boil. Return the fish to the skillet. Spoon the sauce over the fish and heat through. Serve immediately. Yield: 3 to 4 servings.

Donna Hudson (36 years), Beta Master
Cheyenne, Wyoming

WARREN'S FISH FRY

An inexpensive "economy" brand of mustard will work just as well as an expensive one. To test the heat of the oil for deep-frying, float an unlit match on top of the oil; when the match spews, remove it and fry the fish. Serve with hush puppies, coleslaw, fried potatoes, sliced pickles, and sliced onion.

1/2 cup prepared mustard	1 teaspoon garlic powder
2 teaspoons fresh lemon juice	1 cup fresh yellow cornmeal
2 teaspoons Worcestershire sauce	1/3 cupcornstarch
1/2 teaspoon cayenne pepper, or Tabasco sauce to taste	Salt or Tony Chaceres Cajun Seasoning to taste

Combine the first 5 ingredients in a bowl and whisk to blend. Coat fish with the mustard mixture. If fish has a strong fishy flavor, let it stand in a colander in the sink for 30 to 40 minutes so the oils may drip through the colander. Coat the fish with a mixture of the cornmeal, cornstarch and salt and deep-fry in hot oil. Note: If fish is mild, like salmon or white perch, coat with the cornmeal mixture immediately after coating with the mustard mixture. Yield: Varies.

Clair Ledger, Preceptor Kappa
Montrose, Colorado

LINGUINI WITH GARLIC AND TUNA

1/3 cup olive oil	1/2 teaspoon hot red pepper flakes
2 garlic cloves, minced	3/4 cup chicken broth
2 (6-ounce) cans tuna packed in water	16 ounces linguini, cooked, drained
1/4 cup finely chopped parsley	

Heat the olive oil in a saucepan over medium-low heat. Sauté the garlic in the hot oil for 2 minutes. Stir in the undrained tuna, parsley, hot red pepper flakes and chicken broth. Cook over medium heat until heated through. Serve over linguini on a warmed serving platter. Yield: 4 to 6 servings.

Jane Grzybowski, Gamma
Laramie, Wyoming

TUNA AND EGG CASSEROLE

This was a "standby" recipe I got from my mother, who is now ninety-four years old.

1 cup chopped celery	4 hard-cooked eggs, chopped
1/2 cup water	1/2 teaspoon salt
1 (10-ounce) can cream of mushroom soup	1/4 teaspoon pepper
1 (6-ounce) can tuna, drained	1/2 cup shredded Cheddar cheese
2 tablespoons grated lemon zest	1/8 teaspoon paprika

Combine the celery and water in a small saucepan and simmer until softened. Stir in half the cream of mushroom soup and mix well. Combine the tuna, lemon zest and remaining soup in a bowl and mix well. Layer the tuna mixture, chopped egg whites, crumbled egg yolks and soup mixture in a greased 1-quart casserole. Sprinkle with the salt and pepper. Top with the Cheddar cheese and paprika. Bake, covered, at 450 degrees for 15 minutes or until hot and bubbly. Yield: 4 servings.

Delores Schmidt (45 years), Beta Mu Master
Susanville, California

Elaine Cernik, Theta Master, Rogers, Arkansas, promotes her **Best Yet Tuna and Noodles**. Mix a can of albacore tuna with a can of cream of mushroom soup, 1/4 cup mayonnaise, 2 tablespoons prepared mustard, and a can of drained French-style green beans. Fold in 8 ounces cooked noodles and 1/2 can French-fried onions. Spoon into a baking dish, bake at 350 degrees for 25 minutes, top with the remaining onions and bake for 5 minutes longer.

SAVORY SHRIMP AND RICE

We always have this dish on special days like birthdays because it's everyone's favorite.

6 tablespoons butter
1¹/2 cups uncooked rice
1 large onion, finely
  chopped
¹/2 teaspoon salt
¹/2 cup dry white wine
1 cup sliced fresh
  mushrooms
1 (15-ounce) can beef
  broth

1 soup can water
2 tablespoons chopped
  parsley
¹/2 teaspoon thyme
2 teaspoons lemon juice
1 to 1¹/2 pounds small
  shrimp

Melt the butter in a saucepan over medium heat. Add the rice, onion and salt; sauté until golden. Add the wine and mushrooms; cook for 4 minutes, stirring frequently. Add the beef broth, water, parsley, thyme, lemon juice and shrimp. Reduce heat and simmer, covered, for 10 minutes or until shrimp is opaque, rice is tender and liquid is absorbed.
Yield: 6 to 8 servings.

Judy Pettigrew (28 years), Laureate Phi
Pasco, Washington

SAUCY SHRIMP AND RICE

Because we live on the coast, we have easy access to a lot of fresh seafood. This recipe is a great change from fried, fried, fried! Serve with a spinach salad.

¹/3 cup butter
1 pound raw fresh
  shrimp, peeled,
  deveined
¹/2 red bell pepper,
  julienned
¹/2 yellow bell pepper,
  julienned
¹/2 green bell pepper,
  julienned

¹/2 white onion, chopped
2 tablespoons flour
1 cup sour cream
¹/4 cup milk
1 (4-ounce) can sliced
  mushrooms, drained
Salt and pepper to taste
1 (5-ounce) package
  Mahatma yellow
  rice, cooked

Melt the butter in a saucepan over medium heat. Add the shrimp, bell peppers and onion. Sauté for 5 minutes; do not let vegetables brown. Add the flour and stir well. Stir in a mixture of the sour cream and milk. Add the mushrooms, salt and pepper and stir. Simmer, covered, for about 8 minutes. Serve over yellow rice. Yield: 4 to 6 servings.

Anne Kittrell, Laureate Zeta
Orange Beach, Alabama

SHRIMP CREOLE

This dish was a specialty at Paradise Point Restaurant in Mississippi City between Biloxi and Gulfport. My Great-Aunt Myrtle Jones got the recipe in 1955.

3 large green bell
  peppers, diced
3 large onions, diced
3 tablespoons olive oil
Dash of paprika

4 cups chopped
  tomatoes
2 pounds cooked shrimp
Salt and pepper to taste
2 cups cooked rice

Sauté the bell peppers and onions in the olive oil in a skillet over medium-low heat for a few minutes. Add the paprika and tomatoes; simmer for 15 minutes. Add the shrimp and simmer for 10 minutes longer. Season with salt and pepper and serve over hot rice. Yield: 5 servings.

Demetra Toomey, Xi Delta Iota
Athens, Tennessee

MARYLAND CRAB CAKES

We all grew up on the Chesapeake Bay, and this recipe was a summer delight. When our family gets together now, this is the dish we all look forward to most and the one that brings back memories of childhood and home.

1 pound fresh lump crab
  meat, drained
1 teaspoon Old Bay
  seasoning
¹/4 teaspoon salt
1 tablespoon
  mayonnaise

1 teaspoon
  Worcestershire sauce
1 tablespoon baking
  powder
1 egg, beaten
5 or 6 saltines, crushed
  into fine crumbs

Combine the crab meat, Old Bay seasoning, salt, mayonnaise, Worcestershire sauce, baking powder, egg and saltines in a medium bowl and mix well. Shape into 12 cakes and fry in a skillet over medium heat until light brown on both sides.
Yield: 6 servings.

Linda Boyle (27 years), Xi Alpha Zeta
Columbia, Maryland

Julia Gatsos (32 years), Laureate Beta Omicron, New Albany, Indiana, makes **Microwave Tuna Wedges** by beating 2 eggs in a greased pie plate and mixing in 1¹/2 cups cooked rice, ¹/4 cup chopped onion, ¹/2 cup melted butter, ¹/4 teaspoon thyme, a can of drained, flaked tuna and 1 cup fine dry bread crumbs. Spread evenly in the pie plate and microwave, covered with waxed paper, on High for 9 to 11 minutes or until set. Garnish with tomato wedges and shredded cheese.

MEMORIES

My parents always had Christmas at our house. All my aunts, uncles, cousins and grandparents were there—a very large group. Everyone came for the noon meal and stayed for the evening meal. The adults played cards and/or games with all the kids. It was always the best day of the year because everyone was together and so happy to be there! This continued until my mother could no longer handle the large crowd, and some of the younger ones moved too far away to come. But what a great family memory!

Shirley Bird (32 years), Xi Alpha Nu
Eureka Springs, Arkansas

FRIED BAY SCALLOPS

I come from a family of seven, and we were all born in a small fishing village where our daddy made our living on the Gulf. We always had plenty of fish to eat. All the five girls left the homeplace except for me, and I still live there with our eighty-two-year-old mother close by. We all share recipes, especially seafood recipes. I have learned many different ways to prepare the bay scallops we gather in the summer. Everyone is excited when they get to come home, gather some wonderful seafood, and have a big family cookout.

1 pound scallops	1 egg, well beaten
Salt and pepper to taste	1 cup flour
1/2 envelope Sazón Goya	1/2 cup cornmeal
1 cup buttermilk	

Rinse the scallops and drain. Season with salt and pepper and Sazón Goya. Beat the buttermilk and egg together. Combine the flour and cornmeal in a separate bowl and mix well. Roll the scallops in the flour mixture, then in the buttermilk mixture, then in the flour mixture once again. Arrange on a baking sheet; chill, covered, for at least 1 hour. Deep-fry in hot vegetable oil. Watch very closely and remove from oil just as scallops begin to turn golden brown; drain on paper towels. Serve immediately. Yield: 4 servings.

Ann Levingston, Theta Chi
Steinhatchee, Florida

SHRIMP AND CRAB CASSEROLE

I am the oldest of eight children, and Mom could make a pan of this dish to feed us all. Dad shrimped for a living, so such a luxurious meal was easy and economical. It can be refrigerated for 4 days.

1/2 cup (1 stick) margarine	1 cup water
2 ribs celery, chopped	1 (10-ounce) can tomatoes with green chiles
1 small green bell pepper, chopped	2 cups uncooked rice
1 small onion, chopped	2 pounds shrimp, cleaned
1 (10-ounce) can onion soup	2 cups crab meat (optional)
1 (10-ounce) can cream of mushroom soup	Salt and pepper to taste

Melt the margarine in a Dutch oven. Add the celery, green pepper, onion, soups, water, tomatoes with green chiles, rice, shrimp, crab meat, salt and pepper; mix well. Bake, covered, at 350 degrees for 30 minutes; stir. Bake, covered, for 1 hour longer. Stir and serve. Yield: 8 to 10 servings.

Kathy Sterling (31 years), Laureate Eta Nu
Houston, Texas

❖ BASIL SHRIMP WITH FETA AND ORZO

Serve with a mixed green salad and Pinot Grigio.

1/2 cup uncooked orzo	1/4 teaspoon salt
2 teaspoons olive oil	1/4 teaspoon black pepper
1 cup diced fresh tomatoes	Dash of hot red pepper flakes
3/4 cup sliced green onions	3/4 pound uncooked shrimp, peeled, deveined
1/2 cup crumbled feta cheese	1/4 cup chopped fresh basil
1/2 teaspoon grated lemon zest	

Cook the orzo in boiling water in a saucepan for 5 minutes; drain. Place the orzo, olive oil, tomatoes, green onions, feta cheese, lemon zest, salt, black pepper and hot red pepper flakes in a large bowl; toss to combine. Spread the orzo mixture in an 8-inch-square baking pan that has been sprayed with nonstick cooking spray. Combine the shrimp and basil; spread over the orzo mixture. Bake, tightly covered with foil, for 25 minutes. Yield: 2 to 3 servings.

Mary Ellen Cramer, Xi Zeta Psi
Stroudsburg, Pennsylvania

SEAFOOD LASAGNA

My grandchildren ask for this dish on their birthdays. All ten of them love it! You may substitute imitation crab for the crab meat if you like, and frozen shrimp for the canned shrimp.

¹/₂ cup (1 stick) margarine	8 ounces lasagna noodles
4 garlic cloves, crushed	1¹/₂ cups creamed cottage cheese
¹/₂ cup flour	
Salt and pepper to taste	1 (7-ounce) can crab meat, drained
2 cups milk	
2 cups chicken broth	1 (4-ounce) can tiny shrimp, drained
1 teaspoon dried basil leaves	
	¹/₂ cup grated Parmesan cheese
2 cups shredded mozzarella cheese	

Melt the margarine in a 3-quart saucepan over low heat. Add the garlic, flour and salt. Cook until bubbly, stirring constantly. Remove from heat. Stir in the milk, chicken broth and basil. Return to heat and bring to a boil, stirring constantly; boil and stir for 1 minute. Reduce heat and stir in the mozzarella cheese and pepper. Cook over low heat until cheese is melted, stirring constantly. Spread ¹/₄ of the cheese mixture in an ungreased 9×13-inch baking dish. Layer 3 or 4 uncooked lasagna noodles over the cheese mixture, overlapping if necessary. Layer the cottage cheese, ¹/₄ of the cheese mixture, 3 or 4 uncooked noodles, crab meat, shrimp, ¹/₄ of the cheese mixture, the remaining noodles and the remaining cheese mixture over the noodles. Sprinkle with Parmesan cheese. Bake, uncovered, at 350 degrees for 35 to 40 minutes or until hot and beginning to brown. Let stand for 15 minutes before cutting. Yield: 12 servings.

Patricia Riecke (30 years), Laureate Pi
Medford, Oregon

CREAMY SEAFOOD PASTA

Serve with a salad, garlic bread, and a glass of wine.

¹/₂ pound scallops	1¹/₂ cups heavy cream
¹/₂ pound salad shrimp	¹/₂ cup grated Parmesan cheese
1 (8-ounce) can mushrooms, drained	
	3 tablespoons butter
1 green or red bell pepper	Salt and pepper to taste
	¹/₂ teaspoon paprika
16 ounces vermicelli, angel hair or other pasta	

Sauté the scallops in hot oil in a skillet over medium heat for 5 to 10 minutes. Add the shrimp, mushrooms and bell pepper and sauté for 5 minutes longer. Remove from heat. Cook the pasta al dente in boiling water in a kettle; drain. Return pasta to the kettle with the cream, Parmesan cheese and butter. Add salt, pepper and paprika and toss to combine. Heat through. Toss in the scallops mixture and heat through. Add more Parmesan cheese if desired. Yield: 6 servings.

Ellen Turner, Eta Delta
Newport, Oregon

BAKED SEAFOOD SALAD

1 cup chopped green bell pepper	1 (6-ounce) can tuna, drained
¹/₂ cup chopped yellow onion	1 teaspoon Worcestershire sauce
2 cups chopped celery	1 teaspoon salt
2 cups (or less) mayonnaise	Pepper to taste
	Dash of Tabasco sauce
2 (6-ounce) cans crab meat, drained	Crushed potato chips
2 (6-ounce) cans shrimp, drained	

Combine the green pepper, onion, celery, mayonnaise, crab meat, shrimp, tuna, Worcestershire sauce, salt, pepper and Tabasco sauce in a bowl and mix well. Spoon into a 9×13-inch glass baking dish and top with crushed potato chips. Bake, uncovered, at 350 degrees for 30 minutes or until hot. Serve over a bed of lettuce. Yield: 10 servings.

Judith Wade, Preceptor Xi
West LaFayette, Indiana

FETTUCCINI SHRIMP ALFREDO

Florets from ¹/₂ head broccoli	¹/₂ cup (1 stick) margarine
8 ounces cream cheese, cubed	20 to 25 medium shrimp, peeled, cooked
1¹/₂ cups shredded Parmesan cheese	6 ounces fettuccini, cooked, drained
¹/₂ cup milk	

Combine the broccoli and a small amount of water in a microwave-safe bowl. Microwave on High, covered, for 4 minutes; drain. Combine the cream cheese, Parmesan cheese, milk and margarine in a large saucepan over low heat. Cook until melted and smooth, stirring frequently. Add the broccoli, shrimp and fettuccini; toss to combine. Yield: 4 servings.

Jean Van Stelten (40 years), Epsilon Master
Manchester, New Hampshire

GRANDMA'S SEAFOOD CASSEROLE

My Grandma Fara prepared her Seafood Casserole every Christmas Eve. She is ninety years old now, so I'm keeping the tradition going for her. We serve it with thinly sliced grilled marinated sirloin steak, tossed salad, garlic bread, and something chocolate for dessert.

8 ounces mushrooms, sliced	1 pound shrimp, cooked
1/4 cup (1/2 stick) butter	1 pound crab meat, frozen or canned
1 (10-ounce) can cream of shrimp soup	1 (8-ounce) can sliced water chestnuts, drained
2/3 cup milk	
1/4 cup shredded Cheddar cheese	1 (6-ounce) can French-fried onions
1/2 cup mayonnaise	
2 cups crushed uncooked fine noodles	

Sauté the mushrooms in the butter in a skillet over medium heat for a few minutes. Combine the mushrooms, soup, milk, Cheddar cheese and mayonnaise in a large bowl and mix well. Fold in the crushed noodles. Chill, covered, for 2 to 3 hours. Stir in the shrimp, crab meat and water chestnuts. Spoon into a greased 9×13-inch baking dish. Bake, covered, at 325 degrees for 30 minutes. Top with French-fried onions. Bake, uncovered, for 30 minutes longer. Yield: 8 to 10 servings.

Mele Simonson, Xi Chi
Scottsdale, Arizona

COCONUT FRIED SHRIMP

1 1/4 cups flour	1 pound large shrimp, peeled, deveined
1 1/4 cups cornstarch	
6 1/2 teaspoons baking powder	2 1/2 cups flaked coconut
1/2 teaspoon salt	Vegetable oil for deep-frying
1/4 teaspoon Cajun seasoning	1 cup orange marmalade
1 1/2 cups cold water	1/4 cup honey
1/2 teaspoon vegetable oil	

Combine the flour, cornstarch, baking powder, salt and Cajun seasoning in a bowl and mix well. Add the water and the 1/2 teaspoon vegetable oil and stir until smooth. Dip the shrimp in the flour mixture to coat, then dip in the coconut to coat. Heat vegetable oil to 375 degrees in an electric skillet. Fry the shrimp for 3 minutes or until golden brown, a few at a time. Drain on a paper towel. Combine the marmalade and honey in a saucepan over medium-low heat. Cook

until heated through, stirring constantly. Serve as a dipping sauce for the shrimp. Yield: 4 servings.

Maxine Jones (35 years), Alpha Alpha
Decatur, Alabama

SHRIMP BOURBON

If you are a shrimp lover, you will adore this dish.

2 tablespoons butter or margarine	1 cup half-and-half
	1/2 teaspoon ground red pepper
8 large shallots, chopped	
2 garlic cloves, minced	2 pounds medium-size fresh shrimp, peeled, deveined
1 cup chicken broth	
1/2 cup bourbon	

Melt the butter in a Dutch oven over medium-high heat. Add the shallots and garlic and sauté for 3 minutes or until tender. Stir in the chicken broth, bourbon, half-and-half and red pepper. Cook for about 5 minutes until slightly thickened, stirring occasionally. Add the shrimp and cook for 3 minutes or until shrimp turns pink. Remove from heat and serve over fettuccini. Sprinkle with Parmesan cheese. Yield: 8 servings.

Margie Kelarek, Laureate Eta Beta
Hilltop Lakes, Texas

CHEESY SHRIMP CASSEROLE

I got this recipe while living in Tokyo, Japan, for nearly five years. It became a favorite for my family and for company.

2 cups cooked rice	2 tablespoons chopped onion
1 (10-ounce) can cream of mushroom soup	1 tablespoon lemon juice
8 ounces shrimp, peeled, deveined	1/2 teaspoon Worcestershire sauce
1/2 cup cubed Cheddar cheese	1/2 teaspoon dry mustard
2 tablespoons melted butter	1/4 teaspoon black pepper
2 tablespoons chopped green bell pepper	

Combine the rice, cream of mushroom soup, shrimp, Cheddar cheese, butter, green pepper, onion, lemon juice, Worcestershire sauce, mustard and black pepper in a bowl and mix well. Spoon into a greased 1 1/2-quart baking dish. Bake, uncovered, at 375 degrees for 40 minutes. Yield: 4 servings.

Sybil Huskins (57 years), Pi Master
Melbourne, Florida

SHRIMP SCAMPI

I prepare this dish every Valentine's Day for dinner for my husband and myself.

2 pounds Black Tiger jumbo shrimp	2 tablespoons lemon juice
1 onion, chopped	1/2 teaspoon Worcestershire sauce
2 garlic cloves, minced	
1/2 cup (1 stick) butter, melted	1/4 teaspoon Louisiana hot sauce
1/2 teaspoon steak sauce	Hot cooked fettuccini

Peel and devein the shrimp. Sauté the onion and garlic in the butter in a large skillet over medium heat. Add the steak sauce, lemon juice, Worcestershire sauce and hot sauce; bring to a boil. Add the shrimp. Cook for 3 to 5 minutes or until shrimp is pink, stirring constantly. Serve over fettuccini. Yield: 4 servings.

Gina Jones, Preceptor Alpha Epsilon
Eunice, New Mexico

MEMORIES

My husband, his sons and I join my sister and her nine children for a Christmas Eve party each year. Everyone gets to choose at least one item to put on the buffet table. It's the one time of the year the kids can have as much of whatever they want; they can even have soda pop with their meal. As soon as they're old enough to talk, the kids put in requests. Now, as adults, they bring their own children and the same rules apply. Of course, now they want to be sure to have leftovers to take home.

Ava Wilhelm, Preceptor Alpha Beta
Eugene, Oregon

DENISE'S SHRIMP ASPARAGUS CASSEROLE

1 (10-ounce) can asparagus, drained	2 cups rotini, cooked, drained
2 tablespoons margarine	1 pound cooked deveined shrimp, tails removed
2 tablespoons minced garlic	
2 tablespoons flour	2 cups shredded Cheddar cheese
2 cups milk	

Cut the asparagus into 1-inch pieces. Heat the margarine in a medium saucepan over low heat to melt. Add the garlic and cook for 1 minute. Stir in the flour and cook until bubbly, stirring constantly. Add the milk gradually and cook until thick and bubbly, stirring constantly. Remove from heat. Add the rotini, shrimp and asparagus; toss to coat. Pour into a 2-quart casserole. Bake, covered, at 350 degrees for 25 minutes. Sprinkle with Cheddar cheese. Bake, uncovered, for 10 minutes longer. Yield: 4 servings.

Denise Gorham, Alpha Epsilon
Minneapolis, Minnesota

BLACK OLIVE SHRIMP PIZZA

2 (8-count) cans crescent rolls	2 pounds cooked shrimp
16 ounces cream cheese, softened	1 cup chopped green onions
2 (8-ounce) jars cocktail sauce	1 (4-ounce) can chopped black olives, drained

Unroll the dough. Press in a single layer to cover a large pizza pan, pressing perforations to seal. Bake at 350 degrees for 8 to 10 minutes. Cool completely. Spread the cream cheese over the top. Spread with cocktail sauce. Sprinkle with shrimp, green onions and olives. Serve immediately or chill, covered, until serving time. Yield: 6 to 8 servings.

Coylena Kowalski, Eta Delta
Seal Rock, Oregon

CRAB MORNAY

2 pounds Velveeta cheese, melted	Garlic powder to taste
1 pound margarine, melted	8 ounces cream cheese, softened
1 (12-ounce) can evaporated milk	1/2 cup (1 stick) butter, softened
2 pounds fresh white crab meat	1 cup flour, sifted

Combine the Velveeta cheese, margarine and evaporated milk in a large bowl and mix well. Rinse the crab to remove any stray shells; drain well. Stir the crab and garlic powder into the Velveeta mixture. Combine the cream cheese and butter in a bowl and beat until fluffy. Stir in the flour; chill, covered, for 1 hour. Shape into 1-inch balls. Place in shallow 1 3/4-inch ungreased nonstick muffin cups. Press dough against bottom and up side of each cup to form a shell. Bake at 325 degrees for 20 minutes or until golden. Fill with the crab mixture and serve hot. Yield: 2 dozen.

KK LeBlanc, Xi Rho
Carlyss, Louisiana

MEMORIES

*I*n 1979, when I joined Beta Sigma Phi in California, my sisters became my family. We always had the summer social at our house. The men would play golf while the girls gathered at our pool. The men would all come over after golf, and we cooked out and spent the rest of the day in the spa and pool. Events such as these made me forget how much I missed all the family back in Georgia, and appreciated the close friendships I formed with my Beta Sigma Phi sisters. We still stay in touch.

Ann Bedgood, Xi Eta
Birmingham, Alabama

LINGUINI WITH WHITE CLAM SAUCE

2 (6-ounce) cans chopped clams	1/4 cup (1/2 stick) butter
1/2 cup chopped parsley	3 tablespoons olive oil
1 or 2 garlic cloves, minced	16 ounces linguini
	Salt and pepper to taste

Combine the undrained clams, parsley, garlic, butter and olive oil in a skillet over medium heat. Bring to a simmer; cook for 5 to 10 minutes. Cook the linguini in boiling water in a saucepan; drain. Place the linguini on a warm serving platter; pour the clam sauce over the top. Season and serve with grated Romano cheese. Yield: 6 to 8 servings.

Mary Ann Valley, Preceptor Gamma Lambda
Goodrich, Michigan

CRAB ROLLS WITH CREAM CHEESE

A fast, delicious luncheon recipe. Substitute chicken for the crab if you like.

1/4 cup chopped celery	1/4 cup chopped water chestnuts
1/4 cup chopped onion	
2 tablespoons butter, softened	4 cups chopped imitation crab meat
8 ounces cream cheese, softened	1 (8-count) can crescent rolls
1 tablespoon milk	

Cook the celery and onion in 1 cup boiling water in a saucepan for 2 minutes; drain. Combine the butter, cream cheese and milk in a mixing bowl and beat until light and fluffy. Stir in the celery mixture and

water chestnuts. Add the crab meat and mix well. Unroll the dough. Separate into 4 rectangles on a baking sheet, pressing the perforations to seal. Place 2 tablespoons crab filling in the center of each rectangle. Pull the dough edges toward the center and seal to enclose the filling. Bake at 400 degrees for 25 minutes or until hot and golden. Yield: 4 servings.

Mary Tinsley (30 years), Preceptor Alpha Theta
Washington, North Carolina

BAKED CRAB SHELLS

Do not break up the crab meat before mixing it with the other ingredients.

1 pound crab meat	1/2 teaspoon Worcestershire sauce
2 tablespoons bread crumbs	
1 egg, slightly beaten	3 tablespoons chopped onion
1/2 teaspoon prepared mustard	1/4 cup mayonnaise
1 tablespoon parsley	4 unbaked patty shells

Combine the crab meat, bread crumbs, egg, mustard, parsley, Worcestershire sauce, onion and mayonnaise in a bowl and mix well. Place the patty shells on a baking sheet and fill with the crab mixture. Bake at 350 degrees for 20 to 30 minutes or until hot and bubbly. Place 1 teaspoon mayonnaise on top of each crab shell and serve. Yield: 4 servings.

Diane T. Summers (28 years), Preceptor Nu
Frederick, Maryland

SCALLOPED OYSTERS

This recipe, passed down from my maternal great-grandmother, has been served at our family Thanksgiving and Christmas dinners for as long as I can remember.

1 cup (2 sticks) butter, melted	2 cups oysters, deveined
	Salt and pepper to taste
1 cup fine cracker crumbs	3/4 cup coffee cream
2 cups unseasoned bread cubes	

Combine the butter, cracker crumbs and bread cubes in a bowl and mix well. Layer half the crumb mixture and the oysters in a greased 9×13-inch baking dish. Sprinkle with salt and pepper. Layer the remaining crumb mixture over the oysters. Pour the cream evenly over the top. Bake, covered, at 300 degrees for 25 minutes. Uncover and bake for 5 to 15 minutes longer or until hot and browned. Yield: 10 servings.

M. Sue Harwell, Zeta Lambda
Mt. Vernon, Ohio

Vegetables and Side Dishes

On Thanksgiving Day, our family always invited some elderly friends without family to eat with us. The year my daughter was only about three years old disaster struck. We had tucked her into the table in her high chair and I had prepared her plate. Just as we all sat down with Abbie, George, and Bill, our three elderly friends, the entire table collapsed on the floor. Believe it or not, all of the food remained in the serving dishes and was salvageable, except the gravy. That year the only person who had gravy was my daughter sitting in her high chair. Most of those people have left this earth now, but my daughter still remembers having gravy and those of us who are still around laugh at this memory.

Sandee Moline, Xi Delta Beta
Fort Bragg, North Carolina

WESTERN BAKED BEANS

A great side dish for barbecue.

8 slices bacon	1/4 cup barbecue sauce
1/2 pound ground beef	1/3 cup granulated sugar
1 cup chopped onion	1/3 cup packed brown
1 (16-ounce) can pork	sugar
and beans	2 tablespoons molasses
1 (15-ounce) can lima	1 tablespoon chili
beans, drained	powder
1 (16-ounce) can kidney	1 tablespoon prepared
beans, drained	mustard
1 (15-ounce) can pinto	1 teaspoon salt
beans, drained	1 teaspoon pepper
1/4 cup ketchup	

Cook the bacon in a skillet over medium-low heat until crisp. Remove bacon from skillet; drain and crumble. Brown the ground beef with the onion in the bacon drippings, stirring until crumbly; drain. Mix the bacon, ground beef mixture and remaining ingredients in a large bowl and mix well. Spoon into a shallow 3-quart baking dish. Bake, covered, at 350 degrees for 1 hour. Yield: 12 to 15 servings.

Jackie Clevenger, Laureate Delta Epsilon
Independence, Missouri

MEMORIES

*T*his baked beans recipe is special to my family because everyone loves it so much. The aunts in my family bring the beans to all the family gatherings. The dish is eaten hot with dinner and then cold the next day with leftovers. This recipe belongs to my aunt, Mary Lou, but my other aunts, Ann and Madeline, also make them. They all three claim their recipe as the original. I made them once for a family event, but no one ate them. After everyone had left I tried the beans for myself. To my dismay, the beans were crunchy. Since my failing, I only let my aunts bake them. My aunt, Mary Lou Brannon, has always spoken so highly of Beta and her sorority sisters. When I joined, I felt an extra-special connection with her, as though we were doubly related. She is my aunt and now my sister!

Cynthia Waters, Beta Chi
Independence, Iowa

I remember the rush party that was held for the group of pledges when I joined Beta 32 years ago. It was a western theme and everyone had so much fun. The meal was simple: hot dogs and baked beans that had been heated in tin cups. I still have the cup. I knew after meeting these ladies that I would always love to be a member of Beta Sigma Phi. I have been active ever since.

Edna Faye Williams (32 years), Delta Omicron
Kennett, Missouri

SLOW-COOKER BAKED BEANS

1 1/2 pounds dry navy	2 teaspoons dry mustard
beans	2 tablespoons dark
1 onion, chopped	molasses
1 cup ketchup	1 tablespoon salt
1 cup packed brown	4 ounces salt pork, diced
sugar	

Place the navy beans in a kettle. Add enough water to cover. Simmer for about 30 minutes or until beans have tripled in size. Remove from heat and let stand, covered, for 1 1/2 hours or until beans are soft; drain. Combine the beans and the remaining ingredients in a large slow cooker and mix well. Cook on Low for 10 to 12 hours. Yield: Over 30 servings.

Elaine M. Wilson (25 years), Laureate Beta
Warwick, Rhode Island

HARVARD BEETS

My grandma and mom often made this favorite dish, especially at Christmastime. Serve with turkey, ham, or chicken—and double the recipe if you have a larger group to feed. You may use 3 cups of diced, peeled, cooked fresh beets instead of canned if you like.

1/2 cup sugar	1/3 cup boiling water
1 tablespoon cornstarch	1 (10-ounce) can beets,
1/2 teaspoon salt	drained, diced
1/3 cup white vinegar	1 tablespoon butter

Mix the sugar, cornstarch and salt in a saucepan. Stir in the vinegar and boiling water and cook over medium heat until clear, stirring constantly. Remove from heat. Stir in the beets and butter; keep warm until ready to serve. Yield: 4 to 6 servings.

Wanda Rathbone (34 years), Alpha Iota Master
Sault Ste. Marie, Ontario, Canada

CHEESY BROCCOLI CASSEROLE

I first enjoyed this broccoli casserole more than fifteen years ago when I was secretary to the Nuclear Quality Assurance Department at the Mare Island Naval Shipyard. One of the electrical inspectors brought this dish to a holiday potluck, and my family has enjoyed it at Thanksgiving ever since.

2 (10-ounce) packages
  frozen broccoli, or 1¼
  pounds fresh broccoli
1 cup mayonnaise
1 (10-ounce) can cream
  of mushroom soup
½ cup cracker crumbs

2 eggs, well beaten
¼ cup finely chopped
  onion
Salt and pepper to taste
1½ cups shredded
  Cheddar cheese

Cook the broccoli until tender; drain. Combine the mayonnaise, soup, ³/₄ of the cracker crumbs, eggs, onion, salt, pepper and 1 cup of the Cheddar cheese in a large bowl; mix well. Stir in the cooked broccoli. Spoon the mixture into a greased 2-quart casserole. Sprinkle with the remaining Cheddar cheese and cracker crumbs. Bake, covered, at 350 degrees for 35 to 40 minutes or until hot and bubbly.
Yield: 8 to 10 servings.

*Carole Emge (49 years), Laureate Iota Sigma
Vallejo, California*

BAKED BROCCOLI BALLS

I am the proud grandmother of six grandchildren, three of them teenagers. When a family dinner is planned, they always insist that "Meme" prepare her Broccoli Balls. You can double the recipe for a larger crowd.

1 (16-ounce) package
  herb-seasoned
  stuffing mix
2 (10-ounce) packages
  frozen chopped
  broccoli

8 ounces mozzarella
  cheese, shredded
½ onion, finely chopped
¾ cup melted butter
4 eggs

Prepare the stuffing using the package directions. Cook the broccoli using the package directions; drain well. Combine the stuffing, broccoli, mozzarella cheese, onion, butter and eggs in a bowl and mix well. Shape into balls about the size of a small orange. Arrange in a shallow baking dish. Bake at 350 degrees for 20 minutes or until hot and sizzling.
Yield: 6 to 8 servings.

*Lucille H. Crogan (45 years)
Kingwood, West Virginia*

BROCCOLI CHEESE BAKE

Double the recipe for a 9×13-inch baking dish.

2 eggs
2 tablespoons flour
½ teaspoon salt
⅛ teaspoon pepper
1½ cups shredded
  Cheddar cheese

1 (10-ounce) package
  frozen chopped
  broccoli, thawed,
  drained
1 cup cottage cheese

Combine the eggs, flour, salt and pepper in a bowl and mix well. Stir in the Cheddar cheese, broccoli and cottage cheese. Spoon into an 8-inch-square baking dish. Bake, uncovered, at 350 degrees for 30 to 40 minutes or until center is set. Yield: 6 to 8 servings.

*Judith Brown (27 years), Laureate Alpha Theta
Claremore, Oklahoma*

ZESTY MARINATED BRUSSELS SPROUTS

1 cup white vinegar
½ cup sugar
½ teaspoon salt
½ (5-ounce) jar prepared
  horseradish

1 teaspoon dry mustard
1 (10-ounce) package
  frozen brussels
  sprouts, thawed,
  drained

Place the vinegar, sugar, salt, horseradish and mustard in a jar and shake vigorously to combine. Combine the vinegar mixture and uncooked brussels sprouts in a bowl; marinate, covered, in the refrigerator for 8 to 10 hours. Serve cold or at room temperature. Yield: 4 servings.

*Nelda Mavis Wheeldon, Beta Sigma Phi
Rushville, Indiana*

GERMAN SWEET-AND-SOUR RED CABBAGE

This dish reminds me of Germany, where I grew up. Serve with pork chops or veal cutlets.

1 small red cabbage,
  shredded
1 apple, cored, diced
1 onion, peeled, diced
2 tablespoons brown
  sugar

2 teaspoons salt
¼ teaspoon pepper
1½ tablespoons apple
  cider vinegar
2 slices bacon, chopped,
  crisp-cooked

Cook the cabbage, apple and onion in boiling water for about 30 minutes. Remove from heat. Combine the brown sugar, salt, pepper and vinegar and stir into the cabbage mixture. Stir in the bacon. Heat and serve. Yield: 6 servings.

*Erika F. Wells, Eta Rho
Joplin, Missouri*

MEMORIES

I'll never forget the Thanksgiving when each household was in charge of bringing a meat, a side dish, and a pie. We served our plates, said a prayer, and sat down to eat. Then my cousin started to laugh. She had to confess a mishap that occurred when she was making her broccoli-cheese casserole. She had spilled the broccoli on the floor and dog hair got in it. Instead of making a second batch, she proceeded with the broccoli and finished the recipe. Luckily, at the time I didn't like broccoli and so was not eating dog hair broccoli casserole. We all stared at our plates wondering what else she had made for dinner.

Michelle Triano, Eta
Oviedo, Florida

CABBAGE CASSEROLE

1 medium head cabbage	1/2 cup (1 stick)
2 cups diced American	margarine
cheese	1 (6-ounce) package corn
2 tablespoons flour	bread stuffing mix

Trim and shred the cabbage. Cook in boiling water until tender; drain, reserving 2 cups of the cabbage liquid. Spread the cabbage in a greased 9×13-inch baking dish. Combine the cabbage liquid, American cheese and flour in a saucepan over medium heat; cook until thickened, stirring constantly. Pour the cheese mixture evenly over the cabbage layer. Mix the margarine and the stuffing mix in a bowl; sprinkle evenly over the cabbage. Bake, covered, at 350 degrees for 30 minutes. Yield: 8 to 10 servings.

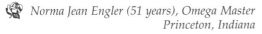 *Norma Jean Engler (51 years), Omega Master*
Princeton, Indiana

CREAMED CABBAGE

My future mother-in-law taught me to prepare this dish when I was sixteen years old. It is a comfort food in many ways.

1 head cabbage	2 cups half-and-half
Butter, salt and pepper	2 to 3 tablespoons apple
to taste	cider vinegar

Quarter and core the cabbage. Cut into 1/2-inch-wide slices; steam until tender. Place in a bowl; add butter, salt and pepper. Cool slightly. Pour the half-and-half into a small bowl; add the apple cider vinegar 1 tablespoon at a time, tasting each time until a small tang has developed. Stir the half-and-half mixture into the cabbage. Serve over mashed potatoes with fried pork chops. Yield: 6 servings.

Patricia Taylor
Garden Grove, California

CABBAGE FRITTATA

My Italian mother-in-law prepared this dish regularly for over sixty years of marriage. It gave me my first real appreciation of this odorous veggie!

1 (3- or 4-pound)	1/4 cup Italian bread
cabbage, cut up	crumbs
1/4 cup grated fresh	2 eggs, well beaten
Romano or Parmesan	3 tablespoons
cheese	vegetable oil
2 garlic cloves, minced	

Cook the cabbage in 4 quarts of boiling water in a saucepan until tender; drain. Combine the cabbage with the Romano cheese, garlic, bread crumbs and eggs in a large bowl; mix well. Heat a thin layer of vegetable oil in a 10- or 12-inch skillet over medium heat. Spoon half the cabbage mixture into the skillet and cook until a brown finish forms on the bottom, pressing down with a spatula. Flip the cabbage mixture over to brown the other side. Remove from the skillet and repeat with the remaining 1/2 of the cabbage mixture. Serve warm. Yield: 8 servings.

Sandra Miletello, Xi Chi
Alexandria, Louisiana

MARINATED CARROTS

When I was in college, I would often visit my girlfriend's parents' home. Her mom prepared fresh country sausage, fried potatoes, and marinated carrots—what a treat after weeks of the college's institutional fare!

2 pounds carrots	1 (10-ounce) can tomato
1 large onion, thinly	soup
sliced (optional)	1 cup vegetable oil
1 green bell pepper,	1 teaspoon dry mustard
thinly sliced	3/4 cup cider vinegar
(optional)	1 teaspoon salt
1 cup sugar	

Peel the carrots and place in a saucepan with water to cover. Simmer for 15 minutes, or until soft but not mushy. Drain and cut into bite-size pieces. Layer the carrots, onion and green pepper in a 9×13-inch glass dish. Whisk the remaining ingredients in a bowl.

Drizzle over the vegetables in the glass dish. Marinate, covered, for 8 to 10 hours, stirring occasionally. Yield: 8 to 10 servings.

Linda Thiele, Preceptor Epsilon Phi
Delaware, Ohio

PARMESAN CAULIFLOWER

My husband and children all enjoy this spicy alternative to bland cauliflower.

1 whole cauliflower, leaves removed	1 tablespoon chopped fresh dill (less if dried)
3/4 cup mayonnaise	
1/2 cup sour cream	1/4 cup grated fresh Parmesan cheese
1/2 teaspoon (or less) cayenne pepper	

Steam the cauliflower for about 10 to 15 minutes or until tender and easily pierced with a fork. Combine the mayonnaise, sour cream, cayenne pepper and dill in a bowl and whisk to blend. Place the cauliflower in a 9×9-inch baking dish and spread with the mayonnaise mixture. Sprinkle with Parmesan cheese. Broil about 6 inches from heat for 3 minutes or until lightly browned. Cut into 1-inch slices and serve. Yield: 4 to 6 servings.

Jolene Korb, Xi Tau
Havre, Montana

SAVORY BAKED EGGPLANT

Everyone enjoys this vegetable with chicken, ham, pork chops, or beef roast. Double the recipe for a potluck dinner.

1 medium eggplant, peeled, cubed	1 teaspoon salt
3 tablespoons butter	1 tablespoon brown sugar
3 tablespoons flour	1 cup shredded Cheddar cheese
1 onion, chopped	
3 large tomatoes, peeled, chopped	1/2 cup fine dry bread crumbs

Place the eggplant in a kettle and add enough salted water to cover. Boil for 10 minutes; drain. Spread the eggplant in a buttered 2-quart casserole. Melt the butter in a saucepan over medium heat. Stir in the flour and sauté for 1 minute. Add the onion, tomatoes, salt and brown sugar. Simmer for 6 to 8 minutes, stirring frequently. Pour the onion mixture over the eggplant. Sprinkle with Cheddar cheese and bread crumbs. Bake at 350 degrees for 30 minutes or until hot and bubbly. Yield: 4 servings.

Esther Colton (43 years), Preceptor Epsilon Delta
Garden Grove, California

MEMORIES

One of my favorite stories is about a dear friend who was very eager to share her favorite corn recipe with a newfound friend on a cruise. As she was leaving the ship, she suddenly remembered that she had forgotten to give her the main ingredient—the corn! We laugh about this often and wonder what the lady did if she ever tried it. It would certainly have been runny and not at all fit to eat.

Laurel Brown
Redmond, Oregon

CORN AND GREEN BEAN CASSEROLE

My bridge club has been meeting every month for the last forty years and has a covered dish luncheon once a year. This Corn and Green Bean Casserole is always gobbled up with compliments.

2 (16-ounce) cans French-style green beans, drained	1/2 cup chopped onions
	3/4 cup shredded Cheddar cheese
1 (10-ounce) can cream of celery soup	1/2 cup sour cream
1 (16-ounce) can Shoe Peg corn	Salt and pepper to taste
	1/2 cup crumbled butter crackers
1/2 cup chopped celery	1/4 cup (1/2 stick) margarine, melted
1/2 cup chopped green bell pepper	1/2 cup sliced almonds

Combine the green beans, soup, Shoe Peg corn, celery, green pepper, onions, Cheddar cheese, sour cream, salt and pepper in a large bowl and mix well. Spoon into a 10-inch-square baking dish. Sprinkle a mixture of the butter crackers, margarine and almonds over the top. Bake at 350 degrees for 30 to 45 minutes or until hot and bubbly. Yield: 10 to 12 servings.

Louise H. Hope (50 years), Epsilon Master
Huntsville, Alabama

Trisha E. Klock, Xi Tau Upsilon, Goodrich, Texas, says her husband created **Cheesy Corn Casserole** 20 years ago when he combined 2 cans cream-style corn, 1 can whole kernel corn, 1/2 cup chopped onion, 1 beaten egg, 2/3 cup milk, 1/4 cup melted margarine, 1 cup shredded Cheddar cheese and 1 cup cracker crumbs and baked at 350 degrees for 1 hour.

❖ PEPPERED CORN FRITTERS

1¼ cups fresh corn or frozen, thawed	2 teaspoons baking powder
1 cup finely chopped red bell pepper	¼ teaspoon salt
1 cup finely chopped green onions	⅛ teaspoon black pepper
1 teaspoon cumin	1 cup milk
1¼ cups flour	2 to 4 tablespoons vegetable oil

Combine the corn, red pepper and green onions in a bowl and mix well. Combine the next 5 ingredients in a separate bowl and mix well. Stir the flour mixture into the corn mixture. Add the milk gradually, stirring until moistened. Heat 2 tablespoons vegetable oil in a skillet over medium-high heat. Drop the batter by ¼ cups in the skillet. Cook for 2 minutes on each side or until golden brown, adding more vegetable oil as needed. Yield: 13 to 14 fritters.

Jane Owen, Xi Xi
Lynchburg, Virginia

MEMORIES

During the Depression days when we were little, Mom and Dad both worked. My sister, who was twelve at the time, tried to help out with dinner. She made creamed potatoes that turned out to be like paste. Our dear Daddy sat down at the table and ate them, never letting her know. What a great time we shared as a family!

Jean Leta, Alpha Xi Master
Sarasota, Florida

POTATO CROQUETTES

4 large potatoes, cooked in skins	¼ teaspoon nutmeg
2 tablespoons butter	½ teaspoon tarragon
Salt and pepper	1 cup bread crumbs
1 egg yolk	Peanut oil for deep-frying
4 eggs	

Peel and cube the potatoes; force through a food mill or potato ricer into a bowl. Add the butter and a generous amount of salt and pepper; mix well. Add the egg yolk and 1 of the whole eggs; mix well with a wooden spoon. Stir in the nutmeg and tarragon. Spread the potato mixture flat on a dinner plate. Chill, covered, for 3 hours. Shape into croquettes. Beat the remaining 3 eggs. Dip the croquettes into the eggs to coat; roll in the bread crumbs. Deep-fry in peanut oil at 375 degrees for 3 to 4 minutes or until brown on both sides. Drain on paper towels. Yield: 4 servings.

Joycee Davis, Laureate Alpha Epsilon
Lowell, Arkansas

POTATO DUMPLINGS

I found out only last year that my mother didn't grow up with this potato dumplings recipe. It was taught to her by my dad after they got married.

4 medium potatoes, peeled, shredded	4 slices bread, dried, crumbled
1 cup mashed potatoes	1 teaspoon salt
2 eggs, beaten	Flour

Combine the shredded potatoes, mashed potatoes, eggs, bread and salt in a bowl and mix well. Stir in enough flour to make a stiff dough. Shape into 2-inch balls. Drop into boiling water and cook for 20 minutes. Yield: 10 servings.

Lois Kotas, Laureate Kappa
Milligan, Nebraska

TWICE-BAKED POTATOES

Everyone seems to love this recipe. When our chapter has a steak fry or potluck dinner, I know what I'll be asked to bring—or someone will hint, hoping this is what I will bring. If you make them ahead of time, reheat them at 350 degrees for about 30 minutes before serving.

4 (7-ounce) potatoes	2 tablespoons butter or margarine
½ cup sour cream	
3 ounces cream cheese, softened	1 teaspoon onion salt
	⅛ teaspoon pepper

Select good well-shaped potatoes that are uniform in size. Scrub with a brush and rub with shortening. Pierce skin several times with a fork. Bake at 425 degrees for 40 to 50 minutes or until tender. Cut a slice from the top of each potato and scoop the pulp into a bowl, leaving ¼-inch shells. Add the sour cream, cream cheese, butter, onion salt and pepper to the pulp and beat until smooth. Spoon the sour cream mixture back into the potato shells. Garnish with paprika or parsley flakes or both.
Yield: 4 servings.

Colleen Breyfogle (49 years), Preceptor Beta Alpha
Sioux City, Iowa

SWEET POTATO PUDDING

**6 cups grated peeled
sweet potatoes
3 cups sugar
5 eggs
1 teaspoon vanilla
extract**

**3/4 cup milk
1/4 cup (1/2 stick) butter
or margarine,
softened**

Combine the sweet potatoes, sugar, eggs, vanilla, milk and butter in a bowl and beat until smooth. Spoon into a 2-quart baking dish. Bake, covered, at 350 degrees for 1 1/2 to 2 hours, stirring 3 times. Yield: 12 to 15 servings.

*Ann Bost, Preceptor Kappa Alpha
Elkhart, Texas*

SWEET POTATO BALLS

Mother always prepared this dish for the holiday meals. She passed away in December 2000, and my two brothers and sister came back home to the old place for Thanksgiving the following year. The looks on their faces were priceless when I served this dish that Mom had served since the 1950s.

**2 cups diced cooked
sweet potatoes
1/2 cup sugar
1/2 cup (1 stick)
margarine**

**8 to 10 marshmallows
2 cups crushed
cornflakes**

Mash the sweet potatoes in a bowl. Stir in the sugar and margarine. Shape into 8 to 10 balls. Press a marshmallow into each ball and roll in the cornflakes. Arrange on a lightly greased baking sheet. Bake at 350 degrees for 10 to 15 minutes or until hot and beginning to brown. Yield: 8 to 10 servings.

*Yvonne Johnson, Preceptor Upsilon
Brantley, Alabama*

SPINACH NOODLE CASSEROLE

**1 (10-ounce) package
frozen spinach,
thawed, drained
1/2 cup half-and-half
1 onion, finely chopped
2 tablespoons chopped
garlic
2 tablespoons olive oil
Salt and pepper to taste**

**7 ounces fresh baby
spinach
1/4 cup (1/2 stick) butter
1 cup sour cream
8 ounces cream cheese,
softened
16 ounces extra-wide
egg noodles, cooked,
drained**

Purée the thawed frozen spinach and half-and-half in a blender. Sauté the onion and garlic in the olive oil in a skillet over medium-low heat for 5 to 10 minutes or until tender. Add salt, pepper and the spinach.

Sauté for about 5 minutes or until spinach wilts. Stir in the butter, sour cream, cream cheese and half-and-half mixture; cook for about 5 minutes or until mixture is uniform and melted, stirring frequently. Spoon into a greased 9×13-inch baking dish. Stir in the noodles. Bake, uncovered, at 375 degrees for 10 minutes or until hot. Yield: 6 to 8 servings.

*Anita Wilson (40 years), Omega Master
Mansfield, Ohio*

SPINACH LOAF

My grandmother was a member of a women's club in San Antonio during the Depression. The ladies pooled their money to buy this recipe—for $25!—from the popular Menger Hotel. The recipe was passed on to my mother, who made it for her new husband in 1941. His first remark was, "Our children will be so lucky. I've never tasted such good spinach!" Throughout the years, no Thanksgiving dinner has been complete without this dish.

**1 (10-ounce) package
frozen chopped
spinach, thawed
2 cups cracker crumbs
3 eggs
1 cup milk
1/2 teaspoon black
pepper
1 teaspoon salt
1/4 teaspoon garlic salt**

**2 tablespoons chopped
green bell pepper
2 teaspoons minced
onion
1/2 teaspoon nutmeg
1/2 cup (1 stick) butter or
margarine, melted
1 (12-ounce) jar Cheez
Whiz**

Combine the spinach, cracker crumbs, eggs, milk, black pepper, salt, garlic salt, green pepper, onion, nutmeg and butter in a bowl; mix well. Spoon into a greased 5×9-inch loaf pan. Place a pan of water on the lower shelf of the oven. Bake the spinach loaf at 375 degrees on the top shelf of the oven for 35 to 45 minutes or until center is firm. Serve topped with Cheez Whiz or homemade cheese sauce. Yield: 8 servings.

*Joanne Jones, Xi Kappa Chi
Refugio, Texas*

KK LeBlanc, Xi Rho, Carlyss, Louisiana, keeps her **Homemade All-Purpose Cajun Spice Mix** ready to use in a dry container by mixing 1/4 cup salt with 2 tablespoons each red pepper and onion powder, 1 tablespoon each black and white pepper, 1 1/2 tablespoons garlic powder, 1 teaspoon paprika, 1/2 teaspoon each dried parsley, cilantro, crushed bay leaves and celery seed, 1/4 teaspoon each dried sage and ground ginger and 1/8 teaspoon thyme.

MEMORIES

A special memory is the annual get-together at the lake with all the family. We took guitars and accordions. Our families would sing songs and tell all these little fishing stories. The one that will always be remembered is the year we got caught at the lake in a bad storm. We were stuck in the mud in our big motor homes. It took us a whole day to get home, which was only 25 miles from where we live now. We still return to the same lake. The road is now paved; back then, there was no pavement.

Jean Yaremko, Beta Phi
Westlock, Alberta, Canada

BUTTERNUT SQUASH CASSEROLE

3 cups diced cooked squash	1/2 teaspoon coconut flavoring
2 eggs, beaten	1 cup milk
3/4 cup sugar	1/2 teaspoon ginger
3/8 cup (3/4 stick) margarine	Crushed butter crackers

Combine the squash, eggs, sugar, margarine, coconut flavoring, milk and ginger in a large bowl and mix well. Spoon into a greased 9×13-inch baking dish. Bake, uncovered, at 325 degrees for 35 minutes. Sprinkle with butter crackers and return to the oven for a few minutes or until crackers turn slightly brown. Yield: 10 to 12 servings.

Edna Scott (47 years), Gamma Kappa
Lakeland, Florida

ZUCCHINI FRITTERS

6 zucchini, peeled, boiled, mashed	2 eggs, beaten
1/2 teaspoon onion powder	1/2 cup grated Parmesan cheese
1/4 cup chopped parsley	1 cup bread crumbs
1 teaspoon oregano	1/4 teaspoon salt
1/2 teaspoon thyme	Dash of pepper

Mix all the ingredients in a bowl. Shape into small cakes. Fry in vegetable oil on a hot griddle until golden brown on both sides. Yield: 4 to 6 servings.

Betty Mershon, Preceptor Nu Omega
San Andreas, California

OLD-FASHIONED SCALLOPED TOMATOES

1/4 cup chopped onion	1/8 teaspoon nutmeg
3 tablespoons butter	1 3/4 cups toasted bread cubes
1 tablespoon light brown sugar	3 cups drained canned tomatoes
Salt and pepper to taste	

Sauté the onion in the butter in a skillet for 5 to 10 minutes or until soft. Remove from heat. Add the brown sugar, salt, pepper and nutmeg; mix well. Stir in the bread cubes. Layer the bread mixture and tomatoes alternately in a 1-quart baking dish, ending with a bread mixture layer. Bake at 350 degrees for 30 minutes or until hot and bubbly. Yield: 6 servings.

Deborah O'Neill
Cookeville, Tennessee

TOMATO PIE

This recipe was given to me by a co-worker at the school from which I retired after thirty-three years of teaching. It was a huge success at my family reunion! You can make two pies, or press the pie shells in a 9×13-inch baking dish to make one large pie.

2 (9-inch) unbaked pie shells	Salt and pepper to taste (optional)
4 unpeeled tomatoes, thinly sliced	1 1/2 cups mayonnaise
1 bunch green onions, finely chopped	1 1/2 cups shredded mild Cheddar cheese
1 teaspoon Cavendar's Greek Seasoning	

Bake the pie shells at 350 degrees for 10 minutes. Arrange the sliced tomatoes on paper towels to drain excess moisture. Layer the tomatoes, green onions, Cavendar's Seasoning, salt and pepper, mayonnaise and Cheddar cheese in the cooled pie shells, 1/2 at a time. Bake at 350 degrees for 30 minutes. Yield: 12 servings.

Diann C. Walters (25 years), Delta Kappa
Ellisville, Mississippi

ELLA'S CREAMY RUTABAGAS

1 large rutabaga or turnip	Salt and pepper to taste
2 tablespoons butter	1/4 cup heavy cream
2 tablespoons sugar	2 tablespoons chopped fresh chives or parsley
3/4 cup chicken stock	
5 garlic cloves, minced	
Pinch each of nutmeg and thyme	

Peel the rutabaga and cut into 1-inch cubes. Cook in boiling water in a large saucepan for 10 to 12 minutes or just until tender; drain. Melt the butter in a large skillet over medium heat. Add the rutabaga and sugar. Cook for 10 minutes, stirring frequently. Reduce heat to low. Stir in the chicken stock and garlic. Cook, covered, for 20 minutes. Uncover the skillet and simmer until liquid has evaporated. Stir in the nutmeg, thyme, salt and pepper. Stir in the cream and heat gently, stirring frequently. Sprinkle with chives just before serving. Yield: 8 servings.

Ella Forbes-Chilibeck, Zeta Mu
Ottawa, Ontario, Canada

ROASTED GARDEN VEGETABLES

I love harvesting vegetables from my garden and cooking something as tasty as this dish. It's a great reward for all the hard work.

3 to 4 medium red potatoes	*1/2 teaspoon salt*
1 onion	*1 teaspoon rosemary*
1 large eggplant	*1 teaspoon basil*
3 garlic cloves, minced	*1/2 teaspoon paprika*
4 parsnips	*1/4 teaspoon cayenne*
1/4 cup olive oil	*pepper*

Clean the potatoes, onion, eggplant, garlic and parsnips and cut into 1-inch cubes. Place the vegetables, olive oil, salt, rosemary, basil, paprika and cayenne pepper in a large bowl; toss to combine. Spoon into a 9×13-inch baking dish. Bake, uncovered, at 425 degrees for 40 minutes, stirring after 20 minutes. Yield: 6 servings.

Kathryn Daly, Xi Alpha Omega
Banner, Wyoming

SAVORY SUCCOTASH

1 (16-ounce) can French-style green beans, drained	*1/2 cup chopped green bell pepper*
	1/2 cup chopped celery
1 (15-ounce) can whole kernel corn, drained	*2 tablespoons chopped onion*
	1 cup soft bread crumbs
1/2 cup mayonnaise	*2 tablespoons butter, melted*
1/2 cup shredded sharp American cheese	

Combine the green beans, corn, mayonnaise, American cheese, green pepper, celery and onion in a bowl and mix well. Spoon into a greased 1-quart baking dish. Sprinkle a mixture of the bread crumbs and

butter over the top. Bake, uncovered, at 350 degrees for 30 minutes or until heated through and crumbs are brown. Yield: 6 servings.

Lillian Vannett (48 years), Laureate Iota
Minot, North Dakota

GRANDMA FOOS' NOODLES

I spent a lot of very special time with my Grandma when I was growing up. She always prepared home-made noodles, and this dish was a favorite dish.

16 ounces noodles	*1 (12-ounce) can*
1 (10-ounce) can cream of chicken or mushroom soup	*evaporated milk or 1 cup heavy cream*
	Salt and pepper to taste
1 cup shredded Cheddar cheese	

Place the noodles in a large amount of cold water in a large saucepan over high heat. Bring to the boiling point and remove from heat; drain. Combine the noodles, soup, Cheddar cheese, evaporated milk, salt and pepper in a large bowl and mix well. Add milk if mixture is dry. Spoon into a 9×13-inch baking dish. Bake, covered, at 350 degrees for 1 hour. Yield: 8 to 10 servings.

Hennie Harris (30 years), Laureate Beta Eta
Plains, Kansas

HOMEMADE EGG NOODLES

My grandmother always had these noodles ready to cook when we came to visit. While her command of the English language was limited, her communication through her German cooking spoke loudly of love and caring.

1 1/3 cups flour	*2 eggs, well beaten*

Combine the flour and eggs in a bowl and mix well, adding a little water if necessary to keep the dough soft. Shape into a ball. Knead the dough on a well-floured cloth-covered board until smooth and elastic. Let stand, covered, in the refrigerator for 1 to 2 hours. Divide the dough into 4 equal portions. Roll the dough one portion at a time into paper-thin rectangles, keeping unrolled portions covered. Place on towels to dry for about 2 hours. If dried too much, the dough will crumble. Cut crosswise into narrow 18-inch strips. Cook in boiling chicken broth for a few minutes or until tender. Yield: 4 servings.

Dee Richter Hall (29 years), Preceptor Gamma Kappa
Victoria, Texas

MEMORIES

I *have many memories of my family, and one of them is of my mother telling about the trip her family took to California in 1919. She was 15 years old and her sister was 17. This memory has become even more vivid as this winter I found four theme book diaries in which she and her sister wrote the day-by-day happenings of that trip. I have been typing those writings into my computer.*

They left the farm in Northeast Missouri in the middle of June 1919, and returned to the farm in mid-October, 1919. They visited family members along the way, and were joined by two of these families to make the trip. There were three cars traveling together. They traveled in an open car and used side curtains when it rained. They wrote of muddy roads, no roads, traveling across fields, opening gates to get through and fording streams. They had to stop, put on chains and take off chains. Sometimes they had to turn back and look for a road to follow, or find one of the cars that was experiencing trouble or stuck in the mud.

They carried tents and camping equipment and would hunt for campgrounds to stop at overnight, or they would just stop and cook their meals. Sometimes they had car trouble and would need a spark plug or battery. Sometimes they had to crank their cars. When they were in larger towns, they would find a hotel or rooms to rent in private homes.

When they were climbing the higher mountain roads in Colorado, all of them except the driver would have to get out and run alongside the car. They carried large rocks, so if the car died they could place the rocks under the wheels to keep the car from rolling back. They traveled at about 30 miles per hour.

A boy cousin of mother's who was traveling in another car with his parents would jump over the doors to get in the car. This irritated my mother and aunt; they were proper young ladies who didn't like the way their cousin got in the car. They would stop at farms

and buy fresh garden vegetables, peaches, apples, watermelons and cantaloupes.

Mother passed away ten years ago. She would be pleased to know that now, 83 years later, we are enjoying the writings of her trip. What a legacy of memories she left behind.

Sharron Connor, Kappa Master
Brookfield, Missouri

SOUTHERN PEACH YAM BAKE

1/2 cup packed brown sugar	2 (17-ounce) cans yams, drained
3 tablespoons flour	1 (16-ounce) can sliced peaches, drained
1/2 teaspoon nutmeg	
2 tablespoons butter	1 1/2 cups miniature marshmallows
1/2 cup chopped pecans	

Combine the brown sugar, flour and nutmeg in a bowl; cut in the butter until mixture resembles coarse crumbs. Stir in the pecans. Arrange the yams and peaches in a 1 1/2-quart casserole. Sprinkle the brown sugar mixture over the top. Bake, uncovered, for 35 minutes. Sprinkle with marshmallows and broil until lightly browned. Yield: 6 servings.

Alisa Hawthorne, Xi Gamma Sigma
Scottsdale, Arizona

SPICED PINEAPPLE

1 (20-ounce) can pineapple in juice	Salt to taste
3/4 cup vinegar	6 to 8 whole cloves
1 1/4 cups sugar	4 cinnamon sticks

Drain the pineapple, reserving the juice. Combine the reserved juice with enough water to make 3/4 cup liquid. Combine the juice mixture, vinegar, sugar, salt, cloves and cinnamon sticks in a saucepan and bring to a boil. Boil for 10 minutes, stirring occasionally. Stir in the pineapple; return to a boil. Remove from heat. Spoon into airtight containers. Store in the refrigerator. Yield: 8 to 10 servings.

Louise Meador (63 years), Alpha Master
Nashville, Tennessee

Gilda Sheets, Alpha Delta, Lynchburg, Virginia, prepares **Cheesy Pineapple Bake** by layering 30 ounces pineapple chunks, a mixture of 1/2 cup each flour and sugar and a mixture of 1 cup each Cheddar cheese and mozzarella cheese. Drizzle with 1/4 cup melted butter. Bake at 350 degrees for 30 minutes.

❖ LAZY PIROGIES

My friend Kim and I both love pirogies but are too lazy to make real ones.

2 cups dry cottage cheese	Salt and pepper to taste
1 egg	9 lasagna noodles, cooked, drained
1 teaspoon onion salt	1 cup chopped onion
1 cup shredded Cheddar cheese	3/4 cup (1 1/2 sticks) margarine or butter
2 cups mashed potatoes	

Combine the cottage cheese, egg and half the onion salt in a bowl and mix well. Combine the Cheddar cheese, mashed potatoes, salt, pepper and the remaining 1/2 teaspoon onion salt in a separate bowl; mix well. Layer 3 of the noodles in a 9×13-inch baking dish. Layer the cottage cheese mixture, 3 noodles, the potato mixture and the remaining 3 noodles over the first noodle layer. Sauté the onion in the margarine for a few minutes and spread over the top noodle layer. Bake, uncovered, at 350 degrees for 30 minutes. Yield: 8 servings.

Karen Taylor, Chi
Edmonton, Alberta, Canada

STUFFED DUMPLINGS (PIROGIES)

My grandmother brought this recipe from Poland in her memory, and this finished version is the result of much love, sharing, trial, and error. On Christmas Eve these little pouches filled with cottage cheese, potatoes, mushrooms, or sauerkraut are an important part of the Festival of the Star, a dinner to commemorate the birth of Christ.

1 egg, beaten	1 egg yolk, beaten
1 cup water	1 1/2 teaspoons sugar
1/2 teaspoon salt	1/4 teaspoon salt
3 cups flour	1 tablespoon butter or margarine, softened
1 1/2 cups cream-style cottage cheese, drained	1 cup chopped onion

Combine the egg, water and salt in a large bowl. Stir in the flour to make a stiff dough. Knead until smooth. Roll paper-thin (less than 1/8-inch thickness) on a floured surface. Cut into 3-inch circles. Combine the cottage cheese, egg yolk, sugar, salt and butter in a bowl and mix well. Place a tablespoon of cottage cheese mixture off center on each dough circle. Fold over dough to enclose the filling, making a half-circle; seal the edges with a fork. Pour 3 quarts of water in a large saucepan and bring to a boil. Drop pirogies in the boiling water, 10 to 12 at a time; boil for 8 to 10 minutes. Drain on paper towels and keep warm.

Repeat until all pirogies are cooked. Sauté the onion in butter or margarine and serve over the pirogies. Yield: 3 dozen.

Susan Foster (35 years), Preceptor Beta
Grand Rapids, Michigan

RICE PILAF

Some of my most cherished childhood memories are my mother and grandmother's trips to the millinery shop to purchase a new hat. In the springtime it was a straw hat; in the fall, a felt hat. It was an agonizing choice: "Should I have a flower added here or a feather there? And what about the color? Does it suit me?" It was a serious decision. So if you are going to purchase a hat today, put your Rice Pilaf together in the morning so you can put it in the oven when you get home and your dinner will be ready in one hour.

2 cups unwashed white rice	2 teaspoons salt
1/2 cup (1 stick) butter	1/4 teaspoon pepper
1 (14-ounce) can chicken broth	1 cup slivered almonds
3 cups water	6 medium mushrooms, sliced (optional)

Sauté the rice in the butter in a large skillet over medium heat until very brown. Stir in the chicken broth, water, salt, pepper, almonds and mushrooms. Spoon into a buttered 2-quart baking dish. Bake, covered, at 350 degrees for 1 hour. Yield: 12 servings.

Marilyn M. Olsen (44 years), Laureate Epsilon Alpha
Eureka, California

GREEN AND YELLOW RICE

1/4 cup (1/2 stick) butter	1 tablespoon Worcestershire sauce
3 cups cooked rice	1/2 teaspoon thyme
4 eggs, beaten	1/2 teaspoon marjoram
1 cup milk	1/2 teaspoon pepper
1 (10-ounce) package frozen chopped spinach	1 tablespoon chopped onion
1 pound Cheddar cheese, shredded	

Stir the butter into the cooked rice. Beat the eggs and milk together. Cook the spinach using the package directions; squeeze dry. Combine the rice mixture, egg mixture and remaining ingredients in a large bowl and mix gently. Spoon into a well-greased 2-quart baking dish. Bake, uncovered, at 350 degrees for 45 minutes or until center is set. Yield: 10 servings.

Betty Pederlick, Beta Delta
Show Low, Arizona

PARMESAN PESTO

Serve 1 or 2 tablespoons of the pesto mixed into a serving of hot pasta; do not heat the pesto or the cheese will melt. It is also good served on chicken breasts.

8 to 10 cups basil leaves	10 to 12 garlic cloves,
2 cups olive oil	chopped
6 ounces Parmesan	8 ounces pine nuts or
cheese, grated	walnuts

Wash the basil and shake dry. Combine the basil and olive oil in a food processor container and pulse. Add the Parmesan cheese, garlic and pine nuts, processing slowly after each addition to combine. Yield: 3 cups.

Leslie Von Bergen, Xi Theta Delta
Sherman, Texas

MEMORIES

I have been in Beta Sigma Phi for 37 years (plus my mom was a member), and the friends I made in this sorority have become my family. No doubt some women see their sorority families more than their own.

Beta Sigma Phi has been a great outlet for me; there's always something to learn and do.

Sue Jedlicka (37 years), Xi Master
Beatrice, Nebraska

PAP'S BARBECUE SAUCE

Our family loves Beta Sigma Phi because of the socials with all the good food. Now and then life got too busy and I would say I must stop doing some of my social activities. My husband always said, "Never leave BSP." I was always glad I stayed.

3/4 cup ketchup	1 1/2 teaspoons ginger
1/2 cup packed brown	1 1/2 teaspoons liquid
sugar	smoke
3 tablespoons soy sauce	2 garlic cloves, mashed

Combine the ketchup, brown sugar, soy sauce, ginger, liquid smoke and garlic in a saucepan over medium-low heat. Cook until sugar is dissolved and mixture is bubbly, stirring frequently. Serve over pork or beef. Yield: 6 servings.

Joyce Williams (30 years), Preceptor Kappa
Bono, Arkansas

PICANTE SAUCE

This delicious picante sauce, first given to me by a very dear friend, makes great gifts.

6 quarts ripe tomatoes,	6 large onions, chopped
chopped	10 teaspoons minced
4 or 5 green bell peppers,	garlic
chopped	1/2 cup vinegar
8 to 10 jalapeño chiles,	6 tablespoons salt
chopped	1 cup sugar

Combine all the ingredients in a large kettle over medium heat. Simmer for 2 to 2 1/2 hours until thickened, stirring occasionally. Ladle into hot sterilized jars, leaving 1/2 inch headspace; seal with 2-piece lids. Process in a boiling water bath for 10 minutes. Yield: 12 to 14 pints.

Janette Stuessel, Xi Tau Tau
Brazoria, Texas

MOCK APPLE BUTTER

My mother used to spend hours making apple butter with real apples. Now I can make a delicious spread in a short time, the easy way, with the ever-plentiful zucchini. My mother would be surprised.

Zucchini	1 teaspoon cinnamon
4 tablespoons vinegar	Dash of allspice
1 teaspoon lemon juice	2 drops red food
2 cups sugar	coloring

Peel, seed and coarsely chop enough zucchini to make 4 heaping cups. Combine the zucchini and vinegar in a blender and process until smooth. Combine the zucchini purée, lemon juice, sugar, cinnamon, allspice and food coloring in a heavy saucepan over medium-low heat. Cook until mixture is of desired thickness, stirring occasionally. Cool and keep in the refrigerator, or seal in hot canning jars. Yield: 3 half-pints.

Dayle L. Nelson (50 years), Beta Master
Cheyenne, Wyoming

Bertha Cooley (25 years), Delta Kappa, Ellisville, Mississippi, makes **Pear Honey** by grating enough peeled and cored pears to yield 12 cups and cooking in a large saucepan until translucent. She then adds a 16-ounce can of undrained crushed pineapple and 12 cups sugar (one 5-pound package plus 2 cups) and mixing well. Bring the mixture to a boil, stirring frequently, and ladle into hot sterilized jars, leaving 1/2-inch space, and seal with 2-piece lids. Process in a boiling water bath for 10 minutes.

MOM'S APPLE BUTTER

My mother used to make delicious homemade apple butter outside in a cast-iron kettle, using a recipe she had invented. She gave me this recipe when I married so that I would be able to make it, too—inside, of course!

1 (14-ounce) can applesauce	2 teaspoons cinnamon
1/2 cup sugar	1/8 teaspoon nutmeg
2 teaspoons apple cider vinegar	1/8 teaspoon ground cloves

Combine the applesauce, sugar, cider vinegar, cinnamon, nutmeg and cloves in a medium saucepan over medium heat. Simmer for 10 to 15 minutes or until a line drawn through a spoonful of the apple butter on a saucer does not cause the apple butter to run. Yield: 1 cup.

Arlene Bunch, Xi Kappa Delta
La Plata, Missouri

RHUBARB BLUEBERRY FREEZER JAM

I first tasted this jam nearly twenty years ago when my future husband and I visited his grandmother. It became my very favorite, and I was so glad when she shared this special recipe with me. She made this jam for us, and now I make it for my daughter.

5 cups finely chopped rhubarb	2 (3-ounce) packages raspberry gelatin
5 cups sugar	
1 (21-ounce) can blueberry pie filling	

Combine the rhubarb and 1 cup water in a saucepan over medium heat. Simmer for 10 minutes or until rhubarb is tender. Add the sugar and cook a few minutes longer, stirring constantly. Add the pie filling and cook 6 to 8 minutes longer, stirring frequently. Remove from heat. Add the dry gelatin mix and stir until completely dissolved. Ladle into hot sterilized jars, leaving 1/2 inch headspace; seal with 2-piece lids. Process in a boiling water bath for 10 minutes. Yield: 3 to 4 pints.

Delinda Pinson, Xi Gamma Delta
Aurora, Colorado

STRAWBERRY FIG PRESERVES

Twenty to twenty-five figs will yield 3 cups mashed figs.

3 cups mashed figs	3 cups sugar
2 (3-ounce) packages strawberry gelatin	

Combine the figs, dry gelatin mix and sugar in a large saucepan over medium heat. Bring to a boil. Boil gently for 3 minutes, stirring occasionally. Pour quickly into hot sterilized jars. Cover with a 1/8-inch layer of hot paraffin or seal with 2-piece lids. Yield: About 6 half-pints.

Sarah Stephens (53 years), Tau Master
Austin, Texas

CRANBERRY WINE JELLY

This recipe was given to me about thirty years ago by a beloved sorority sister, now passed away. This is a "fun" food with a "sparkle," and it reminds me of her. Serve with turkey or ham; it is also great with cream cheese and crackers.

7 cups sugar	1 cup port
3 cups cranberry juice	2 (3-ounce) packages liquid fruit pectin
1/4 teaspoon cinnamon	
1/4 teaspoon ground cloves	

Combine the sugar, cranberry juice, cinnamon and cloves in a Dutch oven or heavy kettle. Bring to a boil, stirring to dissolve the sugar. Boil for 1 minute, stirring frequently. Remove from heat. Stir in the port and pectin. Skim off foam with a metal spoon. Pour quickly into hot sterilized jars, leaving 1/2 inch headspace; cover at once with a 1/8-inch layer of paraffin; seal with lids. Yield: 7 cups.

Doris Blakeney (48 years), Delta Master
Greenville, South Carolina

HEAVENLY CRANBERRY SAUCE

This unusually good cranberry sauce is so easy to make. Serve at Thanksgiving or Christmas with turkey, goose, duck, or chicken.

2 pounds cranberries	Juice and grated zest of 2 lemons
2 cups coarsely chopped walnuts	2 cups orange marmalade
3 cups sugar	

Wash and drain the cranberries. Layer the cranberries, walnuts, sugar, lemon juice, lemon zest and marmalade in a shallow baking dish. Bake, tightly covered, at 350 degrees for 45 minutes. Yield: 2 quarts.

Bernice Burns-Stivers, Alpha Kappa
Hot Springs, Arkansas

JALAPEÑO CRANBERRY JAM

It takes about two large oranges to yield ¹/₂ cup fresh orange juice, and five or six limes to yield ¹/₂ cup fresh lime juice. To avoid skin irritation, wear rubber gloves when working with the jalapeño chiles, or cover hands with plastic bags.

2 (12-ounce) packages fresh or frozen cranberries	Shredded rind of 1 orange
²/₃ cup dried cranberries	¹/₂ cup fresh lime juice
2¹/₂ cups sugar	2 to 4 jalapeño chiles, seeded, minced
¹/₂ cup fresh orange juice	

Combine the fresh cranberries, dried cranberries, sugar, orange juice, orange rind, lime juice, jalapeño chiles and 1¹/₂ cups water in a large saucepan over medium heat. Bring to a boil, stirring occasionally. Boil gently until sugar is dissolved, stirring occasionally. Boil gently for 10 minutes or until thickened, stirring to prevent sticking. It will keep well in the refrigerator for 2 to 3 weeks; or ladle into hot sterilized jars, leaving ¹/₂ inch headspace, seal with 2-piece lids, and process in a boiling water bath for 10 minutes. Yield: About 5 cups.

Sandy Helms (26 years), Laureate Beta
Longview, Washington

✤ CRANBERRY SAUCE CABERNET

Families and friends look forward to this addition to our holiday meals, and they really like it when I make it for "everyday" occasions! It may be kept in the refrigerator for up to two months.

1¹/₄ cups sugar	2 teaspoons grated tangerine zest
1 cup cabernet sauvignon	1 (3-inch) cinnamon stick
12 ounces fresh cranberries	

Combine the sugar and cabernet sauvignon in a medium saucepan over medium-high heat; bring to a boil. Add the cranberries, tangerine zest and cinnamon stick; return to a boil, stirring constantly. Reduce heat and simmer, partially covered, for 10 to 15 minutes or until cranberry skins pop. Remove and discard cinnamon stick. Cool slightly. Serve warm or chill, covered, for 2 hours if desired. Yield: 3¹/₂ cups.

Carolyn Eberts (36 years), Alpha Beta Master
Bethlehem, Pennsylvania

HOLIDAY CRANBERRY SALSA

This recipe, with its sweet tart taste, is colorful and delicious for Thanksgiving and Christmas. It can be served as a salsa, a spread, or a side dish.

1¹/₂ cups fresh cranberries	¹/₂ cup sugar
1 teaspoon grated orange zest	2 tablespoons fresh orange juice
1 large orange, peeled, chopped	¹/₄ to ¹/₂ teaspoon allspice
¹/₂ yellow bell pepper, finely chopped	¹/₄ teaspoon salt
	2 teaspoons light extra-virgin olive oil

Process the cranberries in a blender or pulse 5 or 6 times in a food processor until coarsely chopped. Combine the chopped cranberries, orange zest, orange, yellow pepper, sugar, orange juice, allspice, salt and olive oil in a bowl; stir well. Chill, covered well with plastic wrap or a tight lid, for at least 8 hours. Yield: 6 (¹/₄-cup) servings.

Donna Marie Stiffler (31 years), Xi Epsilon Iota
Acworth, Georgia

SWEET AND SPICY MUSTARD

This was my dad's favorite recipe to make and share with family and friends. When I give this gift at Christmastime, I'm always asked, "Is this your dad's recipe?" What a nice way to remember a parent. Serve with ham, eggs, pork loin, and egg rolls.

5 tablespoons Coleman's dry mustard	¹/₈ teaspoon (or more) hot red pepper flakes
¹/₂ cup sugar	2 eggs, beaten
1 tablespoon flour	¹/₂ cup vinegar
¹/₂ teaspoon salt	1 tablespoon butter or margarine

Combine the dry mustard, sugar, flour, salt and red pepper flakes in the top of a double boiler; stir until blended. Add the eggs and vinegar, stirring until well mixed. Cook over boiling water for 15 minutes or until thickened, stirring constantly. Remove pan from boiling water. Melt the butter in the hot mustard mixture, stirring constantly. Let cool. Store in a covered jar in the refrigerator. Yield: 1¹/₃ cups.

Suzanne Cichocki, Laureate Zeta Phi
Borger, Texas

MEMORIES

*W*hen I was a teenager in the 1950s, we lived near the Niagara Fruit Belt. Every summer my mother would "put down" fresh peaches, pears, tomatoes and beets. For days our house would smell wonderful. After I was married, my husband planted a vegetable garden. I kept busy by freezing beans and making bread and butter pickles and pickled beets, which were his favorite. I used the same recipe that my mother had used and I still think that our pickled beets are the best ever!

Rita Cane, Preceptor Epsilon Lambda
Whitby, Ontario, Canada

MOM'S PICKLE RELISH

12 large cucumbers	*4 teaspoons whole*
4 green bell peppers	*mustard seed*
2 red bell peppers	*1/2 teaspoon ground*
4 large onions	*cloves*
3 1/2 cups vinegar	*3 teaspoons turmeric*
5 cups sugar	*1 teaspoon salt*
4 teaspoons celery seed	

Grind the cucumbers, bell peppers and onions into a cheesecloth-lined colander; squeeze out as much juice as possible. Combine the cucumber mixture, vinegar, sugar, celery seed, mustard seed, cloves, turmeric and salt in a kettle over medium-high heat; bring to a boil. Boil gently for 5 minutes. Ladle into hot sterilized jars, leaving 1/2 inch headspace; seal with 2-piece lids, and process in a boiling water bath for 10 minutes. Yield: 6 to 8 pints.

Florence Peetz, Laureate Alpha Nu
The Dalles, Oregon

Shari Abernathy (36 years), Preceptor Beta Beta, Portland, Oregon, makes **Maple Mustard** for ham and other smoked meats. Bring 3/4 cup apple cider vinegar to a boil, remove from heat and stir in 3/4 cup dry mustard. Let stand, covered, at room temperature for 8 to 10 hours. Beat in 2/3 cup maple syrup and 2 large egg yolks. Cook over low heat until thickened, stirring constantly. Cool to room temperature and store, tightly covered, in the refrigerator.

"END OF THE GARDEN" TOMATO RELISH

This recipe was given to my mother by an old friend and has been a fall ritual for many years.

12 green tomatoes	*2 teaspoons salt*
4 green bell peppers	*1 (6-ounce) jar yellow*
4 red bell peppers	*mustard*
3 yellow onions	*1 quart mayonnaise-*
2 cups sugar	*type salad dressing*
1 tablespoon celery salt	

Grind the tomatoes, bell peppers and onions into a bowl and let stand at room temperature, covered, for 2 hours. Place the tomato mixture in cheesecloth and squeeze as dry as possible. Combine the tomato mixture, sugar, celery, salt and mustard in a heavy 4-quart kettle over medium-high heat; bring to a boil. Boil for 30 minutes, stirring frequently. Stir in the mayonnaise-type salad dressing; return to a boil. Remove from heat. Ladle into pint jars. Chill, covered, until ready to use. Yield: 6 to 8 pints.

Betty S. Jones (34 years), Preceptor Zeta Eta
Camdenton, Missouri

ZUCCHINI RELISH

A summer recipe from a friend who always gave me produce from her garden. This relish takes about four or five large zucchini.

10 cups shredded seeded	*1 teaspoon dry mustard*
zucchini	*1 teaspoon cornstarch*
4 cups finely chopped	*2 teaspoons celery seed*
onion	*2 green or red bell*
5 tablespoons salt	*peppers, finely*
2 1/4 cups vinegar	*chopped*
5 cups sugar	*1/4 teaspoon black*
1 teaspoon nutmeg	*pepper*
1 teaspoon turmeric	

Combine the zucchini, onion and salt in a large bowl; mix well. Let stand at room temperature, covered, for 8 to 10 hours. Rinse in cold water; drain well. Combine the zucchini mixture, vinegar, sugar, nutmeg, turmeric, dry mustard, cornstarch, celery seed, bell peppers and black pepper in a large kettle over medium-high heat; bring to a boil. Boil for 5 minutes. Remove from heat. Ladle into hot sterilized jars, leaving 1/2 inch headspace; seal with 2-piece lids, and process in a boiling water bath for 10 minutes; or let cool to room temperature, then cover and store in the refrigerator. Yield: 6 pints.

Diana A. Burge (38 years), Preceptor Beta Chi
Niles, Michigan

GREEN TOMATO HOT DOG RELISH

Grind the vegetables with a coarse blade.

4 cups ground green tomatoes	1 cup salt
4 cups ground red bell peppers	4 cups vinegar
4 cups ground onions	6 cups sugar
4 cups ground cabbage	2 tablespoons mustard seed
12 pods hot chiles, ground	2 tablespoons celery seed

Combine the tomatoes, bell peppers, onions, cabbage and chiles in a large bowl. Sprinkle with the salt. Let stand at room temperature, covered, for 8 to 10 hours. Rinse and drain well. Combine the vinegar, sugar, mustard seed and celery seed in a bowl; whisk to blend. Combine the tomato mixture and vinegar mixture in a large kettle over medium-high heat; bring to a boil. Ladle into hot sterilized jars, leaving 1/2 inch headspace; seal with 2-piece lids, and process in a boiling water bath for 10 minutes; or let cool to room temperature, then cover and store in the refrigerator. Yield: About 7 pints.

Golda Williamson, Sigma Mu
Simpson, Illinois

SWEET PICKLED OKRA

I found this recipe in my mom's recipe box. I remember her pickled okra, and that it was an unusual offering on relish trays in the forties and fifties in Lubbock County, Texas.

3 pounds young okra	1 quart water
1/2 cup sugar	6 garlic cloves
1 cup uniodized salt	6 teaspoons celery seeds
1 quart white wine vinegar	6 hot pepper pods
	5 teaspoons dillseeds

Cut the okra into 2- to 3-inch pieces. Combine the sugar, salt, wine vinegar and 1 quart water in a large kettle. Stir until sugar dissolves; bring to a boil. Pack the okra, garlic, celery seeds, hot pepper and dillseeds in 6 hot sterilized jars. Add the vinegar mixture, leaving 1 inch headspace; seal with 2-piece lids. Process in a boiling water bath for 7 minutes. Yield: 6 pints.

Sandra Wiley (28 years), Laureate Zeta Sigma
Idalou, Texas

BREAD AND BUTTER PICKLES

12 medium cucumbers	3 cups vinegar
2 green bell peppers, chopped	5 cups sugar
3 garlic cloves, minced	1 1/2 teaspoons turmeric
6 onions, sliced	2 tablespoons mustard seed
1/3 cup canning salt	1 1/2 teaspoons salt

Slice the cucumbers into a clean sink and add the green peppers, garlic and onions; sprinkle with the 1/3 cup canning salt. Spread ice over the vegetables and let stand for 3 hours. Combine the vinegar, sugar, turmeric, mustard seed and the 1 1/2 teaspoons salt in a kettle over high heat. Bring to a boil. Drain the cucumber mixture and add to the vinegar mixture. Bring to a boil again. Ladle into hot sterilized jars, leaving 1/2 inch headspace; seal with 2-piece lids. Process in a boiling water bath for 10 minutes. Yield: About 11 pints.

Joyce Ann Smith (50 years), Laureate Delta Theta
Sylvania, Ohio

GRANNIE'S RHUBARB RELISH

This recipe brings back memories of Mom's delicious roast beef dinners. You may serve it with fish, meat, or poultry.

1 quart rhubarb, chopped	1/2 teaspoon ground cloves
1 quart onions, chopped	1 teaspoon allspice
1 cup cider vinegar	1/2 teaspoon pepper
2 pounds brown sugar	2 teaspoons salt
1 teaspoon cinnamon	

Combine all the ingredients in a large kettle over medium-high heat. Simmer, uncovered, until thickened. Ladle into hot sterilized jars, leaving 1/2 inch headspace; seal with 2-piece lids, and process in a boiling water bath for 10 minutes. Yield: 4 pints.

Gail Shinde (25 years), Xi Gamma Upsilon
Richmond, British Columbia, Canada

Lisa Minardi, Xi Gamma Delta, Aurora, Colorado, says she remembers picking raspberries from her grandparents' raspberry patch and watching her grandmother make this delicious **Raspberry Freezer Jam**. Mix 4 cups crushed raspberries with a package of Pen-Jel pectin and let it stand for 30 minutes. Combine with 1 cup light corn syrup and 6 cups sugar in a saucepan and heat over low heat until the sugar dissolves, stirring frequently. Let stand at room temperature to mellow overnight and store in the freezer.

Breads

I love the memory of my father baking bread.
Once when my mom was sick, Dad hurried to get the
bread started between his farm duties. He would come
running into the house, scrub and clean up, push
the bread down and then rush back out to the horses.
He finally had the loaves ready for the wood stove.
He asked me to take the bread out of the oven
when it was brown. At dinner, we sliced the lovely
loaf of bread. But Dad made one mistake—he had
forgotten to put salt in the dough. After dinner,
Dad quietly put the four loaves in a paper bag and
took the bread to feed to the pigs.

Josephine Heyden, Epsilon Gamma
Barrington, Illinois

BUTTER PECAN COFFEE CAKE

1 (2-layer) package butter pecan cake mix	4 eggs
1 (16-ounce) can coconut-pecan frosting	2/3 cup vegetable oil
	2/3 cup water
	3/4 cup chopped pecans (optional)

Beat the cake mix, frosting, eggs, vegetable oil and water in a mixing bowl at high speed until well mixed. Stir in the pecans. Spoon the batter into a buttered 11×14-inch cake pan. Bake at 350 degrees for about 45 minutes or until cake tests done. Let cool and sprinkle with confectioners' sugar. Yield: 6 to 12 servings.

Carlene Miller, Xi Gamma Omicron
Clarksville, Arkansas

CHOCOLATE CHIP COFFEE CAKE

1 cup (2 sticks) butter, softened	1 teaspoon baking powder
8 ounces cream cheese, softened	1/2 teaspoon baking soda
1 1/2 cups sugar	1/4 teaspoon salt
2 eggs	1/4 cup milk
1 teaspoon vanilla extract	1 cup semisweet chocolate chips
2 cups flour	1/4 cup chopped pecans
	1 teaspoon cinnamon

Cream the butter, cream cheese and 1 1/4 cups of the sugar in a mixing bowl until light and fluffy. Beat in the eggs and vanilla. Mix together flour, baking powder, baking soda and salt. Add to the butter mixture alternately with the milk, mixing well after each addition. Stir in the chocolate chips. Spoon into a greased 9-inch springform pan. Sprinkle a mixture of the pecans, cinnamon and remaining 1/4 cup sugar over the batter. Bake at 350 degrees for 50 to 55 minutes or until the coffee cake tests done. Remove to a wire rack. Run a knife carefully around the edge of the cake and remove the side of the pan. Cool completely before cutting. Yield: 10 to 12 servings.

Faye A. Magers (48 years), Laureate Beta Upsilon
Chester, Illinois

Dorothy Malo (40 years), Laureate Phi, San Diego, California, shares her **Grandmother's Biscuits** thanks to her mother's writing down the measurements. Sift 2 cups flour, 1 teaspoon salt and 1 tablespoon baking powder into a bowl, cut in 5 tablespoons shortening until crumbly and mix in 2/3 cup milk until moistened. Drop by spoonfuls onto a greased baking sheet or roll on a floured surface and cut with a biscuit cutter. Bake at 400 degrees for 20 minutes.

CINNAMON COFFEE CAKE

This recipe was given to me by one of our local school cafeteria chefs. I used it as a part of my seventh-grade home economics curriculum for many years.

2 eggs	1 teaspoon baking soda
2 cups packed light brown sugar	1 teaspoon cinnamon
1/2 cup (1 stick) butter or margarine, softened	2 1/3 cups flour
	2 tablespoons butter
1 cup sour milk	3 tablespoons light brown sugar

Beat the eggs, the 2 cups light brown sugar and the 1/2 cup butter in a mixing bowl until light and fluffy. Stir in the sour milk, baking soda, cinnamon and 2 cups of the flour just until moistened. Spoon into an ungreased 9-inch-square cake pan. Combine the 2 tablespoons butter, 3 tablespoons light brown sugar and the remaining 1/3 cup flour in a small bowl; rub between the fingers until mixture resembles coarse crumbs. Sprinkle over the top of the batter. Bake at 350 degrees for 40 minutes or until a wooden pick inserted in the center comes out clean. Cool slightly. Serve warm or at room temperature.
Yield: 9 to 12 servings.

Grace M. Baylor (30 years), Laureate Theta
Waynesboro, Pennsylvania

APPLE COFFEE CAKE

I won a blue ribbon for this coffee cake at a Harvest Hoedown.

1 (12-ounce) can apple pie filling	1 teaspoon salt
2 teaspoons cinnamon	3 eggs
3 cups flour	1/2 cup packed brown sugar
1 cup sugar	1/2 cup chopped walnuts or pecans
1 1/2 cups milk	2 tablespoons melted margarine
1/2 cup (1 stick) margarine, softened	Simple Glaze
1 tablespoon baking powder	

Place the pie filling in a bowl and stir in the cinnamon. Combine the flour, sugar, milk, softened margarine, baking powder, salt and eggs in a large mixing bowl and beat at low speed for 30 seconds, scraping bowl constantly. Beat at medium speed for 2 minutes, scraping bowl frequently. Layer half the batter (about 2 cups) and half the pie filling mixture in a 9×13-inch cake pan that has been sprayed with nonstick cooking spray. Repeat the layers and sprinkle with a mixture of the brown sugar and walnuts. Drizzle with the melted margarine. Bake at 350 degrees for 45 to 55 minutes or until cake tests done.

Drizzle Simple Glaze over the hot cake. Cool and serve. Yield: 12 to 16 servings.

SIMPLE GLAZE

3/4 cup confectioners' sugar	*1/4 teaspoon vanilla extract*
1 tablespoon softened margarine	*2 to 3 teaspoons hot water*

Mix together the confectioners' sugar, margarine, vanilla and hot water.

Connie Young, Preceptor Alpha Eta
Hagerstown, Maryland

BUTTERMILK COFFEE CAKE

This recipe means a lot to me because my mother used to prepare it for our family of seven children, and we all loved it. You may sprinkle chopped nuts and additional cinnamon over the crumb topping if you like.

2¹/2 cups flour	*1/2 teaspoon baking soda*
1/2 teaspoon salt	*1/2 teaspoon cinnamon*
2 cups packed brown sugar	*1/2 teaspoon nutmeg*
2/3 cup shortening	*1 cup buttermilk or sour milk*
2 teaspoons baking powder	*2 eggs, well beaten*

Combine the flour, salt and brown sugar in a bowl; cut in the shortening until mixture is crumbly. Remove 1/2 cup of the flour mixture and reserve for the topping. Add the baking powder, baking soda, cinnamon and nutmeg to the remaining crumbs and mix well. Stir in the buttermilk and eggs; mix well. Pour into a greased 8-inch cake pan. Sprinkle with the reserved flour mixture. Bake at 375 degrees for 25 to 30 minutes or until cake tests done.
Yield: 9 to 12 servings.

Nancy Owens, Laureate Delta Epsilon
Blue Springs, Missouri

BUBBLE BREAD

Serve this delightful bread whole. Guests pull bubbles from the side of the bread.

1 cup scalded milk	*4¹/2 cups flour*
1/2 cup vegetable oil	*1 teaspoon cinnamon*
1¹/2 cups sugar	*1/2 cup chopped pecans*
1 teaspoon salt	*1/2 cup (1 stick)*
2 envelopes dry yeast	*margarine, melted*
2 eggs, beaten	

Combine the milk, vegetable oil, 1/2 cup of the sugar and salt in a large mixing bowl. Stir in the yeast, eggs and 3 cups of the flour. Beat at medium speed for 3 minutes, gradually adding the remaining 1¹/2 cups flour. Knead lightly on a floured surface until smooth and elastic. Place in a greased bowl, turning to coat the surface. Let rise, covered, in a warm place until doubled in bulk. Punch the dough down. Let rise for 10 minutes longer. Combine the remaining 1 cup sugar, cinnamon and pecans in a bowl and mix well. Pour the melted margarine into a separate bowl. Pinch off and shape bubbles of dough the size of small walnuts. Dip each bubble in margarine, then in the sugar mixture; drop into a well-greased tube pan. Let rise for about 45 minutes. Bake at 350 degrees for 45 minutes. Cool in the pan for 20 minutes. Invert onto a serving plate. Yield: 16 servings.

Patricia Soard, Theta Psi
Cookeville, Tennessee

MEMORIES

Some of my favorite memories as a child were the visits to my grandmother's small house in Bisbee, North Dakota. After being tucked in for the night, my Grandma Ethel would roll and pat me and "put me in the oven to bake until morning." I would awaken just before dawn to a sense of light coming from the kitchen. Then the smells and pan noises would draw me to the kitchen to spend some precious time alone with my grandma before everyone else was awake. I'd walk into the small, warm, steaming kitchen full of the smells of bread rising, bacon frying and coffee perking. Potatoes would be boiling to make lefsa. She would say nice things and ask me what I wanted for breakfast. I could have whatever I wanted. I usually said "Egg Pancakes." I could eat more in her kitchen than anywhere else! I would have one with just butter or sugar and one or two more with homemade chokecherry syrup. Looking back at those times in her kitchen, I realize that she was actually feeding me love. The food was soaked with her love.

Dulci Jensen, Xi Alpha Omicron
Elko, Nevada

MEMORIES

I remember how my dad, two brothers and I were banished to the basement when Mom had sorority meetings at our house. We would laugh and giggle if it was a ritual ceremony and have mock ones ourselves. As I grew older, Mom often hosted the Mexican theme night. I was always in charge of making the sopaipillas. I felt very grown-up. Now I am a Beta Sigma Phi member and I hope to give my children some of the same laughs and giggles and grown-up moments that Mom gave to me.

Krista Soda, Pi Zeta
Waukee, Iowa

PIE FILLING COFFEE CAKE

4 eggs	1 teaspoon baking
1 cup sugar	powder
1 cup vegetable or	1/2 teaspoon salt
canola oil	1 (21-ounce) can fruit
1 teaspoon vanilla	pie filling
extract	Confectioners' sugar
2 cups flour	frosting

Beat the eggs in a large mixing bowl. Add the sugar, vegetable oil and vanilla; beat until smooth. Beat in a mixture of the flour, baking powder and salt. Spread half the batter in a greased and floured 9×13-inch cake pan. Spread the pie filling over the batter. Layer the remaining batter over the pie filling. Bake at 350 degrees for 50 minutes. Drizzle with a confectioners' sugar frosting. Yield: 18 servings.

Esther Gruling (47 years), Preceptor Rho
Merrill, Wisconsin

IZZY'S RAISIN COFFEE CAKE

1 cup lukewarm water	2 to 4 cups flour
1 envelope dry yeast	1 cup (2 sticks) butter
1 3/4 cups sugar	2 teaspoons cinnamon
1/4 cup shortening	1 cup chopped pecans
1 egg	1 cup raisins

Combine the water and yeast in a bowl and let stand for 5 to 10 minutes. Cream 1/4 cup of the sugar and shortening in a mixing bowl until light and fluffy. Beat in the egg. Beat in the yeast mixture. Mix in flour gradually until dough is easy to knead. Knead on a floured surface until smooth and elastic. Place in a greased bowl, turning to coat. Let rise, covered, in a warm place for 2 hours or until doubled in bulk. Punch the dough down. Let rise for 1 hour. Melt the butter and place in a bowl. Mix the remaining 1 1/2 cups sugar, cinnamon and pecans in a separate bowl. Pinch dough into walnut-size pieces; dip in the melted butter, then roll in the sugar mixture. Drop half the dough pieces lightly into a greased 9-inch tube pan. Layer the raisins over the dough. Drop the remaining prepared dough pieces in the pan over the raisins. Let rise for 1 hour. Bake at 350 degrees for about 1 hour or until golden brown. Yield: 12 servings.

Toni Austin (35 years), Preceptor Alpha Beta
Colorado Springs, Colorado

COFFEE TIME ROLLS

This recipe is great for making Kolache, a Czech pastry. When I was growing up in Texas, I watched my aunts prepare Kolache in different ways with different ingredients. They are traditionally made every Friday afternoon or Saturday morning to be enjoyed after church or during the week. Some freeze them to serve to unexpected company. The most popular fillings are poppy seed, prune, and cheese. Sometimes I would bake a few dozen and my dad would take some to work to share with his co-workers at coffee break.

2 cups milk	6 cups flour
1/4 cup (1/2 stick) butter	2 cups packed brown
or margarine	sugar
1/2 cup water	4 teaspoons cornstarch
1/2 cup sugar	1 cup heavy cream
1 teaspoon salt	1 teaspoon vanilla
2 envelopes dry yeast	extract

Heat a mixture of the milk, butter and water to 120 to 130 degrees in the microwave or in a saucepan over medium heat. Pour into a large mixing bowl and add the sugar, salt, yeast and 1 cup of the flour; mix well by hand or with a dough hook. Add the remaining flour gradually, over a period of 5 to 8 minutes while dough hook operates. Roll into an 8×10-inch rectangle on a lightly floured surface. Spread with additional softened butter and sprinkle with sugar and cinnamon to taste. Roll to enclose the filling. Cut into 1-inch slices. Arrange cut side down in 2 greased 9×13-inch baking pans. Let rise in a warm place until doubled in bulk. Combine the brown sugar, cornstarch, cream and vanilla in a saucepan and cook until hot, stirring constantly. Drizzle the warm brown sugar mixture over the raised rolls. Bake at 400 degrees for 15 minutes or until hot and browned. Yield: 40 rolls.

Terry Patlovany, Delta Sigma
Broomfield, Colorado

KOLACHES

I watched my late mother-in-law, Mary Mikeska Svadlenak, make this Czech pastry many times, but I never learned how—she did the "pinch of this" and "pat of that" type of cooking. She was a wonderful cook and her Kolaches were delicious. She used many fillings: apple, apricot, poppy seed, prune, pineapple, and my favorite, cottage cheese. This recipe makes Kolaches that are almost as good as hers, except she made her fillings from scratch.

2 envelopes dry yeast	2 teaspoons salt
1¼ cups sugar	½ cup shortening,
4 eggs, beaten	melted
2 cups warm whole milk	½ cup (1 stick)
5 cups flour	margarine, melted
1 cup evaporated whole milk	

Dissolve the yeast and ½ cup of the sugar in 1 cup of warm water. Let stand for 15 minutes. Stir in the eggs, warm whole milk and flour; let rise, covered, for 15 minutes. Stir in the remaining ¾ cup sugar, evaporated whole milk, salt, shortening and margarine and mix well. Add enough flour to make a very soft dough, about 7 cups. Knead on a floured surface until soft and elastic. Place in a greased bowl, turning to coat the surface. Let rise, covered, in a warm place until doubled in bulk. Punch the dough down. Arrange the dough by tablespoons on a greased baking sheet. Brush the tops with melted butter and let rise until doubled in bulk. Top with canned apple, cherry or blueberry pie filling. To make an apricot filling, soak dried apricots overnight in enough water to cover and cook until soft; drain and mash, adding sugar to taste. Yield: 5 dozen.

Hazel I. Ivey, Beta Epsilon Omicron
Brackettville, Texas

Grace Pender, Xi Alpha Xi, Adamsville, Alabama, is able to serve **Angel Biscuits** at every meal with a bowl of dough always ready in the refrigerator. Dissolve an envelope of yeast in ½ cup warm water. Sift 5½ cups flour, 3 tablespoons baking powder, 2 tablespoons sugar and 1 tablespoon each salt and baking soda into a bowl. Cut in ⅔ cup shortening and stir in a mixture of the dissolved yeast and 2 cups buttermilk. Knead lightly and store, covered, in a greased bowl in the refrigerator. Roll and cut the desired amount of dough and bake on a greased baking sheet at 450 degrees for 20 minutes.

GRANDMA ANDERSON'S KRINGLE

This recipe, my great-great-grandmother's, was passed down to each generation for our sheer enjoyment!

1 envelope yeast	2 cups confectioners'
4 cups flour	sugar
3 tablespoons sugar	1 teaspoon vanilla
1 teaspoon salt	extract
1 cup shortening	1 tablespoon melted
3 egg yolks, beaten	butter
1 cup scalded milk	Coffee
2 (16-ounce) jars apricot	Chopped pecans to taste
or peach preserves	

Dissolve the yeast in 2 cups lukewarm water and let stand for 10 minutes. Sift the flour, sugar and salt into a large bowl. Cut in the shortening until mixture resembles fine crumbs. Stir the egg yolks into the yeast mixture; mix in the milk. Add the egg yolk mixture to the flour mixture and stir. Chill, covered, for 8 to 10 hours; the dough will thicken in the refrigerator. Knead the dough on a lightly floured board until smooth and elastic. Divide into 3 equal portions. Roll each portion into an 8×14-inch rectangle. Spread the preserves over the short half of each rectangle to within 1 inch of the edges. Fold the other half over the filling and press the edges to seal. Place on a greased baking sheet. Bake at 350 degrees for 15 to 20 minutes or until golden brown. Mix together the confectioners' sugar, vanilla, butter and enough coffee to make a thick glaze in a bowl. Glaze the kringle with the coffee mixture; sprinkle with chopped pecans. Yield: 18 servings.

Bonnee Blue Pierson (35 years), Xi Gamma Omicron
Pryor, Oklahoma

KRINGLA

3 tablespoons butter or	½ teaspoon baking soda
margarine	2 teaspoons baking
1 cup sugar	powder
1 egg	1 teaspoon vanilla
½ teaspoon salt	extract
1 cup sour cream	3 cups flour
½ cup buttermilk	¼ to ½ teaspoon nutmeg

Cream the butter, sugar, egg and salt in a mixing bowl until light and fluffy. Beat in the next 5 ingredients. Stir in the flour and nutmeg. Chill, covered, for 8 to 10 hours. Roll dough into pencil-size ropes and shape into figure-eights. Arrange on ungreased baking sheets. Bake at 375 degrees for 10 minutes or until light brown. Yield: 1½ dozen.

Debbie Ward, Xi Delta Epsilon
Brighton, Colorado

GRANDMOTHER'S KUCHEN

My grandmother, who came from Germany, made this coffee cake every Christmas. My mom does now, and if I don't make it to their home in South Dakota for Christmas, she sends me a loaf.

½ cup milk	1 teaspoon orange
1 cup (2 sticks)	extract or grated
margarine	orange zest
2 envelopes dry yeast	¾ cup raisins
½ cup sugar	½ cup chopped dates
3 eggs, slightly beaten	½ cup chopped walnuts
1 teaspoon lemon	or pecans
extract	About 6 cups flour
2 teaspoons almond	
extract	

Combine the milk and margarine in a saucepan over low heat; heat until margarine is melted, stirring occasionally. Stir the yeast into ½ cup warm water in a large bowl and let stand for 10 minutes. Add the milk mixture, sugar, eggs, lemon extract, almond extract, orange extract, raisins, dates and walnuts to the yeast mixture and mix well. Stir in enough flour to make a stiff dough. Knead on a floured surface until smooth and elastic. Place in a greased bowl, turning to coat the surface. Let rise, covered, in a warm place until almost doubled in bulk. Punch the dough down. Shape into 2 loaves in 2 greased loaf pans. Bake at 350 degrees for 40 to 45 minutes or until brown. Frost with chocolate frosting if desired. Yield: 2 loaves.

Sherry Mansheim, Xi Alpha Beta
Sidney, Montana

FUDGENS

My grandmother and mother always made this treat for New Year's. Now my daughter, fourth generation, continues the tradition. Serve with wine soup or fruit soup.

1 envelope dry yeast	3 eggs
1 cup milk, scalded,	1 cup raisins
cooled	3 to 4 cups flour
½ cup (1 stick) butter	Vegetable oil for
1 cup sugar	deep-frying
1 teaspoon salt	

Dissolve the yeast in 1 cup lukewarm water in a large bowl. Stir in the milk, butter, sugar, salt, eggs, raisins and enough flour to make a thick sponge. Let rise, covered, in a warm place until doubled in bulk. Punch the dough down. Let rise until doubled in bulk. Heat the vegetable oil to 375 degrees. Drop the dough by teaspoons into the oil and fry until golden brown. Serve with individual dishes of sugar or powdered sugar. Each person dips hot Fudgens in the sugar. Yield: 2 or 3 dozen.

Delores Dunker (35 years), Kappa Master
Fremont, Nebraska

CHRISTMAS STOLLEN

For many years I made this bread a day or two before Christmas Day and then delivered to friends and neighbors with a basket of homemade goodies. Previous neighbors allowed me to move away on the condition they would still be on the list for "stollen delivery." It is now a tradition in our family to have it during Christmas morning present-opening, served on a special stollen plate given to me by a sorority sister. I serve it with orange juice mixed with champagne and a fresh fruit platter.

1 cup sugar	7¾ to 8 cups flour
½ cup (1 stick) butter,	1 cup raisins
melted	1 cup red and green
2 teaspoons salt	cherries, chopped
2 cups scalded milk	1 cup sliced almonds
2 eggs, beaten	½ teaspoon allspice
2 envelopes fast-rising	1 teaspoon cinnamon
yeast	

Mix the sugar, butter, salt and milk in a bowl. Let stand until cool. Add the eggs and a mixture of the yeast and 3 cups of the flour; mix well. Combine 1 cup of the flour with the raisins, cherries, almonds, allspice and cinnamon in a small bowl; mix well. Stir the raisin mixture into the egg mixture. Gradually add flour until dough is no longer sticky. Knead for about 5 minutes or until smooth and elastic. Let rest for 10 minutes. Shape into 4 long loaves. Flatten the loaves and fold in half lengthwise. Place on greased baking sheets. Let rise, covered, in a warm place until doubled in bulk. Bake at 400 degrees for 10 minutes. Reduce oven heat to 350 degrees and bake for 30 minutes longer or until bread tests done. Yield: 4 loaves.

Deanna Coates (35 years), Omega Master
Kamloops, British Columbia, Canada

Heather Murphy, Preceptor Sigma, Ottawa, Ontario, Canada, makes her own **Biscuit Mix** by mixing 10 cups flour with ⅓ cup baking powder and 1 tablespoon salt and then cutting in 1 pound shortening. Store in an airtight container. Make **Tea Biscuits** by mixing 2½ cups of the biscuit mix with ¾ cup milk, rolling ½ inch thick on a floured surface, cutting into biscuits and baking at 450 degrees for 8 to 10 minutes on a greased baking sheet.

SWEET APPLESAUCE BRAN LOAF

1½ cups flour	1 egg
1 tablespoon baking powder	1 cup applesauce
	½ cup milk
1½ teaspoons cinnamon	¼ cup vegetable oil
½ teaspoon salt	1 cup whole bran cereal
½ cup packed brown sugar	½ cup raisins

Combine the flour, baking powder, cinnamon and salt in a bowl and mix well. Stir in the brown sugar and mix well, breaking up any lumps. Beat the egg with a fork in a separate bowl; blend in the applesauce, milk and vegetable oil. Stir the bran cereal into the applesauce mixture and let stand for 5 minutes. Add the cereal mixture to the flour mixture and stir until moistened. Stir in the raisins with a few quick strokes. Spoon the batter into a greased 5×9-inch loaf pan. Bake at 350 degrees for 45 to 50 minutes or until bread tests done. Cool in the pan for 5 minutes. Invert on a wire rack to cool completely. Yield: 1 loaf.

Sarah Heather Miyauchi, Preceptor Psi
Brooks, Alberta, Canada

BANANA BREAD

I was born and raised in Illinois farm country. I belonged to 4-H for five years and always received blue ribbons for my baked goods entries in 4-H contests. My mother gave me this recipe, and somehow, when we moved to Arizona, it became my specialty. My husband and I lived in Ethiopia for a while, where bananas were so inexpensive that I had to do something with them. I made my Banana Bread. The bread became so popular with the other Americans as well as with the other locals that I had a hard time keeping up with the demand. It remains a favorite with my family today.

½ cup (1 stick) butter, softened	1 teaspoon lemon juice
	2 cups flour
1 cup sugar	1 tablespoon baking powder
2 eggs	
3 large bananas, mashed	½ teaspoon salt

Cream the butter and sugar in a mixing bowl until light and fluffy. Add the eggs 1 at a time, beating well after each addition. Stir in the bananas and lemon juice. Add a mixture of the flour, baking powder and salt, stirring just until moistened. Spoon into a greased loaf pan. Bake for 1 hour or until a wooden pick inserted in the center comes out clean. Yield: 1 loaf.

Donna Fulkerson (33 years), Preceptor Alpha Upsilon
Lake Havasu City, Arizona

LEMON BLUEBERRY BREAD

I received the recipe for this special bread from a friend who runs a Bed and Breakfast.

⅓ cup butter, melted	½ teaspoon salt
1 cup sugar	½ cup milk
3 tablespoons lemon juice	½ cup chopped walnuts or pecans
2 large eggs	1 cup fresh or frozen blueberries, thawed
1½ cups flour	
1 teaspoon baking powder	

Combine the butter, sugar, lemon juice and eggs in a large mixing bowl and beat until smooth. Mix together the flour, baking powder and salt; add to the egg mixture alternately with the milk, mixing well after each addition. Fold in the walnuts and blueberries. Pour into a greased 4×8-inch loaf pan. Bake at 350 degrees for 60 to 70 minutes or until bread tests done. Cool in the pan for 10 minutes. Yield: 1 loaf.

LuAnn Throgmorton, Theta Psi
Cookeville, Tennessee

GEORGIA PEACH BREAD

This recipe is great with fresh peaches, even peaches you have frozen yourself. It always reminds me of summer.

3 cups sliced fresh peaches	1 teaspoon baking soda
	¼ teaspoon salt
6 tablespoons sugar	1 teaspoon cinnamon
½ cup shortening	1 cup finely chopped pecans
1½ cups sugar	
2 eggs	1 teaspoon vanilla extract
2 cups flour	
1 teaspoon baking powder	

Combine the peaches and the 6 tablespoons sugar in a blender container and process until smooth. Cream the shortening and the 1½ cups sugar in a mixing bowl until light and fluffy. Add the eggs 1 at a time, beating well after each addition. Add a mixture of the flour, baking powder, baking soda, salt and cinnamon to the egg mixture and stir just until moistened. Stir in the pecans and vanilla. Spoon the batter into 2 well-greased and floured 5×9-inch loaf pans. Bake at 325 degrees for 55 to 60 minutes or until bread tests done. Cool in the pans for 10 minutes. Remove to a wire rack to cool completely. Yield: 2 loaves.

Carolyn S. Mawyer (33 years), Preceptor Kappa
Charlottesville, Virginia

MEMORIES

*S*ome of my fondest memories of home center in the kitchen of our 100-year old farmhouse. A large kitchen was added on to the house in 1955. I can still smell the baked cinnamon rolls with fresh cream and sugar on top or the pickles with their pungent vinegary juice as we put them in the jars. My mom worked busily cutting up the butchered chickens to freeze, canning beans and tomatoes, freezing corn and peas, washing the cream separator, and listening to the radio for the weather forecast so that she could tell my dad at noon what weather to expect. But even more important than the usual activities in a farm kitchen, I remember the sharing. Mom could generously and enthusiastically stretch a meal for any number of surprise visitors. Friends and family were always welcome. Mom and I had many heart to heart talks as she washed dishes and I dried. Often Mom counseled my adult cousins who would drop in any time to talk through problems. She would hang up the dishtowel and they would sit down to talk. Mom would mostly listen. In the midst of her busy time in the kitchen, my mom always had time for people.

Sharon Senger, Xi Beta Omicron
Excelsior Springs, Missouri

STRAWBERRY BREAD

Serve this delicious bread with anything. It is especially good with finger foods.

3 cups flour	1/2 cup vegetable oil
2 cups sugar	4 eggs, well beaten
1 teaspoon salt	1 1/2 cups chopped
1 teaspoon baking soda	walnuts or pecans
1/2 teaspoon cinnamon	Strawberry Spread
1 (16-ounce) package	
frozen unsweetened	
strawberries, thawed	

Sift the flour, sugar, salt, baking soda and cinnamon into a large bowl. Combine the strawberries, vegetable oil, eggs and walnuts in another bowl and mix well. Add the liquid ingredients gradually to the dry ingredients; mix well. Spoon the batter into 2 foil-lined 4×8-inch loaf pans or 4 smaller loaf pans. Bake at 325 degrees for 1 hour. Serve with Strawberry Spread. Yield: About 18 slices.

STRAWBERRY SPREAD

8 ounces cream cheese, softened	1 (12-ounce) jar strawberry preserves
1/2 cup (1 stick) margarine, softened	

Combine the cream cheese and margarine in a mixing bowl and beat until smooth. Stir in the strawberry preserves. Keep in the refrigerator for up to 1 month.

Jeanne Shear, Gamma Iota
Sabetha, Kansas

SPICED PUMPKIN BREAD

I make this special pumpkin bread once a week in the fall. Friends and family love it.

1 3/4 cups flour	1/8 teaspoon nutmeg
1 1/2 cups sugar	1 (15-ounce) can
1 teaspoon baking soda	pumpkin
1 teaspoon cinnamon	2 eggs
1/4 teaspoon salt	1/2 cup vegetable oil
1/4 teaspoon baking powder	1/3 cup water

Sift the flour, sugar, baking soda, cinnamon, salt, baking powder and nutmeg together. Combine the pumpkin, eggs, vegetable oil and water in a large bowl and blend well. Add the sifted dry ingredients gradually and mix well. Spoon the batter into 2 miniature loaf pans. Bake at 350 degrees for 75 minutes or until bread tests done. Cool completely. Yield: 2 small loaves.

Laura Plaisance, Lambda Alpha
Denham Springs, Louisiana

❖ DILLY BREAKFAST BREAD

This bread was a big hit at brunch the day after my daughter's wedding. I made several loaves in advance, put them in the freezer, and reheated them to serve.

1 onion, chopped	6 slices bacon, crisp-cooked, crumbled
2 tablespoons margarine	1 tablespoon dillweed
1 (1-pound) loaf frozen bread dough, thawed	2 tablespoons dillseeds
3 tablespoons Dijon mustard	1 egg, beaten
4 ounces Swiss cheese, shredded	

Brown the onion in the margarine in a skillet. Roll the bread dough into an 8×12-inch rectangle and spread with the Dijon mustard. Layer the Swiss cheese, browned onion, bacon, dillweed and half the dillseeds over the mustard. Roll as for a jelly roll, sealing the edge. Place seam side down in a 9-inch-round cake pan. Make several 1/4-inch diagonal slashes in the top of the bread. Let rise, covered, in a warm place until doubled in bulk. Brush with beaten egg and sprinkle with the remaining 1 tablespoon dillseeds. Bake at 375 degrees for 25 to 30 minutes or until bread tests done. Yield: 12 servings.

Judy A. Dunbar, Xi Gamma Alpha
Norfolk, Nebraska

POPPY SEED NUT BREAD

3 large eggs	1 (13-ounce) can
2 cups sugar	sweetened condensed
1 cup vegetable oil	milk
3 cups flour	2 ounces poppy seeds
1 1/2 teaspoons baking	1/2 cup chopped walnuts
soda	or pecans (optional)
1 teaspoon salt	

Combine the eggs, sugar and vegetable oil in a large bowl and mix well. Sift together the flour, baking soda and salt in a separate bowl. Add to the egg mixture alternately with the condensed milk, mixing well after each addition. Stir in the poppy seeds and walnuts. Pour the batter into an ungreased tube pan. Bake at 325 degrees for 1 1/4 hours or until cake tests done. Yield: 16 servings.

Laurie Donovan, Xi Omicron Chi
Pleasant Hill, California

MOM'S WALNUT BREAD

My family had a walnut orchard, so we used walnuts a lot, especially during the holidays. This simple bread recipe is terrific.

3 cups flour	1/4 cup vegetable oil
3/4 cup sugar	1 1/2 cups milk
4 teaspoons baking	1 egg, beaten
powder	1 teaspoon vanilla
1 teaspoon salt	extract
1 1/2 cups chopped	Maple Glaze
walnuts	

Sift the flour, sugar, baking powder and salt into a large mixing bowl. Stir in 1 1/4 cups of the walnuts. Add the vegetable oil, milk, egg and vanilla and mix just until blended. Spoon into a greased and floured 5×9-inch loaf pan. Bake at 350 degrees for 60 to 70 minutes or until bread tests done. Let cool in the pan

for 10 minutes. Remove to a wire rack to cool completely. Drizzle Maple Glaze over the cooled bread. Sprinkle with the remaining 1/4 cup chopped walnuts. Yield: 1 loaf.

MAPLE GLAZE

2 tablespoons milk	1 teaspoon maple
1 cup confectioners'	extract
sugar	

Combine the milk, confectioners' sugar and maple extract in a small bowl and beat until smooth.

Nanci Davison, Delta Kappa Iota
Live Oak, California

GRANDMA'S NUT BREAD

This firm bread that has no shortening or oil is good when sliced and toasted. It keeps well and will not fall apart. The date on the recipe is 1924.

1 egg, beaten	1 teaspoon salt
3/4 cup sugar	1/2 cup chopped walnuts
1 1/4 cups whole milk	or pecans
3 cups flour	1/2 cup chopped dates
2 tablespoons baking	(optional)
powder	

Mix the egg, sugar and milk in a large bowl. Add a mixture of the flour, baking powder and salt and stir until moistened. Fold in the walnuts and dates. Spoon the batter into a greased 5×9-inch loaf pan. Bake at 325 degrees for 1 hour. Yield: 12 to 16 slices.

Evelyn M. Oberlander, Rho Master
Allison Park, Pennsylvania

MEMORIES

My fondest memory is of Christmas Eve at my parents' home in Tonkawa, Oklahoma. My five brothers and one sister would bring their families, and there were 20 grandchildren. My parents weren't wealthy, but they loved to give. My father had all the grandchildren line up in a row, and then he gave each one a dollar bill. It always brought to mind that "it is more blessed to give than to receive." Now I only have two brothers and one sister who are still living, as well as my wonderful memories.

Lucylee K. Lively (26 years), Preceptor Iota Sigma
Dallas, Texas

MEMORIES

*O*ne fond memory is of the time my late hus-band, our son and I were down at our doughnut shop making doughnuts when the power went out. It was pitch-black dark inside because there weren't any windows. Praise God for those shoes with the little lights in them! Our little one-year-old son was wearing those shoes. In the total darkness we saw the little patter of his feet take off running across the kitchen, so we knew where to find him. When the lights came back on our precious, "sweet" little boy was covered in frosting! It taught me a lesson: if we follow the light, even if it's just a glimpse, it will lead us to our final destination that will be pure sweet joy! I'm thankful for the time that we spent together (even if it was at 2:00 a.m.).

Julie Persinger, Kappa Eta
Hugoton, Kansas

POTATO DOUGHNUTS

I have no idea where this delicious recipe came from, but it has "always" been in our family. The dough-nuts need no sugar coating.

1 cup sugar	1 tablespoon baking
1 cup mashed cooked	powder
potatoes	3 cups flour
1 cup milk	Vegetable oil for deep-
2 eggs	frying
1 teaspoon nutmeg	

Combine the sugar, mashed potatoes, milk, eggs, nutmeg, baking powder and flour in a large bowl in the order listed, mixing well after each addition. Roll 1/3 of the dough to 1/3-inch thickness on a lightly floured surface. Cut with a floured doughnut cutter. Repeat with remaining dough. Have all doughnuts ready before frying, for they cook very fast. Fry in deep vegetable oil at 375 degrees until brown on both sides, turning once. Drain on paper towels. Yield: 3 1/2 dozen.

Neldalea Dotray, Laureate Gamma Pi
Greenville, Illinois

GARLIC CHEESE BREAD

1 loaf French bread	1 cup mayonnaise
1/2 cup (1 stick) butter or	1 bunch green onions,
margarine, softened	chopped
1 cup shredded asiago	2 garlic cloves, puréed
cheese	
1 cup shredded	
Monterey Jack cheese	

Split French bread loaf into halves horizontally. Combine the butter, asiago cheese, Monterey Jack cheese, mayonnaise, green onions and garlic in a bowl and blend well. Spread the cut side of each bread half with the cheese mixture. Place cheese side up on an ungreased baking sheet. Bake at 350 degrees for 7 minutes. Broil 6 inches from heat source for about 3 minutes or until browned. Slice and serve. Yield: 10 slices.

Karen MacInnis, Xi Beta Theta
Surrey, British Columbia, Canada

✤ SALSA BREAD

2 (8-count) cans Grand	1 cup salsa
Corn Biscuits	1/2 cup melted butter
1 (4-ounce) jar sliced	8 ounces Mexican cheese
black olives, drained	blend, shredded
1 (6-ounce) jar	
marinated artichoke	
hearts, drained, diced	

Cut each biscuit into 8 pieces. Combine the biscuit pieces, olives and artichoke hearts in a large bowl. Stir in the salsa and melted butter. Stir in the cheese. Spoon into an ungreased 9×13-inch baking dish. Bake at 350 degrees for 30 minutes or until hot and lightly browned. Yield: 12 to 15 servings.

Delores Lorraine Keatley (39 years),
Preceptor Alpha Zeta
Omaha, Nebraska

BREAD MACHINE FLAX BREAD

1 1/4 cups warm water	3 tablespoons flax seed
2 tablespoons honey	2 tablespoons sesame
2 tablespoons canola oil	seeds
1 1/2 teaspoons salt	2 tablespoons raw
2 cups all-purpose flour	sunflower seeds
1 cup whole wheat flour	2 teaspoons dry yeast

Place the water, honey, canola oil, salt, flours, flax seed, sesame seeds, sunflower seeds and yeast in the bread machine in the order listed. Bake using the manufacturer's directions. Yield: 1 loaf.

Pat Engebretson, Preceptor Beta Iota
Quesnel, British Columbia, Canada

BREAD MACHINE SWEDISH RYE

My grandma always served us her rye bread when we visited, and she taught me how to make it when I was newly married. She passed away soon after that, and I am the only family member who knows how to make it. I make it for all holidays and I always look forward to giving it to all of my family.

1½ cups water	2 tablespoons molasses
2 tablespoons nonfat dry milk powder	1½ teaspoons salt
2 tablespoons shortening	2 cups dark rye flour
2 tablespoons corn syrup	2¼ cups all-purpose or whole wheat flour
	1 tablespoon anise seeds
	1½ teaspoons dry yeast

Place the ingredients in a bread machine in the order listed. Set the machine on the 2-hour dough mode. Complete the 2-hour cycle, then allow dough to rise for 1 hour. Remove from the bread machine pan to a floured board. Knead slightly and shape into a round. Place in a buttered springform pan. Let rise, covered, in a warm place for 1 hour. Pierce the top of the dough with a wooden pick, making 12 deep holes. Bake at 400 degrees for 40 to 45 minutes or until bread tests done. Yield: 1 loaf.

Kris Weishaupt, Omicron
Fruitvale, British Columbia, Canada

BREAD MACHINE CRANBERRY ORANGE BREAD

1 cup milk, room temperature	1 tablespoon sugar
2 eggs	2 teaspoons grated orange zest
1 tablespoon butter or margarine	1 teaspoon salt
3 cups bread machine flour	¾ cup dried cranberries
	2 teaspoons bread machine yeast

Place the milk, 1 of the eggs, butter, flour, sugar, orange zest, salt, dried cranberries and yeast in the bread machine pan in the order recommended by the manufacturer. Set the machine on the dough mode. When cycle is complete, divide the dough into 16 pieces. Shape each piece into a ball and place the balls in a greased 9-inch springform pan. Let rise, covered with a tea towel, in a warm place until doubled in bulk. Beat the remaining egg and brush lightly over the risen dough. Bake at 375 degrees on the lower oven rack for 20 to 25 minutes or until golden. Remove to a wire rack immediately to cool completely. Yield: 10 servings.

Sharon Hall, Preceptor Beta Beta
Foxboro, Ontario, Canada

SWEET POTATO BREAD

My four-year-old son always helps me knead the dough. He thinks it's just like playdough. I think it means high-quality time with my son!

3 cups warm (110 to 115 degrees) water	4 cups shredded peeled sweet potatoes
1½ cups honey	2 teaspoons salt
2 tablespoons dry yeast	6 cups (about) unbleached flour
7½ cups whole wheat flour	

Combine the water and 1 tablespoon of the honey in a large mixing bowl. Sprinkle the yeast over the honey mixture and let stand for 5 to 10 minutes. Stir in 3 cups of the whole wheat flour. Beat at medium-high speed for 3 minutes. Stir in the sweet potatoes, salt and remaining honey. Place on a floured surface and knead in the remaining 4½ cups whole wheat flour and enough of the unbleached flour to form a workable dough. Knead for 10 minutes and shape into a ball. Place in a lightly oiled bowl, turning to coat the surface. Let rise, covered, in a warm place for 1 hour or until doubled in bulk. Punch the dough down and divide into 3 equal portions. Shape into loaves in 3 greased 5×9-inch loaf pans. Let rise, covered, for 30 to 40 minutes or until doubled in bulk. Bake at 350 degrees for 45 minutes or until browned. Remove to a wire rack to cool. Yield: 3 large loaves.

Dana L. Priddy, Alpha Kappa
Hot Springs, Arkansas

GRANDMA'S ANADAMA BREAD

2 cups boiling water	½ cup light molasses
½ cup cornmeal	1 teaspoon salt
2 tablespoons shortening	1 envelope dry yeast
	5 cups (or more) flour

Pour the boiling water into a large bowl and stir in the cornmeal slowly. Add the shortening and stir until melted. Stir in the molasses and salt. Cool. Dissolve the yeast in ½ cup warm water; stir into the cornmeal mixture. Add enough flour to make a soft dough. Knead until soft and elastic. Let rise, covered, in a warm place for 1 to 1½ hours or until doubled in bulk. Punch the dough down. Knead for 5 minutes longer and shape into loaves in greased loaf pans. Let rise again until doubled in bulk. Bake at 350 degrees for 30 to 35 minutes or until bread tests done. Yield: 3 small loaves.

Denise J. Paquette, Theta Pi
DeKalb Junction, New York

SWISS RYE BREAD

My mother entered eternal life this past December, and while sorting through her belongings, I came across this recipe. While preparing it for a meal, a smile emerged on my face as I remembered how my mother solved the problem when dough didn't rise— she would put it in her car in the warm garage, a perfect solution.

2¹/₄ to 2³/₄ cups unsifted all-purpose flour	1 tablespoon caraway seeds
1¹/₄ cups unsifted rye flour	2 teaspoons salt
³/₄ cup beer	¹/₂ teaspoon garlic powder
2 tablespoons honey	12 ounces Swiss cheese, cubed, room temperature
1 tablespoon margarine	
2 envelopes dry yeast	
¹/₂ cup warm (105 to 115 degrees) water	

Combine 1¹/₂ cups of the all-purpose flour with the rye flour in a bowl. Heat the beer, honey and margarine in a small saucepan until margarine is melted and mixture is warm. Dissolve the yeast in the warm water in a large bowl. Add the warm beer mixture, caraway seeds, salt, garlic powder and 1¹/₂ cups of the flour mixture; beat until smooth. Stir in the remaining flour mixture and enough all-purpose flour to make a soft dough. Knead on a floured surface for about 4 minutes or until smooth. Place in a greased 8-inch-round baking pan, turning to coat the surface. Flatten to fit the pan. Press cubes of Swiss cheese into the dough. Let rise, covered, in a warm place for about 45 minutes or until doubled in bulk. Bake at 375 degrees for 25 to 30 minutes or until bread tests done. Yield: 1 loaf.

Janet Hamilton, Xi Zeta Epsilon
Kalamazoo, Michigan

LIZ'S PIZZA DOUGH

2 teaspoons brown sugar or honey	1 teaspoon dry yeast
1 cup plus 2 tablespoons warm water	3 cups flour
	1 teaspoon salt
	1 tablespoon olive oil

Dissolve the brown sugar in the warm water and sprinkle with the yeast; let stand for 5 minutes. Combine the flour and salt in a large bowl; blend well. Add the yeast mixture and olive oil gradually to the flour mixture; blend well. Knead on a floured surface for 20 minutes. Let rise, covered, in a warm place until doubled in bulk. Punch the dough down. Let rise for 45 minutes longer. Punch down. Let stand for 10 minutes. Roll into a flat circle. Sprinkle with

toppings of choice and bake at 450 degrees for 15 minutes. Note: To prepare the dough in a bead machine, run it through the dough cycle twice. Yield: 8 to 10 servings.

Alice Hutchins, Xi Alpha Lambda
Council, Idaho

WHOLE WHEAT BREAD

My grandma was born in 1888, and she prepared delicious simple meals. This was her recipe, and it was the first bread I made as a teen.

1¹/₂ envelopes fast-rising yeast	1¹/₂ cups whole wheat or graham flour
¹/₂ cup packed brown sugar	2 cups milk, scalded
¹/₂ cup molasses	2 cups boiling water
4 teaspoons salt	4¹/₂ cups (about) all-purpose flour
¹/₄ cup shortening	

Dissolve the yeast in ¹/₃ cup lukewarm water (80 to 85 degrees). Combine the brown sugar, molasses, salt, shortening and whole wheat flour in a large bowl. Pour a mixture of the scalded milk and boiling water over the flour mixture; mix well. Let stand until lukewarm. Stir in the dissolved yeast and enough all-purpose flour to make a stiff dough. Let rise, covered, in a warm place until doubled in bulk. Punch the dough down. Shape into 4 loaves in 4 greased loaf pans. Let rise again until doubled in bulk. Bake at 350 degrees for 50 to 60 minutes or until bread tests done. Remove to wire racks to cool. Brush the tops of the warm loaves with butter. Yield: 4 loaves.

Elsie Johnson, Preceptor Pi
Anoka, Minnesota

MEMORIES

I can remember back to the days in the 1940s when margarine was made by hand. You would dump lard into a bowl and add a yellow color mixture and squeeze it into the lard with your hands, kneading it like flour. The kids would stand around, wait for Mom to finish and then lick the margarine off the bowl and her fingers! I guess when you're poor and you don't know it the best things in life are indeed free!

Bobbi Shannon, Laureate Lambda
Port Saint Lucie, Florida

OLD-FASHIONED WHITE BREAD

I visited my grandmother often when I was a child, and she would be making fresh bread when I arrived. There was a big bowl of dough in front of the fireplace, and I would watch it rise and wonder how it did that. I remember Grandma kneading and pounding the dough with all her might. If you listened closely you could hear her speaking a few German words, then into the oven went the bread. I sat impatiently as it baked, and the smell would make my mouth water and tummy growl. Grandma sliced the bread while it was hot, and butter would melt into it. Sometimes she served it with her homemade jam.

1 envelope yeast	**2 teaspoons salt**
2 tablespoons sugar	**1 cup milk**
2 tablespoons shortening	**5 cups (about) flour**

Dissolve the yeast in ¹/₂ cup warm water. Place the sugar, shortening and salt in a large bowl. Add 1 cup of very hot water and stir until sugar is dissolved. Add the yeast mixture and milk. Stir in enough flour to make a stiff dough. Knead on a floured surface until smooth but not sticky. Place in a greased bowl, turning to coat the surface. Let rise, covered, in a warm place until doubled in bulk. Punch the dough down. Shape into 2 loaves in 2 greased loaf pans. Let rise until doubled in bulk. Bake at 400 degrees for 35 to 40 minutes or until golden and loaves sound hollow when tapped lightly on top. Yield: 2 loaves.

Dawn Hroma, Beta Kappa
Boise, Idaho

WHITE OR WHOLE WHEAT BREAD

2 tablespoons dry yeast	**5 cups whole wheat flour**
¹/₃ cup sugar	**5 cups all-purpose flour**
1¹/₂ tablespoons salt	
¹/₄ cup vegetable oil	

Combine the yeast, sugar, salt, vegetable oil, whole wheat flour and 4¹/₄ cups lukewarm water in a large bowl and mix well. Stir in the all-purpose flour. Knead on a floured surface until smooth and elastic, adding more flour if necessary. Place in a generously greased bowl, turning to coat the surface. Cover and place the bowl in the oven. Turn the temperature to 200 degrees for exactly 1 minute. Turn off the oven. Let the dough stand in the oven for 20 minutes. Punch the dough down and flip over with the fingers. Let stand in the warm oven for 40 minutes longer. Punch the dough down and place into three 1¹/₂-pound or four 1-pound loaf pans. Pierce each deeply several times with a fork. Return to the warm oven and let stand, uncovered, for 30 minutes. Turn oven temperature to 375 degrees and bake the bread for 45 minutes, reducing oven temperature to 350 degrees for the last 10 minutes. Yield: 3 or 4 loaves.

Mildred K. Burk (25 years), Iota Iota
Parker, Kansas

DILLY BREAD

In 1980 my cousin put together a booklet of each family member's three favorite recipes and called it "It's All in the Berg Family." My copy is getting dog-eared and slightly soiled, but it is still my favorite.

1 envelope dry yeast	**1 teaspoon butter**
1 cup creamed cottage cheese	**2 teaspoons dillweed**
1 teaspoon minced onion	**1 egg, unbeaten**
	2¹/₄ cups (about) flour

Soften the yeast in ¹/₄ cup warm water. Heat the cottage cheese to lukewarm in a saucepan or in the microwave oven. Combine the yeast mixture, cottage cheese, onion, butter, dillweed and egg in a large bowl and mix well. Add the flour a little at a time to form a stiff dough, beating after each addition. Let rise, covered, in a warm place until doubled in bulk. Stir the dough down. Shape into a loaf in a greased 5×9-inch loaf pan. Bake at 350 degrees for 40 to 50 minutes or until bread tests done. Yield: 1 loaf.

 Esther Berg Johnson (63 years), Alpha Zeta Master
Watseka, Illinois

DINNER ROLLS

My entire family loves these rolls, and I also used to prepare them for my mother's bridge club.

3 tablespoons yeast	**1 tablespoon salt**
¹/₂ cup vegetable oil	**3 eggs**
³/₄ cup sugar	**10 cups flour**

Dissolve the yeast in a cup of warm water. Combine the vegetable oil, sugar, salt, eggs and flour in a large bowl. Stir in the yeast mixture. Stir in 1³/₄ cups warm water. If dough is sticky, add more water. Knead on a floured surface until smooth and elastic. Place in a greased bowl, turning to coat the surface. Let rise, covered, in a warm place until doubled in bulk. Punch the dough down and divide into 24 portions. Place each portion in a muffin cup that has been sprayed with nonstick cooking spray. Let rise until doubled in bulk. Bake at 400 degrees for 10 minutes or until rolls test done. Yield: 2 dozen.

Clarice Collins, Laureate Omicron
Pahrump, Nevada

FRENCH BREAD

This recipe was passed down through four generations.

2 tablespoons sugar	2 envelopes yeast
2 tablespoons shortening	2 teaspoons sugar
2 teaspoons salt	1/2 cup warm water
2 cups boiling water	6 cups flour

Combine the 2 tablespoons sugar, shortening, salt and boiling water in a large bowl and stir; let stand until cool. Dissolve the yeast and the 2 teaspoons sugar in the warm water in a small bowl. Add the yeast mixture to the shortening mixture and stir to combine. Add the flour gradually with a spoon. Let stand, covered, in a warm place for 40 to 50 minutes, stirring down the dough with a wooden spoon every 10 minutes. Divide into 3 equal portions and let stand for 10 minutes. Roll into three 1/2-inch-thick rectangles. Roll each as for a jelly roll, sealing the edge and ends to form a loaf. Place the loaves well apart on a greased baking sheet. Let rise, covered, in a warm place until doubled in bulk. Cut 3 or 4 diagonal slashes in the top of each. Bake at 400 degrees for 25 minutes or until bread tests done. Yield: 3 loaves.

Janice Roth, Preceptor Beta Psi
Dodge City, Kansas

MEMORIES

I started cooking when I was five or six years old. One of the first recipes that I prepared was corn bread. My mother told me to always follow the directions, so I did. My dad said that it was the best cake that he had ever eaten. I was broken-hearted because the recipe called for more sugar than he was used to. One year for Christmas I made my adult children each a cookbook which included family recipes that had been handed down. It's a cherished keepsake that they love and use. I love to cook and always try something new. I try to get a cookbook wherever I go.

Betty P. Parsons (39 years), Laureate Rho
Jasper, Alabama

BROCCOLI CORN BREAD

My family loves this bread on a cold day or night when we have soup or stew. Serve with butter or cream cheese.

1/2 cup (1 stick) butter, melted	1 (10-ounce) package frozen chopped broccoli, thawed, drained
1/2 cup chopped onion	
1 teaspoon salt	
3/4 cup cottage cheese	1 (8-ounce) package corn bread mix
4 eggs, beaten	
3/4 cup shredded Cheddar or Swiss cheese	

Combine the butter, onion, salt, cottage cheese, eggs, Cheddar cheese and broccoli in a medium bowl and mix well. Stir in the dry corn bread mix. Spoon into a greased 9×12-inch baking dish. Bake at 400 degrees for 30 minutes. Yield: 15 to 18 servings.

Mary Meza (29 years), Laureate Zeta Gamma
Deer Park, Texas

DILLY CORN BREAD

A group of twenty-six women, Mountain Mommas, takes a trip to a lodge for cross-country skiing every January. This recipe is one of our favorites.

2 tablespoons shortening	1 cup flour
3/4 cup yellow cornmeal	1 tablespoon baking powder
1/2 cup sugar	1/2 cup milk
1/2 teaspoon salt	2 eggs, beaten
1/2 cup plain yogurt	1 tablespoon dillweed

Place the shortening in an 8-inch cast-iron skillet and place the skillet in the oven. Turn oven temperature to 425 degrees; shortening will melt while oven is preheating. Combine the cornmeal, sugar, salt, yogurt, flour, baking powder, milk, eggs and dillweed in a large bowl; stir just until moistened. Remove the skillet from the oven and swirl to coat the bottom of the skillet. Pour the rest of the melted shortening into the cornmeal mixture and stir to blend. Spoon the batter into the hot skillet. Bake for 20 minutes or until bread tests done. Yield: 8 to 10 servings.

Martha Setterstrom, Preceptor Alpha Psi
Cross Lanes, West Virginia

TEXAS CORN BREAD

2 cups corn bread mix
1²/3 cups milk
1/3 cup vegetable oil
2 eggs, beaten
2 tablespoons sugar

4 slices bacon, crisp-
 cooked, crumbled
2/3 cup cream-style corn
2 jalapeño chiles, finely
 chopped

Preheat a greased 10¹/2-inch iron skillet in a 400-degree oven. Combine the dry corn bread mix, milk, vegetable oil, eggs, sugar, bacon, cream-style corn and jalapeño chiles in a large bowl and mix well. Pour the batter into the hot iron skillet. Bake for 20 to 25 minutes or until brown. Yield: 6 to 8 servings.

Kathy G. Fowler, Preceptor Eta Alpha
Azle, Texas

CORN LIGHT BREAD

This recipe belongs to my sister's mother-in-law, a wonderful lady of German descent. We have had Corn Light Bread at every family reunion for forty years. It's wonderful with ham and fresh vegetables.

3 cups self-rising
 cornmeal
1 cup sugar
3/4 cup self-rising flour

1/2 cup vegetable oil
1/2 teaspoon salt
3 cups buttermilk

Combine the cornmeal, sugar, flour, vegetable oil, salt and buttermilk in the order listed in a large mixing bowl; mix well. Spoon into a greased tube pan and bake at 350 degrees for 1 hour.
Yield: 10 to 12 servings.

Linda Rhodes, Preceptor Alpha Pi
McMinnville, Tennessee

VERY CORNY MUFFINS

1 cup flour
4 teaspoons baking
 powder
1/4 cup sugar
1 cup yellow cornmeal
1/2 teaspoon salt

1 egg
2 egg whites
1¹/4 cups milk
1 (15-ounce) can cream-
 style corn

Combine the flour, baking powder, sugar, cornmeal and salt in a large bowl; blend well. Beat the egg and egg whites in a medium bowl until light and smooth. Stir in the milk and cream-style corn. Add to the dry ingredients and stir just until moistened. Fill 12 muffin cups that have been sprayed with nonstick cooking spray. Bake at 350 degrees for 20 to 25 minutes or until muffins test done. Yield: 1 dozen.

Bev Dewis, Xi Delta
Portage la Prairie, Manitoba, Canada

AUNT KAY'S BLUEBERRY STREUSEL MUFFINS

Beginning in the mid-1960s, we made a yearly trip to northern New Hampshire to spend time with my aunt at her cottage on Conway Lake. The wild blueberries would be out in profusion in mid-July, and it became a ritual to pick the berries along the causeway or out on the small islands, enough so that Aunt Kay could make her blueberry muffins. If we were lucky, we would gather enough to freeze for several more batches later on. Forty years later we still make the trip every summer, and I still look forward to picking the blueberries and making these delectable muffins.

1/2 cup packed brown
 sugar
1 teaspoon cinnamon
1/4 cup chopped pecans
 or walnuts
1 cup rolled oats
1 cup orange juice
3 cups flour
1 teaspoon salt

1/2 teaspoon baking soda
4 teaspoons baking
 powder
1 cup vegetable oil
1 cup sugar
3 eggs, beaten
3 cups blueberries, fresh
 or frozen

Place the brown sugar, cinnamon and pecans in a small bowl. Combine the rolled oats and orange juice in another small bowl and let stand for at least 10 minutes. Sift the flour, salt, baking soda and baking powder into a large bowl. Stir in the vegetable oil and sugar. Stir in the eggs and the rolled oats mixture. Add the blueberries, stirring gently to keep them whole. Spoon the batter into 24 to 36 greased or paper-lined muffin cups. Sprinkle the brown sugar mixture over the top. Bake at 400 degrees for 15 minutes or until muffins test done. The muffins do not freeze well, but they will keep for several days if covered with foil. Note: If you use frozen blueberries, reduce the amount of orange juice by 3 tablespoons. Yield: 2 to 3 dozen.

Jackie Elrick (40 years), Laureate Delta
Claymont, Delaware

Carla Nelson, Delta Mu, Otho, Iowa, makes a special treat for warm bread with her *Cinnamon Honey Butter*. Blend 1/2 cup honey with 1/2 cup softened butter, 1/2 cup confectioners' sugar and 1/2 teaspoon cinnamon.

MEMORIES

*W*hen I was very young, Daddy owned a gas station that he ran with the help of his brother. He usually ran the station from the time he finished the city mail route in Abbeville, Georgia, until closing. Mama was at home with my sister and me. She would finish supper that always included homemade biscuits that were kept warm in the oven with a dishcloth covering them. Then she would take my sister and me to swing in the front porch swing. We would take turns guessing which car would be Daddy's. He was never too tired to pick up the two of us when we ran out to greet him. He would give us a ride back to the house while Mama went directly to the kitchen to put supper on the table.

Cheryl Howard, Epsilon Sigma
Hawkinsville, Georgia

SUPER-MOIST BRAN MUFFINS

I ate these muffins often when I was expecting. My children love them, especially with shredded apples and sunflower seeds, and served with fresh fruit.

1¹/₂ cups bran	1 teaspoon baking soda
2 cups whole wheat flour	Pinch of salt
³/₄ cup wheat germ	1¹/₄ cups nonfat yogurt, flavor of choice
Shredded apples, chopped nuts or raisins (optional)	¹/₄ cup vegetable oil or applesauce
1 teaspoon baking powder	¹/₂ cup honey
	¹/₄ cup molasses
	1 egg or 2 egg whites

Combine the bran, whole wheat flour, wheat germ, fruit or nuts, baking powder, baking soda and salt in a large bowl; mix well. Combine the yogurt, vegetable oil, honey, molasses, egg and 1 cup water in a medium bowl; blend well. Stir the yogurt mixture into the flour mixture just until moistened. Fill greased or paper-lined muffin cups. Bake at 350 degrees for 20 to 25 minutes or until lightly browned and top springs back when touched.
Yield: 12 to 18 muffins.

Joanne Berarducci, Xi Epsilon Phi
Smithers, British Columbia, Canada

BEER MUFFINS

The cook at my mother's large Southern Baptist church in Oklahoma gave Mom this recipe only if she promised not to share (because of the BEER). Well, Mom, rest in peace—this recipe is now in print!

4 cups baking mix	1 (12-ounce) can of beer
2 tablespoons sugar	

Beat all the ingredients in a mixing bowl at high speed for 30 seconds. Fill 12 greased or paper-lined muffin cups ²/₃ full. Bake at 375 degrees for 15 minutes or until golden brown. Serve hot. Yield: 1 dozen.

Nedra J. Murphy, Xi Phi Iota
Victorville, California

YORKSHIRE PUDDING POPOVERS

Mom said the secret to success was letting the ingredients come to room temperature on the kitchen counter and then making sure the shortening was hot. This is nothing like the infamous dry popovers!

¹/₂ cup flour	Pinch of salt
¹/₂ cup milk	6 teaspoons shortening
3 or 4 eggs	

Combine the flour, milk, eggs and salt in a bowl and whisk until smooth. Let stand, covered, for 2 to 3 hours, whisking occasionally. Place 1 teaspoon shortening in each of 6 ovenproof custard cups. Place the custard cups in a baking dish. Heat in a 450-degree oven until shortening is almost smoking; remove from oven. Pour the batter into the cups. Bake for about 20 to 25 minutes or until puffed and golden. Serve immediately with roast beef and gravy. Yield: 6 servings.

Barbara Slater, Laureate Delta Eta
Sault Ste. Marie, Ontario, Canada

ICE CREAM MUFFINS

My grandmother cut out this newspaper recipe when I was a child (I'm now fifty-seven). She made it often. To make Banana-Nut Muffins, *use homestyle butter pecan ice cream, baking mix, ¹/₂ cup chopped pecans, and 3 mashed bananas.*

2 cups self-rising flour or baking mix	2 cups softened vanilla ice cream

Combine the flour and ice cream in a bowl and beat until smooth, adding a little more ice cream if necessary to make a creamy mixture. Grease 12 muffin cups and fill ³/₄ full. Bake at 425 degrees for 25 minutes or until golden. Yield: 12 muffins.

Patricia McDade, Xi Delta Gamma
Milledgeville, Georgia

BLUE RIBBON MUFFINS

My grandmother used to make these early in the morning to serve with boiled potatoes, fried salt pork, and coffee to the hired men on the farm after they finished milking. My sister and I spent lots of time at the farm with our grandparents, and these muffins were our favorite. After moving to Albuquerque in 1954, I entered these muffins and other baked items in the New Mexico State Fair, winning several blue ribbons.

1 cup whole wheat or graham flour	1 cup sour milk
1 cup all-purpose flour	1/4 cup melted butter or vegetable oil
1/4 cup brown sugar	1 teaspoon baking soda
2 eggs, beaten	1/2 teaspoon salt

Combine the flours and brown sugar in a large bowl and blend well. Stir in the eggs. Add the sour milk, butter, baking soda and salt; stir just until moistened. Fill greased or paper-lined muffin cups just over 1/2 full. Bake at 425 degrees for 15 to 20 minutes or until muffins test done. Note: If you do not have sour milk, omit the baking soda and use 2 teaspoons baking powder stirred into 1 cup sweet milk.
Yield: 12 to 15 muffins.

Wanda E. Dudley (44 years), Laureate Alpha
Albuquerque, New Mexico

PUMPKIN CRANBERRY MUFFINS WITH STREUSEL TOPPING

1 1/4 cups flour	1 egg, beaten
1/4 cup sugar	1/3 cup vegetable oil
1/2 cup nonfat dry milk	2 cups pumpkin purée or canned pumpkin
1 tablespoon baking powder	1 cup cranberries, finely chopped
1 teaspoon cinnamon	1 1/2 cups chopped walnuts, pecans or other nuts
1/4 teaspoon nutmeg	
1/2 teaspoon salt	
1 1/2 cups packed brown sugar	Streusel Topping

Combine the flour, sugar, dry milk, baking powder, cinnamon, nutmeg, salt and brown sugar in a large bowl; mix well. Combine the egg, vegetable oil and pumpkin purée in a separate bowl; mix well. Add the egg mixture to the flour mixture and blend. The batter should be scoopable, sliding off the spoon, but not runny. If batter is the consistency of mashed potatoes, it is too thick; add water, milk, or pumpkin to thin it. Stir in the cranberries and chopped walnuts. Fill greased or paper-lined muffin cups 2/3 full. Bake at 325 degrees for 40 to 45 minutes or until muffins spring back when lightly pressed in the center. Sprinkle a small amount of Streusel Topping over each muffin. Yield: 2 to 2 1/2 dozen

STREUSEL TOPPING

1/3 cup baking mix	2 tablespoons chopped walnuts or other nuts
3 tablespoons brown sugar	1 tablespoon butter or margarine, softened
1 teaspoon cinnamon	

Combine the ingredients in a bowl and mix well. Mixture will be crumbly.

Judy Davey, Preceptor Gamma Mu
Lakewood, Colorado

BLUEBERRY MUFFINS

2 cups flour	2 eggs, beaten
1 cup sugar	1/2 cup vegetable oil
1/2 teaspoon salt	1/2 teaspoon vanilla extract
1/2 teaspoon baking soda	
1 teaspoon baking powder	1 cup sour cream
	1 cup fresh blueberries

Combine the flour, sugar, salt, baking soda and baking powder in a medium bowl and mix well. Blend the eggs, vegetable oil, vanilla and sour cream in a large bowl. Add the flour mixture to the egg mixture and stir until moistened. Fold in the blueberries. Bake at 400 degrees for 18 to 20 minutes or until muffins test done. Yield: 12 large muffins.

Alda Lou Geiger (51 years), Alpha Master
Surprise, Arizona

SUGAR-CRUSTED MUFFINS

2 cups flour	1 egg
2 tablespoons sugar	3/4 cup milk
2 1/2 teaspoons baking powder	1/2 cup (1 stick) butter, melted
3/4 teaspoon salt	1/2 cup sugar
1/3 cup shortening	1 teaspoon cinnamon

Sift the flour, the 2 tablespoons sugar, baking powder and salt into a large bowl. Cut in the shortening until mixture resembles coarse crumbs. Beat the egg and milk together in a small bowl and add all at once to the flour mixture; stir just until moistened. Fill 10 greased muffin cups 2/3 full. Bake at 450 degrees for 20 minutes. Dip the top of each muffin in melted butter and shake at once in a paper bag containing a mixture of the 1/2 cup sugar and cinnamon. Serve hot. Yield: 10 muffins.

Phylis Hyland (31 years), Preceptor Delta Alpha
Sturgis, Michigan

SUGARLESS FRUIT NUT MUFFINS

1 cup chopped dates	2 eggs, beaten
1/2 cup raisins	1 teaspoon vanilla
1/2 cup chopped prunes	extract
1 cup water	1 cup flour
1/2 cup (1 stick)	1 teaspoon baking soda
margarine, cut up	1/2 cup chopped walnuts
1/4 teaspoon salt	or pecans

Combine the dates, raisins, prunes and water in a saucepan over medium-high heat; bring to a boil. Boil, uncovered, for 5 minutes. Stir in the margarine and salt. Remove from heat; let stand until cool. Add the eggs, vanilla, flour, baking soda and walnuts to the date mixture; stir just until moistened. Fill 18 greased regular muffin cups or 32 miniature ones. Bake at 350 degrees for 10 to 20 minutes or until muffins test done. Yield: 18 or 32 muffins.

Dorothy Wilson (37 years), Preceptor Eta Omicron
West Sacramento, California

AUNT GERTRUDE'S SWEETHEART CRESCENTS

This recipe came from my great-aunt in South Texas. My Grandmomie made the Crescents very often and my mother made them at times, but now I hardly cook. That does not keep me from remembering how delicious they were for breakfast, brunch, tea time, or with coffee. They are light, flaky, and not too sweet.

4 cups flour	1 cup sour cream
1/2 teaspoon salt	4 teaspoons vanilla
1 envelope dry yeast	extract
1 cup (2 sticks)	3 egg whites
margarine	1 cup sugar
3 egg yolks	3/4 cup ground pecans

Combine the flour, salt and yeast in a large bowl. Cut in the margarine until mixture resembles coarse crumbs. Combine the egg yolks, sour cream and 1 teaspoon of the vanilla in a small bowl; mix until smooth. Add the sour cream mixture to the flour mixture and stir to form a dough. Beat the egg whites at high speed until stiff peaks form; beat in the sugar and the remaining 1 tablespoon vanilla. Fold in the pecans. Divide the dough into 8 equal portions. Roll each portion into a circle. Spread pecan filling evenly over each circle to within 1/2 inch of the edge. Cut each circle into 8 wedges; roll up each wedge from the wide end. Shape into crescents on a greased baking sheet. Bake at 375 degrees for 5 to 10 minutes or until beginning to brown. Yield: 64 crescents.

Marcella L. Bell, Xi Iota Delta
Denver City, Texas

MEMORIES

I grew up in North Dakota during the Depression in the 1930s. Freshly baked home-made bread and cinnamon rolls were always waiting for us when we got home from school. As I walked the twelve blocks home from school in the 48-degree-below-zero weather, I used to daydream of the bread baking. What a joy to walk in the house and enjoy something so tasty! There was always a pot of beans cooking on the wood stove. My sister and I would cuddle up behind the pot-bellied stove and eat to our heart's content.

Virginia Williams, Preceptor Beta Omega
Lakewood, Washington

QUICK HOMEMADE CINNAMON ROLLS

You cannot go wrong with this recipe!

3/8 cup (6 tablespoons)	51/2 cups flour
sugar	1/4 cup (1/2 stick) butter
1/2 cup vegetable oil	or margarine, melted
3 tablespoons dry yeast	1 cup sugar
13/4 cups warm water	1 tablespoon cinnamon
11/2 teaspoons salt	Maple Frosting
2 eggs	

Combine the 3/8 cup sugar, vegetable oil, yeast and warm water in a large bowl; let stand for 15 minutes. Stir in the salt, eggs and flour; roll immediately into 2 rectangles on a lightly floured surface. Brush melted butter over the rectangles and sprinkle evenly with a mixture of the 1 cup sugar and cinnamon. Roll as for a jelly roll. Cut into 2-inch-wide slices; arrange the dough slices on a greased baking sheet. Let rise for 15 minutes. Bake at 375 degrees for 20 minutes or until golden brown. Frost immediately with Maple Frosting. Yield: 12 large rolls.

MAPLE FROSTING

3 cups confectioners'	1/2 cup maple-flavored
sugar	syrup
1/3 cup butter or	
margarine, softened	

Combine the confectioners' sugar, butter and syrup in a mixing bowl; beat until smooth.

Tyanna Bischoff, Alpha Epsilon
Idaho Falls, Idaho

FAST CINNAMON ROLLS

This dough may be refrigerated overnight, but be sure to let it rise before baking.

2 envelopes yeast	1½ tablespoons
2½ cups warm water	cinnamon
1 (2-layer) package	½ cup chopped pecans
yellow cake mix	or walnuts (optional)
4½ cups flour	
1 cup packed brown	
sugar	

Dissolve the yeast in the warm water in a large bowl. Stir in dry cake mix and flour. Knead for about a minute or until smooth and elastic. Roll to ¼-inch thickness and spread with a mixture of the brown sugar, cinnamon and chopped pecans. Roll as for a jelly roll and cut into ½-inch slices. Butter a 10×15-inch cake pan and sprinkle with additional brown sugar. Arrange the rolls over the brown sugar layer. Let rise until doubled in bulk. Bake at 350 degrees for 15 to 20 minutes or until golden. Spread with frosting if desired. Yield: 2 dozen.

Joy Gee Rasmussen, Xi Omega
Malta, Idaho

MEMORIES

*A*fter my Grandmother Cally would roll out her hot rolls, she would find a special place for them to rise. One of her favorite places was the rear window of the back seat of the car. She always said that the rolls would rise better with natural warmth.

Dana Pules, Zi Zeta Lambda
Fort Stockton, Texas

QUICK AND EASY STICKY ROLLS

These yummy, gooey rolls are quick and easy for Sunday mornings and holidays.

½ (36-count) package	1 (4-ounce) package
frozen dinner rolls	vanilla cook-and-
½ cup brown sugar	serve pudding
½ teaspoon cinnamon	
¼ cup (½ stick)	
margarine or butter,	
melted	

Cut the frozen rolls in half and arrange cut side down, still frozen, in a greased 9×13-inch baking dish. Sprinkle a mixture of the brown sugar and cinnamon over the rolls. Drizzle with melted margarine; sprinkle evenly with the dry pudding mix. Let rise, covered, in the refrigerator for 8 to 10 hours. Bake at 300 degrees for 30 minutes. Yield: 12 to 18 servings.

Patricia Perry, Xi Alpha Mu
Bonners Ferry, Idaho

PAVITICA (CROATIAN NUT ROLL)

My husband's grandparents are from Croatia, and his family has been making this Croatian nut roll for all holidays for hundreds of years. My mother-in-law taught me how to make it in 1971, and I've been making it for all holidays for our family ever since.

1 cup milk	8 cups (about) flour,
1 teaspoon salt	sifted
3 tablespoons sugar	4 or 5 eggs, room
6 tablespoons butter	temperature, beaten
2 envelopes dry yeast	Pecan Raisin Filling

Combine the milk, salt, sugar and butter in a saucepan over low heat; heat to lukewarm. Dissolve the yeast in ½ cup warm water. Combine 4 cups of the flour, the warm milk mixture, eggs and yeast mixture in a large bowl; mix well. Knead on a floured surface until smooth and elastic, adding the remaining flour as you knead. Place in a buttered bowl, turning to coat the surface. Let rise, covered, in a warm place for 1½ hours or until doubled in bulk. Punch the dough down. Cut in half and roll each half into a 12-inch circle. Brush melted butter over each circle, then spread with Pecan Raisin Filling to within ½ inch of edge. Roll each circle into a long roll. Twist each roll around so it will fit in a buttered 8×8-inch baking pan. Let rise for 30 minutes. Bake at 350 degrees for 45 minutes or until pastry tests done. Yield: 20 to 30 servings.

PECAN RAISIN FILLING

1 pound shelled pecans	¾ teaspoon cinnamon
or walnuts	½ cup honey or syrup
1 pound raisins, soaked,	1 cup milk
drained	¼ cup sugar

Grind the pecans and raisins into a bowl. Add the cinnamon, honey, milk and sugar and mix well.

Carolyn Sepich (29 years), Kappa Master
Raleigh, North Carolina

SWEET ROLLS

The dough for this failproof recipe can be refrigerated overnight. The rolls freeze well, too.

1 tablespoon sugar	1/2 cup sugar
1 envelope dry yeast	2 teaspoons salt
1/2 cup warm water	3 eggs, beaten
1/2 cup vegetable oil	4 1/2 cups flour
1 cup milk	

Combine the 1 tablespoon sugar, yeast and warm water in a large bowl and whisk well. Let stand until foamy. Combine the vegetable oil and milk in a small bowl and microwave for 1 1/2 minutes or until warm; whisk in the 1/2 cup sugar, salt and eggs. Add the egg mixture to the yeast mixture and mix well. Gradually work in the flour, mixing just until dough is no longer sticky. Let rise, covered, in a warm place until doubled in bulk. Punch the dough down. Shape into 36 balls. Place 3 balls in each of 24 greased muffin cups to make cloverleaf rolls. Let rise for 30 minutes. Bake at 350 degrees for 18 to 20 minutes or until golden brown. Yield: 2 dozen.

Dolores B. Mattson (40 years), Master Gamma
Spearfish, South Dakota

CORNMEAL ROLLS

My mother bakes these rolls on holidays, and we really look forward to having them.

1 envelope dry yeast	1/2 cup shortening
1/3 cup cornmeal	2 cups milk
1/2 cup sugar	2 eggs, beaten
2 teaspoons salt	4 cups flour

Dissolve the yeast in 1/4 cup warm water. Combine the cornmeal, sugar, salt, shortening and milk in a saucepan over medium-low heat; cook until thickened, stirring constantly. Remove from heat and let stand until slightly cooled. Combine the dissolved yeast, eggs and cornmeal mixture in a large bowl; beat at medium speed until smooth. Add enough flour, a little at a time, to make a soft dough. Knead lightly on a floured surface until smooth and elastic. Place in a greased bowl, turning to coat. Let rise, covered, in a warm place for 2 hours or until doubled in bulk. Punch the dough down. Roll to 1-inch thickness. Cut rounds with a biscuit cutter. Arrange the rounds on a greased baking sheet; brush with melted butter. Sprinkle with additional cornmeal. Let rise, covered, in a warm place until doubled in bulk. Bake at 375 degrees for 15 minutes or until golden and crispy. Yield: 1 1/2 dozen.

Stacy Smith, Xi Theta Zeta
Concordia, Missouri

GRANDMA'S HOT CLOVERLEAF ROLLS

Anything goes well with these melt-in-your-mouth hot rolls. My grandmother gave me this recipe and taught me a love for cooking. Whenever my Beta Sigma Phi sisters decide we will cater a planned meal, guess who makes the hot rolls? Not just one batch, but two or three. My sisters know I will do it because I love to cook, and I love to please people with my ability to cook.

3 tablespoons butter or	1 teaspoon salt
margarine	2 1/4 teaspoons or
2 cups milk	1 envelope dry yeast
2 tablespoons sugar	4 to 5 cups flour

Melt the butter in a large bowl in the microwave. Add the milk. Heat the butter and milk until baby-bottle-temperature warm; you will never kill the yeast if you follow that rule. Stir in the sugar, salt and yeast; stir until yeast is dissolved. Stir in the flour, 1 cup at a time, until dough forms a ball. Knead on a floured surface until smooth and elastic. Place in a greased bowl, turning to coat the surface. Let rise, covered, in a warm place for about 1 hour or until doubled in bulk. Punch the dough down. Shape into 1-inch balls. Place 3 balls in each of 18 greased muffin cups to make cloverleaf rolls. Let rise for 30 minutes. Bake at 350 degrees for 15 to 20 minutes or until golden brown. Brush butter over the tops of the rolls when they are removed from oven. Yield: 18 rolls.

Dawn Norwood, Xi Zeta Rho
Lamar, Missouri

BUTTERHORN ROLLS

This is one of the first breads I learned to bake, and after fifty years of marriage and trying other recipes, it is still everyone's favorite.

1 envelope dry yeast	1/2 cup melted butter
1 1/4 cups warm water	1/2 cup sugar
4 cups flour	1/2 teaspoon salt
2 eggs, well beaten	

Dissolve the yeast in the warm water. Mix flour, eggs, butter, sugar and salt in a large mixing bowl. Stir in the yeast mixture and mix well. Place in a greased bowl, turning to coat the surface. Let rise, covered, in a warm place until doubled in bulk. Punch the dough down. Roll into 1 or 2 circles. Cut into wedges; roll up from the wide ends. Shape into crescents on a greased baking sheet. Bake at 375 degrees for 20 minutes or until golden brown. Yield: 1 to 2 dozen.

Mildred Ormiston (51 years), Laureate Beta Eta
Kismet, Kansas

EASY-DOES-IT DOUGH

To make whole wheat bread, substitute whole wheat flour for half the bread flour.

1 cup warm (115 degrees) water	2 tablespoons vegetable oil
3 tablespoons sugar	1 teaspoon salt
1 envelope fast-rising yeast	2¹/₂ cups bread flour

Combine the water, sugar, yeast and vegetable oil in a large bowl; let stand for 10 minutes. Stir in the salt and flour, adding more flour if necessary to make a tacky dough. Place in a greased bowl, turning to coat the surface. Let rise, covered, in a warm place for 30 minutes. Punch the dough down. Shape into a loaf or rolls; or roll into a circle to make a pizza shell. Bake at 375 degrees for 25 minutes or until bread tests done. Yield: 1 loaf.

Marlene B. Lacey (35 years), Alpha Mu Master
Pueblo, Colorado

POTATO ROLLS

1 envelope yeast	3/4 cup sugar
1 cup warm water	1 teaspoon salt
1 cup mashed cooked potatoes	6 cups flour
	1 cup ice water
1 cup shortening	

Dissolve the yeast in the warm water. Combine the mashed potatoes, shortening, sugar and salt in a mixing bowl; beat until smooth. Stir in the yeast mixture. Let stand, covered, at room temperature for 2 hours. Add the flour and ice water alternately, mixing well after each addition. Let rise, covered, in a warm place for about 2 hours or until doubled in bulk. Punch the dough down and knead a few strokes. Let rise again until doubled in bulk; punch down and knead. Shape into 1-inch balls. Arrange in shallow baking pans that have been greased with shortening. Let rise until doubled in bulk. Bake at 450 degrees for 15 to 20 minutes or until browned. Yield: 3 dozen.

Margaret Doherty, Xi Alpha Alpha Omicron
Ennis, Texas

Gloria Olson (37 years), Laureate Gamma Kappa, Lakewood, Washington, shares her mother's prize **Thistledown Dumplings.** Sift 3/4 cup sifted flour, 2¹/₂ teaspoons baking powder and ¹/₂ teaspoon salt together. Whisk 1 egg and ¹/₃ cup milk together and mix gently into the flour mixture just until moistened. Drop by teaspoonfuls into simmering broth or gravy and simmer, tightly covered, for 15 minutes.

BAKING POWDER BISCUITS

This recipe for baking powder biscuits, although very simple, evokes many fond memories. These biscuits were a staple in our family, and I well remember my mother baking them every day. They are especially good when taken from the oven and served warm with beehive corn syrup.

3 cups flour	1 tablespoon lard
1 tablespoon baking powder	1¹/₂ cups milk
	1 cup shredded aged
Pinch of salt	Cheddar cheese

Stir together the flour, baking powder and salt in a large bowl. Cut in the lard until mixture resembles fine crumbs. Stir in 1 cup of the milk and the Cheddar cheese. Stir in the remaining ¹/₂ cup milk gradually, adding a little more if necessary to make the dough slightly moist. Roll quickly to ¹/₂-inch thickness. Cut into rounds with a water glass. Arrange on an ungreased baking sheet. Bake at 450 degrees for 11 to 12 minutes or until beginning to brown. Yield: About 15.

Marie Morrison, Alpha Eta
Nanton, Alberta, Canada

❖ AMISH FASNACHTS

3 envelopes yeast	1 cup sugar
3/4 cup warm water	2 eggs, beaten
Pinch of sugar	1 tablespoon salt
Pinch of nutmeg	1 quart milk, scalded
2 or 3 potatoes, peeled	5 pounds flour
¹/₂ cup shortening	Shortening for
¹/₂ cup (1 stick) margarine	deep-frying

Stir together the yeast, water, the pinch of sugar and nutmeg in a bowl. Cut the potatoes into large pieces. Boil in enough water to barely cover for 20 minutes or until tender. Mash the potatoes in the potato water. Measure 2 cups of the mashed potatoes. Combine the mashed potatoes, shortening, margarine, sugar, eggs, salt and yeast mixture in a large bowl. Add the flour and milk alternately to the potato mixture, mixing well after each addition. Knead on a floured surface for 10 minutes. Place in a very large greased bowl, turning to coat. Let rise, covered, in a warm place until doubled in bulk. Punch the dough down. Roll to ¹/₂-inch thickness. Cut into squares. Arrange the squares on baking sheets and let rise, covered, until doubled in bulk. Deep-fry until golden brown, turning once. Drain on paper towels and roll in confectioners' sugar. Yield: 100 doughnuts.

Sylvia Doyle (42 years), Preceptor Laureate Beta
Lancaster, Pennsylvania

MEMORIES

My mom never really emphasized cooking when I was a child, but my dad always loved to cook. Almost every weekend we would make a big breakfast. We would finish cooking at around ten o'clock and gather around the table and enjoy! He would usually get some help from my brother and me, as if he was teaching us how to cook! He did teach me how to make really great biscuits and gravy.

Melody Johnson, Theta Rho
Clarksville, Arkansas

LIGHTEST PANCAKES EVER

My mother-in-law has been a Beta Sigma Phi member for over fifty years. She lives in Eldon, Missouri, and is known as one of the best cooks around. Her recipes are passed on to everyone, and I hope everyone enjoys this recipe as we have.

3 eggs	2 tablespoons baking
1/3 cup sugar	powder
1/2 cup vegetable oil	1/2 teaspoon salt
1 1/3 cups buttermilk	2 cups sifted flour
1 tablespoon baking soda	1 1/3 cups sweet milk

Beat the eggs, sugar and vegetable oil in a mixing bowl. Stir in a mixture of the buttermilk, baking soda and baking powder. Stir in a mixture of the salt and flour. Stir in the sweet milk. Place in a pitcher to pour onto a hot, lightly greased griddle. Cook until bubbles appear on the surface and the underside is golden brown. Turn the pancake. Yield: 8 to 10 servings.

Shirley Wolfe, Preceptor Alpha Lambda
Springfield, Missouri

FRUITY FRENCH TOAST

1 loaf French bread	1 (20-ounce) package
5 eggs	frozen strawberries,
3/4 cup milk	thawed
1/4 teaspoon baking	4 ripe bananas, sliced
powder	1 cup sugar
1 tablespoon vanilla	1 tablespoon apple pie
extract	spice mix

Cut bread into 8 or more thick slices and place them in a deep bowl. Combine the eggs, milk, baking powder and vanilla in a bowl and whisk to blend. Pour the egg mixture over the bread. Chill, covered, for 8 to 10 hours. Mix together the strawberries, bananas, sugar and apple pie spice. Spread the strawberry mixture in a greased 9×13-inch baking dish. Layer the soaked bread over the fruit. Sprinkle with cinnamon sugar. Bake at 450 degrees for 20 to 25 minutes or until hot and lightly browned. Yield: 8 to 10 servings.

Margie McMilian (26 years), Laureate Pi
Independence, Missouri

OVEN FRENCH TOAST

1 (12-ounce) loaf French	1/2 teaspoon cinnamon
bread	1/2 cup (1 stick) butter,
8 eggs, beaten	softened
2 cups milk	1 cup packed brown
2 cups half-and-half	sugar
2 teaspoons vanilla	2 tablespoons dark corn
extract	syrup
1/2 teaspoon nutmeg	1 cup chopped pecans

Cut the bread into 1-inch-thick slices and layer in the bottom of a greased 9×13-inch baking dish. Combine the eggs, milk, half-and-half, vanilla, nutmeg and cinnamon in a large mixing bowl and beat until smooth. Pour the egg mixture evenly over the bread layer. Press down gently with a wooden spoon. Chill, covered, for 2 to 24 hours. Combine the butter, brown sugar, corn syrup and pecans in a small bowl and mix well. Spoon the butter mixture over the soaked bread. Bake, uncovered, at 325 degrees for 1 hour or until golden brown and puffed. Let stand for 15 minutes and serve. Yield: 10 to 12 servings.

Sheila Barthel, Xi Tau
Havre, Montana

BREAKFAST CEREAL

3 cups rolled oats	1/3 cup vegetable oil
1/2 cup wheat germ	1/3 cup honey
1/4 cup shredded coconut	1 teaspoon vanilla
2 teaspoons cinnamon	extract
1 cup chopped walnuts	4 cups cornflakes,
or almonds	crushed
2 tablespoons brown	1 cup crisp rice cereal
sugar	1/2 cup raisins

Combine the first 6 ingredients in a large bowl. Combine the vegetable oil, honey and vanilla in a small microwave-safe bowl. Microwave on High for 1 minute and stir until smooth. Drizzle the honey mixture over the oats mixture and stir until well mixed. Let the mixture cool. Stir in the cornflakes, crisp rice cereal and raisins. Yield: About 10 cups.

Diane Bright, Preceptor Xi Eta
Weldon, California

Cakes and Pies

When we talk about the sleepovers that we used
to have back in the early sixties, a fond memory that
my high school friends still recall concerns my
mother and her cooking. My mother made a great
four- to six-layer, freshly grated coconut cake with
seven-minute frosting and freshly grated coconut on top.
She served it on a dinner plate with a ladle of
homemade chicken and dumplings over the cake.
My girlfriends nearly died thinking how disgusting
it was, but, being nice young ladies, they accepted it and
were very surprised at what a wonderful combination
it turned out to be. After that, when I invited them,
they would request that my mother make coconut cake
to go with the chicken and dumplings. They enjoyed it
once they got over the initial shock!

Walda Weaver (37 years), Xi Gamma Omicron
Pryor, Oklahoma

CHOCOLATE CAKE WITH SEAFOAM ICING

My grandmother loved to bake cakes for her grand-children, and I never ever remember her not having a wonderful cake on the dining room buffet. She pre-pared this cake every Christmas Eve. My sister and I would sit and watch her prepare the Seafoam Icing, not truly understanding what seafoam icing could be. I use a packaged cake mix, but the icing is made the way my grandmother made it. Serve the cake with cold eggnog or custard.

1 (2-layer) package chocolate cake mix	2 egg whites
1 (1-pound) package brown sugar	1 teaspoon vanilla extract
	Pecan halves

Prepare and bake the cake mix using the package directions for two 8-inch-round cake pans. Let cool for 10 minutes. Place the brown sugar and egg whites in the top of a double boiler over boiling water. Cook while beating with an electric mixer until stiff peaks form. Mix in the vanilla. Spread the icing between the layers and over the top and side of the warm cake. Decorate cake top with pecan halves.
Yield: 8 servings.

Phyllis N. Crim (30 years), Preceptor Beta Gamma
Prairieville, Louisiana

MOM'S ONE-PAN CHOCOLATE CAKE

My mom made this delicious cake often when I was a small girl. It was fun to help put the ingredients in the holes and listen to the vinegar bubble.

3 cups flour	1 tablespoon vanilla extract
2 cups sugar	2/3 cup vegetable oil
9 tablespoons baking cocoa	2 tablespoons vinegar
2 teaspoons baking soda	2 cups water
1 teaspoon salt	

Sift the flour, sugar, baking cocoa, baking soda and salt into a greased 8×8-inch cake pan. Make 3 holes in the flour mixture. Pour the vanilla into one hole, the vegetable oil into the second and the vinegar into the third. Pour the water over the entire mixture and whisk until well blended. Bake at 325 degrees for 20 to 25 minutes or until a wooden pick inserted in the center comes out clean. Frost as desired.
Yield: 9 to 12 servings.

Kim Morrison, Tau Omega
Macedonia, Ohio

GRANDMA'S DARK CHOCOLATE CAKE

My maternal grandmother's family lived on a farm where they milked cows, gardened, and raised dogs and chickens. Every Christmas Grandma baked this cake with its raisin filling and fudge frosting—it made Christmas very special.

2 ounces baker's unsweetened chocolate	2 1/2 cups flour
	2 eggs
	1 teaspoon baking soda
2 egg yolks	1 cup heavy cream
2 cups sugar	1 (16-ounce) package raisins
2 3/4 cups milk	
1/2 cup (1 stick) butter	Fudge Frosting
2/3 cup buttermilk	

Combine the chocolate, the 2 egg yolks, 1 cup of the sugar, milk and butter in a heavy saucepan. Bring to the boiling point, stirring constantly; remove from heat. Stir in a mixture of the buttermilk, flour, 2 eggs and baking soda. Spoon the batter into two 8- or 9-inch cake pans. Bake at 350 degrees for 25 minutes or until a wooden pick inserted in the center comes out clean. Remove to a wire rack to cool. Combine the heavy cream and remaining 1 cup sugar in a heavy saucepan. Bring just to the boiling point, stirring con-stantly. Remove from heat. Stir in the raisins. Cool slightly. Spread between the cake layers. Frost the cake with the Fudge Frosting. Yield: 12 servings.

FUDGE FROSTING

1 1/4 cups sugar	2 teaspoons (heaping) baking cocoa
Pinch of salt	1/3 to 1/2 cup milk
1/4 cup plus 1 teaspoon (level) shortening	

Combine the sugar, salt, shortening, baking cocoa and 1/3 cup milk in a heavy saucepan and bring to a boil, stirring constantly. Boil for 1 minute and remove from heat. Beat at medium-high speed until mixture is of spreading consistency, adding more milk if necessary.

Sandra McIntyre, Preceptor Gamma Mu
Waterville, Kansas

Carolyn M. Hughes (47 years), Xi Alpha Mu, Flagstaff, Arizona, makes a **Black Russian Cake** by mixing a yellow cake mix with 1/2 cup sugar and a large package of chocolate instant pudding mix and adding 1 cup vegetable oil, 4 eggs, 1/4 cup each vodka and Kahlúa and 3/4 cup water. Beat for 4 minutes. Bake in a greased and floured bundt pan for 45 to 55 minutes, invert and sprinkle with confectioners' sugar.

MEMORIES

We were a family of nine and our mother would make a chocolate cake each week from scratch. She would cut just nine pieces for a meal and one of my brothers would study each piece to see which one was the largest. Then he would mark it and claim it as his.

Martha Baumgartner (58 years), Preceptor Rho
Fort Wayne, Indiana

BEST CHOCOLATE CAKE EVER

When preparing the cake mixes, remember to double the ingredient amounts listed on a single package.

2 (2-layer) packages Swiss chocolate cake mix	2 (16-ounce) packages milk chocolate frosting
2 teaspoons vanilla extract	1/2 cup broken walnuts
2 tablespoons butter flavoring	2 tablespoons shortening
1 teaspoon salt	1 cup semisweet chocolate chips

Prepare the cake mixes using the package directions. Add the vanilla, butter flavoring and salt; beat at low speed until batter is smooth. Pour the batter into a buttered and floured tube pan. Bake at 350 degrees for about 1 hour or until cake tests done. Cool in the pan. Invert onto a serving plate and frost the cooled cake. Decorate top and side with walnuts. Let the cake stand for 2 hours. Melt the shortening and chocolate chips; mix until smooth. Drizzle the chocolate chip mixture over the cake. Yield: 16 servings.

JoAnn Bauer, Eta Nu
Morrisville, Pennsylvania

AUNT LORETTA'S FUDGE CAKE

My Aunt Loretta was one of the best cooks I have ever known.

2 1/2 cups sugar	1 cup buttermilk
3/4 cup vegetable oil	1 teaspoon vanilla extract
2 eggs	1 cup boiling water
2 1/2 cups flour	2 teaspoons baking soda
1/2 cup baking cocoa	Fluffy Cocoa Frosting
1/2 teaspoon salt	

Combine the sugar, vegetable oil and eggs in a mixing bowl and beat until smooth. Sift the flour, baking cocoa and salt together. Add to the egg mixture alternately with the buttermilk, mixing well after each addition. Stir in the vanilla. Stir in a mixture of the boiling water and baking soda. Pour the batter into a greased and floured bundt pan or 9×13-inch cake pan. Bake at 350 degrees for 40 to 45 minutes or until cake tests done. Spread Fluffy Cocoa Frosting over the cooled cake. Yield: 16 servings.

FLUFFY COCOA FROSTING

3/4 cup baking cocoa	1 teaspoon vanilla extract
1 (1-pound) package confectioners' sugar	1/2 cup evaporated milk
1/2 cup (1 stick) margarine	

Mix together the baking cocoa and confectioners' sugar. Cream the margarine and half the cocoa mixture in a mixing bowl until light and fluffy. Blend in the vanilla and half the evaporated milk. Blend in the remaining cocoa mixture and the remaining evaporated milk. Beat until mixture is of desired consistency, adding more milk if necessary.

Beverly Land (28 years), Laureate Delta Delta
Parkville, Missouri

BUTTERMILK CHOCOLATE CAKE

This yummy cake can be frosted while still hot and served warm if desired.

3/4 cup margarine	3 cups sugar
3/4 cup shortening	3 cups flour
6 tablespoons baking cocoa	3/4 cup buttermilk
1 1/2 cups water	1 1/2 teaspoons baking soda
3 eggs, beaten	
1 1/2 teaspoons vanilla extract	

Combine the margarine, shortening, baking cocoa and water in a heavy saucepan and bring to the boiling point, stirring frequently; remove from heat. Mix in the eggs, vanilla, sugar, flour and a mixture of the buttermilk and baking soda. Pour into a generously greased and floured 9×13-inch cake pan. Bake at 400 degrees for 25 minutes or until cake tests done. Frost and serve. Yield: 15 servings.

Shirlene Cusolito (36 years), Alpha Alpha
Ruidoso Downs, New Mexico

MEMORIES

My sister and I decided to bake a cake for our parents' 25th wedding anniversary. She was twelve and I was nine. As we read the recipe, we saw it called for "confectioners' sugar." We knew what powdered sugar was, so we assumed that confectioners' sugar was another name for regular sugar. Our extremely sweet cake should have been labeled "uneatable," but our folks raved and ate the sickening sweet mess, proving once again what people will do for love!

Ann Hall, Xi Theta Beta
Oak Grove, Missouri

BAKED CHOCOLATE PUDDING CAKE

Serve with ice cream or whipped cream.

1 cup flour	3 tablespoons baking
2 teaspoons baking	cocoa
powder	2 tablespoons butter,
3/4 cup sugar	softened
1/2 cup milk	1 teaspoon vanilla
1/2 cup chopped walnuts	extract
or pecans (optional)	Cocoa Topping
1/2 teaspoon salt	

Combine the flour, baking powder, sugar, milk, walnuts, salt, baking cocoa, butter and vanilla in a bowl and mix well. Spread the batter in a greased 9×9-inch cake pan. Drizzle the Cocoa Topping over the batter. Bake at 350 degrees for 35 to 45 minutes or until cake tests done. Yield: 9 servings.

COCOA TOPPING

1/2 cup sugar	1/4 cup baking cocoa
1/2 cup packed brown	1 cup hot water
sugar	

Combine the sugar, brown sugar and baking cocoa in a bowl and mix well. Drizzle the hot water over the sugar mixture; mix well.

Angela Tieskotter
Humeston, Iowa

CHOCOLATE SHEET CAKE

2 cups sugar	1/2 cup milk
2 cups flour	2 tablespoons vinegar
1/2 teaspoon salt	2 eggs
1 cup water	1 teaspoon vanilla
1/2 cup (1 stick)	extract
margarine	1 teaspoon baking soda
1/2 cup vegetable oil	Chocolate Icing
1/4 cup baking cocoa	

Sift the sugar, flour and salt into a large bowl. Combine the water, margarine, vegetable oil and baking cocoa in a saucepan and bring to the boiling point. Pour a mixture of the milk, vinegar, eggs, vanilla and baking soda over the dry ingredients. Stir in the hot cocoa mixture. Spread in a greased and floured 10×15-inch cake pan. Bake at 400 degrees for 20 minutes. Spread Chocolate Icing over the hot cake. Yield: 15 servings.

CHOCOLATE ICING

1/2 cup (1 stick)	1/2 teaspoon vanilla
margarine	extract
1/4 cup baking cocoa	1/2 cup chopped walnuts
1/3 cup milk	or pecans
1 (1-pound) package	
confectioners' sugar	

Combine the margarine, baking cocoa and milk in a saucepan and bring to a boil. Remove from heat and mix in the confectioners' sugar, vanilla and walnuts.

Teresa Ray, Theta
Vincennes, Indiana

LOW-FAT CHOCOLATE PUDDING CAKE

You may use 1% milk when preparing the pudding.

1 (4-ounce) package	1/2 cup crushed walnuts
chocolate sugar-free	or pecans (optional)
pudding mix	1/2 cup chocolate chips
1 (2-layer) package	(optional)
low-fat chocolate	
cake mix	

Prepare the pudding mix in a mixing bowl using the package directions. Add the dry cake mix and beat until smooth. Pour into a greased and floured 9×13-inch cake pan. Sprinkle walnuts and chocolate chips over the top. Bake at 350 degrees for 25 to 30 minutes or until cake tests done. Yield: 15 servings.

Christina Duffy, Delta Omicron
Mason, New Hampshire

MICROWAVE CHOCOLATE CAKE

This cake is so good, and I make it while I am preparing dinner. Sometimes I serve it with whipped topping instead of the Chocolate Sauce.

1 1/2 cups flour	1 cup cold water
1 cup sugar	1/3 cup vegetable oil
3 tablespoons baking cocoa	1 tablespoon vinegar
1/4 teaspoon salt	1 teaspoon vanilla extract
1 teaspoon baking soda	Chocolate Sauce

Combine the flour, sugar, baking cocoa, salt and baking soda in a bowl; mix well. Add the water, vegetable oil, vinegar and vanilla; mix well. Spread in an ungreased 8-inch-square microwave-safe dish. Microwave on High for 6 to 8 minutes or until a wooden pick inserted near the center comes out clean, turning the dish every 2 minutes. Pour the hot Chocolate Sauce evenly over the warm cake. Yield: 12 servings.

CHOCOLATE SAUCE

1 cup sugar	1 cup boiling water
3 tablespoons cornstarch	Dash of salt
2 tablespoons baking cocoa	1 tablespoon butter
	1 teaspoon vanilla extract

Combine the sugar, cornstarch and baking cocoa in a 1-quart microwave-safe bowl. Stir in the boiling water and salt. Microwave on High for 2 to 3 minutes or until mixture boils, stirring once or twice. Microwave for 1 minute. Stir in the butter and vanilla.

Norma Jean Jones (39 years), Epsilon Master
Broken Arrow, Oklahoma

POTATO DEVIL'S FOOD CHOCOLATE CAKE

1 (2-layer) package devil's food cake mix	1 cup unsalted mashed cooked potatoes
3 eggs	2 (16-ounce) cans coconut pecan frosting
1/2 cup vegetable oil	
1 1/3 cups water	

Prepare the cake batter using 3 eggs, 1/2 cup vegetable oil, 1 1/3 cups water and mashed potatoes. Pour the batter into 2 greased and floured 9-inch cake pans. Bake at 350 degrees for 30 to 40 minutes or until a wooden pick inserted in the center comes out clean. Spread the frosting between the layers and over the top and side of the cooled cake. Yield: 12 servings.

Betty Arlene Fox, Preceptor Iota Iota
Houston, Texas

MEMORIES

I made a cake shaped like a running shoe for my daughter's birthday because she had recently completed a triathalon. As we were sitting down and I was cutting the cake, I realized I didn't have my camera to catch the "Kodak moment." While I was out of the room, my other daughter's boyfriend cut a piece of the cake and took a bite! Well, needless to say, we pieced the cake back together and a photo was taken along with lots of laughter!

Jennifer Kobayashi, Laureate Alpha Phi
Surrey, British Columbia, Canada

BUTTERMILK DEVIL'S FOOD CAKE

2 cups sifted flour	1 1/4 cups buttermilk
1 7/8 cups sugar	3 eggs
1 teaspoon baking soda	2 1/2 ounces unsweetened chocolate, melted
1 teaspoon salt	
2/3 cup shortening	

Sift the flour, sugar, baking soda and salt into a large mixing bowl. Add the shortening and a little more than 1/2 of the buttermilk. Beat at medium speed for 2 minutes. Add the remaining buttermilk, eggs and melted chocolate. Beat for 2 minutes longer. Pour the batter into 2 greased and floured 8- or 9-inch cake pans. Bake at 350 degrees for 30 to 35 minutes or until cake tests done. Spread Penuche Icing between the layers and over the top and side of the cooled cake. Yield: 12 servings.

PENUCHE ICING

2 2/3 cups packed brown sugar	2/3 cup shortening
2/3 cup milk	1/3 teaspoon salt

Combine the brown sugar, milk, shortening and salt in a saucepan over low heat; stir well. Turn heat to high and bring rapidly to a full boil, stirring constantly. Boil at 220 degrees for exactly 1 minute. Remove from heat. Beat until the mixture loses its gloss, is lukewarm and of spreading consistency.

Cheryl Shatzer, Alpha Phi
Paris, Missouri

THREE-CHOCOLATE CHERRY CAKE

Very easy.

1 (4-ounce) package chocolate cook-and-serve pudding	2 cups milk
1 (2-layer) package chocolate cake mix (without pudding)	2 (15-ounce) cans pitted dark sweet cherries
1 cup semisweet chocolate chips	1/2 cup sugar
	2 tablespoons lemon juice
	1/4 cup cornstarch
	1/4 cup rum (optional)

Prepare and cook the pudding mix in a saucepan using the package directions. Remove from heat to a mixing bowl. Stir in the dry cake mix and beat until well mixed and glossy. Stir in half the chocolate chips. Spread the chocolate mixture in a greased and floured 9×13-inch cake pan; sprinkle with the remaining chocolate chips. Bake at 350 degrees for 25 to 35 minutes or until top springs back when touched lightly. Combine the undrained cherries, sugar, lemon juice, cornstarch and rum in a saucepan over medium heat. Cook until thickened, stirring constantly. Serve over individual pieces of cake. Yield: 12 large servings.

Jean Milnes, Laureate Xi
Coldwater, Michigan

CHOCOLATE APPLESAUCE CAKE

This recipe has been in our family for over thirty years. Dad calls it his "going-away cake" because Mom makes it for him when she is going out of town to visit my sister.

1/2 cup shortening	1 (16-ounce) can applesauce
1 cup sugar	1/4 cup sugar
2 eggs	1 cup semisweet chocolate chips
2 cups flour	1 cup chopped walnuts (optional)
1/2 teaspoon cinnamon	
1/2 teaspoon salt	
11/2 teaspoons baking soda	
3 tablespoons baking cocoa	

Cream the shortening and the 1 cup sugar in a mixing bowl until light and fluffy. Add the eggs, flour, cinnamon, salt, baking soda, baking cocoa and applesauce and mix well. Pour the batter into a greased 9×13-inch cake pan. Sprinkle with a mixture of the 1/4 cup sugar, chocolate chips and walnuts. Bake at 350 degrees for 30 minutes. Yield: 12 to 15 servings.

Tracy Kaufman, Preceptor Delta Delta
Leawood, Kansas

CHOCOLATE BEET CAKE

Kids love this cake; they can't taste the beets! Serve with peppermint icing or a dollop of whipped topping.

11/2 cups sugar	1/4 teaspoon peppermint extract
2 large eggs	6 tablespoons baking cocoa
1 cup vegetable oil	13/4 cups flour
1 (19-ounce) can beets, drained, mashed	11/2 teaspoons baking soda
1 teaspoon vanilla extract	

Combine the sugar and eggs in a large mixing bowl. Stir in the vegetable oil, beets, vanilla and peppermint extract. Add the baking cocoa, flour and baking soda. Beat at medium speed for 2 minutes, scraping down the side of the bowl occasionally. Spread in a buttered 9×9-inch cake pan. Bake at 350 degrees for 45 to 50 minutes or until a wooden pick inserted in the center comes out clean. Yield: 10 to 12 servings.

Dianne Fleming, Xi Eta Nu
Deep River, Ontario, Canada

SOUR CREAM CHOCOLATE CAKE

My mother, who was born in 1911, used to make this cake the old-fashioned way. She was so happy when "instant" pudding came out, and was even happier when she could buy cake mix. She served this cake at every occasion with ice cream on the side.

4 ounces German's sweet chocolate	1/2 cup water
1 (2-layer) package yellow cake mix	4 large eggs
1 (3-ounce) package vanilla instant pudding mix	1 cup dairy sour cream
1/2 cup vegetable oil	1 cup semisweet chocolate chips
	1 cup chopped pecans
	1 cup shredded coconut

Break the chocolate into pieces and chop fine or process in a food processor for 10 to 15 seconds or until it appears grated. Combine the cake mix, pudding mix, vegetable oil and water in a large mixing bowl. Add the eggs 1 at a time, mixing well after each addition. Stir in the sour cream, grated chocolate, chocolate chips, pecans and coconut. Spoon the batter into a well-greased bundt or tube pan. Bake at 350 degrees for 55 to 60 minutes or until a tester or broom straw inserted in the center comes out clean. Spread frosting of choice over the cooled cake. You may press pecan halves into the cake or sprinkle with additional coconut if desired. Yield: 12 servings.

Eve Oppedisano, Epsilon Xi
Page, Arizona

MEMORIES

A sorority sister and very good friend of mine decided to make a special birthday cake for her daughter's first birthday. We made the cake and cut the pieces to form a clown with a pointed hat. We worked for hours decorating the cake with bright colored frosting. We sat the beautiful clown cake in front of her and she started crying and screaming. She was scared of the clown face cake! We ended up cutting off a little piece of white cake and put it on a plate with her candle in it. She wanted nothing to do with the clown cake at all.

Cynthia Jeffords, Preceptor Beta Nu
Swain, New York

GRANDMA'S SPOTTED CAKE

I bake this cake for our family get-togethers. My granddaughter came up with the name when she was three.

1 (2-layer) package
   white cake mix
1 (2-layer) package
   chocolate cake mix
3 tablespoons butter,
   melted
4 cups confectioners'
   sugar
Milk
1 cup miniature
   chocolate chips

Prepare the cake batter using the directions on the packages, using a separate bowl for each flavor. Drop large tablespoons of the white cake batter in a checkerboard pattern into a greased 12×18-inch cake pan. Drop large tablespoons of the chocolate cake batter in the holes left by the white cake batter. Draw a knife through the batter several times in each direction until the top looks like marble. Bake for 35 to 40 minutes or until edges begin to pull away from the sides of the pan. Combine the butter, confectioners' sugar and enough milk to make of a spreading consistency in a bowl; mix well. Frost the cooled cake with the butter frosting and sprinkle with the chocolate chips. Yield: 35 to 40 servings.

Mary Connor (30 years), Preceptor Xi
Devils Lake, North Dakota

APPLE CAKE

This recipe was originally my eighty-three-year-old mother's. I've been baking and eating it for over forty years. One bite and you'll want the recipe!

1½ cups sugar
1 cup vegetable oil
2 eggs
1 egg white
1 teaspoon vanilla
   extract
2 cups flour
½ teaspoon salt
1 teaspoon baking soda
2 teaspoons cinnamon
3 cups chopped peeled
   apples
1 cup chopped walnuts
   or pecans
Vanilla Frosting

Combine the sugar and vegetable oil in a mixing bowl and blend. Mix in the eggs, egg white and vanilla. Add a mixture of the flour, salt, baking soda and cinnamon; blend well. Stir in the apples and walnuts. Spread the batter in a greased 9×13-inch cake pan. Bake at 350 degrees for 40 minutes. Frost with Vanilla Frosting. Yield: 12 to 15 servings.

VANILLA FROSTING

½ cup (1 stick)
   margarine, softened
1½ cups confectioners'
   sugar, sifted
1 egg yolk
½ teaspoon vanilla
   extract

Beat the margarine, confectioners' sugar, egg yolk and vanilla in a mixing bowl until smooth.

Fran Bushfield, Xi Eta Eta
Harrison City, Pennsylvania

MOM'S APPLESAUCE CAKE

1 cup sugar
½ cup shortening
1½ cups applesauce
1 teaspoon vanilla
   extract
1 egg, beaten
2 cups sifted flour
½ teaspoon salt
1 tablespoon cinnamon
½ teaspoon ground
   cloves
2 teaspoons baking soda
¾ cup raisins
½ cup chopped walnuts
   or pecans (optional)

Combine the sugar, shortening and applesauce in a saucepan; bring to the boiling point. Remove from heat and cool slightly. Combine the applesauce mixture, vanilla and egg in a mixing bowl; mix well. Stir in a mixture of the flour, salt, cinnamon, cloves and baking soda. Fold in the raisins and walnuts. Spread in a greased 9×13-inch cake pan. Bake at 350 degrees for 30 minutes or until cake tests done.
Yield: 10 to 12 servings.

Jerry Lee Lalonde (39 years), Preceptor Beta Rho
Spokane, Washington

MEMORIES

My mother taught herself how to cook and over the years shared her cooking with friends and family. She loved her kitchen, going from a wood stove to a gas stove. I learned to cook from her and so did my children. She entered her baked goods into the Medocino County Fair each year and always won first, second or third prize.

Sylvia Farebrother (34 years), Preceptor Xi Epsilon
Harlingen, Texas

❖ BANANAS FOSTER CAKE

I prepare my sister's birthday dinner every year, and every year she requests a feast New Orleans style—shrimp Creole or jambalaya, dirty rice, corn bread, and Bananas Foster for dessert. After years of either setting the kitchen on fire or not being able to get the pan to "flambé" correctly, I decided to try the dessert as a cake. She liked it so much last year that she's informed me she wants it again this year . . . and next year . . . and the year after that . . .

1/3 cup butter	1/2 cup (1 stick) butter,
1 cup light brown sugar	melted
1/2 teaspoon cinnamon	1 1/2 cups milk
4 to 6 tablespoons rum	2 eggs
3 large bananas, sliced	
1 (2-layer) package	
butter cake mix	
(without pudding)	

Lightly butter the side of a 10-inch cast iron skillet or 10-inch-round cake pan. Melt the 1/3 cup butter in the skillet over low heat. Remove from heat and add the brown sugar, cinnamon and 2 to 4 tablespoons rum; spread the rum mixture over the bottom of the skillet with a fork. Layer banana slices in the skillet to cover the rum mixture. Combine the cake mix, the 1/2 cup butter, milk, eggs and the remaining 2 tablespoons rum in a mixing bowl; mix until smooth. Pour the milk mixture carefully over the banana layer. Bake at 350 degrees for 45 minutes or until top springs back when touched lightly. Remove from oven. Run a knife around the edge to release the cake. Invert onto a serving plate. Serve with vanilla ice cream and toasted slivered almonds. Yield: 10 to 12 servings.

Cindy Lefler, Xi Beta Epsilon
Haddonfield, New Jersey

BANANA CAKE

This moist cake may be eaten and enjoyed with no frosting or topping, although you may serve with fresh sliced bananas and whipped cream if you prefer. If you have no sour milk, stir 2 teaspoons lemon juice or vinegar into fresh milk.

1/2 cup (1 stick) butter,	1 teaspoon vanilla
softened	extract
1 1/2 cups sugar	1 cup mashed ripe
1/2 teaspoon salt	bananas
1/2 teaspoon baking	1/4 cup sour milk
powder	2 eggs, beaten
2 cups flour	separately
3/4 teaspoon baking soda	

Cream the butter and sugar in a mixing bowl until light and fluffy. Add the salt, baking powder, flour, baking soda, vanilla, mashed bananas and sour milk; mix well. Fold in the eggs 1 at a time. Spread in a greased and floured 9×13-inch cake pan. Bake at 375 degrees for 30 minutes. Cool and cut into squares. Yield: 15 servings.

Sylvia A. Swanson, Xi Alpha Xi
Burnsville, Minnesota

BLACKBERRY WINE CAKE

1 (2-layer) white cake	1/2 cup vegetable oil
mix	1 cup blackberry wine
1 (3-ounce) package	1/2 cup chopped pecans
blackberry gelatin	Blackberry Wine Glaze
4 eggs	

Combine the dry cake mix, dry gelatin mix, eggs, vegetable oil and blackberry wine in a mixing bowl. Beat at low speed for 30 seconds; beat at medium speed for 2 minutes. Sprinkle the pecans in the bottom of a greased and floured bundt pan. Pour the batter into the pan. Bake at 325 degrees for 45 to 50 minutes or until cake tests done. Pour half the Blackberry Wine Glaze over the warm cake in the pan; let stand for 30 minutes. Invert onto a serving plate and drizzle the remaining glaze over the cake. Yield: 10 to 12 servings.

BLACKBERRY WINE GLAZE

1/2 cup butter	1 cup confectioners'
1/2 cup blackberry wine	sugar

Melt the butter in a heavy saucepan over medium-high heat. Stir in the remaining ingredients. Bring to a boil, stirring frequently.

Paula Lyens (41 years), Preceptor Epsilon Theta
Treasure Island, Florida

CARROT COCONUT CAKE

2 cups flour
2½ teaspoons baking
   soda
2 teaspoons cinnamon
1 teaspoon salt
1 cup vegetable oil
2 cups sugar
3 eggs

1 (8-ounce) can crushed
   pineapple, drained
1⅓ cups shredded
   carrots
2 cups shredded coconut
½ cup chopped pecans
Cream Cheese Frosting

Combine the flour, baking soda, cinnamon and salt in a large mixing bowl. Combine the vegetable oil, sugar and eggs in a medium bowl; blend well. Add the egg mixture to the flour mixture; beat until smooth. Stir in the pineapple, carrots, coconut and pecans. Spread in a greased 9×13-inch cake pan. Bake at 350 degrees for 50 minutes or until cake tests done. Frost the cooled cake with Cream Cheese Frosting. Yield: 15 servings.

CREAM CHEESE FROSTING

⅓ cup butter, softened
8 ounces cream cheese,
   softened
½ teaspoon vanilla
   extract

1 (1-pound) package
   confectioners' sugar

Combine the butter, cream cheese and vanilla in a mixing bowl; beat until smooth and creamy. Add the confectioners' sugar; beat until smooth.

Kathy L. Thompson, Preceptor Chi
Pineville, West Virginia

AUNT CARRIE'S CARROT CAKE

Great-Aunt Carrie was a wonderful cook who cooked and baked on a coal stove. I will always remember our family visits to her home and the wonderful aromas that came from her kitchen.

2 cups sugar
1½ cups vegetable oil
2¼ cups flour
4 eggs
2 teaspoons baking soda
2 teaspoons cinnamon

½ teaspoon salt
2½ cups grated carrots
   (not packed)
½ cup chopped pecans
Maple Cream Cheese
   Frosting

Beat the sugar, vegetable oil, flour and eggs in a large bowl until smooth. Add the baking soda, cinnamon and salt; mix well. Stir in the carrots and pecans. Spread in a greased and floured 9×13-inch cake pan. Bake at 350 degrees for 50 minutes or until cake tests done. Frost the cooled cake with Maple Cream Cheese Frosting. Yield: 12 or more servings.

MAPLE CREAM CHEESE FROSTING

8 ounces cream cheese,
   softened
¼ cup (½ stick) butter,
   softened

1 (1-pound) package
   confectioners' sugar
1 tablespoon maple
   extract

Combine the cream cheese, butter, confectioners' sugar and maple extract in a mixing bowl. Beat until smooth.

Kitty A. Maurer (31 years), Laureate Epsilon Sigma
Chambersburg, Pennsylvania

CHERRY NUT POUND CAKE

My teenage son could bake this cake better than I could. The last time he baked it was for a church charity. It sold before he could set it down for $25.00. That was sixteen years ago, and he died shortly after. The cake hasn't been made since; it will always be his cake.

1½ cups shortening
3 cups sugar
6 eggs
½ teaspoon each
   almond and vanilla
   extract

3¾ cups flour
¾ cup milk
5 ounces maraschino
   cherries, drained,
   chopped
Coconut Cherry Frosting

Cream the shortening and sugar in a mixing bowl until light and fluffy; beat for 10 to 15 minutes. Beat in the eggs 1 at a time. Blend in the almond and vanilla extracts. Add the flour to the creamed mixture alternately with the milk, mixing well after each addition. Stir in the cherries. Pour into a greased tube pan and place in an unheated oven. Turn oven heat to 275 degrees and bake for 2 hours and 10 minutes. Frost the cooled cake with Coconut Cherry Frosting. Garnish with a few whole cherries and a little coconut of desired. Yield: 16 servings.

COCONUT CHERRY FROSTING

8 ounces cream cheese,
   room temperature
¼ cup (½ stick) butter,
   room temperature
1 teaspoon almond
   extract
1 teaspoon vanilla
   extract

1 (1-pound) package
   confectioners' sugar
1 cup shredded coconut
1 cup chopped walnuts
5 ounces maraschino
   cherries, drained,
   chopped

Combine the cream cheese, butter, almond extract and vanilla in a mixing bowl; beat until creamy. Add the confectioners' sugar gradually, beating until smooth. Fold in the coconut, walnuts and cherries.

Linda McConnell, Preceptor Iota Sigma
Carrollton, Texas

PUMPKIN SPICE CAKE

When I came home from school and Mother had baked this cake, the wonderful aroma came all the way out to the gate and made me feel happy all over.

1/2 cup (1 stick) margarine	1 teaspoon cinnamon
1 1/4 cups sugar	1/2 teaspoon ginger
2 eggs, well beaten	1/2 teaspoon nutmeg
2 1/4 cups sifted flour	1 teaspoon salt
1/2 teaspoon baking soda	1 cup canned pumpkin
2 1/2 teaspoons baking powder	3/4 cup milk
	1/2 cup chopped walnuts or pecans

Cream the margarine and sugar in a mixing bowl until light and fluffy. Blend in the eggs. Sift the flour, baking soda, baking powder, cinnamon, ginger, nutmeg and salt into a bowl. Add to the egg mixture alternately with a mixture of the pumpkin and milk, mixing well after each addition. Stir in the chopped nuts. Spread the batter in two 9-inch cake pans that have been sprayed with nonstick cooking spray. Bake at 350 degrees for 30 minutes or until cakes test done. Frost the cooled cake with your favorite butter frosting, using orange juice and grated orange zest for added flavor. Yield: 12 servings.

Betty B. Stevenson (35 years), Xi Kappa
Corvallis, Oregon

GRANDMA'S RAISIN CAKE

1 pound seedless raisins	3 tablespoons lard or 1/4 cup shortening
1 (1-pound) package dark brown sugar	1 teaspoon salt
1 teaspoon ground cloves	1 teaspoon baking soda
1 teaspoon cinnamon	3 cups flour
1 teaspoon allspice	Brown Sugar Frosting

Combine the raisins, brown sugar, cloves, cinnamon, allspice, lard, salt and 2 cups water in a kettle and bring to a boil. Boil gently for 5 minutes; remove from heat. Whisk the baking soda into 1/2 cup cold water and stir into the cooled raisin mixture. Stir in the flour. Pour into a greased tube pan. Bake at 350 degrees for 1 hour and 15 minutes. Frost with Brown Sugar Frosting. Yield: 16 servings.

BROWN SUGAR FROSTING

1 (1-pound) package light brown sugar	1 (5-ounce) can evaporated milk
1/2 cup (1 stick) margarine	

Combine the brown sugar, margarine and evaporated milk in a heavy saucepan. Cook over medium heat to 234 to 240 degrees on a candy thermometer, soft-ball stage. Let cool before frosting the cake.

Arlette S. Hiler (25 years), Xi Alpha Iota
Gretna, Virginia

LUNAR RHUBARB CAKE

This very old recipe has been in the family for many years. If you have no buttermilk, use 1 or 2% milk with a drop of vinegar.

1/2 cup (1 stick) butter	1 teaspoon baking soda
1 1/2 cups sugar	1/2 teaspoon salt
1 egg	1 cup buttermilk
1 teaspoon vanilla extract	2 cups (1/2-inch) rhubarb pieces
2 cups flour	Cinnamon Topping

Cream the butter and sugar in a mixing bowl until light and fluffy. Mix in the egg and vanilla. Sift the flour, baking soda and salt into a bowl. Add the sifted dry ingredients and buttermilk to the egg mixture alternately, mixing well after each addition. Toss the rhubarb with 1 tablespoon flour and fold into the batter. Spoon into a greased 9×13-inch cake pan. Sprinkle evenly with Cinnamon Topping. Bake at 350 degrees for 45 minutes. Yield: 15 servings.

CINNAMON TOPPING

1/4 cup (1/2 stick) butter	1 cup packed brown sugar
2 teaspoons cinnamon	

Cut the butter into a mixture of the cinnamon and brown sugar until mixture resembles coarse crumbs.

Nancy Leduc, Preceptor Zeta Alpha
Tweed, Ontario, Canada

MEMORIES

My memories of Beta are of food, sisters, laughing and friendship. I am a Legacy (nine years going on ten) full-fledged sister. I was brought up by sisters in Beta and couldn't ask for a better family. My fondest memories are of helping to prepare for sorority night—the cleaning, cooking and waiting for that doorbell to ring. It's like coming home all over again!

Charlena M. Wilson, Xi Lambda Theta
Canton, Ohio

STRAWBERRY RHUBARB CAKE

My grandmother used to make this delicious cake in the summer when we would visit her. Now it's my turn to make it for my children.

4 cups chopped rhubarb	1 (2-layer) yellow cake
1 cup sugar	mix
4 cups small	1/2 cup packed brown
marshmallows	sugar
3 tablespoons dry	1/2 teaspoon cinnamon
strawberry gelatin	

Layer the rhubarb, sugar, marshmallows and dry gelatin mix in a greased 9×13-inch cake pan in the order listed. Prepare the yellow cake batter using the package directions. Pour the batter evenly over the gelatin layer. Sprinkle with a mixture of the brown sugar and cinnamon. Bake at 350 degrees for 35 to 40 minutes or until cake tests done. Cool and serve with whipped topping. Yield: 15 servings.

Paula Stark, Beta Delta
Waukesha, Wisconsin

MEMORIES

When my sister and I were around the ages of eight and ten we made a layer cake for a family birthday gathering. We used an inch of salt instead of a pinch of salt! I don't remember anyone refusing a piece, but I doubt they went back for seconds.

Janice Cygan, Preceptor Beta Xi
Webster, New York

STRAWBERRY SUPREME CAKE

1 (2-layer) package	1 (10-ounce) package
white cake mix	frozen strawberries,
1 (3-ounce) package	thawed
strawberry	1/4 cup (1/2 stick) butter,
gelatin	softened
1/2 cup vegetable oil	3/4 (1-pound) package
4 eggs	confectioners' sugar

Combine the dry cake mix, dry gelatin mix, vegetable oil, eggs, 3/4 of the strawberries and 1/4 cup water in a large mixing bowl; beat until light and creamy. Pour into a greased and floured 9×13-inch cake pan. Bake at 350 degrees for 50 minutes. Cool in the pan. Combine the remaining strawberries, butter and confectioners' sugar in a mixing bowl; beat until fluffy. Spread over the warm cake.
Yield: 15 to 18 servings.

Angel Grissom, Sigma Xi
Gatewood, Missouri

DARK RICH CHRISTMAS CAKE

Mom said she's never been able to find a dark cake as good as this one. I went back "home" to Ontario last Christmas, and my mom asked if I could make Dark Rich Christmas Cake for the upcoming Christmas. Then we found out that my dad had to have a biopsy and now radiation treatments for a recurring cancer problem. So I came home, made this cake, and sent it to them by Greyhound so they could enjoy it and have a treat while Dad is receiving his treatments.

1 1/2 pounds seedless	12 ounces brown sugar
raisins	8 eggs, beaten
1/2 pound candied	Juice and grated zest of
cherries	1 lemon
1 pound currants	1 teaspoon cinnamon
1/2 pound chopped mixed	1 teaspoon ground
citrus peel	cloves
1/2 pound candied	Dash of nutmeg
pineapple	1 pound flour (4 cups)
1 pound butter, softened	

Place the raisins, candied cherries, currants, mixed citrus peel and candied pineapple in a large bowl and toss with a few tablespoons of flour. Beat the butter until creamy in a huge mixing bowl; beat in the brown sugar. Mix in the eggs, lemon juice and zest, cinnamon, cloves and nutmeg. Add the flour to the fruit alternately with the egg mixture, mixing well after each addition. When mixing becomes difficult, roll up your sleeves and mix with your hands. Press into a heavy 3 1/2-inch-deep by 8 1/2-inch-round cake pan lined with very lightly buttered parchment paper. Bake at 250 degrees for 5 to 5 1/2 hours. Cool completely. Yield: 20 to 30 servings.

Jan Jarvie (32 years), Laureate Rho
Sherwood Park, Alberta, Canada

Sandy Petersen, Preceptor Delta Theta, Brookpark, Ohio, turns plain cake into a *Fruit-Glazed Angel Food Cake* by combining 1/4 cup frozen orange juice concentrate with 1/4 cup applesauce-apricot baby food and 1/2 cup sugar in a saucepan. Bring to a boil over low heat, stirring constantly. Let stand until cool and spread over an angel food cake either home-made or store-bought.

MEMORIES

The memories of my mother, grandmother, my childhood and friendships are renewed when I smell pound cake, pot roast and other foods cooking. I have treasured recipes that have been passed down to me by my family and friends. The most treasured of these are the handwritten recipes from my mother and grandmother who are now deceased. The sharing of these recipes through generations is the best way to preserve the goodness of both the recipe and the good memories!

Joyce E. Thornton, Xi Alpha Eta
Simpsonville, South Carolina

FROSTED CHOCOLATE POUND CAKE

This recipe was given to me by the wife of my husband's best college buddy. After we were first married over twenty-five years ago, we two couples spent a week together at the beach every summer, and Susan always brought one of these delicious cakes.

3 cups flour	3 cups sugar
1/4 cup baking cocoa	5 eggs
1/2 teaspoon baking powder	1 cup milk
1/2 teaspoon salt	1/2 cup shortening
1 cup (2 sticks) butter	Cocoa Frosting

Sift the flour, baking cocoa, baking powder and salt into a bowl. Cream the butter and sugar in a mixing bowl until light and fluffy. Add the eggs 1 at a time, beating well after each addition. Add the sifted dry ingredients and milk alternately, mixing well after each addition. Beat in the shortening. Pour into a well-greased tube pan. Bake at 325 degrees for 1 hour and 15 minutes. Invert onto a serving plate. Frost the cooled cake with Cocoa Frosting. Yield: 16 servings.

COCOA FROSTING

1 cup (2 sticks) margarine	2 eggs
1 1/2 (1-pound) packages confectioners' sugar	1 teaspoon lemon juice
6 tablespoons baking cocoa	1 teaspoon vanilla extract

Cream the margarine and confectioners' sugar in a mixing bowl until light and fluffy. Mix in the baking cocoa. Add the eggs 1 at a time, beating well after each addition. Beat in the lemon juice and vanilla.

Charlene Williams, Xi Zeta Pi
Pryor, Oklahoma

CREAM CHEESE POUND CAKE

It's very good alone, or serve with strawberries or other fruit and whipped cream.

1 1/2 cups (3 sticks) butter, softened	3 cups sifted flour
3 cups sugar	1 1/2 teaspoons vanilla extract
6 eggs	
8 ounces cream cheese, softened	

Cream the butter and sugar in a mixing bowl until light and fluffy. Add the eggs 1 at a time, beating well after each addition. Mix in the cream cheese, flour and vanilla. Pour into a greased bundt pan. Bake at 325 degrees for 1 hour and 15 minutes or until cake tests done. Invert onto a serving plate. Yield: 16 servings.

Denise Jordan (25 years), Xi Gamma Phi
Amarillo, Texas

MOM'S POUND CAKE

My mom always had pound cake in the kitchen, and this recipe is the best ever. Be sure to sift the dry ingredients three times—that's the secret!

3 1/2 cups flour	6 eggs
1 teaspoon baking soda	1 cup milk
1/2 teaspoon salt	1 teaspoon vanilla extract
1 1/4 cups (2 1/2 sticks) butter, softened	1 teaspoon lemon extract
1/2 cup vegetable oil	
3 cups sugar	

Sift the flour, baking soda and salt three times and set aside. Cream the butter, vegetable oil and sugar in a mixing bowl until light and fluffy. Add the eggs 1 at a time, beating well after each addition. Add the flour mixture to the sugar mixture alternately with the milk, mixing well after each addition, starting and ending with flour mixture. Mix in the vanilla and lemon extracts. Pour the batter into a tube pan that has been greased and lined with waxed paper on the bottom only. Bake at 325 degrees for 1 hour and 15 minutes. Loosen the cake from the side of the pan. Cool in the loosened pan for 20 minutes. Invert onto a serving plate. Yield: 20 servings.

Lillie Mae Merriman, Xi Epsilon Omega
Spencer, Virginia

MISS LIZZIE'S POUND CAKE

Miss Lizzie was one of my Grandma Brand's prized Rhode Island Red laying hens. Grandma Brand said the largest brown egg that we gathered each day was happily laid by Miss Lizzie. Grandma and I carefully checked each nest to find each and every one of the large brown eggs, whose colors ranged from light tan to a deep brown. Some of the eggs were small, and some seemed almost too large for my hands to hold. I gathered the eggs into an old wire basket, and Grandma used her apron. Fresh water and a generous supply of chopped corn were awarded to the hens for their generosity. One spring afternoon a quick storm came up, and Grandma and I hurried to get the chickens in their shelter, but one mother hen with many fuzzy yellow chicks was caught in the rain. Grandma and I ran to get her, gathered the chicks into Grandma's apron, and carried them inside to the washroom. An old wood stove was in the corner of the room, and Grandma filled it with wood and started a fire. I towel-dried each of the little yellow chicks, and the mother hen sat by the warm fire, very thankful that we had saved her little family. When the storm was over we carried them back to the comfort of the chicken house. Miss Lizzie and the other hens were so glad to see that they were safe.

I always cracked the four brown eggs when we made this wonderfully dense yellow cake. "Only brown eggs will work for this cake," my grandma would say. She mixed the flour, sugar, milk, and other ingredients, and poured them into a large cake pan. I could hardly wait for the cake to finish baking.

Today I still bake Miss Lizzie's wonderful pound cake. I have updated the recipe a little, but I never bake it without large brown eggs. Enjoy!

1 (2-layer) package yellow cake mix	4 brown eggs
1 (4-ounce) package vanilla instant pudding mix	1 cup water 1/3 cup vegetable oil

Combine the dry cake mix, dry pudding mix, eggs, water and vegetable oil in a large mixing bowl. Beat at medium speed for 2 minutes. Pour into a bundt pan that has been sprayed with nonstick cooking spray. Bake at 350 degrees for 50 to 60 minutes or until cake tests done. Cool in the pan for 25 minutes. Invert onto a serving plate. Yield: 12 servings.

Sue Scott
Rogers, Arkansas

For years, I watched my mom go to sorority meetings on Tuesday nights. Having been a member of Beta Sigma Phi since she was in college, her charm bracelet seemed to weigh a ton as I put it on my own small wrist. I would help my mom get ready for the Christmas social, which was always at our house.

Six months ago, one of my long-time friends asked me to join a friendly venture called Beta Sigma Phi, a chapter now named Eta Lambda. I was amazed at how quickly I bonded with these other young career women, and fully realized the wonder of sisterhood my mother had enjoyed for so many years.

Lori Johnston, Eta Lambda
Medford, Oregon

❖ SHMOO TORTE

6 eggs, separated	2 cups whipping cream, whipped
1/4 teaspoon cream of tartar	1 cup heavy cream
1 cup sugar	3 tablespoons butter
1/2 cup flour	1 1/2 cups packed brown sugar
1 teaspoon baking powder	
1 cup finely chopped pecans	

Oil the bottom of a 10-inch tube pan. Beat the egg whites in a large bowl until light. Beat in half the sugar. Beat the egg yolks in a small bowl; fold into the egg white mixture. Fold in the flour and baking powder. Fold in the pecans. Pour the batter into the prepared tube pan. Bake at 325 degrees for 1 hour. Invert on a funnel to cool completely. Remove from pan. Slice cake into 2 equal layers. Stir the remaining 1/2 cup sugar into the whipped cream. Spread between the layers and over the top and side of the torte. Combine the heavy cream, butter and brown sugar in a saucepan; bring to a boil. Remove from heat and let cool. Drizzle some of the cream mixture over the torte just before serving. Serve the remaining cream mixture in a glass dish for those who want more calories! Yield: 16 servings.

Maureen Crerar, Laureate Gamma Alpha
Peachland, British Columbia, Canada

ONE-TWO-THREE-FOUR CAKE

My mother had wonderful recipes she had gotten from her father's German bakery in Philadelphia. This was one of his delicious cakes, and it was served at family events.

4 eggs, separated	1 teaspoon salt
1 cup shortening	1 cup milk
2 cups sugar	1 teaspoon vanilla
3 cups sifted flour	extract
1 teaspoon baking	Strawberry Goo
powder	

Beat the egg whites in a mixing bowl until stiff peaks form. Cream the shortening and sugar in a large mixing bowl until light and fluffy; beat in the egg yolks. Mix the flour, baking powder and salt together. Add to the creamed mixture alternately with a mixture of the milk and vanilla, beating well after each addition. Fold in the egg whites. Spoon into a greased and floured bundt pan. Bake at 350 degrees for 1 hour. Serve with Strawberry Goo. Yield: 10 to 12 servings.

STRAWBERRY GOO

1 cup sugar	1 cup sliced strawberries
1 egg white	

Combine the sugar, egg white and strawberries in a large mixing bowl and beat at medium-high speed for 20 minutes. Chill, covered, for at least 6 hours before use. Serve cold.

Jeanne Griffin (36 years), Pi Phi
Sebring, Florida

SWEET CINNAMON CAKE

My mother sometimes made this warm sweet cake in the morning for breakfast. We would put butter on a piece and dunk it in coffee, or simply have a piece with milk while we listened to "Fibber Magee and Molly" on the radio. These are my fondest memories.

1 tablespoon shortening	1 teaspoon baking soda
1 cup packed brown	1/2 teaspoon baking
sugar	powder
1 cup sweet or sour	3 to 4 cups flour
milk	Sugar and cinnamon

Cream the shortening and brown sugar in a mixing bowl until smooth. Mix in the milk, baking soda and baking powder. Stir in the flour 1 cup at a time to form a dough. Press into a greased 8-inch-square cake pan. Sprinkle with sugar and cinnamon to taste. Bake at 350 degrees for 35 minutes or until edges are brown. Variation: Roll the dough on a floured sur-

face. Cut with a cookie cutter and bake on a greased cookie sheet. Yield: 6 servings.

Judy Harrar, Delta Delta
Myrtle Beach, South Carolina

PINA COLADA CAKE

This is the first cake my mother let me bake by myself. It is delicious, and easy enough for a ten-year-old to bake.

1 1/2 cups sugar	1/2 teaspoon salt
2 eggs	1 1/2 teaspoons baking
1 (15-ounce) can crushed	soda
pineapple	Coconut Pecan Topping
2 cups sifted flour	

Combine the sugar, eggs and undrained pineapple in a large bowl and mix well. Add the flour, salt and baking soda; mix well. Pour into a greased 9×13-inch cake pan. Bake at 350 degrees for 30 minutes. Spread Coconut Pecan Topping over the hot cake. Cool and serve. Yield: 15 servings.

COCONUT PECAN TOPPING

1/2 cup (1 stick) butter	1 cup toasted chopped
1 cup sugar	pecans
3/4 cup evaporated milk	1 cup toasted coconut
1 teaspoon vanilla	
extract	

Combine the butter, sugar and evaporated milk in a heavy saucepan over medium-high heat. Bring to a boil. Boil gently for 10 minutes, stirring frequently. Remove from heat. Stir in the vanilla, pecans and coconut.

Leslie Weiss
Brenham, Texas

OLD-FASHIONED GINGERBREAD

1/2 cup shortening	1 teaspoon cinnamon
1/2 cup sugar	1 teaspoon ginger
1 egg, beaten	1/2 teaspoon ground
1 cup molasses	cloves
2 1/2 cups flour	1/2 teaspoon salt
1 1/2 teaspoons baking	1 cup hot water
soda	

Cream the shortening and sugar in a mixing bowl until light and fluffy. Mix in the egg and molasses. Sift together the flour, baking soda, cinnamon, ginger, cloves and salt. Add the flour mixture to the creamed mixture and blend. Blend in the hot water. Beat until smooth, making a very soft batter. Pour into a greased 9×9-inch cake pan. Bake at 350 degrees for 35 minutes or until gingerbread tests done. Yield: 16 servings.

Pat McMurray, Preceptor Alpha
Riverview, New Brunswick, Canada

WHITE LOAF CAKE

3 cups sifted flour
1 tablespoon baking
 powder
1/4 teaspoon salt
1 cup (2 sticks) butter,
 softened
1 1/2 teaspoons vanilla
 extract

1/4 teaspoon almond
 extract
2 cups sugar
1 cup milk
6 egg whites

Grease the bottom of a 10-inch tube pan and line it with waxed paper. Sift the flour, baking powder and salt; set aside. Cream the butter, vanilla and almond extract in a mixing bowl until smooth. Add 1 cup of the sugar gradually, creaming until fluffy after each addition. Add the sifted dry ingredients in fourths and the milk in thirds, beating only until smooth after each addition. Beat the egg whites until frothy. Add the remaining 1 cup sugar gradually, beating well after each addition. Beat until rounded peaks form and egg whites do not slide. Spread the egg white mixture over the batter and fold in gently. Spoon into the tube pan. Bake at 350 degrees for 1 hour or until cake tests done. Cool on a wire rack for 15 minutes. Invert onto a serving plate. Yield: 16 servings.

Juanita W. Gray (44 years), Xi Omicron
Bluefield, West Virginia

QUEEN ELIZABETH CAKE

My aunt gave me this old-fashioned recipe. It had been handed down in her family for years.

1 cup chopped dates
1 cup boiling water
1 teaspoon baking soda
1/2 cup (1 stick) butter
1 cup sugar

1 egg
1 1/2 cups flour
1 teaspoon baking
 powder
Coconut Frosting

Combine the dates, boiling water and baking soda in a small bowl; let stand for 10 minutes. Cream the butter and sugar in a mixing bowl until light and fluffy. Beat in the egg. Mix in the date mixture, flour and baking powder. Pour into a greased 9×13-inch cake pan. Bake at 350 degrees for 30 minutes. Frost the cooled cake with Coconut Frosting. Yield: 18 servings.

COCONUT FROSTING

2 egg yolks
1/2 cup packed brown
 sugar
1/2 cup (1 stick) butter
1/2 cup evaporated milk

1 tablespoon vanilla
 extract
1 cup shredded coconut
1 cup chopped pecans or
 walnuts

Combine the egg yolks, brown sugar, butter, evaporated milk and vanilla in a heavy saucepan; bring to a boil. Boil for 3 minutes, stirring constantly. Stir in the coconut or pecans or both.

Julie Whitacre, Laureate Iota
Cross Junction, Virginia

MATRIMONIAL CAKE

2 cups rolled oats
2 cups flour
1 teaspoon baking
 soda
1 cup (2 sticks) butter,
 softened

1 cup packed brown
 sugar
1 cup finely chopped
 dates
1 cup water
1 cup sugar

Beat the rolled oats, flour, baking soda, butter and brown sugar in a mixing bowl until smooth. Combine the dates, water and sugar in a saucepan and bring to a boil; boil gently until thickened, stirring constantly. Layer half the oat mixture, the date filling and the remaining oat mixture in a greased 9×13-inch cake pan. Bake at 350 degrees for 35 minutes or until cake tests done. Yield: 24 servings.

Eileen Atchison (34 years), Laureate Lambda
Sherwood Park, Alberta, Canada

MEMORIES

*T*wenty-four years ago, my daughter was living in Newport News, Virginia, and was expecting her first child, my first grandchild. I was unable to travel to Virginia at that time and felt very bad about it. My sorority sisters had a lovely shower and I was able to send my daughter some wonderful gifts. My daughter did not know many people in Newport News and was so thrilled to have a baby shower by mail. I am still a member of the same chapter and truly cherish their friendships. Beta Sisters are the best.

Sara Westfahl (42 years), Gamma Epsilon Master
Eureka, California

MEMORIES

My grandfather, Toney Schimmels, was a wonderful man. I can't remember when he didn't walk with a cane. He and my grandma had over 25 grandchildren. Grandpa's favorite way to tease us was to pretend to hook us with his cane as we walked by. If we came too close, he caught us and hugged or kissed us quick! He had a wonderful sense of humor and a gentle nature that he passed on to my dad. I only hope my grandkids will remember me as fondly as I remember him.

Jeanné Hayden, Preceptor Upsilon
Boise, Idaho

SHOO-FLY CAKE

My grandmother made this cake often for our family gatherings. All my aunts, uncles, and cousins came every Sunday to make homemade ice cream, play games, and have a family singalong. I have lots of fond memories when I make this yummy cake.

4 cups flour	1 (16-ounce) bottle light
2 cups packed light	molasses
brown sugar	1 tablespoon baking soda
1 cup shortening	2 cups boiling water
1/4 teaspoon cinnamon	

Combine the flour and brown sugar in a bowl. Cut in the shortening until mixture resembles coarse crumbs. Reserve 1 cup of the crumbs. Stir in the cinnamon and molasses. Dissolve baking soda in 1/4 cup boiling water. Stir the remaining boiling water into the molasses mixture gradually. Stir in the baking soda mixture. Pour into a greased 9×13-inch cake pan. Sprinkle with the reserved crumbs. Bake at 375 degrees for 45 minutes. Serve with whipped cream or ice cream or both. Yield: 20 to 24 servings.

Phyllis Davis, Beta Sigma
Santa Cruz, California

LAZY DAISY CAKE

2 eggs, beaten	1 teaspoon baking
1 cup sugar	powder
1 teaspoon vanilla	1/2 cup milk
extract	1 tablespoon melted
1/2 teaspoon salt	butter
1 cup flour	Lazy Topping

Combine the eggs, sugar and vanilla in a mixing bowl and beat until smooth. Sift together the salt, flour and baking powder and stir into the egg mixture. Add the milk and butter; mix well. Spread the batter in a greased 8-inch-square cake pan. Bake at 350 degrees for 25 to 30 minutes or until cake tests done. Spread Lazy Topping over the hot cake. Return to the oven and bake for 2 to 3 minutes or until topping is slightly golden. Yield: 9 to 12 servings.

LAZY TOPPING

3 tablespoons melted	1 cup shredded coconut,
butter	or 1/2 cup chopped
2 tablespoons milk	walnuts
5 tablespoons brown	
sugar	

Combine the butter, milk, brown sugar and coconut in a bowl; mix well.

Sue Flagel (26 years), Omicron
Trail, British Columbia, Canada

CHOCOLATE BUTTERMILK CAKE

2 cups flour	2 eggs, well beaten
2 cups sugar	1/2 cup buttermilk
1/2 teaspoon salt	1 teaspoon baking soda
1/2 cup shortening	1 teaspoon cinnamon
1/2 cup (1 stick)	1 teaspoon vanilla
margarine	extract
1 cup water	Chocolate Pecan
3 tablespoons baking	Frosting
cocoa	

Sift together the flour, sugar and salt. Combine the shortening, margarine, water and baking cocoa in a saucepan and bring to a boil. Pour the cocoa mixture over the flour mixture. Combine the eggs, buttermilk, baking soda, cinnamon and vanilla in a bowl and mix until smooth. Add the buttermilk mixture to the flour mixture; mix well. Spread in a greased and floured 10×15-inch cake pan. Bake at 350 degrees for 20 minutes. During last 5 minutes of baking, make the Chocolate Frosting. Spread Chocolate Frosting over the hot cake. Cool and serve. Yield: 12 servings.

CHOCOLATE PECAN FROSTING

1/2 cup (1 stick)	1 (1-pound) package
margarine	confectioners' sugar
3 tablespoons baking	1 teaspoon vanilla
cocoa	extract
6 tablespoons milk	1/2 cup chopped pecans

Heat the margarine, baking cocoa and milk in a saucepan over low heat, stirring occasionally; do not boil. Remove from heat. Stir in the confectioners' sugar, vanilla and pecans; mix well.

Karen Henderson, Xi Alpha Delta
Eugene, Oregon

MIMI'S FRENCH CAKE

Mimi was a wonderful friend. She treasured this seventy-year-old recipe to the point that when someone asked for it, she made little alterations so it would never come out the same. But I got the real thing.

2³/₄ cups flour	1¹/₂ cups sugar
1³/₄ teaspoons baking powder	6 eggs, separated
	1¹/₄ cups milk
1¹/₄ cups (2¹/₂ sticks) butter, softened	1 teaspoon vanilla extract
2¹/₂ cups confectioners' sugar	

Sift together the flour and baking powder. Cream the butter and sugars in a large mixing bowl until light and fluffy. Add the egg yolks; mix well. Beat the egg whites in a bowl until stiff peaks form. Add the flour mixture to the creamed mixture alternately with the milk, mixing well after each addition, beginning and ending with flour mixture. Stir in the vanilla. Fold in the stiffly beaten egg whites. Spoon into a greased 10×14×2-inch cake pan. Bake at 350 degrees for 40 to 45 minutes or until cake tests done. Wrap while still warm in a tea towel. Cool, remove towel and serve. Yield: 16 servings.

Arlene Radel, Chi Omicron
Naperville, Illinois

SPONGE SHORTCAKE

This recipe is the one my mother used for strawberry shortcake. It is still preferred by my family.

2 eggs	1 cup sugar
Heavy cream or evaporated milk	1 cup flour
¹/₂ teaspoon vanilla extract	1 teaspoon baking powder

Break the eggs into a 1-cup measuring cup. Add enough cream to fill to the 1-cup line. Combine the egg mixture, vanilla and sugar in a mixing bowl and beat well. Add the flour and baking powder; beat at medium speed for 2 minutes. Pour into a greased 9-inch-square cake pan. Bake at 375 degrees for 20 minutes or until set. Serve warm with strawberries and whipped cream. Yield: 6 servings.

Joan R. Smith (45 years), Laureate Beta Mu
Benton Harbor, Michigan

COUNTRY LOAF CAKE

When I was a young girl, my grandmother sometimes made this dessert on a Sunday afternoon. After a huge meal at noon, we would rest and get ready for this "surprise" dessert, served around 2:30 in the afternoon. That was Gramma's way of keeping all her grandchildren with her for a full Sunday afternoon. Otherwise we would all stay for lunch and then "split" for an afternoon movie with our friends.

1 (2-layer) package chocolate cake mix	Vanilla ice cream
1 (2-layer) package white cake mix	2 cups sliced strawberries
1 (2-layer) package yellow cake mix	Marshmallow creme or vanilla pudding
	Confectioners' sugar

Prepare the chocolate, white and yellow cake mix batter in separate bowls using the package directions, reducing the water by 2 tablespoons. Pour each bowl of batter into a greased and floured 5×9-inch loaf pan. Bake at 350 degrees for 30 to 35 minutes or until a wooden pick inserted in the center comes out clean. Cool. Cut each cake into ¹/₂-inch slices. Layer the slices with ice cream, strawberries and marshmallow creme. Sprinkle heavily with confectioners' sugar if desired. Garnish with a peppermint leaf, an orange slice and two grapes, one green and one purple. Serve immediately. Yield: 20 servings.

Joycee Davis, Laureate Alpha Epsilon
Lowell, Arkansas

OLD-FASHIONED JELLY ROLL

3 eggs	³/₄ cup sifted flour
1 cup sugar	2 teaspoons baking powder
¹/₄ cup cold water	
1 teaspoon vanilla extract	¹/₂ teaspoon salt
	Your favorite jelly

Break the eggs into a mixing bowl and beat until light. Add the sugar gradually, continuing to beat until light and fluffy. Add the water and vanilla; stir until smooth. Stir in the flour, baking powder and salt a little at a time. Pour the batter into a waxed paper-lined jelly roll pan. Bake at 375 degrees for 12 to 15 minute or until set. Dust a clean kitchen towel with confectioners' sugar. Invert the cake onto the towel. Remove the waxed paper and trim the edges. Spread jelly to the edge. Roll the warm cake as for a jelly roll from the short side and wrap in the towel. Place on a wire rack to cool. Yield: 10 servings.

Kelli E. Canevit, Xi Mu Phi
Canton, Illinois

JAM CAKE

I was raised on a ranch during the war years, and the highlight of the summer was spending a week with my grandparents at their home. Grandmother was a very good cook who loved to bake when I was there. Mom was busy with chores at the ranch, including baking bread for "us kids" and Dad, so she didn't have time to bake many cakes at that time. Hence, Gran's cakes were a special treat.

1 cup (2 sticks) butter	3 cups flour
2 cups sugar	1/4 teaspoon salt
5 eggs	1 teaspoon ground
1 cup blackberry or	cloves
black raspberry jam	1 teaspoon nutmeg
1 cup coarsely chopped	1 teaspoon cinnamon
pecans	1 teaspoon baking soda
1 cup raisins	1 cup buttermilk

Cream the butter and sugar in a mixing bowl until light and fluffy. Add the eggs 1 at a time, beating well after each addition. Add the blackberry jam and beat well. Dredge the pecans and raisins in some of the flour. Sift the remaining flour, salt, cloves, nutmeg and cinnamon together. Dissolve the baking soda in the buttermilk. Add to the creamed mixture alternately with the flour mixture, mixing well after each addition. Stir in the pecan mixture. Pour into 3 waxed paper-lined 8-inch cake pans. Bake at 325 degrees for 30 to 40 minutes or until cakes test done. Serve plain or frosted with caramel frosting. Yield: 24 to 36 servings.

Phyllis Kraich, Laureate Beta Epsilon
Akron, Colorado

MOON CAKE

Serve with ice cream or fruit salad.

3 cups sifted cake flour	1 cup milk
1 tablespoon baking	1 teaspoon vanilla
powder	extract
1/2 teaspoon salt	5 egg whites, stiffly
2/3 cup butter or	beaten
shortening, softened	Moonglow Lemon
2 cups sugar	Frosting

Measure the sifted cake flour; add the baking powder and salt and sift 3 times. Cream the butter and sugar in a mixing bowl until light and fluffy. Add the sifted flour mixture to the creamed mixture alternately with the milk, a small amount at a time, mixing until smooth after each addition. Mix in the vanilla. Fold in the egg whites. Pour the batter into 3 greased 9-inch cake pans. Bake at 325 degrees for 15 minutes. Turn oven temperature to 350 degrees and bake for 15 minutes longer. Spread Moonglow Lemon Frosting between the layers and over the top and side of the cooled cake. Yield: 12 to 15 servings.

MOONGLOW LEMON FROSTING

2 egg yolks	4 1/2 cups confectioners'
Grated zest of 1 lemon	sugar
1/4 cup fresh lemon juice	

Combine the unbeaten egg yolks and the lemon zest and juice in a bowl and mix well. Add the confectioners' sugar gradually, beating constantly. Beat in additional lemon juice if necessary to make of spreading consistency.

Beverly J. Steele (34 years), Preceptor Mu
Havana, Illinois

MAYONNAISE CAKE

My grandparents had six children, and Grandfather died during the Depression. My grandmother raised the children alone. This was the cake she made for them. It is best when served with a light dusting of confectioners' sugar and a glass of cold milk.

2 cups flour	1 cup mayonnaise-type
1 cup sugar	salad dressing
2 teaspoons baking soda	1 teaspoon vanilla
1/4 cup baking cocoa	extract
1 cup water or milk	

Measure and sift together the flour, sugar, baking soda and baking cocoa 3 or 4 times; sift into a large mixing bowl. Combine the water, mayonnaise-type salad dressing and vanilla in a bowl and whisk until smooth. Add to the flour mixture and beat for 2 minutes. Pour into a lightly oiled 9×13-inch baking dish. Bake at 350 degrees for 25 to 30 minutes or until cake tests done. Yield: 15 servings.

Linda Huhman
Williamsport, Ohio

MEMORIES

I grew up in the country with three sisters and three brothers. My mother was a great cook. I wish I knew her syrup cake recipe. Mom cooked the syrup cake and then we would eat it while it was still hot with butter spread on it.

Maxine Hoff (33 years), Alpha Nu
Breckenridge, Texas

SYRUP CAKE

1 cup pure cane syrup	3 egg yolks
1/2 cup (1 stick) butter	1 cup sugar
1 teaspoon cinnamon	2 cups milk
1 teaspoon nutmeg	1 cup evaporated milk
1 teaspoon (scant) baking soda	2 tablespoons cornstarch
2 cups cake flour	

Combine the cane syrup and 1 cup water in a saucepan over medium-high heat; bring to a boil. Remove from heat. Stir in the butter, cinnamon and nutmeg; let cool. Dissolve the baking soda in 1/4 cup water. Stir the baking soda mixture and cake flour into the cooled syrup mixture. Pour into a greased 10×12-inch cake pan. Bake at 350 degrees for 20 minutes or until set. Combine the egg yolks and sugar in a mixing bowl and beat until creamy. Add the milk and evaporated milk and beat until smooth. Pour the mixture into a heavy saucepan over medium heat; bring to the boiling point. Add the cornstarch gradually and cook until thickened, whisking constantly. Remove from heat. Pour the cooled egg yolk mixture over the hot cake.
Yield: 15 servings.

Kathy Gerald, Xi Alpha Omega
Bogalusa, Louisiana

VINEGAR CAKE

I have eleven brothers and sisters, and this cake was the favorite of all twelve of us! The cake tastes best when served warm, and it reheats well in the microwave.

3 cups flour	4 teaspoons vinegar
2 cups sugar	2 teaspoons vanilla extract
Dash of salt	
2 teaspoons baking soda	2 cups water
1/4 cup baking cocoa	Cocoa Frosting
2/3 cup vegetable oil	

Combine the flour, sugar, salt, baking soda, baking cocoa, vegetable oil, vinegar, vanilla and water in a large bowl and mix well. Pour into a greased and floured 9×13-inch cake pan. Bake at 350 degrees for 30 to 40 minutes or until cake tests done. Cut the hot cake into serving pieces. Pour hot Cocoa Frosting over the hot cake. Yield: 15 servings.

COCOA FROSTING

2 cups sugar	1/2 cup milk
1/2 cup (1 stick) butter or margarine	1 teaspoon vanilla extract
1/4 cup baking cocoa	1 cup pecan pieces

Combine the sugar, butter, baking cocoa and milk in a heavy saucepan over medium-high heat and bring to a vigorous boil. Boil over medium heat for 5 minutes. Remove from heat and stir in the vanilla and pecan pieces.

Patricia Jean Morgan (28 years), Xi Tau Tau
Brazoria, Texas

VICTORY CAKE

My parents were childhood sweethearts. Before they were married during World War II, Dad joined the Navy. Mom would ride her bike to his mother's house and watch her make this cake. Shortening was very hard to get during the war, and since this cake had no shortening, Grandma called it Victory Cake. My mother has made this light, yellow, angel food-type cake with fluffy marshmallow icing for as long as I can remember. It is always a hit.

7 large eggs, separated	1/2 teaspoon cream of tartar
1/3 cup water	
1 teaspoon vanilla extract	Dash of salt
	Marshmallow Icing
1 cup sugar	
1 cup cake flour, sifted 3 times	

Beat the egg yolks at medium speed until very thick and pale yellow, 20 minutes or longer. Add the water and vanilla; beat until thickened. Add the sugar and beat until dissolved. Add the flour gradually, beating well. Beat the egg whites in a separate bowl until foamy; add the cream of tartar and salt. Beat until stiff but not dry peaks form. Fold the egg whites into the batter. Spoon into an ungreased tube pan. Bake at 325 degrees for 1 hour. Invert on a bottle to cool completely. Loosen the cake from the side of the pan. Invert onto a cake plate. Frost with Marshmallow Icing. Yield: 12 servings.

MARSHMALLOW ICING

3 egg whites	1 cup sugar
1/3 teaspoon cream of tartar	1/3 cup water

Beat the egg whites until stiff peaks form. Combine the cream of tartar, sugar and water in a heavy saucepan over medium-high heat; bring to a boil. Boil until the mixture spins a long thread when a little is dropped from a spoon held above the saucepan. Add the egg whites and beat at high speed until of spreading consistency.

Sandy Bartholomew, Xi Epsilon Iota
Ballwin, Missouri

DEPRESSION CAKE

My grandmother created this cake during the Great Depression.

2 cups raisins
4 cups water
1/4 cup shortening
2 cups sugar
4 cups flour

2 teaspoons cinnamon
2 teaspoons nutmeg
2 teaspoons baking soda
1 teaspoon salt

Combine the raisins and water in a saucepan over medium-high heat. Simmer, uncovered, until 2 cups of water remain. Cream the shortening and sugar in a mixing bowl until light and fluffy. Sift the flour, cinnamon, nutmeg, baking soda and salt over the shortening mixture. Add the raisin mixture and mix well. Spoon into a greased 9×13-inch cake pan. Bake at 350 degrees for 35 minutes or until cake tests done. Serve with whipped topping. Yield: 15 servings.

Susan O'Brien, Preceptor Nu
Portland, Maine

KENTUCKY WHISKEY CAKE

I usually make this cake in late September or early October, and by Christmas it's wonderful.

8 ounces red candied
cherries
8 ounces green candied
cherries
1 pint bourbon whiskey
3/4 cup (1 1/2 sticks) butter
2 cups sugar
1 cup packed brown
sugar

6 eggs, separated
5 cups flour
2 teaspoons nutmeg
1 teaspoon baking
powder
4 cups broken walnuts
8 ounces raisins

Soak the red and green candied cherries in the whiskey for 8 to 10 hours. Cream the butter and sugars in a mixing bowl until light and fluffy. Add the egg yolks and beat well. Add the soaked fruit with its soaking liquid. Stir in the flour, nutmeg and baking powder. Fold in the egg whites, walnuts and raisins. Spoon into a greased tube pan. Bake at 300 degrees for 3 to 4 hours or until cake tests done. Invert on a funnel to cool completely. Loosen the cake from the side of the pan. Remove from the pan and place in an airtight container. Stuff the center of the cake with a whiskey-soaked cheesecloth. Keep the cake in a cool place for several months, basting occasionally with whiskey. Yield: 20 to 25 servings.

Ginny Thomas (35 years), Preceptor Gamma Eta
Merritt Island, Florida

POPPY SEED CAKE

1 (2-layer) package
yellow cake mix
1 (4-ounce) package
vanilla instant
pudding mix
1 cup hot water

1/2 cup vegetable oil
3 tablespoons poppy
seeds
4 eggs
1 teaspoon rum or
vanilla extract

Combine the dry cake mix, dry pudding mix, hot water, vegetable oil, poppy seeds, eggs and rum in a large mixing bowl; beat until smooth. Pour into a greased bundt pan. Bake at 350 degrees for 1 hour or until cake tests done. Glaze the warm cake with a mixture of confectioners' sugar, rum and a little lemon juice. Yield: 12 servings.

Irene Hurt, Preceptor Zeta Beta
Shelbina, Missouri

PISTACHIO CAKE

1 (2-layer) package
white or yellow cake
mix
1 (4-ounce) package
pistachio instant
pudding mix
1/2 cup orange juice

1/2 cup water
4 eggs
1/2 cup vegetable oil
1/2 cup sugar
1 cup semisweet
chocolate chips
3/4 cup chocolate syrup

Combine the first 7 ingredients in a large mixing bowl and blend to moisten. Beat at medium speed for 2 minutes. Stir in the chocolate chips. Layer 3/4 cup of the batter in a greased bundt pan. Drizzle with the chocolate syrup. Layer the remaining batter over the chocolate syrup. Bake at 350 degrees for 1 hour. Yield: 16 servings.

Susan Thomason, Xi Eta Chi
Amarillo, Texas

HARVEST PECAN CAKE

I have shared this cake with my family and friends for forty years. Very rich, it stands alone.

4 1/2 cups sifted flour
1/4 teaspoon salt
1 teaspoon baking
powder
6 eggs, separated
3 tablespoons instant
coffee
3 tablespoons hot water

2 cups (4 sticks) butter,
softened
1 (1-pound) package
brown sugar
1/2 cup milk
1 teaspoon vanilla
extract
4 cups chopped pecans

Sift together the flour, salt and baking powder. Grease the bottom of a 10-inch tube pan. Beat the egg yolks in a small bowl until thick and pale yellow. Beat the egg whites in a separate bowl until stiff.

Dissolve the coffee in the hot water. Cream the butter and brown sugar in a large mixing bowl until light and fluffy. Add the beaten egg yolks; mix well. Mix the milk, vanilla and coffee mixture together. Add to the creamed mixture alternately with the dry ingredients, mixing well after each addition. Fold in the pecans and egg whites. Pour into the prepared tube pan. Bake at 325 degrees for 1½ hours or until cake tests done. Cool in the pan on a wire rack; remove from pan. Sprinkle with confectioners' sugar or top with whipped topping and serve. Yield: 24 servings.

Blanche N. Goldsmith (50 years), Eta Master
Las Cruces, New Mexico

WALNUT TORTE

2 tablespoons flour	4 eggs
2½ teaspoons baking powder	1 cup walnut pieces
	Vanilla Coffee Frosting
¾ cup sugar	¼ cup toasted almonds

Combine the flour and baking powder in a small bowl. Combine the sugar and eggs in a blender container and process until frothy and smooth. Add the walnuts and pulse 3 or 4 times. Add the flour mixture and process just until mixed. Pour into two 8-inch greased and floured cake pans. Bake at 350 degrees for 20 minutes. Spread Vanilla Coffee Frosting between the layers and over the top and side. Sprinkle with toasted almonds. Yield: 8 servings.

VANILLA COFFEE FROSTING

1 teaspoon instant coffee granules	⅓ cup sugar
2 teaspoons vanilla extract	1½ cups whipping cream, whipped

Dissolve the coffee in the vanilla. Beat the coffee mixture and sugar into the whipped cream until thick.

C. Lorraine Gainer, Xi Beta Epsilon
Chilliwack, British Columbia, Canada

Carol Montgomery, Preceptor Phi, Goldsboro, North Carolina, has learned to make *Delicious Fast Icing* from those leftover chocolate bunnies, pumpkins and Christmas Santas. She has made the frosting from mixed kinds of chocolate as well as candy filled with peanut butter or creamy fruit-flavored fillings. Place the unwrapped candy in a microwave-safe bowl and microwave for 30 seconds at a time until the candy is smooth and creamy, adding a drop or two of milk as needed to make the mixture of a pourable consistency. Pour over a freshly baked cake.

COCONUT CRUMB CAKE

1 cup (2 sticks) margarine	½ cup milk
2 cups sugar	1 cup chopped walnuts or pecans
6 eggs	1 (7-ounce) package flaked coconut
1 (12-ounce) package vanilla wafers, crushed	

Cream the margarine and sugar in a mixing bowl until light and fluffy. Add the eggs 1 at a time, beating well after each addition. Add the vanilla wafer crumbs to the creamed mixture alternately with the milk, mixing well after each addition. Fold in the chopped nuts and coconut. Spoon into a greased tube pan. Bake at 300 degrees for 1½ to 2 hours or until the cake tests done. Yield: 8 to 10 servings.

Monica Samson, Chi Omicron
Naperville, Illinois

MOM'S WHITE BOILED ICING

My mom still has the aluminum cake pan she used to store desserts. Every day when I returned home from school, I would go directly to this cake pan to see what my mom had baked. Sometimes it was cookies or pies or candy, and everything was made from scratch. I am now a mom myself with a grown child, but when I visit my mom, I still walk over to the cake pan to see what she has baked.

1 cup sugar	2 egg whites
⅓ cup water	1 teaspoon vanilla extract or other flavor such as almond, orange
1 tablespoon light corn syrup	
⅒ teaspoon salt	

Combine the sugar, water, corn syrup and salt in a saucepan over medium-high heat; stir to blend well. Boil gently without stirring until the mixture spins a long thread when a little is dropped from a spoon held above the saucepan. Place the egg whites in a large mixing bowl and beat at high speed for about 2½ minutes or until stiff but moist peaks form, scraping the bowl while beating. Pour the hot syrup slowly over the egg whites while beating at high speed. Beat until mixture is fluffy. Blend in 1 teaspoon vanilla. Spread over a cooled devil's food cake. Yield: Enough icing for 1 cake.

Paulette M. Counce, Gamma Delta
New Iberia, Louisiana

MEMORIES

I now live in New Mexico, but I lived in San Jose, California, for 40 years. I cherish my sisters there and I visit their chapter often. Even though I am not in their chapter now, I feel I am one of them because of their friendships with me over the years. They will always be my Beta sisters, who went through all the beautiful rituals and wonderful years together.

Helen M. Finch (40 years), Laureate Alpha
Albuquerque, New Mexico

PECAN TARTS

If you want to make tarts shiny, you can glaze them with an egg wash before baking.

3 ounces cream cheese, softened	1 tablespoon butter, softened
1/2 cup (1 stick) butter, softened	3/4 cup sugar
1 cup flour	1 teaspoon vanilla extract
1 egg	Chopped pecans to taste

Combine the cream cheese, the 1/2 cup butter and flour in a bowl and mix well. Shape into 21 balls. Press each ball into a small tart or muffin cup, forming a shell. Combine the egg, the 1 tablespoon butter, sugar and vanilla in a bowl and mix well. Fill each pastry shell 1/2 full. Sprinkle with chopped pecans. Bake at 325 degrees for 25 minutes or until beginning to brown. Yield: 21 servings.

Lavonda Ruttman, Xi Beta Epsilon
Woodward, Oklahoma

PUMPKIN PECAN PIE

I like pecan pie, but it is so rich. I found this recipe years ago. It is a big hit with family and friends, and the pumpkin cuts down on the sweetness.

3 eggs, slightly beaten	1/2 teaspoon cinnamon
1 cup canned or mashed cooked pumpkin	1/4 teaspoon salt
1 cup sugar	1 unbaked (9-inch) pie shell
1/2 cup dark corn syrup	1 cup chopped pecans
1 teaspoon vanilla extract	

Combine the eggs, pumpkin, sugar, corn syrup, vanilla, cinnamon and salt in a bowl and mix well. Pour into the pie shell and top with pecans. Bake at 350 degrees for about 40 minutes or until a knife inserted halfway between the center and edge comes out clean. Chill, covered, until ready to serve. Serve with whipped cream or whipped topping. Yield: 6 to 8 servings.

Evelyn Wayenberg (49 years), Laureate Alpha Pi
Soap Lake, Washington

GOLDEN AMBROSIA PECAN PIE

3 large eggs, beaten	1 teaspoon grated orange zest
3/4 cup light corn syrup	1/8 teaspoon salt
1/2 cup sugar	1 1/2 cups chopped pecans
3 tablespoons brown sugar	2/3 cup shredded coconut
2 tablespoons melted margarine	1 unbaked (9-inch) pie shell
3 tablespoons fresh orange juice	

Combine the eggs, corn syrup, sugar, brown sugar, margarine, orange juice, orange zest and salt; mix well. Stir in the pecans and coconut. Pour into the pie shell. Bake at 350 degrees for 50 to 55 minutes or until a knife inserted near the center comes out clean. Yield: 8 servings.

R. Jeanette Beard, Laureate Gamma Nu
Adrian, Missouri

SOUTHERN PECAN PIE

As a high school sophomore, I signed up for Home Ec class and was surprised to find that my teacher had been my mother's teacher more than twenty years before. This pie was my successful cooking item from that class, and I have served it to rave reviews for many years.

1/4 cup (1/2 stick) butter, softened	1/2 teaspoon vanilla extract
1 cup sugar	32 pecan halves
2 tablespoons flour	1 unbaked (9-inch) deep-dish pie shell or 2 regular shells
2 eggs, well beaten	
1/8 teaspoon salt	
1/2 cup dark corn syrup	

Cream the butter and sugar in a mixing bowl until light and fluffy. Mix in the flour, eggs, salt, corn syrup and vanilla. Pour into the pie shell. Cover with pecan halves. Bake at 350 degrees for about 30 minutes. Yield: 8 servings.

Polly Simpson, Preceptor Alpha Nu
Cordova, Tennessee

COCONUT PRALINE DREAM PIE

This pie may be prepared days in advance and refrigerated, or it can be frozen for a month.

1/2 cup chopped pecans	2 3/4 cups cold milk
1/3 cup packed light brown sugar	1 teaspoon vanilla extract
1/3 cup butter or margarine	2 (4-ounce) packages vanilla instant pudding mix
1 baked (9-inch) pie shell	1 1/3 cups shredded coconut
2 envelopes whipped topping mix	

Combine the pecans, brown sugar and butter in a small saucepan over medium-high heat; bring to a boil, stirring constantly. Boil gently for exactly 30 seconds. Spread the hot pecan mixture in the bottom of the cooled pie shell; let stand until cool. Combine the whipped topping mix, 1 cup of the milk, vanilla and dry pudding mix in a large mixing bowl; beat at high speed for about 6 minutes or until thickened and firm. Add the remaining 1 3/4 cups milk and blend at low speed. Beat at high speed for 2 minutes. Stir in 1 cup of the coconut and spoon into the prepared pie shell. Chill, covered, for at least 4 hours or until firm. Sprinkle with the remaining 1/2 cup coconut.
Yield: 8 to 10 servings.

Veronica Graves, Theta Master
Rogers, Arkansas

MAGNOLIA PIE

1 egg	1 teaspoon vanilla extract
3 egg yolks	1/4 teaspoon salt
1 cup sugar	1 cup evaporated milk
1 cup packed brown sugar	1/2 cup chopped pecans
1 tablespoon cornmeal	1 unbaked (10-inch) deep-dish pie shell
1 tablespoon flour	
1/4 cup butter, softened	

Mix together the egg, egg yolks, sugar, brown sugar, cornmeal, flour, butter, vanilla, salt, evaporated milk and chopped pecans in the order listed in a large bowl. Pour into the pie shell. Bake at 400 degrees for 15 minutes. Reduce oven heat to 300 degrees and bake for 30 minutes longer or until set.
Yield: 8 to 10 servings.

Lizette L. Pryor (40 years)
Raleigh, North Carolina

VANILLA CUSTARD PIE

My mom made this for my birthday every year. When I grew up, she continued the tradition. Now she makes two pies and takes one to my workplace for all my co-workers to enjoy.

4 eggs, slightly beaten	1/2 teaspoon vanilla extract
1/2 teaspoon salt	1 unbaked (9-inch) pie shell
1/2 cup sugar	
3 cups milk, scalded, cooled	

Preheat the oven to 450 degrees. Combine the eggs, salt and sugar in a large mixing bowl; beat until smooth. Add the milk and vanilla gradually, beating constantly. Pour into the pie shell and sprinkle with nutmeg. Bake for 10 minutes. Reduce oven heat to 325 degrees and bake for 30 to 40 minutes longer or until a knife inserted near the center comes out clean.
Yield: 6 to 8 servings.

Lucille Monti (32 years), Preceptor Beta Lambda
Rochester, New York

BUTTERSCOTCH CHOCOLATE PIE

No one will guess that this pie is a low-calorie dessert.

1 (4-ounce) package butterscotch sugar-free instant pudding mix	1 (4-ounce) package chocolate sugar-free instant pudding mix
1 1/3 cups nonfat dry milk powder	1 cup light whipped topping
2 1/2 cups water	2 tablespoons chopped pecans
1 chocolate-flavored pie crust	1 tablespoon miniature chocolate chips

Combine the dry butterscotch pudding mix, 2/3 cup of the dry milk powder and 1 1/4 cups of the water in a medium bowl; whisk well to blend. Pour into the pie crust. Combine the dry chocolate pudding mix, the remaining 2/3 cup dry milk powder and the remaining 1 1/4 cups water in a medium bowl; whisk well to blend. Pour gently over the butterscotch layer. Chill, covered, for at least 15 minutes. Spread whipped topping evenly over the chocolate layer before serving. Sprinkle with pecans and chocolate chips and serve. Yield: 6 servings.

Pam Buckalew, Xi Psi
Chariton, Iowa

OATMEAL PIE

For my bridal shower—thirty years ago—everyone brought her favorite recipe written on a recipe card. This is the recipe my eighty-three-year-old grand-mother gave me. I still use the original card that was written by her.

3/4 cup light corn syrup
3/4 cup milk
1/2 cup melted margarine
1 teaspoon vanilla extract
1/2 cup sugar
1/2 cup packed brown sugar

2 eggs, beaten
Dash of salt
1/2 cup pecan halves
3/4 cup quick-cooking oats
3/4 cup coconut flakes
2 unbaked (9-inch) pie shells

Combine the corn syrup, milk, margarine, vanilla, sugar, brown sugar, eggs and salt in a large mixing bowl. Beat at medium speed until well blended. Stir in the pecans, oats and coconut. Pour into the pie shells. Bake at 375 degrees for 40 minutes.
Yield: 12 to 16 servings.

Marcia Carter, Theta
Vincennes, Indiana

FLAPPER PIE

1 1/4 cups fine graham cracker crumbs (about 7 double graham crackers)
1/2 cup granulated or packed brown sugar
1/4 cup melted butter
1/2 teaspoon cinnamon
2 cups milk

2 eggs, separated
2 tablespoons cornstarch
1/4 cup sugar
1 teaspoon vanilla extract
3 tablespoons confectioners' sugar

Combine the graham cracker crumbs, the 1/2 cup sugar, butter and cinnamon in a bowl and mix well. Remove 1/2 cup of the cracker mixture to a small bowl and reserve for topping the pie. Line the bottom of a 9-inch pie plate with the remaining cracker mixture. Combine the milk, egg yolks, cornstarch, the 1/4 cup sugar and vanilla in a saucepan over medium-low heat; whisk until smooth. Cook until thickened, stirring constantly. Spread the hot filling in the graham cracker shell. Beat the egg whites until stiff peaks form; beat in the confectioners' sugar and spread over the filling. Sprinkle with the reserved cracker mixture. Bake at 350 degrees for 20 minutes. Serve warm or cold. Yield: 8 to 10 servings.

Barbara Dawson, Alpha Eta
Nanton, Alberta, Canada

GREAT-AUNT EVELYN'S GRAHAM CRACKER PIE

18 single graham crackers, crushed
1/3 cup margarine, melted
1/4 teaspoon cinnamon
1 cup sugar
Pinch of salt

2 cups milk
2 egg yolks, beaten
3 tablespoons cornstarch
1 teaspoon vanilla extract
2 egg whites

Combine the cracker crumbs, margarine, cinnamon, 1/4 cup of the sugar and the salt; mix well. Press the crumb mixture into a greased 9-inch pie plate to form a shell. Combine the milk, 1/2 cup of the sugar, egg yolks, cornstarch and vanilla in a saucepan over medium-low heat; whisk until smooth. Cook until thickened, stirring constantly. Pour into the pie shell. Beat the egg whites until stiff peaks form; beat in the remaining 1/4 cup sugar and 2 tablespoons water. Spread over the vanilla filling. Bake at 300 degrees for 15 minutes. Let stand at room temperature for 1 hour. Chill, covered, for at least 2 hours.
Yield: 8 servings.

Gloria I. Bunker, Xi Kappa Kappa
Homestead, Florida

MINCEMEAT FOR PIES

This recipe came from my Pennsylvania Dutch grandmother. My mother had to persuade her to measure the ingredients so we could have a recipe.

7 pounds ground beef
10 pounds apples, peeled, cored, ground
5 pounds sugar
2 pounds seedless raisins
3 tablespoons (heaping) cinnamon
2 teaspoons nutmeg

2 teaspoons ground cloves
1 1/2 teaspoons salt
1 1/2 quarts apple cider
3/4 cup plus 2 tablespoons vinegar
2 tablespoons whiskey
1 fifth of apricot or peach brandy

Brown the ground beef in a skillet, stirring until crumbly; drain. Combine the ground beef, apples, sugar and raisins in a large kettle; mix well. Stir in a mixture of the cinnamon, nutmeg, cloves and salt. Stir in the remaining ingredients. Simmer, partially covered, for about 2 hours, stirring occasionally. Divide among 8 containers or plastic bags. Freeze until ready to use. To bake a pie, fill a 9-inch double-layer pie crust with mincemeat and bake at 350 degrees for 45 to 55 minutes or until hot and browned. Yield: 8 pies.

Nancy J. Whitlow, Zeta Nu
Lancaster, Missouri

COTTAGE CHEESE PIE

²/₃ cup milk
2 tablespoons flour
¹/₂ cup sugar
1 egg yolk, beaten
2 tablespoons butter,
   softened

1 cup cottage cheese
Juice and grated zest of
   1 lemon
1 baked (9-inch) pie
   shell
1 recipe meringue

Scald the milk; do not boil. Combine the flour and sugar in the top of a double boiler over boiling water. Add the milk gradually, stirring constantly. Cook until thickened, stirring constantly. Stir in the egg yolk and cook until thick and smooth, stirring constantly. Stir in the butter, cottage cheese and lemon juice and zest. Pour into the pie shell. Cover with meringue, sealing to the edge. Bake for a few minutes or until browned. Yield: 6 to 8 servings.

Ruth Corley, Laureate Zeta Eta
Bryan, Texas

BLACK BOTTOM PIES

Our sorority sister Martha Laxson, who passed away in February 2002 at the age of eighty, served us this pie many times. It is well worth the effort to make it.

1 cup sugar
1 tablespoon cornstarch
4 extra-large egg yolks
2 cups milk, scalded
1 cup semisweet
   chocolate chips
1 teaspoon vanilla
   extract

2 baked (9-inch) pie
   shells
1 envelope unflavored
   gelatin
¹/₄ cup cold water
4 egg whites
1 cup whipping cream,
   whipped

Combine ¹/₂ cup of the sugar and cornstarch in a small bowl; mix well. Place the egg yolks in the top of a double boiler and beat well; stir in the milk gradually. Stir in the sugar mixture. Cook over boiling water until mixture coats a spoon, stirring constantly. Remove all but 1 cup of the custard to a bowl. Add the chocolate chips to the remaining hot custard in the top of the double boiler; stir until chocolate melts. Stir in the vanilla. Pour into the cooled pie shells; chill. Soften the gelatin in the cold water and add to the 1 cup hot custard; stir to dissolve. Chill until slightly thickened. Beat the egg whites in a bowl until stiff peaks form; beat in the remaining ¹/₂ cup sugar. Fold in the gelatin mixture. Pour evenly over the chocolate layer. Chill until set. Garnish with whipped cream and chocolate decorettes. Yield: 6 to 8 servings per pie.

Mary Ann Freels, Laureate Xi
Paducah, Kentucky

MEMORIES

My grandma rarely wrote down recipes or used a cookbook. Cooking and baking were her hobbies. When we spent weekends there, we were allowed to join her in the kitchen and make a mess while getting our favorite foods! Chocolate Pie was everyone's request for every holiday meal. It was also a quick dessert. Since these ingredients were always on hand, there was no need for a trip to the grocery store.

When I was a young newlywed, I wanted to learn how to make her Chocolate Pie. I took a trip to Grandma's and wrote everything down as we made it together. That was tricky because Grandma never used any measuring cups or spoons! She used the "eyeball, pour and dump" method. We used two sets of bowls. As she poured the ingredient into one bowl, I emptied it out into a measuring cup or spoon and then poured it into the second bowl. My recipe card is now 24 years old and stained with cocoa.

Carol Anderson, Xi Zeta Rho
Le Mars, Iowa

CHOCOLATE PIE

1 (12-ounce) can
   evaporated milk, or
   1¹/₂ cups milk
2 tablespoons baking
   cocoa
3 egg yolks
1 cup sugar

2 tablespoons flour
1 tablespoon butter
¹/₂ teaspoon vanilla
   extract
1 baked (9-inch) pie shell
3 egg whites
2 tablespoons sugar

Combine the evaporated milk, baking cocoa, egg yolks, the 1 cup sugar, flour and butter in a saucepan over medium heat; whisk until smooth. Cook until thickened, stirring constantly. Remove from heat. Stir in the vanilla. Pour the cocoa mixture into the cooled pie shell. Beat the egg whites in a small bowl until soft peaks form. Add the 2 tablespoons sugar gradually, beating until stiff peaks form. Top the pie with the meringue, sealing to the edge. Bake at 350 degrees for a few minutes or until meringue is brown. Yield: 6 to 8 servings.

Frances Ann Jeans
Center, Texas

MEXICAN CHOCOLATE PIE

24 large marshmallows
1 cup semisweet
  chocolate chips
1/2 cup milk
2 tablespoons Kahlúa

2 tablespoons crème
  de cacao
1 cup whipped topping
Chocolate wafer crust

Combine the marshmallows, chocolate chips and milk in a microwave-safe 3-quart bowl. Microwave until melted, stirring occasionally until smooth. Let cool. Stir in the Kahlúa and crème de cacao. Chill for at least 30 minutes. Fold the whipped topping into the chocolate mixture. Pour into the chocolate wafer crust. Cover and freeze. Remove from the freezer about 5 to 10 minutes before serving.
Yield: 8 servings.

Nancy Hearn, Preceptor Eta Gamma
West Chester, Ohio

CHOCOLATE BAR PIE

1/2 cup milk
15 large marshmallows
6 small almond-
  chocolate candy
  bars

1 cup whipping cream,
  whipped
1 baked (9-inch) graham
  cracker or other pie
  shell

Heat the milk and marshmallows in the top of a double boiler over boiling water. Break the candy bars into pieces and add to the marshmallow mixture. Heat until all is melted; stir to blend well. Remove from heat and let stand until completely cooled. Fold the whipped cream into the cooled chocolate mixture. Pour into the graham cracker shell. Chill until firm. Yield: 6 to 8 servings.

Mari Vandersloot, Xi Tau
Havre, Montana

CHOCOLATE PIZZA

2 cups (4 sticks) butter,
  softened
2 1/4 cups sugar
12 eggs
1 cup baking cocoa
6 ounces unsweetened
  chocolate, chopped,
  melted
6 peaches, peeled, sliced

6 kiwifruit, peeled,
  sliced
2 cups hulled
  strawberries
1 cup Grand Marnier
3/4 cup raspberry jam
2 ounces white
  chocolate, shaved
1 cup almonds, chopped

Cream the butter and sugar in a mixing bowl until light and fluffy. Break the eggs into a separate large mixing bowl and beat at low speed until smooth. Add the creamed mixture and beat at medium speed. Sift the baking cocoa into the egg mixture; beat at medium speed, scraping the bowl. Add the chocolate.

Beat until blended. Spread over two 12-inch-round pans. Bake at 250 degrees for 1 hour or until slightly firm. Cool in the pans. Place the peaches, kiwifruit and strawberries in 3 separate bowls and drizzle each with 1/3 cup Grand Marnier; let stand for 1 hour. Remove the crusts from the pans to serving plates. Spread the raspberry jam evenly over the crusts. Spread peaches, kiwifruit and strawberries to within 1/2 inch of the edges of the crusts. Sprinkle with white chocolate shavings. Press the almonds into the 1/2-inch border of each crust. Serve immediately.
Yield: 16 servings.

Belinda Wright, Xi Beta Epsilon
Rockview, West Virginia

CHOCOLATE PEANUT BUTTER PIE

My husband Jim and I always ordered Chocolate Peanut Butter Pie at a favorite restaurant, but we could never find a recipe we could use. So Jim made this up! Now he always makes one when there is a meeting at our house.

1 1/2 cups sugar
1/4 cup flour
3 tablespoons baking
  cocoa
Dash of salt
3 egg yolks
2 cups milk
1/4 cup (1/2 stick) butter

2 tablespoons (heaping)
  crunchy or regular
  peanut butter
1 teaspoon vanilla
  extract
1 baked (9-inch) pie
  shell
Meringue

Combine the sugar, flour, baking cocoa and salt in a bowl and blend well. Beat the egg yolks in another bowl; beat in a small portion of the cocoa mixture. Combine the egg mixture, sugar mixture and milk in a saucepan over medium-high heat; bring to a boil. Boil gently for 1 minute. Remove from heat. Blend in the butter, peanut butter and vanilla. Pour into the pie shell. Top with meringue, sealing to the edge. Bake at 350 degrees for a few minutes or until beginning to brown. Let stand until cool. Chill and serve. Yield: 8 servings.

MERINGUE

3 egg whites
1/2 teaspoon cream of
  tartar

1/2 cup sugar
1 teaspoon vanilla
  extract

Beat the egg whites with cream of tartar in a mixing bowl until soft peaks form. Add the sugar and vanilla gradually, beating until stiff peaks form.

Betty Chiasson, Laureate Theta Kappa
Pt. Neches, Texas

PEANUT BUTTER PIE

½ cup peanut butter, softened	1 (3-ounce) package vanilla instant pudding mix
¾ cup confectioners' sugar	1¾ cups milk
1 baked (9-inch) pie shell	Whipped topping

Blend the peanut butter and confectioners' sugar together. Spread all but 2 tablespoons of the mixture in the pie shell. Blend the pudding mix and milk in a bowl. Pour the pudding mixture over the peanut butter layer. Spread with whipped topping. Dot with the reserved peanut butter mixture and garnish with a sprinkle of additional confectioners' sugar. Chill, covered, for at least 2 hours. Yield: 6 to 8 servings.

Mary Ann Cavalier (38 years), Preceptor Zeta Psi
Follansbee, West Virginia

MAMAW MAXEY'S PEANUT BUTTER PIE

My husband's grandmother gave me this recipe before she passed away in 1968. My grown sons love this pie as much as their dad does.

1 unbaked (9-inch) pie shell	1 cup sugar
6 tablespoons (heaping) peanut butter, softened	2 eggs, beaten
	1 cup milk

Prick the pastry shell all over with a fork and bake at 350 degrees for about 10 minutes. Cream the peanut butter and sugar in a mixing bowl until light and fluffy. Add the eggs and beat well. Add the milk; mix well. Pour into the partially baked pie shell and bake at 350 degrees for about 45 minutes or until filling is firm in the center. Cover the crust edge with foil if necessary to prevent overbrowning. Serve with sweetened whipped cream or vanilla ice cream and chocolate syrup. Yield: 8 servings.

Marilyn Maxey (35 years), Preceptor Beta Eta
Ft. Smith, Arkansas

GRANDMA'S FRIED APPLE PIES

1½ cups mashed cooked potatoes	3 tablespoons melted lard
1¾ cups sugar	4 teaspoons baking powder
1 teaspoon ginger	6 to 8 cups flour
¾ cup milk	Apple Filling
2 eggs, beaten	
1 teaspoon nutmeg	

Stir together the warm mashed potatoes, sugar, ginger, milk, eggs and nutmeg in a large bowl. Stir in the lard, baking powder and enough flour to make a dough the consistency of pastry dough. Break off a piece of dough the size of a walnut. Roll to ⅛-inch thickness on a floured surface. Spread a spoonful of Apple Filling over half the dough. Fold the dough and seal and flute the edges to enclose the filling. Pan-fry in additional lard for about 5 minutes or until brown on both sides, turning once. Yield: 2 dozen.

APPLE FILLING

24 ounces dried apples	½ teaspoon allspice
1 cup sugar	

Place the dried apples and enough water to cover in a saucepan over medium heat. Simmer until tender, stirring frequently. Beat with a hand mixer until mashed. Stir in the sugar and allspice.

Natalie Stout, Upsilon Sigma
St. Elmo, Illinois

APPLESAUCE PIE

2 eggs, beaten	½ cup milk
¾ cup sugar	1½ cups applesauce
½ teaspoon salt	1 unbaked (9-inch) pie shell
1 teaspoon lemon juice	

Preheat the oven to 425 degrees. Combine the eggs, sugar, salt, lemon juice, milk and applesauce in a bowl and mix well. Pour into the pie shell. Bake for 15 minutes. Reduce oven temperature to 350 degrees and bake for 40 minutes longer. Sprinkle cinnamon over the top of the hot pie. Let cool. Yield: 6 to 8 servings

Maureen Echols (38 years), Preceptor Zeta
Warner Robins, Georgia

MEMORIES

We raised our three children on our farm. Most of our company arrived close to meal-time. We always had a garden, so it was easy to add more vegetables and we served lots of bread and butter. We all enjoyed ourselves and the food was delicious. Those were good times and family and friends still talk about the fun they had sitting around our table.

Beth Menefee, Xi Beta Alpha
Artesia, New Mexico

MEMORIES

Because she grew up during the Depression my mother never wasted a thing. If she made an apple pie, the skins and cores were boiled and made into apple jelly. All leftover bread, cakes and rolls were transformed into bread pudding. Soured milk was left to turn into buttermilk and used to make buttermilk pancakes. No roast or ham escaped ending up as a casserole. Nothing was thrown out if it could be salvaged and everything was a delicious dish and memory.

Grace Arlene Knipe (42 years), Kappa Master
Staten Island, New York

APPLE CRANBERRY PIE

1¼ cups sugar
3 tablespoons flour
1 recipe (2-crust) pie pastry
4 cups thinly sliced peeled cored apples
1 cup halved fresh cranberries
¼ cup mincemeat
2 tablespoons orange juice
½ teaspoon salt

Blend together the sugar and flour. Sprinkle ¼ cup of the sugar mixture in a pastry-lined 9-inch pie plate. Preheat the oven to 400 degrees. Combine the apples, cranberries and mincemeat and mix well. Layer the apple mixture in the pastry shell and drizzle with a mixture of the orange juice and salt. Sprinkle the remaining sugar mixture over the top. Cut the remaining pastry into strips. Arrange lattice-fashion over the pie. Bake for 10 minutes. Reduce oven temperature to 350 degrees and bake for 30 to 40 minutes or until golden brown. Yield: 8 servings.

Jacqueline Craig (43 years), Alpha Master
L'Orignal, Ontario, Canada

FRENCH APPLE PIE

Mom made the filling from apples that grew on trees on our farm. It was so great to take apples out of the freezer in midwinter and make that warm apple pie.

6 medium tart apples, cored, quartered
½ cup sugar
1 tablespoon flour
1 teaspoon cinnamon
Pastry
⅓ cup sugar
¼ cup (½ stick) margarine
½ cup flour

Combine the apples and 1 cup water in a saucepan over medium-high heat. Cook for 10 minutes or until tender-crisp; drain. Stir in the ½ cup sugar, the 1 tablespoon flour and cinnamon. Spoon into a pastry-lined pie plate. Sprinkle with a mixture of the ⅓ cup sugar, margarine and the ½ cup flour. Bake at 425 degrees for 1 hour. Yield: 6 to 8 servings.

EGG PASTRY

4 cups flour
1 teaspoon salt
1 teaspoon baking powder
1⅓ cups shortening
1 egg
1 tablespoon vinegar

Combine the flour, salt and baking powder in a bowl. Cut in the shortening until mixture resembles coarse crumbs. Beat the egg and vinegar in a 1-cup measuring cup; add water to the ¾-cup line. Pour the egg mixture over the flour mixture and blend. Shape into 3 balls. Roll into 12-inch circles and fit into three 9-inch pie plates. Freeze two of the pastry-lined plates for later use.

Sherry Craig, Xi Iota Beta
Webster City, Iowa

MOCK APPLE PIE

When we were young in the 1960s, Mom had to stretch our grocery money to feed our family of six. I recently came across this old recipe that she used back then. It still amazes me that you can use butter crackers and a few other simple ingredients to make a pie that tastes exactly like apple pie.

1¼ cups sugar
3 cups water
1 tablespoon cream of tartar
45 whole butter crackers
1 baked deep-dish (10-inch) pie shell

Combine the sugar, water and cream of tartar in a medium saucepan and bring to a boil. Remove from heat and stir in the butter crackers. Let stand for 10 or 20 minutes. Fill the pie shell with the cracker mixture. Dot with butter and sprinkle with cinnamon. Bake at 425 degrees for 35 minutes. Yield: 6 to 8 servings.

Pamela S. Jones, Epsilon Alpha
Garland, Texas

SWEDISH APPLE PIE

1 (21-ounce) can apple pie filling
2 tablespoons flour
¾ cup sugar
Pinch of salt
1 egg
1 teaspoon vanilla extract
½ cup sour cream
1 unbaked (9-inch) pie shell
Cinnamon Topping

Mash the apples slightly in a bowl. Mix in the flour, sugar and salt. Beat the egg in a small bowl; beat in the vanilla. Stir the egg mixture into the apple mixture. Stir in the sour cream. Pour into the pie shell. Bake at 350 degrees for 40 minutes. Remove from oven. Sprinkle with Cinnamon Topping. Return to oven and bake for 15 minutes longer.
Yield: 6 to 8 servings.

CINNAMON TOPPING

1/3 cup sugar	*1/2 cup (1 stick) butter,*
1/3 cup flour	*softened*
1 teaspoon cinnamon	

Blend the sugar, flour and cinnamon together. Cut in the butter until mixture resembles coarse crumbs.

Frances Sullivan (25 years), Xi Rho Theta
Ennis, Texas

BANANA CARAMEL PIE

This pie has become a family tradition for all holidays. I usually prepare several cans of condensed milk at one time and keep them on hand for the times I need a fast but delicious dessert.

1 (14-ounce) can	*1 cup whipped topping*
sweetened condensed	*1 large chocolate candy*
milk	*bar*
3 bananas	
1 (9-inch) graham	
cracker pie shell	

Place the unopened can of condensed milk in a saucepan over medium heat. Cover with water and bring to a boil. Boil gently for 4 to 4 1/2 hours, adding water to the pan when necessary. Let stand until cool. Slice the bananas into the pie shell. Pour the cooled caramelized milk over the bananas. Top with the whipped topping, sealing to the edge and making swirls with the back of a spoon. Break the candy bar into pieces and garnish the top of the pie. Chill, covered, until serving time. Yield: 6 to 8 servings.

Voncille Hale, Xi Alpha Kappa
Guymon, Oklahoma

BANANA CREAM PIE

2 cups milk	*3 large bananas*
2 eggs, separated	*1 baked (9-inch) pie*
1/2 teaspoon salt	*shell*
1/2 cup sugar	*2 tablespoons sugar*
1/2 cup flour	
1 teaspoon vanilla	
extract	

Pour 1 1/2 cups of the milk into a saucepan over medium heat. Cook until hot; do not boil. Pour the remaining 1/2 cup milk into a medium bowl. Beat the egg yolks lightly and add to the cold milk. Add a mixture of the salt, the 1/2 cup sugar and flour; mix well. Stir into the hot milk gradually. Cook until thickened, stirring constantly. Remove from heat. Stir in the vanilla. Cool, stirring occasionally. Slice the bananas into the pie shell. Pour the egg mixture evenly over the bananas. Beat the egg whites in a mixing bowl until soft peaks form. Add the 2 tablespoons sugar gradually, beating until stiff peaks form. Top the pie with the meringue, sealing to the edge. Bake at 350 degrees for 10 to 15 minutes or until golden brown. Yield: 6 to 8 servings.

Marguerite J. Wells (27 years), Alpha Tau
Carroll, Iowa

BANANA SPLIT CREAM PIE

1 cup sliced banana (1	*2 cups Diet Mountain*
medium)	*Dew or water*
2 cups sliced fresh	*1 (4-ounce) package*
strawberries	*banana sugar-free*
1 (6-ounce) graham	*instant pudding mix*
cracker pie shell	*2/3 cup nonfat dry milk*
1 (4-ounce) package	*powder*
vanilla sugar-free	*1 (8-ounce) can crushed*
cook-and-serve	*pineapple in juice*
pudding	*1/2 cup nonfat whipped*
1 (4-ounce) package	*topping*
strawberry sugar-free	*2 tablespoons chopped*
gelatin	*pecans*

Layer the banana and strawberries in the graham cracker shell. Combine the dry vanilla pudding mix, dry strawberry gelatin mix and 1 1/3 cups of the Mountain Dew in a saucepan over medium heat. Cook until thickened and mixture starts to boil, stirring constantly. Spoon the hot mixture evenly over the fruit. Chill, covered, for 1 hour or until set. Place the dry banana pudding mix, dry milk powder, undrained pineapple and remaining 1/2 cup Diet Mountain Dew in a medium bowl; mix well. Blend in the whipped topping. Spread the pineapple mixture evenly over the set pie filling. Sprinkle with pecans. Chill, covered, for at least 30 minutes. Note: To prevent the banana from turning brown, mix with 1 teaspoon lemon juice or sprinkle with Fruit Fresh. Yield: 8 to 10 servings.

Sally Jones, Preceptor Alpha Iota
Gladstone, Missouri

CHERRY CREAM CHEESE PIE

When I was about five or six we began to make this pie every Christmas for Santa, serving it with a big glass of milk. Then when I was about ten years old I received a letter from Santa that told me that even though the pie was delicious, he would now prefer to get a lighter snack of chocolate chip cookies and milk. When I got older I learned that Santa actually did not care for this delicious pie! I nearly died laughing. My dad had eaten the pie all those years even though it was not his favorite.

8 ounces cream cheese, softened	1 tablespoon vanilla extract
1¹⁄₃ cups sweetened condensed milk	1 baked (9-inch) pie pastry
¹⁄₃ cup lemon juice, fresh or bottled	1 (21-ounce) can cherry pie filling

Combine the cream cheese, condensed milk, lemon juice and vanilla in a bowl; beat until creamy. Pour into the pie shell. Chill, covered, for 2 to 3 hours. Spread the pie filling over the top. Serve cold. Yield: 6 to 8 servings.

Angea Sue Carroll, Xi Xi Sigma
Copperas Cove, Texas

MAGIC CHERRY PIE

My mom always made this pie for my overnight parties. I never saw her making it, but when we raided the refrigerator after midnight, there it was. We thought it was the best thing we ever ate.

1 (21-ounce) can cherries	1 (14-ounce) can condensed milk
¹⁄₄ cup sugar	
1 tablespoon cornstarch	¹⁄₂ cup whipping cream, whipped
Red food coloring	
¹⁄₃ cup lemon juice	1 (9-inch) graham cracker pie shell
1 teaspoon vanilla extract	
¹⁄₂ teaspoon almond extract	

Drain the cherries, reserving the juice. Combine the cherry liquid, sugar, cornstarch and a few drops of red food coloring in a saucepan over medium heat. Cook until thickened, stirring constantly. Remove from heat; cool. Stir in the cherries. Combine the lemon juice, vanilla, almond extract and condensed milk in a mixing bowl; blend until smooth. Fold in the whipped cream. Pour into the pie shell. Top with the cherry mixture. Chill, covered, until ready to serve. Yield: 6 to 8 servings.

Betty Randol, Laureate Delta Epsilon
Independence, Missouri

RHUBARB CHERRY PIE

2 cups sliced rhubarb	³⁄₄ cup sugar
1 (21-ounce) can cherry pie filling	2¹⁄₂ tablespoons tapioca
	1 (2-crust) pie pastry

Combine the rhubarb, pie filling, sugar and tapioca in a bowl; mix well. Let stand for 15 minutes. Pour the rhubarb mixture into a pastry-lined 9-inch pie plate. Cut the remaining pastry into strips. Arrange lattice-fashion over the pie. Bake at 400 degrees for 40 to 45 minutes or until golden brown.
Yield: 6 servings.

Shirley Haubach (45 years), Preceptor Delta Mu
Lena, Illinois

CHERRY ALMOND CRANBERRY PIE

¹⁄₂ cup sugar	2 tablespoons sugar
³⁄₄ cup flour	¹⁄₂ cup sliced almonds
¹⁄₃ cup butter or margarine	1 (21-ounce) can cherry pie filling
1 (16-ounce) can whole cranberry sauce	1 unbaked (9-inch) deep-dish pie shell

Preheat the oven to 400 degrees. Combine the ¹⁄₂ cup sugar and flour in a bowl. Cut in the butter until mixture resembles coarse crumbs. Layer the cranberry sauce, the 2 tablespoons sugar, almonds, cherry pie filling and flour mixture in the pie shell. Decorate the top of the pie with additional almonds if desired. Bake for 10 minutes. Reduce oven temperature to 325 degrees and bake for 40 minutes longer or until lightly browned. Yield: 8 servings.

Nancy McCreary (27 years), Xi Epsilon Beta
Maurertown, Virginia

CURRANT TARTS

1 (10-ounce) package currants	¹⁄₂ teaspoon salt
	³⁄₄ cup sugar
1 (2-crust) pie pastry	1 teaspoon lemon extract
4 eggs, beaten	

Place the currants in a bowl and add just enough water to cover. Let stand for at least 15 minutes. Roll the pastry on a floured surface. Cut into 3-inch circles. Fit the pastry into muffin cups; flute the edges. Drain the currants. Mix the remaining ingredients in a bowl. Fill the pastry cups and sprinkle with a little nutmeg. Bake at 425 degrees for about 25 minutes or until done to taste. Remove from oven and cool. Remove cooled tarts from muffin cups with a knife. Yield: 12 servings.

Elaine K. Benton (34 years), Laureate Beta Eta
Lorain, Ohio

MEMORIES

My grandmother was a wonderful cook. Before she retired, she was a cook at the high school where her children went to school. I always enjoyed visiting the school and tasting what she cooked for the day. She had a family of six kids to cook for and always had a garden. Everything she made was wonderful and fresh. She always had so much food and so many desserts. We lived ten hours away, so we would spend summers and holidays with her and I would learn so much from her in the kitchen. I will always cherish the memories I have of her. She died in May 1996, and I continue to share her recipes and her enjoyment of cooking with my family and friends.

*Michelle Slavens, Delta Upsilon
Eldon, Missouri*

LIGHT KEY LIME PIE

1 (4-ounce) package
  vanilla cook-and-
  serve pudding
1 (3-ounce) package lime
  gelatin
2 cups cold water

16 ounces whipped
  topping
1 baked (9-inch) pastry
  or graham cracker pie
  shell

Combine the dry pudding mix, dry gelatin mix and 2 cups cold water in a saucepan. Bring to the boiling point, stirring constantly. Let cool until set. Blend 3 cups of the whipped topping into the cooled pudding mixture; pour into the pie shell. Cover with the remaining whipped topping. Chill, covered, for 24 hours. Yield: 8 to 10 servings.

*Janice M. DiBeneditto (35 years), Theta Master
Waterbury, Connecticut*

LEMON CAKE PIE

1 cup sugar
2 tablespoons (heaping)
  flour
2 tablespoons melted
  butter
2 egg yolks

1 cup milk
Juice and grated zest of
  1 lemon
2 egg whites
1 unbaked (9-inch) pie
  shell

Preheat the oven to 450 degrees. Combine the sugar and flour in a bowl. Add the butter, egg yolks and milk; stir until smooth. Stir in the lemon juice and zest. Beat the egg whites until stiff peaks form; fold into the lemon mixture. Spoon into the pie shell. Bake for 15 minutes. Reduce oven temperature to 350 degrees. bake for 20 minutes longer or until cake surface is firm. Yield: 6 to 8 servings.

*Joan Broseke (43 years), Laureate Beta Mu Master
Kenton, Ohio*

LEMON MERINGUE PIE

My mother's lemon meringue pie was my favorite dessert, and she made it without a recipe. I urged her to write it down for me, but she never seemed to have the time. She passed away seven years ago this month. At Christmas I was helping my father move from their apartment and among her personal things I found a handwritten copy of her lemon pie recipe just for me.

1 cup sugar
1¼ cups water
1 tablespoon butter
¼ cup cornstarch
3 tablespoons cold
  water
6 tablespoons fresh
  lemon juice

1 teaspoon grated lemon
  zest
3 egg yolks
2 tablespoons milk
1 baked (8-inch) pastry
  or graham cracker pie
  shell
Lemon Meringue

Combine the sugar, water and butter in a heavy saucepan over medium-low heat. Cook until sugar is dissolved, stirring constantly. Stir in a mixture of the cornstarch and cold water. Cook over low heat for about 8 minutes or until thickened and clear. Stir in the lemon juice and zest; cook for about 2 minutes longer. Beat together the egg yolks and milk and add to the lemon mixture. Bring to the boiling point. Remove from heat and let cool. Pour into the pie shell. Top with the Lemon Meringue, sealing to the edge. Bake at 350 degrees for 13 to 15 minutes or until lightly browned. Yield: 6 to 8 servings.

LEMON MERINGUE

3 egg whites
6 tablespoons sugar

1 teaspoon fresh lemon
  juice

Beat the egg whites until stiff but not dry peaks form. Add the sugar gradually, beating constantly. Add the lemon juice last.

*Marlene Baulk, Preceptor Epsilon Nu
Kitchener, Ontario, Canada*

FROZEN LEMON PIE

I was a five-year-old only child in 1943, and I can still picture my mother cooking. She was not well during my teenage years, and a wonderful couple who lived next door helped my father care for me. Sadly, we lost my mother when I was a senior in college. I have this recipe in my mother's handwriting on the original 3×5-inch card from 1943.

1 cup evaporated milk	Grated zest of 1/4 lemon
2 eggs, separated	1 tablespoon sugar
1/2 cup sugar	1 cup graham cracker
1/3 cup fresh lemon juice	crumbs

Freeze the evaporated milk in a metal pan until crystals begin to form. Beat the egg yolks in the top of a 1-quart double boiler. Stir in the 1/2 cup sugar, lemon juice and lemon zest. Cook over rapidly boiling water for about 10 minutes or until thickened, stirring constantly. Remove from heat. Remove lemon zest with a fine-mesh strainer. Let lemon mixture stand until completely cool. Beat the egg whites until soft peaks form. Add the 1 tablespoon sugar and beat until stiff peaks form. Fold into the cooled lemon custard. Pour the partially frozen evaporated milk into a large bowl; beat until stiff peaks form. Fold the beaten evaporated milk into the custard. Sprinkle half the graham cracker crumbs in a buttered 5×9-inch metal freezer pan. Pour the lemon custard over the crumb layer. Sprinkle the remaining graham cracker crumbs over the top. Freeze until ready to serve. To serve, make diagonal cuts to make wedges. Note: The pie may be frozen in a round metal pan if desired. Yield: 6 to 8 servings.

Shirley M. Leslie (29 years), Preceptor Delta Mu
Farmington, Missouri

PUMPKIN MINCEMEAT PIE

1/4 cup packed light brown sugar	1 cup canned pumpkin
1/2 teaspoon cinnamon	1 egg, lightly beaten
1/2 teaspoon ginger	3/4 cup hot milk
1/8 teaspoon ground cloves	1 1/2 cups mincemeat
1/4 teaspoon salt	1 unbaked (9-inch) pie shell

Preheat the oven to 425 degrees. Combine the brown sugar, cinnamon, ginger, cloves and salt in a bowl; blend well. Stir in the pumpkin. Stir in the egg and hot milk. Spread the mincemeat in the pie shell. Pour the pumpkin mixture evenly over the mincemeat layer. Bake for 10 minutes or until pastry begins to brown. Reduce oven temperature to 350 degrees and bake for 35 to 40 minutes longer or until a knife

inserted near the center of the pumpkin layer comes out clean. Serve with whipped cream.
Yield: 6 to 8 servings.

Joanna J. Ralston, Xi Lambda Tau
DeLand, Florida

GRANDMA YOUNG'S PUMPKIN CUSTARD PIE

The six girls in our family always looked forward to Mom's baking a pie so we could taste the "leftover" batter. We think she made extra batter so we could have this treat while we sat waiting in the kitchen!

4 cups canned pumpkin or fresh cooked pumpkin purée	1 teaspoon vanilla extract
2 cups sugar	4 egg whites, room temperature
1 quart milk	2 unbaked (9-inch) pie shells
3 teaspoons flour	

Combine the pumpkin, sugar, milk, flour and vanilla in a large mixing bowl and beat until smooth. Beat the egg whites until stiff peaks form. Fold the egg whites into the pumpkin mixture. Pour into the pie shells. Bake at 375 degrees for 15 minutes. Reduce oven temperature to 325 degrees and bake for 40 minutes longer. Serve with whipped cream.
Yield: 12 to 16 servings.

Sue Young, Xi Theta Chi
Valley City, Ohio

❖ PRALINE PUMPKIN PIE

1/3 cup packed brown sugar	3 eggs, lightly beaten
1/3 cup chopped pecans	1/2 cup granulated sugar
3 tablespoons butter	1/2 cup packed brown sugar
1 unbaked (9-inch) pie shell	1 1/2 teaspoons pumpkin pie spice
1 cup evaporated milk	1 teaspoon salt
1/2 cup water	1/2 cup whipping cream, whipped
1 1/2 cups canned pumpkin	

Mix together the 1/3 cup brown sugar, pecans and butter. Spread the pecan mixture in the pie shell. Bake at 400 degrees for 10 minutes. Stir the evaporated milk and water together in a saucepan; scald over medium heat. Remove from heat. Combine the next 6 ingredients in a large bowl and mix well. Beat in the scalded milk mixture. Pour into the prepared pie shell. Bake at 350 degrees for 50 minutes. Serve with whipped cream. Yield: 6 to 8 servings.

Ellen F. Boyd (39 years)
Elmira, New York

RAISIN PIE

8 ounces raisins	2 teaspoons vanilla
2 cups sugar	extract
2 cups milk	2 small (2-crust) pie
7 tablespoons flour	pastries

Combine raisins with water to cover in an iron skillet over medium-low heat. Cook until water evaporates. Add the sugar and cook until caramel-colored. Combine the milk and flour in a bowl and whisk well; strain into the raisin mixture. Cook until thickened, stirring constantly. Stir in the vanilla. Pour into 2 pastry-lined pie plates. Top with remaining pastries, sealing edges and cutting vents. Bake at 350 degrees for 30 minutes or until browned. Yield: 2 small pies.

Linda O'Corr, Alpha Kappa
Hot Springs, Arkansas

SOUR CREAM RAISIN PIE

1 cup sugar	1/4 cup (1/2 stick)
1 teaspoon cinnamon	margarine or butter,
1/8 teaspoon salt	softened
2 eggs, slightly beaten	1 cup sour cream
1 cup raisins, cooked,	1 unbaked (9-inch) pie
cooled	shell

Combine the sugar, cinnamon, and salt in a large bowl. Stir in the eggs, raisins, margarine and sour cream. Pour into the pie shell. Bake at 425 degrees for 15 minutes. Reduce oven temperature to 350 degrees and bake for 30 to 40 minutes longer or until set. Add meringue if desired. Yield: 8 servings.

Debbie Snyder, Eta Chi
Cheney, Kansas

SOUR CREAM RHUBARB PIE

4 cups chopped rhubarb	1/2 cup flour
1 1/2 cups sugar	1/2 cup packed brown
1/3 cup flour	sugar
1 cup sour cream	1/4 cup butter
1 unbaked (9-inch) pie	
shell	

Place the rhubarb, sugar and the 1/3 cup flour in a large bowl; toss to combine. Add the sour cream and mix well. Spoon into the pie shell. Combine the 1/2 cup flour and brown sugar in a small bowl. Cut in the butter until the mixture resembles coarse crumbs. Sprinkle over the pie. Bake at 450 degrees for 15 minutes. Reduce oven temperature to 350 degrees and bake for 30 minutes longer. Yield: 6 to 8 servings.

Nancy Bobick (30 years), Laureate Delta
Saskatoon, Saskatchewan, Canada

MEMORIES

I guess a lot of my warm memories originated in the kitchen. I would help my grandma with her pies, my mom ice her cakes, my mother-in-law make fudge, my grandmother-in-law make buns and biscuits and my aunt make rolls and fried chicken. Thanks to these ladies and my hubby (who in his own right is a darn good cook) I love to bake and cook as often as possible. At times I bake so much that I have to give stuff away so that it will be eaten. This does not make my family or my friends the least bit angry!

Cheryl K. Miller (34 years),
Preceptor Laureate Delta Lambda
East Sparta, Ohio

SWEET POTATO PIE

1/4 cup (1/2 stick) butter	3 eggs, slightly beaten
1/2 cup packed brown	1/3 cup corn syrup
sugar	1/3 cup milk
1 teaspoon cinnamon	Pinch of salt
1/2 teaspoon ginger	1 teaspoon vanilla
1/4 teaspoon ground	extract
cloves	1 unbaked (9-inch) pie
1 1/2 cups mashed cooked	shell
sweet potatoes	

Preheat the oven to 425 degrees. Cream the butter, brown sugar, cinnamon, ginger and cloves in a mixing bowl until light and fluffy. Add the sweet potatoes and eggs; mix well. Mix together the corn syrup, milk and salt; stir into the egg mixture. Finally, stir in the vanilla. Spoon the mixture into the pie shell. Bake for 10 minutes. Reduce oven temperature to 325 degrees and bake for 45 minutes longer. Yield: 6 large or 8 small servings.

Mary Belle Morgan (51 years), Zeta Xi
Dongola, Illinois

Sherri Bland, Xi Beta Epsilon, Pineville, West Virginia, makes **Easy Cherries-in-a-Cloud Pie** by beating 8 ounces softened cream cheese with 1/3 cup sugar until fluffy, stirring in 8 ounces whipped topping and spreading in a pie plate. Top with a can of cherry pie filling and chill before serving.

OLD-FASHIONED COCONUT PINEAPPLE PIE

1 cup sugar	3 eggs, beaten
3 tablespoons flour	1 teaspoon vanilla
1 cup light corn syrup	extract
1 cup flaked coconut	1 unbaked (9-inch) pie
1 (8-ounce) can crushed	shell
pineapple in heavy	1/4 cup (1/2 stick) butter
syrup	or margarine, melted

Combine the sugar and flour in a large bowl. Add the corn syrup, coconut, undrained pineapple, eggs and vanilla; mix well. Pour into the pie shell; drizzle melted butter over the top. Bake at 350 degrees for 50 to 55 minutes or until a knife inserted near the center comes out clean. Cover pie loosely with foil if top browns too quickly. Cool on a wire rack. Chill, covered, until serving time. Yield: 8 servings.

Nell Lister (47 years), Gamma Lambda Master
Wichita Falls, Texas

PINEAPPLE PIE

My beloved late mother-in-law served this family favorite. I will someday pass it along to my daughters-in-law.

1 (14-ounce) can	1 1/2 cups drained crushed
condensed milk	pineapple
1/4 cup lemon juice	1 teaspoon vanilla
3 ounces cream cheese,	extract
softened	1 baked (9-inch) pie
2 egg yolks	shell

Combine the condensed milk and lemon juice in a mixing bowl; beat until smooth. Combine the cream cheese and egg yolks in a separate mixing bowl; beat until smooth. Add the cream cheese mixture to the condensed milk mixture; beat until smooth. Mix together the pineapple and vanilla; fold into the cream cheese mixture. Pour into the pie shell. Chill, covered, until serving time. Serve with whipped cream. Yield: 6 servings.

Connie E. Jennings, Xi Alpha Gamma Zeta
Baytown, Texas

TRIED AND TRUE MERINGUE

3 egg whites	1/4 teaspoon cream of
2 1/2 tablespoons cold	tartar
water	6 tablespoons sugar
Pinch of salt	

Add the water, salt and cream of tartar to the egg whites one at a time, beating well after each addition. Add the sugar 1 tablespoon at a time. Beat until stiff peaks form. Spread over cream pie filling, sealing to the crust. Bake at 375 to 400 degrees for 8 to 10 minutes or until light brown. Yield: 1 meringue.

Joyce Symank, Laureate Eta Alpha
Valley Mills, Texas

SECRETS OF MAKING FLAKY PIE CRUST IN TEN MINUTES

• *Don't play with the dough. The colder it stays and the less you handle it, the flakier the crust will be.*
• *Use a rolling pin cover or the top of a man's white sock to cover the rolling pin. Use a pastry cloth or large piece of muslin on the work surface. Flour the cover and cloth, and add more flour as needed.*
• *Try to roll the dough only once. Roll gently in one direction until the patty is doubled in length, then turn over and finish rolling into a circle. Place the pie plate gently on top to check for size. Fold the dough in half and place carefully in the pie plate. Unfold. Press gently toward the center and then to the edges of the pan, being careful not to stretch the dough. If it tears, simply moisten the edge with a little water on your finger and seal the tear. If an edge seems a little short, simply add a little dough from a larger side. Trim the edges with a knife.*
• *Don't be afraid of the pie dough. Just remember to work gently and lightly.*
• *Spread a little milk over the top pastry with your fingers before baking. If you are making a fruit pie, sprinkle with a little sugar.*

6 cups flour	1 egg, slightly beaten,
1 pound lard, or 2 cups	plus cold water to fill
shortening	1 cup
1 tablespoon salt	

Combine the flour, lard and salt in a large mixing bowl. Beat at medium speed for a few minutes or until entire mixture is crumbled together, moving the mixing blades rapidly across and around the bowl. Do not overmix; stop immediately when mixture is crumbled together. Add the egg and water. Move the mixer at medium or high speed rapidly and briefly through the mixture until it forms a ball, scraping down the beaters a little if necessary; do not overmix. Shape into six 4-inch-round 1 1/2-inch-high patties, working lightly with a spatula or your hands. Place each patty in a small plastic bag. The dough patties may be stacked in a large freezer bag to be used later or rolled immediately to make piecrust. If frozen, thaw briefly before using. Yield: 6 piecrusts.

Jackie Cicora, Preceptor Epsilon Phi
Temple, Texas

Cookies and Candy

For the past seventeen years, my two daughters-in-law and I have designated the first Sunday in December as "baking day" when we make dozens and dozens of Christmas cookies. We make at least eight different kinds. When the grandchildren were babies, the dads helped out by baby-sitting, but now as the little ones have grown older they are permitted to help. They wash their hands and begin rolling balls and decorating. The girls all have special aprons for the occasion. At the end of the day, all available table space is covered with cookies. What a beautiful sight! We are tired, but have dozens of cookies ready for colleagues and friends who look forward to their plate of Christmas treats.

Frances Wicks (53 years), Psi Master
Ann Arbor, Michigan

BANANA COOKIES

3/4 cup shortening
3/4 cup packed brown
  sugar
1 egg
1 teaspoon vanilla
  extract

2 ripe bananas, mashed
1/4 teaspoon salt
1 teaspoon baking soda
2 cups flour
Creamy Brown Sugar
  Frosting

Cream the shortening and the brown sugar in a mixing bowl until light and fluffy. Add the egg, vanilla and bananas; beat until smooth. Add a mixture of the salt, baking soda and flour; beat until smooth. Drop by teaspoonfuls 2 inches apart onto a greased cookie sheet. Bake at 350 degrees for 10 minutes or until done to taste. Remove to a wire rack to cool. Frost the cooled cookies with Creamy Brown Sugar Frosting. Yield: 40 cookies.

CREAMY BROWN SUGAR FROSTING

6 tablespoons brown
  sugar
1/4 cup heavy cream
1/4 cup milk

Confectioners' sugar
1/2 teaspoon vanilla
  extract

Combine the brown sugar, cream and milk in a heavy saucepan over medium-high heat. Bring to the boiling point; remove from heat. Mix in enough confectioners' sugar to make of spreading consistency. Stir in the vanilla.

Pam Butler (27 years), Xi Eta Kappa
Sterling, Kansas

PINA COLADA BARS

1 (2-layer) package
  pineapple cake mix
1 (4-ounce) package
  coconut cream
  instant pudding mix
1/2 cup vegetable oil
2 eggs

2 cups vanilla chips
1 cup flaked coconut
1 cup chopped walnuts
  or pecans
3 tablespoons rum
2 tablespoons butter

Mix the first 4 ingredients in a large bowl. Mix in 1 cup of the vanilla chips, coconut and 1/2 cup of the chopped nuts. Press the mixture into a lightly greased 9×13-inch baking dish. Bake at 350 degrees for 25 to 35 minutes or until golden brown. Combine the remaining 1 cup vanilla chips, rum and butter in a small saucepan over low heat. Heat until melted, stirring until smooth. Drizzle over the warm baked coconut mixture. Sprinkle with the remaining 1/2 cup chopped nuts. Cool and cut into bars. Yield: 3 dozen.

Juanita Bean (34 years), Theta Master
Sparks, Nevada

MOM'S PUMPKIN COOKIES

My mother's family used to gather at our house on Christmas night when I was a child. My mother "knocked herself out" preparing lots of good food for us. We children enjoyed listening to the grownups talk about their childhoods. My grandfather had the wanderlust, and he had taken his family around the country. There were four children, and each was born somewhere different. Grandpa was a forest ranger in Minnesota, homesteaded in Canada, and worked as a cowboy out West somewhere. My mother was born in Canada. They always came back to Marion, Ohio, where my grandfather's family lived. We children loved hearing our parents and grandparents tell of their lives of adventure. Now our own children enjoy hearing about the adventures of their great-grandparents, aunt, and uncles.

1 cup packed brown
  sugar
1 cup granulated sugar
3/4 cup shortening
2 cups canned pumpkin
1 egg
3 1/2 cups flour

1 teaspoon salt
1/2 teaspoon allspice
1 teaspoon baking soda
1 teaspoon baking
  powder
1/2 teaspoon cinnamon
Canned frosting

Combine the brown sugar, granulated sugar, shortening and pumpkin in a large mixing bowl; cream until light and fluffy. Beat in the egg. Mix together the flour, salt, allspice, baking soda, baking powder and cinnamon in a separate bowl. Add the flour mixture to the creamed mixture gradually, beating well after each addition. Drop by teaspoonfuls 2 inches apart onto a greased cookie sheet. Bake at 375 degrees for 10 minutes or until done to taste. Frost the cooled cookies with canned frosting. Yield: 3 to 3 1/2 dozen.

Sharon Bargar, Eta
Tennyson, Indiana

ROSE'S LEMON WHIPS

1 (2-layer) package
  lemon cake mix
2 cups whipped topping

1 egg
1/2 cup sifted
  confectioners' sugar

Combine the dry cake mix, whipped topping and egg in a large bowl; mix well. Drop by teaspoonfuls into the confectioners' sugar and roll to coat. Place 1 1/2 inches apart on greased cookie sheets. Bake at 350 degrees for 10 to 15 minutes or until light golden brown. Remove to a wire rack to cool. Yield: 4 dozen.

Mary Helen Goldberg, Lambda Mu
Plattsburg, Missouri

FRUITCAKE COOKIES

My mother's sister, one of my sisters, and I would go to Mother's house every November and make 300 of these cookies—what a wonderful time we had. My mother passed away in 1990 at the age of ninety-one. Her sister and I still make cookies.

1 cup (2 sticks) butter, softened	**1/2 pound red candied pineapple, chopped**
1 cup firmly packed light brown sugar	**1/2 pound green candied pineapple, chopped**
3 eggs, well beaten	**1/2 pound red candied cherries, chopped**
3 cups flour	
1 1/2 teaspoons baking soda	**1/2 pound green candied cherries, chopped**
1 tablespoon cinnamon	**1/2 pound pitted dates, chopped**
1/2 cup sherry	
7 cups mixed nuts, chopped	**3/4 pound white raisins**

Cream the butter and brown sugar in a mixing bowl until light and fluffy. Mix in the eggs. Sift together the flour, baking soda and cinnamon. Add to the creamed mixture alternately with the sherry, mixing well after each addition. Add the mixed nuts, red and green candied pineapple, red and green candied cherries, dates and raisins, mixing with the hands if necessary. Drop by teaspoonfuls onto greased cookie sheets and shape into mounds. Bake at 300 degrees for 20 to 25 minutes or until firm and beginning to brown. Remove to a wire rack to cool.
Yield: 100 cookies.

Inez L. Hyatt (29 years), Laureate Mu
Blythewood, South Carolina

MEMORIES

Memories of Mom! She always had warm cookies and milk on the table when we got home from school. It was talk time then! You could tell her anything—from your first beau to the latest bus words. She would tell you which ones you could use and which ones not to say again. Her favorite expression was "Don't do anything you wouldn't like to see on the front page of the paper!"

Marilyn J. Schwartz (30 years), Laureate Beta
Lafayette, Louisiana

CARROT DROP COOKIES

3/4 cup shortening	**1 teaspoon vanilla extract**
1 cup sugar	
1 egg	**2 cups flour**
1 cup mashed cooked carrots	**2 teaspoons baking powder**
Grated zest of 1 orange	**1/4 teaspoon salt**

Cream the shortening and sugar in a mixing bowl until light and fluffy. Mix in the egg, carrots, orange zest and vanilla. Blend in a mixture of the flour, baking powder and salt. Drop by teaspoonfuls 2 inches apart onto a greased cookie sheet. Bake at 375 degrees for 10 to 12 minutes. Remove to a wire rack to cool. Frost the cooled cookies with a mixture of 1 cup confectioners' sugar and enough orange juice to make of spreading consistency. Yield: 3 dozen.

Donna Patry (33 years), Xi Delta Pi
Horton, Kansas

GREAT CHOCOLATE CHIP COOKIES

1 cup (2 sticks) butter, softened	**1 teaspoon vanilla extract**
1/4 cup granulated sugar	**2 eggs**
3/4 cup packed brown sugar	**2 1/4 cups flour**
	1 teaspoon baking soda
1 (4-ounce) package vanilla instant pudding mix	**2 cups semisweet chocolate chips**
	1 cup chopped pecans

Combine the butter, granulated sugar, brown sugar, dry pudding mix and vanilla in a large mixing bowl. Beat until smooth and creamy. Mix in the eggs. Stir together the flour and baking soda and add gradually to the egg mixture. Stir in the chocolate chips and pecans. Batter will be stiff. Drop by teaspoonfuls 1 inch apart onto an ungreased cookie sheet. Bake at 375 degrees for 10 minutes or until lightly browned; do not overbake. Yield: 3 dozen.

Georgeana Rainwater (41 years)
Preceptor Gamma Gamma
Broken Arrow, Oklahoma

Della Warner (30 years), Preceptor Delta, Coffeyville, Kansas, makes *Jiffy Cookies* by mixing a large cake mix (any flavor) with 1/3 cup oil and 2 beaten eggs. The mixture will be stiff but can be shaped into two ropes on a lightly floured surface and cut into 1/2-inch or larger pieces, shaped into balls and baked on a cookie sheet at 350 degrees for 8 to 10 minutes.

MEMORIES

When I was a young girl at home my sister, Barbara, loved to cook and bake. I would wake up to the smell of chocolate chip cookies baking in the oven. She would let me taste the dough, lick the beaters and eat the warm delicious cookies. Now that we are both married and live a distance from each other, those memories are cherished ones. One morning my husband lit my Yankee candle in the kitchen. As I came down the stairs my excitement grew. I thought that Barbara was in the kitchen baking. Now when I need her close by, I just light my candle. She is a wonderful sister, and she is also a Beta Sigma Phi sister.

Carole J. Whitney, Preceptor Zeta Omega
Antioch, Illinois

✤ CARAMEL-FILLED CHOCOLATE COOKIES

1 cup granulated sugar	2 teaspoons vanilla
1 cup firmly packed	extract
brown sugar	1 cup chopped pecans
1/2 cup (1 stick)	48 cherry caramels in
margarine, softened	milk chocolate,
1/2 cup (1 stick) butter,	unwrapped
softened	1 tablespoon sugar
2 1/2 cups flour	4 ounces vanilla-
3/4 cup baking cocoa	flavored candy
1 teaspoon baking soda	coating
2 eggs	

Combine the 1 cup granulated sugar, brown sugar, margarine and butter in a large mixing bowl; beat until light and fluffy. Combine the flour, baking cocoa and baking soda in a medium bowl and mix well. Add the eggs to the butter mixture and mix well. Add the flour mixture and blend well. Stir in 1/2 cup of the chopped pecans. Chill, covered, for 30 minutes for easier handling. Preheat the oven to 350 degrees. With floured hands, shape about 1 tablespoon of the dough around each cherry caramel, enclosing it completely. Combine the remaining 1/2 cup chopped pecans and the 1 tablespoon sugar in a small bowl. Press each dough-wrapped caramel into the pecan mixture. Place 2 inches apart, pecan side up, on ungreased baking sheets. Bake for 7 to 10 minutes or until cookies are set and slightly cracked.

Cool for 2 minutes on the cookie sheets; remove to a wire rack to cool for 15 minutes. Melt the candy coating in a small saucepan over low heat, stirring constantly until smooth. Drizzle over the cookies. Yield: 3 to 4 dozen.

R. Gene Farley (36 years), Laureate Gamma Iota
Tallahassee, Florida

SNICKERS BAR COOKIES

1 cup (2 sticks) butter	1 teaspoon vanilla
1 cup granulated sugar	extract
1 cup packed brown	1 teaspoon baking
sugar	powder
2 eggs	1 teaspoon baking soda
1 cup creamy peanut	3 cups flour
butter	4 dozen miniature
1/2 teaspoon salt	Snickers Bars

Cream the butter, granulated sugar and brown sugar in a large mixing bowl until light and fluffy. Combine the next 7 ingredients in a medium bowl and mix well. Mix the peanut butter mixture into the creamed mixture to make a firm dough. Wrap a heaping tablespoonful of dough around each unwrapped Snickers Bar to enclose. Arrange 2 inches apart on greased cookie sheets. Bake at 350 degrees for 9 to 10 minutes or until dough is set and lightly browned; do not overbake. Yield: 4 dozen.

Sara Moler, Pi Beta
Clear Lake, Iowa

CHOCOLATE TOFFEE BARS

My mom just passed away, and this is the last recipe she had wanted to prepare for my husband, whom she spoiled. Since she had already gotten the ingredients, I made it for him. Just proves that even after she has died, she is still spoiling him . . .

1/2 cup (1 stick) butter,	1 cup semisweet
melted	chocolate chips
1 3/4 cups crushed	1 cup chopped pecans
chocolate graham	1/2 cup chopped walnuts
crackers	1 (14-ounce) can
1 1/4 cups almond brickle	sweetened condensed
chips	milk
6 small English toffee	
bars, crushed	

Preheat the oven to 325 degrees. Line a 9×13-inch baking pan with foil large enough so its edges extend beyond the pan's edges. Spray nonstick cooking spray over the foil. Pour in the melted butter and tilt to spread evenly. Sprinkle the graham crackers crumbs in the pan; press firmly. Bake for 5 minutes.

Layer the almond brickle chips, English toffee bars, chocolate chips, pecans and walnuts evenly over the graham cracker crust in the order given; press firmly. Pour the condensed milk evenly over the top. Bake for 30 minutes or until edges are light brown. Cool completely in the pan. Lift the foil from the pan and peel away from the baked toffee mixture. Cut into bars. Yield: 2 dozen.

D-Ann Berry, Alpha Xi Psi
Liberty, Texas

MAGIC PEANUT BUTTER MIDDLES

1/2 cup (1 stick) butter, softened	*1 teaspoon vanilla extract*
1 cup creamy peanut butter	*1 1/2 cups flour*
1/2 cup granulated sugar	*1/2 cup baking cocoa*
1/2 cup packed brown sugar	*1/2 teaspoon baking soda*
1 egg	*3/4 cup confectioners' sugar*

Preheat the oven to 375 degrees. Cream the butter, 1/4 cup of the peanut butter, granulated sugar and brown sugar in a mixing bowl until light and fluffy. Blend in the egg and vanilla. Stir in a mixture of the flour, baking cocoa and baking soda. Blend together the remaining 3/4 cup peanut butter and confectioners' sugar to make the filling. Shape into 30 (1-inch) balls. Wrap a tablespoon of dough around each ball to enclose. Arrange on ungreased baking sheets. Flatten each ball slightly with the bottom of a glass dipped in granulated sugar. Bake for 7 to 9 minutes or until cookies begin to firm and brown. Remove to a wire rack to cool. Cooled cookies may be decorated with icing if desired. Yield. About 30.

Kay Dunning, Xi Delta Psi
Erie, Kansas

PEANUT BUTTER TART COOKIES

1 (18-ounce) package peanut butter cookie mix	*1 egg*
	1 (13-ounce) package Reese's Peanut Butter Cups
1/3 cup vegetable oil	

Preheat the oven to 350 degrees. Prepare the cookie dough using the package directions with 1/3 cup vegetable oil and 1 egg. Shape into 3 dozen balls and drop into greased muffin cups or tart pans. Bake for 7 minutes. Push an unwrapped Reese's Peanut Butter Cup into each warm cookie. Let cool. Remove from pan, using a thin knife to loosen if necessary. Yield: 3 dozen.

Millissa A. Duffey, Theta
Vincennes, Indiana

"M & M'S" PARTY COOKIES

1 cup shortening	*2 1/2 cups sifted flour*
1 cup packed brown sugar	*1 teaspoon baking soda*
1/2 cup granulated sugar	*1 teaspoon salt*
2 teaspoons vanilla extract	*1 1/2 cups "M & M's" Plain Chocolate Candies*
2 eggs	

Cream the shortening, brown sugar and granulated sugar in a mixing bowl until light and fluffy. Beat in the vanilla and eggs. Sift together the flour, baking soda and salt; add to the sugar mixture and mix well. Stir in 1/2 cup of the "M & M's." Drop by spoonfuls 2 inches apart onto ungreased cookie sheets. Decorate tops of cookies with remaining "M & M's." Bake at 375 degrees for 10 to 12 minutes or until golden brown. Yield: 6 dozen.

Mary Margaret Odom, Preceptor Theta Lambda
Miami, Florida

BON BON COOKIES

1/2 cup (1 stick) butter, softened	*1 1/2 cups flour*
3/4 cup confectioners' sugar	*1/8 teaspoon salt*
	Pecan or walnut halves
1 tablespoon vanilla extract	*Small gumdrops, halved horizontally*
	Bon Bon Icing

Combine the butter, confectioners' sugar and vanilla in a mixing bowl and beat until smooth. Add a mixture of the flour and salt; blend completely using the hands. Wrap a level tablespoonful of dough around each pecan half or around the bottom half of each gumdrop. Arrange 1 inch apart on ungreased cookie sheets. Bake at 350 degrees for 12 to 15 minutes or until set but not brown. Dip the tops of the warm cookies in Bon Bon Icing. Top each with a pecan half or the top half of a gumdrop. Sprinkle with colored sugar if desired. Yield: 2 dozen.

BON BON ICING

1 cup confectioners' sugar	*1 teaspoon vanilla extract*
2 tablespoons milk	

Combine the confectioners' sugar, milk and vanilla in a small mixing bowl and beat until smooth. Beat in food coloring if desired.

Carol Ann Ferguson, Preceptor Gamma Epsilon
Marion, Ohio

MEMORIES

I grew up in the country over 60 years ago. The wood stove, which provided all our heat, was the center of our activities in the cold winters. The upstairs bedrooms got very little of the heat! At night, as small children, we would get into our p.j.s by the stove. Mom would carefully take a hot brick from the oven, wrap it in newspaper and a towel, and send us up to be tucked into a cold bed piled high with homemade quilts. This brick was our hot water bottle, and it would still be warm in the morning. The smells of hot brick and newspaper always come back with fond memories. I loved that smell and I still get that feeling when a fire is lit with newspaper.

Anne Willcox (37 years), Laureate Alpha Epsilon
Kitchener, Ontario, Canada

BRANDY ALMOND BISCOTTI

*1 cup toasted chopped
   almonds
1 cup sugar
1/2 cup (1 stick) butter,
   melted
1/4 cup brandy
3 eggs*

*3 cups flour
1/2 teaspoon baking
   powder
1/4 teaspoon salt
1 cup semisweet
   chocolate chips*

Combine the almonds, sugar, butter, brandy and eggs in a bowl and mix well. Stir in a mixture of the flour, baking powder and salt. Knead briefly. Shape into a long loaf about 2 inches in diameter. Place on an ungreased cookie sheet. Bake at 350 degrees for 25 minutes or until it has a cakelike texture. Remove from oven and cool for about 15 minutes. Cut into 1/2-inch slices and arrange cut side down on ungreased cookie sheets. Bake for 20 minutes or until both sides are lightly browned, turning once. Melt the chocolate chips in the top of a double boiler over boiling water. Dip each cookie halfway in the melted chocolate and cool on waxed paper. Yield: 2 dozen.

Carole Michael, Delta Nu Alpha
Mariposa, California

ALMOND SLICES

*3/8 cup vegetable oil
1 cup sugar
6 large eggs
2 tablespoons pure
   anise oil
4 cups flour*

*2 tablespoons baking
   powder
1 cup almond slices,
   chopped
Pinch of salt*

Combine the vegetable oil, sugar, eggs and anise oil in a mixing bowl and mix until smooth. Add the flour, baking powder, almonds and salt. Mix with floured hands until smooth and dough does not stick to hands, adding a little flour if necessary. Shape into loaves 12 inches long and 2 inches in diameter on greased baking sheets. Bake at 375 degrees for 12 to 15 minutes or until light brown. Remove from oven and cool slightly. Cut into 1/2-inch-thick diagonal slices with a sharp knife. Arrange slices cut side down on a greased baking sheet. Bake at 425 degrees for 5 minutes or until golden brown, watching closely. Yield: 2 to 3 dozen.

Kathy Marchese, Laureate Delta Epsilon
Lees Summit, Missouri

ITALIAN WEDDING CAKES

*4 large eggs
1 cup milk
1 cup vegetable oil
4 teaspoons anise
   extract
1 1/2 cups granulated
   sugar*

*5 cups flour
5 teaspoons baking
   powder
Anise Icing*

Combine the eggs, the 1 cup milk, vegetable oil and the 4 teaspoons anise extract in a bowl and mix well. Mix in the sugar. Add a mixture of the flour and baking powder gradually; dough will be stiff and sticky. Shape into 1-inch balls with floured hands. Arrange on greased cookie sheets. Bake at 350 degrees for 10 to 15 minutes or until bottom is light golden color; top of cookie will remain white. Cool. Dip in Anise Icing and let harden on waxed paper. Yield: 6 dozen.

ANISE ICING

*2 cups confectioners'
   sugar*

*Milk
Anise extract to taste*

Mix the confectioners' sugar with enough milk to make icing just thin enough for dipping cookies. Flavor with anise extract.

Debbie Meegan, Preceptor Beta Phi
Lemont Furnace, Pennsylvania

CREAM CHEESE COOKIES

1 cup (2 sticks) butter, softened	1 egg
3 ounces cream cheese, softened	1½ teaspoons vanilla extract
1 cup sugar	2½ cups flour

Cream the butter, cream cheese and sugar in a mixing bowl until light and fluffy. Beat in the egg and vanilla. Add the flour gradually, beating until well blended. Dough may be refrigerated for easier handling. Press through a cookie press or roll on a floured surface and cut with cookie cutters. Arrange on greased cookie sheets. Bake at 325 degrees for 10 to 15 minutes or until done to taste. Frost or decorate as desired. Yield: 5 dozen.

Linda Herring, Laureate Alpha Eta
Oneonta, New York

FORGOTTEN COOKIES

This is the recipe that was the answer to bedtime pleas of: "Mom, I'm supposed to take refreshments," or "Mom, we are having a bake sale." You can substitute candy bar chips, chopped pecans, crushed peppermint candy, or another ingredient you have on hand for the chocolate chips.

2 egg whites	1 cup semisweet chocolate chips
⅔ cup sugar	
1 teaspoon vanilla extract	

Preheat the oven to 350 degrees. Line a cookie sheet with foil. Beat the egg whites until foamy. Add the sugar gradually while beating at top speed; beat until stiff peaks form. Fold in the vanilla and chocolate chips. Drop by teaspoonfuls 2 inches apart onto the foil. Place in the preheated oven; turn off the oven immediately. Let cookies stand in oven for 5 to 10 hours. Yield: About 3 dozen.

Bea Lawler, Xi Pi Mu
Kilgore, Texas

FRYING PAN COOKIES

½ cup butter	2 cups crisp rice cereal
1 cup sugar	1 cup chopped walnuts or pecans
1 egg, beaten	
1 cup dates, chopped	6 ounces shredded coconut
½ teaspoon salt	

Melt the butter in a large skillet over low heat. Add the sugar and blend well. Remove from heat and cool for 5 minutes. Stir in the egg, dates and salt. Return to the stovetop and cook over low heat for 5 minutes. Remove from heat. Stir in the crisp rice cereal and walnuts. When cool enough to handle, shape into 2-inch balls with buttered hands and roll in coconut to coat. Arrange on a tray to cool. Yield: 3 dozen.

Kathleen Priddy (45 years), Preceptor Beta Psi
Indio, California

❖ FROSTED CASHEW COOKIES

This recipe belonged to my mother. She made hundreds of these cookies for our wedding reception in 1961.

½ cup (1 stick) butter, softened	¾ teaspoon baking powder
1 cup firmly packed brown sugar	¾ teaspoon baking soda
1 egg	¼ teaspoon salt
½ teaspoon vanilla extract	⅓ cup dairy sour cream
2 cups sifted flour	1¾ cups salted cashews
	Golden Butter Frosting

Cream the butter and brown sugar in a mixing bowl until light and fluffy. Beat in the egg and vanilla. Mix together the flour, baking powder, baking soda and salt. Add to the creamed mixture alternately with the sour cream, mixing well after each addition. Fold in the cashews carefully. Drop by teaspoonfuls 2 inches apart onto greased cookie sheets. Bake at 375 degrees for 10 minutes. Remove to a wire rack to cool. Frost with Golden Butter Frosting. Yield: About 4½ dozen.

GOLDEN BUTTER FROSTING

½ cup (1 stick) butter	2 cups confectioners' sugar
3 tablespoons half-and-half	
¼ teaspoon vanilla extract	

Melt the butter in a skillet over medium heat and cook until lightly browned. Remove from heat. Stir in the half-and-half and vanilla. Stir in the confectioners' sugar; beat until thick enough to spread.

Marianne Hilleren, Epsilon Delta
Benson, Minnesota

Rosemary Cronin, Xi Zeta Rho, Le Mars, Iowa, makes a **Butter Cream Frosting** for raisin bars that would be delicious on other cookies or cake. Blend a cup of brown sugar with ½ cup melted butter in a saucepan and boil for 2 minutes, stirring constantly. Add ¼ cup milk and bring to a full rolling boil, stirring constantly. Let stand until cool and beat in 2 cups confectioners' sugar.

BUTTERSCOTCH YUM YUMS

1 cup (2 sticks) butter or
  margarine, softened
1½ cups packed brown
  sugar
2 eggs
1 teaspoon vanilla
  extract
½ teaspoon baking soda
2½ cups flour
1 (12-ounce) package
  butterscotch morsels
1 cup chopped pecans

Cream the butter and brown sugar in a mixing bowl until light and fluffy. Add the eggs 1 at a time, beating well after each addition. Add the vanilla, baking soda and flour; beat well. Add the butterscotch morsels and pecans and mix well. Drop by rounded teaspoonfuls 2 inches apart onto a lightly greased cookie sheet. Bake at 375 degrees for 8 to 10 minutes or until browned. Yield: 5 dozen.

Sarah C. Byerly (35 years), Laureate Chi Chapter
Salisbury, North Carolina

ELEPHANT EAR COOKIES

My mother experimented until she came up with this delicious recipe.

1 teaspoon salt
2 cups packed brown
  sugar
3 cups flour
1 cup shortening
3 eggs, slightly beaten
½ cup milk
1 teaspoon baking soda
3 tablespoons sour milk
1 cup chopped walnuts
  or pecans
1 cup raisins (optional)

Mix together the salt, brown sugar and flour in a large bowl. Mix in the shortening, eggs and milk. Dissolve the baking soda in the sour milk and stir into the flour mixture. Fold in the chopped nuts and raisins. Drop by large spoonfuls 2 inches apart onto greased cookie sheets. Bake at 375 degrees for 10 minutes or until edges are slightly brown, with centers remaining a little soft. Yield: 2 to 4 dozen.

Mary M. Fronczak, Laureate Gamma Nu
Oviedo, Florida

NUTMEG COOKIES

Fifty-three years ago after we had just married, my husband brought a little cookbook home to me, and I have enjoyed cooking from it all these years.

3 cups flour
1 teaspoon baking soda
½ teaspoon nutmeg
1 cup shortening
1 cup sugar
2 eggs
5 tablespoons milk

Sift together the flour, baking soda and nutmeg. Cream the shortening and sugar in a mixing bowl.

Add the eggs 1 at a time, beating well after each addition. Add the milk; mix well. Drop by teaspoonfuls 2 inches apart onto an ungreased cookie sheet. Press gently with the tines of a fork. Bake at 350 degrees for 12 minutes or until done to taste.
Yield: About 5 dozen.

Rena Hopkins, Laureate Beta Epsilon
Arkansas City, Kansas

K.J.'S STIR-AND-DROP COOKIES

I have a large family, and sharing recipes is part of our family tradition. I loved going to my grandmother's house when I was a young girl, and smelling all the wonderful smells that came from her kitchen. As my own children were growing up, I decided to fill my kitchen with the same cookie smells. I always had to leave enough dough in the bowl for them to fight over. These childhood spoon fights reminded me of my sisters and myself fighting over our mother's and grandmother's cookie dough. What great memories and fun.

¾ cup sugar
⅔ cup vegetable oil
2 tablespoons vanilla
  extract
Grated lemon zest
  (optional)
2 eggs
2 cups self-rising flour

Combine the sugar, vegetable oil, vanilla, lemon zest and eggs in a large bowl; blend well. Add the flour ½ cup at a time, mixing well after each addition. Spoon onto ungreased cookie sheets about 2 inches apart. Bake at 400 degrees for 5 to 10 minutes or until brown. Yield: 2 dozen.

Karen Jo Smith, Laureate Omicron
Franklin, Tennessee

WHITE COOKIES

¾ cup shortening
1 cup sugar
2 eggs
2 tablespoons milk
½ teaspoon vanilla
  extract
½ teaspoon almond
  extract
½ teaspoon salt
½ teaspoon baking soda
5 to 6 cups flour

Cream the shortening and sugar in a mixing bowl until light and fluffy. Beat in the eggs, milk, vanilla and almond extract. Stir in a mixture of the salt, baking soda and enough flour to make a workable dough. Roll thin and flat on a floured surface. Cut with a cookie cutter. Place on an ungreased cookie sheet. Bake at 350 degrees for 8 to 10 minutes or until done to taste. Cool on a wire rack. Yield: 1 to 2 dozen.

Jacqueline Jump (26 years), Beta Sigma Phi
Necedah, Wisconsin

MEMORIES

*W*hen we moved to a small farming community in northern Minnesota, I had to learn a lot about survival in the cold and deep snow. Going to the store was often out of the question. One Saturday, my daughter and her friend decided to make cookies. At eleven years old they knew how to read, or so I thought. Checking on how they were doing, I noticed that they were measuring out a cup of salt. Just before they added it to the dough, I stopped them and asked them to re-read the recipe. They almost died when they realized that it said 1 teaspoon of salt!

Helen Marquis, Epsilon Rho
Colorado Springs, Colorado

FRIGIDAIRE COOKIES

The name of these cookies tells you how old this recipe is. I got it at a cooking school in the 1930s.

1¹/₂ cups shortening	2 teaspoons cinnamon
1 cup packed brown sugar	Melted chocolate and vanilla (optional)
¹/₃ cup granulated sugar	Shredded coconut (optional)
3 eggs	
4 cups flour	Chopped nuts and
1 teaspoon baking soda	raisins or chopped
1 teaspoon salt	dates (optional)

Cream the shortening and sugars in a mixing bowl until light and fluffy. Add the eggs 1 at a time, beating well after each addition. Sift together the flour, baking soda, salt and cinnamon. Stir into the creamed mixture. Divide the dough into 3 portions. Add melted chocolate and vanilla to 1 portion, shredded coconut to another and nuts and raisins or chopped dates to the third. Shape each portion into a sausage-like roll and wrap in waxed paper. Chill for 8 to 10 hours or until baking time. Slice very thin and place on a nonstick cookie sheet. Bake at 450 degrees for 8 to 10 minutes or until done to taste.
Yield: 3 to 4 dozen.

 Pegeen K. Blackford (50 years)
Neodesha, Kansas

SHORTBREAD

This recipe has been handed down through at least four generations.

2 cups (4 sticks) butter, softened	1 teaspoon vanilla , orange or lemon extract
¹/₂ cup sugar	
2 cups flour	1 (1-pound) package confectioners' sugar
¹/₂ cup cornstarch	
Walnut Filling	
8 ounces cream cheese, softened	

Cream 1 cup of the butter and sugar in a mixing bowl until light and fluffy. Stir in a mixture of the flour and cornstarch. Pat gently into an ungreased 11×17-inch shallow baking pan. Bake at 325 degrees for 15 minutes. Cool for at least 20 minutes while preparing Walnut Filling. Spread the Walnut Filling evenly over the shortbread. Bake at 350 degrees for 25 minutes. Let stand until completely cool. Combine the remaining 1 cup butter and remaining ingredients in a bowl and mix well. Beat until creamy. Frost the cooled shortbread. Let stand for a while until frosting sets. Cut into pieces. Place cut cookies between layers of waxed paper and store in containers or in the freezer. Yield: 4 dozen.

WALNUT FILLING

4 large eggs	1 pound shelled
4 tablespoons flour	walnuts, chopped
¹/₂ teaspoon baking powder	1 (1-pound) package brown sugar
2 teaspoons vanilla, orange or lemon extract	1 (14-ounce) package shredded coconut

Combine the ingredients in a large bowl and mix well. Mixture will be stiff.

Trish Patterson, Laureate Eta Iota
Running Springs, California

Peg Stephenson (30 years), Pi Phi, Sebring, Florida, makes **Canadian Shortbread** by beating 1 pound softened butter, 1 tablespoon vanilla extract, 1 teaspoon almond extract, 1 cup confectioners' sugar, ¹/₂ cup cornstarch and 3 cups flour together until the consistency of heavy whipped cream. Drop the dough onto ungreased cookie sheets using a small ice cream scoop and flatten slightly. Bake at 325 degrees until just before the cookies start to brown around the edge. Drizzle with a small amount of vanilla or almond-flavored glaze.

SCOTCH BREAD

I am allergic to eggs, and my mother always tried to come up with recipes for desserts that I could eat. This was and still is one of my favorites. It was my "birthday cake" several times. Mom often baked "my Scotch Bread" and put it in a tin just for me.

1 cup butter, softened   2 cups flour
1/2 cup sugar

Cream the butter and sugar in a mixing bowl until light and fluffy. Stir in the flour. Press into an ungreased 9×13-inch baking pan. Bake at 300 degrees for 35 to 40 minutes or until lightly browned. Cut into squares. Yield: 3 dozen squares.

Kathy Rand, Xi Alpha Pi
Madison, Wisconsin

MARION'S SAND TARTS

This was my mom's (Marion's) recipe, and making these cookies was and still is a Christmas tradition. As we roll the dough, we remember her saying, "Thinner, thinner."

3 1/2 cups flour   2 cups sugar
3/4 teaspoon baking soda   2 eggs
1 cup (2 sticks) butter

Sift together the flour and baking soda. Cream the butter and sugar in a mixing bowl until light and fluffy. Beat in the eggs. Stir in the flour mixture. Chill, covered, for at least 30 minutes. Roll very thin on a well-floured surface. Cut into shapes and place on a nonstick cookie sheet. Brush with egg whites and sprinkle with cinnamon sugar. Bake at 350 degrees for 12 to 15 minutes or until done to taste. Cool on a wire rack. Yield: 3 to 4 dozen.

Linda M. Miller (30 years), Laureate Epsilon Sigma
Scotland, Pennsylvania

MEMORIES

My *mother's parents owned a bakery, so my mom inherited their recipes for rolls, pies, cakes and cookies. She was a stay-at-home mom and every afternoon she had something coming out of the oven for my brother and me when we got off the school bus. We came home from school to wonderful aromas and sweet treats.*

Mary Elizabeth Maze, Preceptor Alpha Psi
Scott Depot, West Virginia

SANTA CLAUS COOKIES

For over forty years my mother-in-law made these cookies on Christmas Eve for her next-door neighbor, and in return she received homemade tamales. So every Christmas Eve we have tamales for dinner and the neighbors anxiously await their Santa Claus Cookies. My mother-in-law has never given this recipe to anyone who wasn't family, so it wasn't easy getting her permission to use it.

1 cup shortening   1 teaspoon baking soda
1 teaspoon vanilla   1 teaspoon salt
  extract   1 cup evaporated milk
2 cups sugar   1 tablespoon lemon
2 eggs, separated   juice
4 cups flour

Cream the shortening, vanilla and sugar in a mixing bowl until light and fluffy. Add the egg yolks 1 at a time, beating well after each addition. Add a mixture of the flour, baking soda and salt; mix well. Mix in the evaporated milk and lemon juice. Beat the egg whites until soft peaks form. Fold into the flour mixture. Drop by teaspoonfuls 2 inches apart onto a greased cookie sheet. Bake at 375 degrees for 10 minutes or until done to taste. Press 2 chocolate chips point side down into each warm cookie to make Santa's eyes. Remove cookies to a wire rack to cool. Use red icing to make Santa's nose and his cap. Use white icing quickly sprinkled with shredded coconut for his beard. Yield: 4 dozen.

Joyce Martin, Delta Lambda
El Centro, California

CANDY CANE PINWHEELS

I made these cookies for our family at Christmastime for years. When our middle daughter went off to school, she called and asked for them for Christmas!

1 cup (2 sticks) butter,   1 1/2 teaspoons vanilla
  softened   extract
1 cup confectioners'   2 1/2 cups flour
  sugar   1 teaspoon salt
1 egg, beaten   Crushed candy canes
1 1/2 teaspoons almond
  extract

Cream the butter and confectioners' sugar in a mixing bowl until light and fluffy. Beat in the egg, almond extract and vanilla. Stir in a mixture of the flour and salt. Refrigerate, covered, until completely chilled. Roll to 1/8-inch thickness, working with 1 portion at a time; cut into 2 1/2-inch squares. Make a 1 1/2-inch cut from each corner toward the center. Fold the points alternately to the center; press to secure.

Place on a nonstick cookie sheet and sprinkle with crushed candy canes. Bake at 375 degrees for 8 to 10 minutes or until done to taste. Yield: 4 dozen.

Jenean Patrick, Preceptor Rho
Worland, Wyoming

GRANDMA'S VANILLA WAFERS

My Grandma Fraser always let me help her make these cookies in her old-fashioned farm kitchen. They were best when made with her homechurned butter. Six years after her death, I still think of her daily.

1¹/₄ cups butter, softened	2 tablespoons milk
1 cup sugar	3¹/₂ cups flour
2 eggs	1 teaspoon baking
¹/₂ teaspoon vanilla	powder
extract	

Cream the butter and sugar in a mixing bowl until light and fluffy. Beat in the eggs. Blend in the vanilla and milk. Sift together the flour and baking powder and add to the creamed mixture. Stir well. Shape into small balls and place 2 inches apart on a greased cookie sheet. Flatten with a glass that has been dipped in sugar. Bake at 375 degrees for 12 to 14 minutes or until done to taste. Cool on the cookie sheet for several minutes. Remove to a wire rack to cool completely. Yield: 5 dozen.

Dawna Davis (31 years)
Henryetta, Oklahoma

MOLASSES SPICE CRISPS

This recipe was created by my Aunt Esther in 1959, and our family has been making the cookies ever since

³/₄ cup shortening	1 teaspoon ginger
1 cup sugar	1 teaspoon cinnamon
1 egg	2 tablespoons light
2¹/₂ cups flour	molasses
2 teaspoons baking soda	2 tablespoons dark
1 teaspoon ground	molasses
cloves	

Cream the shortening and sugar in a mixing bowl until light and fluffy. Beat in the egg. Mix together the flour, baking soda, cloves, ginger and cinnamon. Add to the creamed mixture alternately with the light and dark molasses, mixing well after each addition. Shape into walnut-size balls and dip in sugar. Place sugar side up on a nonstick cookie sheet. Bake at 350 degrees for 10 to 12 minutes. Cool and serve.
Yield: About 4 dozen.

Roberta Hersom, Mu Mu
Emmetsburg, Iowa

MEMORIES

*W*hen I was growing up my mom, my grandma and I would get together every year a week before Christmas and make ten different kinds of Christmas cookies. We would bake everything from toffee bars and date balls to Russian teacakes. We would decorate holiday-shaped cut-out cookies with colored frostings and sprinkles. My favorite treats were the layered cookies with chocolate chips, butterscotch chips and coconut. We would have so much fun talking about everything from Grandma's life as a girl to my life. Since then I have moved away and am no longer able to be at my mom's house for "cookie day." My mom and grandma, who is now in her eighties, still get together every year. I make a point of calling them on that day.

Ann Lancaster, Beta Psi
Lexington, Kentucky

OLD-FASHIONED CRYBABIES

2 teaspoons baking soda	1 cup shortening
1 cup warm milk	1 egg
About 5 cups flour	1 teaspoon cinnamon
1 cup molasses	1 teaspoon salt
1 cup sugar	Raisins

Dissolve the baking soda in the milk. Combine the milk mixture, flour, molasses, sugar, shortening, egg, cinnamon, salt and raisins as desired in a bowl; mix well. Drop by teaspoonfuls 2 inches apart onto a greased cookie sheet. Bake at 350 degrees for 8 to 10 minutes. Yield: 4 to 5 dozen.

Kathleen Shafer, Xi Theta Eta
Mifflinburg, Pennsylvania

Ann Latoski, Xi Delta, Portage la Prairie, Manitoba, Canada, prepares **Carrot or Zucchini Bars** by beating 4 eggs for 5 minutes and blending in 1¹/₄ cups vegetable oil. Add a mixture of 2 cups each flour and sugar and 2 teaspoons each baking soda and cinnamon and mix well. Stir in 3 cups shredded carrots or zucchini and bake in a greased 10×15-inch baking pan for 35 minutes. Cool and frost with a favorite frosting.

GRANDMA'S OLD-FASHIONED SPICE COOKIES

Our Grandpa and Grandma Peters had a sorghum mill when we were kids, and we used to watch them make molasses. They had sixteen children and lots of grandchildren, and this is one of Grandma's cookie recipes.

1/4 cup lard, vegetable oil or margarine	1/2 teaspoon salt
2 cups sugar	2 tablespoons cinnamon
2 large eggs	2 tablespoons ginger
1/2 cup medium molasses	1 tablespoon ground cloves
4 cups flour	1/4 teaspoon nutmeg
4 teaspoons baking soda	

Cream the lard and sugar in a mixing bowl until light and fluffy. Beat in the eggs and molasses. Sift together the flour, baking soda, salt, cinnamon, ginger, cloves and nutmeg. Add to the molasses mixture and beat until smooth. Chill, wrapped in plastic wrap, for 1 to 10 hours. Preheat the oven to 375 degrees about 15 minutes before baking. Shape the dough into 1-inch balls and dip in sugar. Place sugar side up about 2 inches apart on a nonstick cookie sheet. Bake at 375 degrees for 10 to 12 minutes or until done to taste. Yield: 3 to 4 dozen.

Glendola King, Xi Gamma Omicron
Pryor, Oklahoma

MOM'S GINGERBREAD COOKIES

1 cup (2 sticks) margarine	2 cups flour
2 cups sugar	1/2 teaspoon salt
1 egg	2 teaspoons ginger
1/2 cup molasses	2 teaspoons cinnamon
2 cups quick-cooking oats	2 teaspoons baking soda

Cream the margarine and sugar in a mixing bowl until light and fluffy. Beat in the egg and molasses. Add a mixture of the oats, flour, salt, ginger, cinnamon and baking soda; mix well. Drop by teaspoonfuls 2 inches apart onto a greased cookie sheet. Bake at 375 degrees for 10 to 12 minutes or until done to taste. Yield: About 3 dozen.

Emmeline Hammer (31 years), Preceptor Gamma Tau
Sorrento, British Columbia, Canada

GINGER SNAPS

This is a recipe that belonged to my grandmother. I can remember her sending me a box of these cookies when I was in college, back in the '50s. These cookies are one of my "comfort" foods, and I always baked them at Christmas when my children were growing up. The dough makes excellent gingerbread men (or women).

1 1/2 cups molasses	1 teaspoon salt
1 cup shortening	1 cup sugar
1 tablespoon baking soda	2 tablespoons ginger
1/2 cup hot water	1 tablespoon cinnamon
	6 1/2 cups flour

Place the molasses in a heavy saucepan over medium-high heat and bring to a boil. Add the shortening and boil for 5 minutes. Remove from heat. Dissolve the baking soda in the hot water. Combine the molasses mixture, baking soda mixture, salt, sugar, ginger, cinnamon and flour in a large bowl. Mix well to make a stiff dough. Roll very thin on a floured surface. Cut as desired with cookie cutters. Place on nonstick cookie sheets. Bake at 350 degrees for 7 minutes or until done to taste. Frost if desired, but the cookies keep particularly well if left unfrosted. Yield: 4 to 6 dozen.

Mary Sumner Beamer, Xi Delta Xi
Oakridge, Oregon

BRANDY SNAPS

These cookies spread as they bake and become thin and crisp.

3/4 cup (1 1/2 sticks) butter	3/4 teaspoon grated orange zest
1/2 cup granulated sugar	3/4 teaspoon cinnamon
1/4 cup packed dark brown sugar	1 1/2 cups flour
1/2 cup molasses	1 tablespoon brandy
3/8 teaspoon ginger	

Preheat the oven to 300 degrees. Combine the butter, sugars, molasses, ginger, orange zest and cinnamon in a saucepan over low heat. Heat until butter melts and sugars are liquefied, stirring frequently to blend well. Remove from heat. Whisk in the flour; whisk until smooth. Stir in the brandy. Drop by teaspoonfuls 3 inches apart onto an ungreased cookie sheet. Bake for 10 to 12 minutes or until golden brown. Let stand on the cookie sheet for a few minutes. Remove carefully with a spatula and place on a flat surface to cool. Yield: 2 dozen.

Sonya Lee, Xi
Brandon, Mississippi

MEMORIES

On one occasion, many people had gathered in our home. I was getting too rambunctious to suit my mother and her eyes told me to settle down. I loudly proclaimed, "Mom, don't look at me with your black eyes." Her friends laughed, knowing my mother and her quiet ways. I was thoroughly reprimanded later.

Kelly Anne Gunn (44 years), Laureate Lambda
Sherwood Park, Alberta, Canada

OATMEAL COOKIES

1 cup shortening	1/4 cup hot water
2 cups packed brown sugar	1 tablespoon vanilla extract
2 eggs, beaten	2 cups rolled oats
1 teaspoon baking soda	2 cups flour

Cream the shortening and brown sugar in a mixing bowl until light and fluffy. Beat in the eggs. Dissolve the baking soda in the hot water. Add the baking soda mixture and vanilla to the creamed mixture and beat until smooth. Stir in the rolled oats and flour; mix well. Drop by teaspoonfuls 2 inches apart onto a well-greased cookie sheet. Bake at 375 degrees for 10 to 12 minutes or until done to taste. Yield: 3 dozen.

Irma G. Miller, Delta Delta
Myrtle Beach, South Carolina

OATMEAL MACAROONS

1 cup vegetable oil	2 eggs, slightly beaten
4 cups quick-cooking oats	1 tablespoon flour
2 cups packed brown sugar	1 teaspoon salt
1 tablespoon vanilla extract	1 cup chopped walnuts or pecans
	1 cup raisins

Combine the vegetable oil, oats and brown sugar in a bowl and mix well. Let stand, covered, at room temperature for 8 to 10 hours. Add the vanilla, eggs, flour and salt and mix well. Stir in the chopped nuts and raisins. Drop onto cookie sheets that have been sprayed with nonstick cooking spray. Bake at 325 degrees for 15 minutes or until done to taste. Yield: About 3 dozen.

Beverly Vanatta, Preceptor Iota Mu
Fountain Valley, California

OATMEAL CARMELITAS

This is one of my husband's favorites. He remembers his grandmother baking them for him.

32 caramels	1 cup rolled oats
5 tablespoons evaporated milk	1/2 teaspoon baking soda
1 cup flour	1/4 teaspoon salt
3/4 cup packed brown sugar	3/4 cup (1 1/2 sticks) butter, melted
	1 cup chocolate chips

Cook the caramels and evaporated milk in a saucepan over low heat until caramels are melted, stirring frequently. Remove from heat. Combine the flour, brown sugar, rolled oats, baking soda, salt and butter in a bowl; mix well. Press half the oats mixture in a greased 9×13-inch baking dish. Bake at 350 degrees for 10 minutes. Layer the chocolate chips, caramel mixture and remaining oats mixture over the top. Bake for 15 to 20 minutes longer or until lightly browned. Cool and cut into squares.
Yield: 2 to 3 dozen.

Kathleen Kennedy, Xi Omega
Worland, Wyoming

CHEWY OATMEAL COOKIES

This recipe comes from a very small paperback cookbook from the early 1960s. I made them the first time I baked cookies, and my whole family loved them. As my two younger sisters grew up, they baked these cookies, too, as they were already hooked. I have baked and shared them over the years, and many of our friends have come to love this family cookie of choice.

1 1/4 cups flour	2 eggs, unbeaten
1 teaspoon baking powder	1 teaspoon vanilla extract
1/2 teaspoon baking soda	2 1/2 cups quick-cooking oats
1 teaspoon salt	
3/4 cup (1 1/2 sticks) butter	1 cup chopped walnuts or pecans
1/2 cup granulated sugar	
1 1/2 cups packed brown sugar	1 cup shredded coconut

Sift together the flour, baking powder, baking soda and salt. Cream the butter and sugars in a mixing bowl until light and fluffy. Beat in the eggs and vanilla. Blend in the sifted dry ingredients. Stir in the oats, chopped nuts and coconut. Drop by rounded teaspoonfuls 2 inches apart onto a lightly greased cookie sheet. Bake at 375 degrees for 12 to 15 minutes or until done to taste. Cool on a wire rack. Store in airtight containers. Yield: 3 to 4 dozen.

Deborah J. Collins, Preceptor Alpha
North Little Rock, Arkansas

MEMORIES

Members of Laureate Epsilon Beta in Brandon, Florida, are very special sisters. When I had knee replacement surgery over a year ago, they truly came to my aid. Besides visits, flowers and phone calls, I even got my laundry done! When my father passed away recently, a sister gave of her time to take me to the funeral home and assist me with arrangements. My wonderful chapter attended the memorial service and provided an entire meal for my family. They surely have demonstrated "the aims and purposes" of sisterhood. I want to thank them from the bottom of my heart.

Joanna Anderson (43 years), Laureate Epsilon Beta
Valrico, Florida

LACE COOKIES

Parchment paper may be reused—just wipe clean with a paper towel between uses.

1 cup packed brown sugar	1 teaspoon baking powder
1 egg	1 teaspoon vanilla extract
1/2 cup melted butter	1/2 teaspoon salt
2 cups rolled oats	

Combine the brown sugar, egg, butter, oats, baking powder, vanilla and salt in a bowl; mix well. Drop dough by teaspoonfuls 3 inches apart onto parchment paper-lined cookie sheets. Bake at 350 degrees for 10 minutes or until deep golden brown and crisp. If cookies are soft in the center, return them to the oven for a few minutes. Let cool. Remove from parchment paper. Yield: 5 dozen.

Barbara Henson (25 years), Iota Master
Calgary, Alberta, Canada

CHOCOLATE LACE

You can grind the almonds by processing 1/2 cup whole blanched and shelled almonds in the blender.

1/2 cup (1 stick) butter	3/4 cup ground almonds
1 tablespoon flour	4 ounces semisweet chocolate
1/2 cup sugar	
1 tablespoon heavy cream	1/2 to 1 ounce cocoa butter (available in drugstores)
1 tablespoon milk	

Preheat the oven to 350 degrees. Combine the butter, flour, sugar, cream and milk in a small saucepan over low heat. Heat until butter melts. Stir in the almonds. Spoon 5 well-spaced teaspoonfuls onto a large greased and floured cookie sheet. Bake for 8 to 9 minutes. Cool on the cookie sheet for 1 minute. Invert onto paper towels. Bake cookies 5 at a time until all flour mixture is used. Melt the chocolate and cocoa butter in the top of a double boiler over boiling water. Drizzle over the cooled lace cookies. Chill to harden. Yield: 2 1/2 dozen.

Catherine Colangelo (59 years), Gamma Rho Master
San Diego, California

ALICE COOKIES

In 1964 I entered a recipe in the Five Roses Flour Young Canada Bake-Offs. My recipe for Alice Cookies gave me the opportunity to travel to our capital city, St. John's, Newfoundland, for a Bake-Off with six other young girls. My mom, who taught me to bake, accompanied me on the trip. It was a great experience for a fifteen-year-old girl to travel on a plate and stay in a hotel, all expenses paid for myself and my mom. I was not a finalist in the contest, but the experience alone was wonderful.

1/2 cup (1 stick) butter	1 cup rolled oats
3/4 cup sugar	1 cup flour
2 eggs	1 teaspoon baking powder
1/2 cup milk	
1/2 cup shredded coconut	1 teaspoon cinnamon
1 cup raisins	Dash of salt
1 cup chopped walnuts or pecans	

Cream the butter and sugar in a mixing bowl until light and fluffy. Beat in the eggs and milk. Stir in the coconut, raisins and walnuts. Add a mixture of the oats, flour, baking powder, cinnamon and salt; mix well. Drop by teaspoonfuls 2 inches apart onto a cookie sheet that has been lined with greased waxed paper. Bake at 350 degrees for 12 to 15 minutes. Yield: 3 dozen.

Donna Jones (25 years), Tau
Happy Valley-Goosebay, Newfoundland, Canada

Gloria J. Feddersen, Xi Pi Epsilon, Big Spring, Texas, makes **Sour Cream Honey Cookies** by blending 1 cup sugar, 1 cup honey and 1 cup sour cream together and adding a mixture of 4 cups flour, 2 teaspoons baking soda and 1 teaspoon nutmeg. Drop by teaspoonfuls onto ungreased cookie sheets and bake at 350 degrees for 10 minutes.

MRS. LEWIN'S COOKIES

My grandmother had rheumatic fever as a young girl and was not permitted to work outside or inside when she grew up, so she cooked just enough to get by. She was known for her delicious square cookies. The cookie dough all ran together as it baked, and she squared the baked dough into cookie-size portions with her spatula.

1 cup (2 sticks) margarine	1 egg
1/2 cup granulated sugar	2 cups flour
1/2 cup packed brown sugar	1/2 teaspoon salt
1 teaspoon vanilla extract	1 teaspoon baking soda
	1 1/2 cup rolled oats
	1 1/2 cups flaked coconut
	Chocolate stars or kisses

Cream the margarine and sugars in a mixing bowl until light and fluffy. Beat in the vanilla and egg. Add a mixture of the flour, salt and baking soda a little at a time, beating well after each addition. Stir in the oats and coconut. Shape the dough into small or medium balls and arrange them on a nonstick cookie sheet. Press a chocolate star into each ball. Bake at 350 degrees for 12 to 15 minutes. Yield: 2 to 4 dozen.

Gail Lewin, Preceptor Alpha Zeta
DePere, Wisconsin

WORLD'S BEST COCONUT COOKIE

1 cup (2 sticks) butter, softened	1/2 cup shredded coconut
1 cup granulated sugar	1 cup crushed cornflakes
1 cup packed brown sugar	1/2 cup chopped pecans or walnuts
1 egg	3 1/2 cups flour
1 cup vegetable oil	1 teaspoon salt
1 cup rolled oats	1 teaspoon vanilla extract

Cream the butter and sugars in a mixing bowl until light and fluffy. Beat in the egg and vegetable oil Mix in the oats, coconut, cornflakes, pecans, flour, salt and vanilla. Drop by teaspoonfuls 2 inches apart onto a greased cookie sheet. Bake at 350 degrees for 10 minutes or until light brown. Yield: 1 dozen.

Joyce Grizzle
Fayetteville, North Carolina

Lois Helm Webb, Laureate Chi, Toledo, Ohio, makes **Lemon Balls** by mixing a large lemon cake mix with 2 eggs, 8 ounces of whipped topping and adding a second lemon cake mix. Chill the dough. Shape into balls, roll in confectioners' sugar and bake at 350 degrees for 8 minutes.

AUNT TILLIE'S HERMITS

1/2 cup (1 stick) butter, softened	3 cups flour
1 1/2 cups packed brown sugar	1/2 teaspoon cinnamon
2 eggs	1/2 teaspoon nutmeg
2 tablespoons sour cream	1 cup raisins
1 teaspoon baking soda	1 cup currants
	1/2 cup chopped pecans
	Grated zest of 1 orange

Cream the butter and brown sugar in a mixing bowl until light and fluffy. Beat in the eggs and a mixture of the sour cream and baking soda. Sift together the flour, cinnamon and nutmeg. Add to the creamed mixture and mix well. Stir in the raisins, currants, pecans and orange zest. Wrap in plastic wrap and chill. Shape the dough into 3/4-inch balls and place on nonstick cookie sheets. Bake at 375 degrees for 7 minutes. Yield: 8 dozen.

Suzanne Butler, Xi Phi
Bowie, Maryland

MOM'S STONE JAR COOKIES

My mom is ninety-six years young now, and she still makes these cookies. My little sister and I would come home from school to these warm cookies, and later we would put them away in a stone jar. When I had children of my own, we did the same thing, and now my daughters do the same with their own children.

1 cup shortening	1/4 cup milk
1 teaspoon salt	1 cup raisins, ground
1 teaspoon vanilla extract	2 cups packed brown sugar
1 teaspoon nutmeg (optional)	3 cups flour, or 2 cups flour and 1 cup quick-cooking oats
2 eggs	
1 teaspoon baking soda	

Combine the shortening, salt, vanilla and nutmeg in a large mixing bowl and beat until smooth. Add the eggs, baking soda, milk, raisins, brown sugar and flour and mix well. Let stand for 10 minutes. Drop by teaspoonfuls 2 inches apart onto a greased cookie sheet. Flatten with a sugared glass. Bake at 350 degrees for about 10 to 12 minutes. Cool completely before storing in a jar. Yield: 3 dozen.

Glee Tappan (44 years), Preceptor Beta Alpha
Vancouver, Washington

RAISIN FORK COOKIES

This recipe belonged to my Grandma Kelb, and I truly believe she made a batch every single day. She had them available in a cookie jar for my cousins and myself, and also for my children as they were growing up.

1 cup (2 sticks) butter, softened	1 cup ground raisins
2 cups sugar	2 eggs
4 cups sifted flour	6 tablespoons milk
1½ teaspoons cream of tartar	1 teaspoon vanilla extract
1½ teaspoons baking soda	¾ cup chopped walnuts or pecans (optional)

Cream the butter and sugar in a mixing bowl until light and fluffy. Add a mixture of the flour, cream of tartar and baking soda and mix well. Add the raisins, eggs, milk, vanilla and walnuts; mix well. Dough will be very stiff. Shape into walnut-size balls and place on a nonstick cookie sheet. Press down with a fork that has been dipped in milk. Bake at 375 degrees for 8 to 10 minutes or until brown. Yield: 4 dozen.

Shirley Golembeck (25 years), Laureate Delta Theta
St. Charles, Missouri

RAISIN-FILLED COOKIES

1 cup shortening	2 teaspoons cream of tartar
2 cups packed brown sugar	2 teaspoons baking soda
2 eggs	½ cup milk
5 cups flour	Raisin Filling

Beat the shortening and brown sugar in a mixing bowl until light and fluffy. Add the eggs. Mix the flour, cream of tartar and baking soda. Add to the creamed mixture alternately with the milk, mixing well after each addition. Roll ⅛ inch thick on a floured surface. Cut into circles with a biscuit cutter. Place a spoonful of Raisin Filling in the center of half the circles. Top with the remaining dough circles and press edges to seal. Place on a nonstick cookie sheet. Bake at 375 degrees for 15 minutes. Yield: 2 to 3 dozen.

RAISIN FILLING

1 cup ground raisins	2 cups packed brown sugar
Juice of 1 lemon	½ cup water
2 teaspoons flour	

Combine the raisins, lemon juice, flour, brown sugar and water in a saucepan over medium-low heat. Cook until thickened, stirring frequently.

Ruth A. Johnson, Xi Kappa Mu
Keystone Heights, Florida

❖ FROG BELLIES

These cookies remind me of cold winter days in Nova Scotia with filled cookies and a cup of hot tea.

1 cup (2 sticks) butter, softened	5½ cups flour
1 cup granulated sugar	2 teaspoons cream of tartar
1 cup packed brown sugar	1 teaspoon baking soda
2 eggs	1 teaspoon salt
2 teaspoons vanilla extract	1 cup sour cream
	Raisin Filling

Cream the butter and sugars in a mixing bowl until light and fluffy. Beat in the eggs and vanilla. Mix together the flour, cream of tartar, baking soda and salt. Add to the creamed mixture alternately with the sour cream, mixing well after each addition. Roll to ⅛-inch thickness on a floured surface. Cut with a 2½-inch-round cookie cutter. Drop 1 teaspoon Raisin Filling in the center of half the dough circles. Top with the remaining dough circles and crimp edges to seal. Place on greased cookie sheets. Bake at 350 degrees for 12 to 15 minutes or until golden brown. Cool completely. Store in an airtight container to allow cookies to soften slightly. Yield: 5 dozen.

RAISIN FILLING

3 cups raisins	1 cup water
1 cup granulated sugar	2 tablespoons lemon juice
2 tablespoons flour	

Combine the raisins, sugar and flour in a saucepan over medium-high heat. Stir in the water and lemon juice and bring to a boil. Reduce heat and simmer, uncovered, for about 10 minutes or until thickened. Remove from heat and cool completely.

Jean K. Dunn, Laureate Gamma
Halifax, Nova Scotia, Canada

GRANDMA'S SOFT SUGAR COOKIES

3 cups flour	3 eggs
1 teaspoon baking powder	1 cup (2 sticks) butter, softened
1 teaspoon baking soda	1 cup sour cream
1 cup granulated sugar	1 teaspoon vanilla extract
1 cup packed light brown sugar	

Mix the flour, baking powder and baking soda in a large bowl. Add the sugars, eggs, butter, sour cream and vanilla and mix well. Drop by teaspoonfuls 2 inches apart onto a greased cookie sheet.

Bake at 350 degrees for 10 to 12 minutes or until edges are golden brown. Cool on a wire rack. Yield: 1 to 2 dozen.

Kandee Graham (32 years), Alpha Lambda Master
Hershey, Pennsylvania

GRANDMA'S FROSTED SUGAR COOKIES

2/3 cup shortening	2 cups sifted flour
1 teaspoon vanilla extract	1 1/2 teaspoons baking powder
3/4 cup sugar	1/4 teaspoon salt
1 egg	Coffee Frosting
4 teaspoons milk	

Cream the shortening, vanilla and sugar in a mixing bowl until light and fluffy. Beat in the egg and milk. Sift together the flour, baking powder and salt. Blend into the creamed mixture. Chill the dough, covered, for at least 1 hour before baking. Roll 1/8 inch thick on a floured surface. Cut with a cookie cutter. Place on an ungreased cookie sheet. Bake at 375 degrees for 8 to 10 minutes. Remove to a wire rack to cool. Frost the cooled cookies with Coffee Frosting. Yield: 3 dozen.

COFFEE FROSTING

1 tablespoon milk	1 teaspoon margarine, softened
1 teaspoon vanilla extract	Confectioners' sugar
1 tablespoon coffee	

Combine the milk, vanilla, coffee and margarine and beat until smooth. Beat in enough confectioners' sugar to make of spreadable consistency.

Vicki Butler, Xi Iota Gamma
Exline, Iowa

SUGAR TOP COOKIES

This is an old recipe from the 1930s that my mother fixed a lot while I was growing up. It's a real melt-in-your-mouth comfort cookie served with a glass of cold milk.

1/2 cup (1 stick) butter, softened	1/2 teaspoon salt
1 cup sugar	1/2 cup finely chopped walnuts or pecans
1/2 teaspoon vanilla extract	2 egg whites
2 eggs	1 teaspoon vanilla extract
1 1/2 cups flour	1 cup packed brown sugar
1 teaspoon baking powder	

Cream the butter and sugar in a mixing bowl until light and fluffy. Add the vanilla and eggs; beat until creamy. Sift the flour, baking powder and salt into the butter mixture and stir to blend. Spread in a well-greased 9×13-inch baking dish. Sprinkle with chopped nuts. Bake at 350 degrees for 20 minutes. Beat the egg whites until stiff peaks form. Beat in the vanilla and fold in the brown sugar. Spread over the cookie dough layer, sealing to the edge. Bake for a few minutes or until light brown. Cool and cut into squares. Yield: 2 to 3 dozen.

Karen L. Chabot (27 years), Alpha Upsilon
Snyder, Colorado

MOM'S YUMMY SUGAR COOKIES

The cookie recipe makes me think of my mom.

1 cup (2 sticks) butter or margarine, softened	1 teaspoon baking powder
2 cups sugar	1 teaspoon salt
3 eggs	2 teaspoons vanilla extract
1 cup sour cream	5 cups flour
1 teaspoon baking soda	

Cream the butter and sugar in a mixing bowl until light and fluffy. Add the next 6 ingredients; mix well. Add the flour and mix well. Chill, covered, for at least 1 hour. Roll to 1/8-inch thickness. Cut the dough with a cookie cutter and place on a greased cookie sheet. Sprinkle with sugar. Bake at 350 degrees for 10 to 12 minutes or until done to taste. Frost cooled cookies with butter frosting and decorate if desired. Yield: 4 to 5 dozen.

Cathy Gilliland, Alpha Kappa
Rose Hill, Iowa

STIR-AND-DROP SUGAR COOKIES

This is my mother's recipe from the 1960s when I was in grade school. She is gone now, but I treasure seeing her handwriting on the recipes. Never e-mail recipes to your children. Send them in your own handwriting. It will be a part of your identity left to their world.

2 eggs	2 teaspoons vanilla extract
3/4 cup sugar	2 cups sifted flour
2/3 cup vegetable oil	1/2 teaspoon salt
1 teaspoon grated lemon zest	

Combine the eggs, sugar, vegetable oil, lemon zest and vanilla in a large bowl and mix well. Stir in a mixture of the flour and salt. Drop by teaspoonfuls 2 inches apart onto an ungreased cookie sheet. Flatten with a fork and sprinkle with sugar. Bake at 400 degrees for 8 minutes. Yield: 4 dozen.

Margo S. Caley, Preceptor Beta Zeta
Manhattan, Kansas

OLD-FASHIONED SUGAR COOKIES

I have used this recipe for fifty-one years. My three children loved helping me bake the cookies, and they still request them—as do their children, my grand-children.

1 cup shortening or margarine	4 cups flour
2 cups sugar	4 teaspoons baking powder
2 eggs	1/2 teaspoon salt
6 tablespoons whole milk	1/4 teaspoon nutmeg
2 teaspoons vanilla extract	

Cream the shortening and sugar in a mixing bowl until light and fluffy. Beat in the eggs, milk and vanilla. Sift together the flour, baking powder, salt and nutmeg. Work the flour mixture by hand into the creamed mixture, adding an additional 1 to 1 1/2 cups flour until dough does not stick to the hands. Dough should be soft. Roll to 1/4 inch thick on a floured surface beneath a sheet of waxed paper. Cut with a cookie cutter and place on a nonstick cookie sheet. Bake at 350 degrees for 10 to 12 minutes. Frost and decorate if desired. Yield: 5 dozen.

Wilma Palmer Valentine, Iota Lambda
Warfordsburg, Pennsylvania

BROWN SUGAR COOKIES

This is a very old recipe from my grandmother, who lived to be 103 years old. I got the recipe when we went back to Pennsylvania for her 100th birthday.

1 cup (2 sticks) butter, softened	1 teaspoon baking soda
3 cups packed brown sugar	1 tablespoon baking powder
3 eggs	1 tablespoon vanilla extract
1 1/2 cups milk	Flour

Cream the butter and brown sugar in a mixing bowl until light and fluffy. Add the eggs 1 at a time, beating well after each addition. Beat in the milk, baking soda, baking powder and vanilla. Mix in enough flour to make a dough that can be rolled. Chill, covered, for 2 to 10 hours. Roll 1/8 inch thick on a floured surface. Cut with a cookie cutter and place on a greased cookie sheet. Bake at 350 degrees for 10 to 12 minutes. Yield: 2 to 3 dozen.

Alice Dorene Prior (36 years), Preceptor Beta Rho
Spokane, Washington

AUNTIE'S SUGAR COOKIES

These cookies have become my trademark, and my nephew, who loves them, gave them their name.

1 cup (2 sticks) butter, softened	2 eggs, beaten
1 cup sugar	1 teaspoon vanilla extract
1 cup confectioners' sugar	4 cups flour
3/4 cup plus 2 tablespoons vegetable oil	1 teaspoon baking soda
	1/2 teaspoon salt

Cream the butter, sugar and confectioners' sugar in a mixing bowl until light and fluffy. Beat in the next 3 ingredients. Add a mixture of the flour, baking soda and salt and mix well. Chill, covered, for 2 hours. Place tablespoon-size balls of dough on ungreased cookie sheets. Flatten each with the bottom of a glass that has been dipped in sugar. Bake at 350 degrees for 12 to 15 minutes. Yield: About 4 dozen.

Kaylen Hagens-Cooper, Xi Beta Tau
Columbus, Wisconsin

MOM'S CUTOUT SUGAR COOKIES

1 cup confectioners' sugar	4 3/4 cups flour
1 cup sugar	1 teaspoon salt
1 cup (2 sticks) butter, softened	1 teaspoon cream of tartar
1 cup vegetable oil	1/2 cup (1 stick) butter, melted
2 eggs	1 (1-pound) package confectioners' sugar
1 teaspoon each vanilla and butter extracts	Evaporated milk

Combine the 1 cup confectioners' sugar, sugar, 1 cup butter and vegetable oil in a large mixing bowl and beat until smooth. Beat in the eggs, vanilla and butter flavoring. Sift together the flour, salt and cream of tartar and add gradually to the sugar mixture, beating well after each addition. Chill, covered, for 1 hour. Roll 1/8 inch thick on a pastry sheet dusted with confectioners' sugar. Cut with a cookie cutter and placed on a greased cookie sheet. Bake at 375 degrees for 8 to 10 minutes or until edges are slightly golden. Remove to a wire rack and cool. Combine the 1/2 cup butter and the 1 pound confectioners' sugar in a mixing bowl and beat until smooth. Beat in enough evaporated milk until of spreading consistency. Separate into several portions and tint with different colors of food coloring. Frost cookies and sprinkle with candy sprinkles. Yield: 5 dozen.

Dana Elza (31 years), Preceptor Nu Zeta
Granbury, Texas

MOM'S COFFEE BARS

My dad always asked that Mom bake these bars so he could take them to his men's group.

1 cup raisins	1/2 teaspoon baking soda
3/4 cup hot strong coffee	1 cup confectioners'
1/2 teaspoon cinnamon	sugar
3/4 cup shortening	2 tablespoons butter,
1 cup sugar	softened
2 eggs	1/2 teaspoon vanilla
1 1/2 cups flour	extract
1/2 teaspoon salt	1 tablespoon (about)
1/2 teaspoon baking	milk
powder	

Plump the raisins in a mixture of coffee and cinnamon in a small bowl. Cream the shortening and sugar in a mixing bowl until light and fluffy. Beat in the eggs and a mixture of the flour, salt, baking powder and baking soda. Spread in a thin layer in a nonstick 10×15-inch baking pan. Bake at 350 degrees for 15 to 20 minutes or until lightly browned. Beat the confectioners' sugar, butter and vanilla with enough milk to make a thin icing. Glaze the warm baked layer with the icing. Cool and cut into bars.
Yield: 1 dozen.

Gail J. Robinson, Xi Gamma
St. Joseph, Missouri

CHERRY WINKS

I am from a family of thirteen children, and this meant lots of fun and work for all of us. We loved to help Mother cook. Now I have the pleasure of making cookies with an electric mixer, but when I was young, we had to beat the ingredients until smooth with a spoon. It was very tiring, but worth the effort because the cookies were so good and mother would always praise us. We used a woodstove until 1951 when we got electricity and our first electric stove.

2 1/4 cups flour	2 teaspoons vanilla
1 teaspoon baking	extract
powder	1 cup pecans, chopped
1/2 teaspoon baking soda	1 cup dates, chopped
1/2 teaspoon salt	1/3 cup chopped
3/4 cup shortening	maraschino cherries
1 cup sugar	2 1/4 cups crushed
2 eggs	cornflakes
2 tablespoons milk	

Preheat the oven to 350 degrees. Sift the flour, baking powder, baking soda and salt together into a bowl. Combine the shortening, sugar, eggs, milk and vanilla in a separate mixing bowl and beat well.

Add the flour mixture; mix well. Stir in the pecans, dates and cherries. Shape the dough into 3/4-inch balls and roll in cornflakes. Place on a nonstick cookie sheet and bake for 10 minutes. Press a maraschino cherry half into each warm cookie. Let cool. Yield: 4 dozen.

Syble A. Shoults (30 years), Xi Mu
Bessemer, Alabama

MEMORIES

My husband's mother, Eva Rose Petersen, was an excellent cook and loved to entertain family and friends. They owned a small grocery store and lived in an apartment in the back of the store. When company was coming, Eva would simply go to their grocery store and pick out what she needed for the meal. My four children would help her by rolling the food cart around the store aisles and "shopping" for the menu that she was cooking. When we were leaving to go home, the grandparents would allow each child to "shop" the candy case for a treat to take home. The children would always select a Cherry Mash candy bar for me as well.

Shirley Petersen (27 years), Laureate Kappa
Beatrice, Nebraska

CRANBERRY SQUARES

Cranberries are native to Cape Cod, and they freeze well.

1 cup (2 sticks)	1 teaspoon baking
margarine	powder
2 cups flour	2 eggs, slightly beaten
1 1/2 cups sugar	2 cups cranberries

Melt the margarine in a large saucepan. Remove from heat. Add the flour, sugar and baking powder to the margarine and blend well. Add the eggs and mix well. Add the cranberries; mix well. Spread in a greased 9×13-inch baking dish and sprinkle with 2 tablespoons sugar. Bake at 350 degrees for 20 to 25 minutes or until lightly browned. Cool and cut into squares. Yield: 15 squares.

Jeanne Thomas, Delta Nu
Hyannis, Massachusetts

OATMEAL CRUNCHIES

2 cups margarine	1 teaspoon baking soda
2 cups granulated sugar	1 teaspoon baking
2 cups packed brown	powder
sugar	1 teaspoon salt
1 tablespoon vanilla	4 cups rolled oats
extract	4 cups cornflakes,
4 eggs	crushed
4 cups flour	2 cups shredded coconut

Combine the margarine, sugars, vanilla and eggs in a large mixing bowl; beat until smooth. Sift together the flour, baking soda, baking powder and salt; stir into the sugar mixture. Stir in the oats, cornflakes and coconut. Shape into 3/4-inch balls and arrange on a lightly greased cookie sheet. Flatten slightly. Bake at 325 degrees for 15 to 20 minutes or until golden brown. Yield: 7 to 8 dozen.

Marilyn Giesbrecht, Eta Omicron
Clearwater, British Columbia, Canada

SEVEN-LAYER BARS

1/2 cup (1 stick) butter or	1 cup butterscotch chips
margarine, melted	1 cup shredded coconut
1 1/2 cups graham cracker	1 cup chopped pecans
crumbs	1 (8-ounce) can
1 cup semisweet	sweetened condensed
chocolate chips	milk

Layer the butter, graham cracker crumbs, chocolate chips, butterscotch chips, coconut and pecans in the order listed in a 9×13-inch baking dish. Drizzle with the condensed milk. Bake at 425 degrees for 10 to 12 minutes or until hot and bubbly and top is lightly browned. Cool slightly and cut into bars. Yield: 2 dozen.

Ramona Mitchell, Beta Sigma Phi
Woodward, Oklahoma

LONDON COCONUT BARS

1 cup flour	1 teaspoon vanilla
1 1/2 cups packed brown	extract
sugar	3 tablespoons flour
1/2 cup (1 stick) butter,	1/2 teaspoon salt
softened	1 1/2 cups shredded
2 eggs, beaten	coconut

Mix together the 1 cup flour and 1/2 cup of the brown sugar in a bowl. Cut in the butter until mixture resembles coarse crumbs. Pat into a greased 9×13-inch baking dish. Bake at 375 degrees for 10 minutes. Combine the remaining 1 cup brown sugar, eggs, vanilla, the 3 tablespoons flour, salt and coconut in a bowl and mix well. Pour evenly over the hot crust.

Bake for 20 minutes longer or until set and browned. Cool and cut into squares. Yield: 2 dozen.

Janice Underwood, Laureate Kappa
Vancouver, Washington

CONGO SQUARES

It was not always easy for my parents to take their eight children on a vacation. That meant a trip to my grandparents' home was very special. On a Friday evening my mother would have us bathed and in our pajamas, eagerly waiting by the window for my father's arrival home from work. They would pile us into the back of the family station wagon with our pillows and blankets. When we got to our grandparents' house, my father and grandpa would carry us to bed. The next morning we would awaken to my grandma making us Congo Squares. I remember my grandma fondly every time I bake these cookies.

2 3/4 cups flour	1 (1-pound) package
2 1/2 teaspoons baking	brown sugar
powder	3 eggs
1/2 teaspoon salt	1 cup chopped walnuts
2/3 cup shortening,	or pecans (optional)
melted	2 cups chocolate chips

Mix the flour, baking powder and salt in a bowl. Combine the shortening, brown sugar and eggs in a separate bowl and mix well. Cool slightly. Stir in the flour mixture. Fold in the walnuts and chocolate chips. Spread in a greased 10×15-inch cake pan. Bake at 350 degrees for 25 to 30 minutes or until lightly browned. Cut into 2-inch squares when almost cool. Yield: 4 dozen.

Mary Fisch, Xi Gamma Upsilon
Palm Harbor, Florida

CHOCOLATE CHIP TOFFEE BARS

Once a month the staff of Coronado High School held an "Extra Special Person" or E.S.P. luncheon for deserving students. Students were recommended by teachers for their outstanding contributions to the school. I served on the E.S.P. committee . . . and was praised over and over for my contribution of Chocolate Chip Toffee Bars!

2 1/3 cups flour	2 cups semisweet
2/3 cup packed light	chocolate chips
brown sugar	1 (14-ounce) can
3/4 cup (1 1/2 sticks)	sweetened condensed
butter, softened	milk
1 egg, beaten	1 (10-ounce) package
1 cup coarsely chopped	toffee bits
walnuts or pecans	

Mix together the flour, brown sugar and butter in a large bowl; stir in the egg. Stir in the walnuts and 1 1/2 cups of the chocolate chips. Remove 1 1/2 cups of the flour mixture to a small bowl and set aside. Press the remaining flour mixture in a greased 9×13-inch baking dish. Bake at 350 degrees for 10 minutes. Pour the condensed milk evenly over the crust. Sprinkle evenly with 1 1/2 cups of the toffee bits. Sprinkle the 1 1/2 cups flour mixture and the remaining 1/2 cup chocolate chips over the top. Bake for 25 to 30 minutes or until hot and bubbly and lightly browned. Sprinkle with the remaining 1/2 cup toffee bits. Cool completely. Cut into bars. Yield: 2 to 3 dozen.

Sherrie Maule, Laureate Alpha Zeta
Scottsdale, Arizona

PEANUT BUTTER CRISP SQUARES

1 cup sugar	6 cups crisp rice cereal
1 cup light corn syrup	3 cups chocolate chips
1 cup creamy peanut butter	1 1/3 cups butterscotch chips

Place the sugar and corn syrup in a microwave-safe bowl. Microwave on High, loosely covered, for 2 minutes. Stir until sugar dissolves. Add the peanut butter and mix until smooth. Place the rice cereal in a large bowl. Pour the peanut butter mixture over the cereal and stir to coat completely. Pat into a greased 9×13-inch baking dish with your hand covered by a plastic sandwich bag. Place the chocolate chips and butterscotch chips in a large microwave-safe bowl. Microwave on High for 2 1/2 to 3 minutes. Stir until smooth. Spread over the cereal layer. Chill 1/2 hour to set. Cut into small squares. Yield: 50 squares.

Elaine Hackenberg, Preceptor Alpha Upsilon
Nesquehoning, Pennsylvania

TRIPLE CHOCOLATE FUDGE BARS

1 (2-layer) package chocolate cake mix	1 cup chopped peanuts, walnuts or pecans
1/4 cup vegetable oil	1 cup chocolate chips
1 egg	1 (14-ounce) can sweetened condensed milk
1 teaspoon vanilla extract	

Combine the dry cake mix, vegetable oil, egg and vanilla in a mixing bowl. Beat until crumbly. Stir in the chopped nuts. Press all except 1 1/2 cups of the cake mixture in a 9×13-inch baking dish that has been lightly sprayed with nonstick cooking spray. Melt the chocolate chips in the condensed milk in a saucepan over low heat or in the microwave; stir until smooth. Pour evenly over the top of the crust. Sprinkle with the reserved cake mixture. Bake at 350 degrees for 30 minutes. Cool completely in the pan. Cut into bars. Yield: 24 large bars or 36 small ones.

Cincy Lefler, Xi Beta Epsilon
Haddonfield, New Jersey

MEMORIES

Family and friends are so important. Five years ago I was diagnosed with breast cancer. I knew that I could count on my family, but I didn't know that my sorority sisters would become some of my greatest supporters. Prayers, flowers, cards and phone calls were their ways of showing that they really cared. This past January I celebrated five years of being cancer-free. I came to the regular meeting that week with a box of dark chocolates (my favorite). I was not engaged or going to have a baby, so my sisters were a little confused when I presented the chocolates during the meeting. But confused looks soon turned into broad smiles and applause when I announced that I had hit my five-year mark and that this all happened with the help of my sorority sisters.

Barbara Accordino (25 years), Xi Mu
Louisville, Kentucky

CHOCOLATE SODA CRACKER BARS

Soda crackers	2 cups chocolate chips
1 1/2 cups packed brown sugar	Sliced almonds (optional)
1 1/2 cups (3 sticks) butter	

Preheat the oven to 375 degrees. Line a large shallow baking dish or cookie sheet with soda crackers. Combine the brown sugar and butter in a saucepan and bring to a boil. Boil gently for 3 minutes, stirring constantly. Pour slowly and evenly over the cracker layer. Bake for 5 minutes. Sprinkle the chocolate chips over the hot sugared soda cracker layer. Let stand for 10 minutes; spread evenly with a spoon. Sprinkle with sliced almonds. Freeze for 2 hours. Break into pieces. Yield: Varies.

Sandra Moyer, Xi Pi
Brandon, Manitoba, Canada

CHOCOLATE REVEL BARS

This recipe was given to me by a neighbor lady when I was first married. She was always there when I needed a cup of sugar or some cooking help. This recipe is still good thirty years later.

1 cup (2 sticks) butter, softened	2¹/₂ cups flour
2 cups packed brown sugar	1 teaspoon baking soda
2 large eggs	1 teaspoon salt
2 teaspoons vanilla extract	3 cups quick-cooking oats
	Chocolate Filling

Cream the butter and brown sugar in a mixing bowl until light and fluffy. Stir in the eggs, vanilla, flour, baking soda, salt and oats in the order listed. Mixture will be quite thick. Pat ²/₃ of the oats mixture in a greased 10×15-inch cake pan. Spread Chocolate Filling over the oats layer. Sprinkle with the remaining oats mixture. Bake at 350 degrees for 25 to 30 minutes. Cool and cut into bars. Yield: 3 dozen.

CHOCOLATE FILLING

2 cups chocolate chips	¹/₂ teaspoon salt
1 (15-ounce) can sweetened condensed milk	1 cup chopped walnuts
	2 teaspoons vanilla extract
2 tablespoons butter	

Combine the chocolate chips, condensed milk, butter and salt in the top of a double boiler over boiling water; heat until melted, stirring frequently to mix well. Remove from heat and stir in walnuts and vanilla.

Claudia M. Long, Kappa Kappa
Meriden, Kansas

BROWNIES

I vividly remember coming home from grade school and having my mom greet me at the door with brownies. I thought she had spent the whole day making the brownies, when in reality she had two babies under the age of two and a huge house to care for!

2 cups flour	¹/₂ cup vegetable oil
2 cups sugar	¹/₂ cup buttermilk
¹/₂ teaspoon salt	2 eggs
¹/₂ cup (1 stick) margarine	1 teaspoon baking soda
1 cup water	1 teaspoon vanilla extract
¹/₄ cup baking cocoa	Brownie Frosting

Mix together the flour, sugar and salt in a large bowl. Combine the margarine, water, baking cocoa and vegetable oil in a saucepan over medium-high heat; bring to a boil, stirring frequently. Pour over the flour mixture. Add the buttermilk, eggs, baking soda and vanilla and mix well. Spread in a greased 11×16-inch baking pan. Bake at 400 degrees for 20 minutes or until done to taste. Remove from pan and frost immediately. Cut into bars. Yield: 2 to 3 dozen.

BROWNIE FROSTING

¹/₂ cup (1 stick) margarine	1 cup chopped pecans or walnuts
¹/₄ cup baking cocoa	1 teaspoon vanilla extract
¹/₃ cup buttermilk	
1 (1-pound) package confectioners' sugar	

Combine the margarine, baking cocoa and buttermilk in a saucepan over medium-high heat; bring to a boil, stirring frequently. Remove from heat. Stir in the confectioners' sugar, chopped nuts and vanilla.

Cyndi Fischer, Xi Beta Phi
Bend, Oregon

QUEEN'S BROWNIES

A family friend shared this recipe with me, and it is requested at all social occasions. Serve warm with ice cream.

¹/₃ cup baking cocoa	4 eggs, beaten
³/₄ cup (1¹/₂ sticks) butter	1 teaspoon vanilla extract
2 tablespoons peanut butter	¹/₂ cup chocolate chips
1 cup flour	Chopped walnuts or pecans (optional)
2 cups sugar	

Combine the baking cocoa, butter and peanut butter in a saucepan over medium-high heat. Bring to a boil, stirring constantly. Remove from heat and cool immediately in a sink of ice water. Combine the flour, sugar, eggs and vanilla in a large bowl and mix well with a wooden spoon. Add the peanut butter mixture and stir until smooth. Stir in the chocolate chips and chopped nuts. Spread in a greased 8¹/₂×11-inch baking dish. Bake at 320 degrees for 35 to 40 minutes or until brownies are seen to be moist when a knife is inserted near the center; do not overbake.
Yield: 12 servings.

Joyce Linton McHone, Zeta Alpha
Sheridan, Arkansas

CREME DE MENTHE BROWNIES

1 cup sugar
1 cup flour
4 eggs, beaten
1 teaspoon vanilla
    extract
1/2 teaspoon salt
1 (16-ounce) can
    chocolate syrup

2 cups confectioners'
    sugar
1/2 cup (1 stick) butter,
    softened
2 tablespoons crème de
    menthe
1 cup chocolate chips
6 tablespoons butter

Combine the first 6 ingredients in a bowl and mix well. Press into a greased 9×13-inch baking dish. Bake at 350 degrees for 30 minutes. Cool completely in the pan. Combine the confectioners' sugar, the 1/2 cup butter and crème de menthe in a small bowl; mix until smooth. Spread over the cooled brownies. Melt the chocolate chips and the 6 tablespoons butter in a heavy saucepan over medium heat, stirring constantly until smooth. Pour evenly over the crème de menthe layer. Cool until top is firm. Cut into 11/2-inch squares. Yield: 11/2 to 2 dozen.

Judy Dorsey, Laureate Delta
Wilmington, Delaware

BLONDE BROWNIE CARAMEL CUPS

I made hundreds of these for the soldiers camped in the desert during the Gulf War. Helping the soldiers take their minds off the desert for just a while was the highlight of my twenty years living in Saudi Arabia.

1/2 cup (1 stick) butter
1 cup packed brown
    sugar
1 teaspoon vanilla
    extract
1 egg
1 cup flour
1 teaspoon baking
    powder

1/4 teaspoon salt
1/2 cup chopped walnuts
    or pecans
1/2 cup semisweet
    chocolate chips
20 caramels
1 tablespoon water
1/4 to 1/2 cup chopped
    walnuts or pecans

Melt the butter in a saucepan over low heat. Remove from heat and stir in the brown sugar. Add the vanilla and egg and mix well. Blend in a mixture of the flour, baking powder and salt. Stir in the 1/2 cup chopped nuts. Divide the batter evenly among 16 paper-lined muffin cups. Bake at 350 degrees for 16 to 20 minutes or until golden brown. Press a few chocolate chips into the center of each cupcake. Melt the caramels with the water and walnuts in a saucepan over low heat, stirring constantly until smooth. Spoon a scant tablespoonful of the caramel mixture over each cupcake. Yield: 16 servings.

Jan Lincoln, Alpha Alpha
Ruidoso, New Mexico

ROCKY ROAD FUDGE BROWNIES

This treat is a family favorite, perfect with or without nuts.

1 (20-ounce) package
    brownie mix
1 cup chopped walnuts
    or pecans
3 cups miniature
    marshmallows
1/2 cup (1 stick) butter or
    margarine

1/3 cup milk
2 ounces unsweetened
    chocolate
1/2 teaspoon vanilla
    extract
1 (1-pound) package
    confectioners' sugar,
    sifted

Prepare the brownie mix using the package directions. Stir in the walnuts. Spread the batter in a greased 9×13-inch baking dish. Bake at 350 degrees for 25 minutes. Sprinkle the marshmallows evenly over the hot brownies. Combine the butter, milk and chocolate in a heavy saucepan over low heat; cook until melted, stirring frequently. Remove to a medium mixing bowl. Add the vanilla and the confectioners' sugar gradually while beating at low speed. If frosting is too thick for spreading, add 1 tablespoon of milk, stirring until smooth. Spread over the cooled brownies. Cut into bars.
Yield: 1 dozen.

Lindsay Hamilton, Chi
Albany, Oregon

CARAMEL CHOCOLATE MICROWAVE BROWNIES

1 (14-ounce) package
    caramels
2/3 cup evaporated milk
1 (18-ounce) package
    German chocolate
    cake mix

3/4 cup (11/2 sticks)
    margarine, softened
1 cup chopped pecans
2 cups chocolate chips

Place the caramels and 1/3 cup of the evaporated milk in a glass bowl. Microwave on Medium-High for 31/2 minutes. Stir until smooth. Cool. Combine the dry cake mix, margarine and the remaining 1/3 cup evaporated milk in a bowl and mix with a wooden spoon. Press 2/3 of the cake mixture into a greased and sugared 9×13-inch microwave-safe dish. Microwave on High for 4 minutes with the dish elevated on a microwave saucer. Sprinkle the pecans and chocolate chips over the microwaved layer. Spread caramel mixture over the nuts and chips. Crumble the remaining cake mixture over the caramel layer. Microwave on High for 4 to 5 minutes longer. Refrigerate to cool. Cut into squares.
Yield: 30 brownies.

Sarah Kapla, Chi Omicron
Romeoville, Illinois

GRAHAM CRACKER BROWNIES

Thirty-two graham cracker squares yield 2 cups of crumbs.

2 cups graham cracker crumbs	1/4 teaspoon salt
1 cup chocolate chips	1 (14-ounce) can sweetened condensed milk
1 teaspoon baking powder	

Combine the graham cracker crumbs, chocolate chips, baking powder, salt and condensed milk in a bowl and mix well. Spread in a greased 8-inch-square baking dish. Bake at 350 degrees for 25 to 30 minutes or until center is set and a wooden pick inserted in the center comes out clean. Cool and serve. Yield: 16 brownies.

*Liz Zerr, Gamma Zeta
Mobridge, South Dakota*

BOURBON BALLS

3 cups finely ground vanilla wafers	3 tablespoons light corn syrup
1 cup finely ground pecans	1/2 cup bourbon
1 cup confectioners' sugar	

Combine the vanilla wafers, pecans and confectioners' sugar in a bowl and mix well. Add a mixture of the corn syrup and bourbon to the wafer mixture and mix well. Shape into cherry-size balls. Dust with confectioners' sugar. Yield: 4 to 5 dozen.

*Lottie Kelm (47 years), Iota Master
New Braunfels, Texas*

AUNT MADGE'S NUTTY CARAMELS

Every Christmas for many years my husband's Aunt Madge would give each of us a big bag of her delicious homemade caramels.

2 cups sugar	2 cups chopped walnuts
2 cups light corn syrup	1 teaspoon vanilla extract
1/2 cup (1 stick) butter	
1 (14-ounce) can sweetened condensed milk	

Combine the sugar, corn syrup, butter and condensed milk in a heavy 8-quart kettle over medium heat. Cook, stirring constantly with a large wooden spoon to prevent sticking or burning. Bring to a full rolling boil, and cook to 242 degrees on a candy thermometer. Remove from heat. Stir in the walnuts and vanilla. Pour into a heavily greased 9×13-inch baking dish. Let stand for 2 hours or until cool. Cut into pieces of desired size, perhaps 3/4×1-inch. Wrap each piece separately in a square of waxed paper, twisting the ends closed. Yield: About 4 dozen.

*Georgia Schaefer (43 years), Beta Nu
Joseph, Oregon*

CARAMELS

2 cups granulated sugar	2 cups heavy cream
1 cup packed brown sugar	1 cup (2 sticks) butter
1 cup corn syrup	1 1/4 teaspoons vanilla extract
1 cup evaporated milk	

Combine the sugars, corn syrup, evaporated milk, cream and butter in a medium saucepan. Bring to a full rolling boil. Cook to 250 degrees on a candy thermometer. Remove from heat. Stir in the vanilla. Pour into a greased 12×15-inch baking pan. Let stand until cool. Cut into pieces and wrap individually in waxed paper. Yield: 5 dozen.

*Kathie Vigliotti, Xi Tau
Havre, Montana*

CHOCOLATE CARAMELS

My mother made these caramels every year at Christmastime. Now her great-grandson enjoys them with the rest of our family.

1 cup sugar	Dash of salt
1 cup light corn syrup	1/4 teaspoon vanilla extract
1 cup light cream or half-and-half	Chopped walnuts or pecans (optional)
1/4 cup (1/2 stick) butter	
1 ounce unsweetened chocolate	

Combine the sugar, corn syrup, cream, butter, chocolate and salt in a medium saucepan over medium-low heat. Cook until butter and chocolate are melted, stirring until mixed and smooth. Bring to a full rolling boil. Cook to 242 degrees on a candy thermometer or until a small amount of the mixture dropped in cold water forms a firm but not brittle ball, stirring occasionally at the beginning and more frequently toward the end of the cooking process. Remove from heat. Stir in the vanilla and pour at once into a greased 8 1/2×4 1/2-inch loaf pan or 8×8-inch baking pan, being careful not to scrape the mixture. Let stand until firm. Cut into pieces and wrap individually. Yield: Varies.

*Anne M. Livak, Xi Beta Upsilon
Salamanca, New York*

CARAMEL NUT EASTER EGGS

My husband belonged to the Darlington Volunteer Fire Department when we were first married, and one Firemen's Ladies Auxiliary Fund-Raiser was making Easter Eggs, beginning in late January and working until Easter Sunday. We made Fruit and Nut Eggs, Maple Nut Eggs, Coconut Eggs, Peanut Butter Eggs, and Caramel Nut Eggs. The firemen and wives would meet three to four nights a week to make the eggs. The men's job was to stir the caramel mixture, as that took the most time. As we all worked we laughed and talked about family and community happenings. Those were happy and simpler times.

4 cups sugar	3 cups chopped walnuts
1¹/2 cups light corn syrup	or pecans
1 cup (2 sticks) butter	2 teaspoons vanilla
2 cups evaporated milk	extract

Combine the sugar, corn syrup and butter in a heavy saucepan and bring to a boil. Stir in the evaporated milk. Cook over medium heat until mixture becomes "chewy," stirring constantly. Remove from heat. Stir in the chopped nuts and vanilla. Cool. Knead until smooth and pliable. Shape into eggs. Brush with a mixture of beaten egg white and a little water; roll in finely chopped nuts. Yield: 5 to 6 dozen.

Patricia Donaldson, Eta Beta
Alachua, Florida

HOMEMADE MARSHMALLOWS

2¹/2 tablespoons	¹/4 teaspoon salt
unflavored gelatin	2 tablespoons pure
1¹/2 cups sugar	vanilla extract
1 cup light corn syrup	

Combine the gelatin and ¹/2 cup cold water in a mixing bowl, beating with the whisk attachment. Let stand for 30 minutes. Combine the sugar, corn syrup, salt and an additional ¹/2 cup water in a heavy saucepan over low heat. Cook until sugar is dissolved, stirring constantly and washing down the side of the pan with a wet pastry brush to dissolve sugar crystals. Bring to a full rolling boil. Cook without stirring to 244 degrees on a candy thermometer, firm-ball stage. Remove from heat immediately. Pour the hot syrup slowly and carefully into the gelatin mixture, beating constantly at low speed. Beat at high speed for about 15 minutes or until mixture is very thick and white and almost tripled in volume. Beat in the vanilla. Pour the marshmallow mixture into an 8×12-inch glass baking dish that has been generously dusted with confectioners' sugar. Let stand, uncovered, for 8 to 10 hours or until dry.

Remove to a board. Cut into 1¹/2-inch squares with a dry hot knife and dust with additional confectioners' sugar. Yield: 40 marshmallows.

Laura Hannan, Xi Eta Theta
Wamego, Kansas

MY MOTHER'S HALVA

When I was a child, my father would freeze the backyard so we seven children could skate. This would keep us outside while my mother made this sweet candy. I remember coming inside cold and hungry to that sweet cinnamon smell. The sweet Halva, a Greek candy, was good with hot chocolate.

1¹/2 cups vegetable oil	1 cup sugar
2 cups flour	1 tablespoon cinnamon
¹/2 cup crushed walnuts	2 dozen whole cloves
¹/2 cup honey	

Heat the vegetable oil in a heavy saucepan over medium-high heat until a bit of flour sizzles when dropped in the oil. Add a mixture of the flour and walnuts to the hot oil gradually, stirring constantly until smooth. Cook for 1 minute, stirring constantly. Add the honey and cook until thickened, stirring constantly. Fill a big soup spoon with the honey mixture and wrap a clean "throwaway" towel around the spoon and honey mixture; squeeze hard to draw out the excess oil. Wipe off the outside of the spoon and slide the honey mixture into a mixture of the sugar and cinnamon, coating well. Repeat the procedure to make 2 dozen pieces. Press a clove in the center of each. Yield: 2 dozen.

Sophia McMillon, Preceptor Kappa
Montrose, Colorado

PEANUT BUTTER PRETZEL CANDY

2 cups peanut butter	2 tablespoons creamy
chips	peanut butter
1 (1-pound) package	2 cups unsalted peanuts
white or yellow	2 cups thin pretzel
chocolate wafers,	sticks
broken	

Combine the first 3 ingredients in the top of a double boiler over boiling water. Cook until melted and warm, stirring until mixed well. Remove from heat. Stir in the unsalted peanuts. Break pretzel sticks in half and stir into the peanut butter mixture. Spread over a foil-lined baking sheet or 9×13-inch baking dish. Chill for 15 minutes and break into bite-size pieces. Yield: 2 pounds.

Mona Mae Russo (42 years), Laureate Epsilon Phi
Pittsburgh, Pennsylvania

MEMORIES

My mother makes peanut butter fudge. When my sisters and I were little, she would make sure there was enough left in the pan for two of us and the other one got the spoon. My dad was kind enough just to eat the fudge after it set and leave the "scrapings" for us. The scrapings were the creamy, smooth, warm part left after the cooking process was done. It is what we thought was the best part.

Debra C. Burchette, Xi Alpha Xi
Lenoir, North Carolina

JIM'S PEANUT BUTTER FUDGE

My husband got this recipe when he was in high school and would make it at home on the farm. After we got married (forty-five years ago), I acquired the recipe and the job of making the fudge. The recipe can be doubled and placed in a 9×13-inch baking dish.

2 cups sugar	1 teaspoon vanilla
1/2 cup milk	extract
Dash of salt	1 cup peanut butter,
1 tablespoon butter	plain or chunky

Combine the sugar, milk and salt in a heavy saucepan over medium heat; bring to a boil. Cook over medium heat to 234 to 240 degrees on a candy thermometer, soft-ball stage. Remove from heat. Stir in the butter and vanilla. While the butter melts, stir in the peanut butter. Stir until mixture begins to get stiff. Pour into a buttered 9×9-inch baking dish. Let stand in the refrigerator until firm. Yield: 1 pound.

Joanne H. Greene (39 years), Laureate Mu
Parkersburg, West Virginia

VELVEETA CHEESE FUDGE

1 pound Velveeta cheese	4 (1-pound) packages confectioners' sugar
2 cups margarine	1 cup baking cocoa
2 teaspoons vanilla extract	2 cups chopped walnuts or pecans

Place the Velveeta cheese and margarine in a microwave-safe bowl. Microwave on Medium for 5 minutes or until cheese and margarine are melted. Stir in the vanilla. Combine the confectioners' sugar and baking cocoa in a large bowl. Stir in the cheese mixture. Add the chopped nuts; mix well. Spread in

2 lightly greased 9×13-inch baking dishes. Cool until firm. Cut into squares. Yield: 8 dozen.

Norma J. Boyer (25 years), Xi Epsilon Nu
Colorado Springs, Colorado

EASY MICROWAVE FUDGE

To vary this recipe, use 1 cup raspberry chips and 2 cups chocolate chips.

3 cups semisweet chocolate chips	Dash of salt
1 (14-ounce) can sweetened condensed milk	1/2 to 1 cup chopped walnuts or pecans
	1 1/2 teaspoons vanilla extract

Combine the chocolate chips, condensed milk and salt in a glass 1-quart measuring container with a handle. Microwave on High for 3 minutes or until chips are melted, stirring after each 1 1/2 minutes. Stir in the chopped nuts and vanilla. Pour into a greased 8×8-inch baking dish. Let cool until firm. Cut into squares. Yield: 2 pounds.

Judy Chenowith (29 years), Laureate Beta Beta
Elkhart, Indiana

PEANUT BUTTER PEANUT BRITTLE

2 cups smooth peanut butter	2 cups raw peanuts
1 1/2 cups sugar	1 teaspoon sifted baking soda
1 1/2 cups light corn syrup	1 teaspoon vanilla
1/4 cup water	extract
2 tablespoons butter	

Butter two large baking sheets. Warm the peanut butter in the top of a double boiler over simmering water. Butter the inside of a heavy 2-quart saucepan. Combine the sugar, corn syrup and water in the prepared saucepan over medium-high heat. Bring to a boil, stirring constantly. Cook to 275 degrees on a candy thermometer, soft-crack stage, stirring frequently. Reduce heat to medium. Add the butter and stir until melted. Add the peanuts. Cook for five minutes longer or until candy begins to turn brown and thermometer registers 295 degrees, stirring frequently. Remove from heat. Sprinkle the baking soda quickly over the peanut mixture, stirring constantly. Stir in the vanilla. Add the warm peanut butter, stirring gently until well combined. Working quickly, pour the candy immediately onto the prepared baking sheets; spread as thin as possible with a spatula. Let stand until cool and break into pieces. Yield: 3 pounds.

Kathy Young, Laureate Beta Beta
Cave Junction, Oregon

Desserts

I have many memories of family dinners on my grandparents' farm. In the summertime, dessert was often homemade ice cream. Water was frozen in cardboard milk containers and kept on hand just for this use. Grandma mixed up the fresh ingredients while Grandpa broke the ice. The freezer was not electric so we all took turns turning the crank. No matter how many of us were there, Grandma's long-handled spoon always found enough ice cream in that freezer for everyone. If you have ever been in Iowa on a hot and muggy day, you know what I mean when I say that that dessert hits the spot!

Cheryl Wissler, Preceptor Alpha Nu
Leighton, Iowa

CLASSIC STRAWBERRY SHORTCAKE

2 cups flour
1/4 cup sugar
1 tablespoon baking
    powder
1 teaspoon salt
1 1/2 cups cold heavy
    cream

1 1/2 cups whipping
    cream
Sugar to taste
Fresh Strawberry Sauce
12 ounces California
    strawberries,
    stemmed, sliced

Combine the flour, sugar, baking powder and salt in a bowl and mix well. Add the cream gradually, stirring gently with a fork just until moistened. Shape gently into 6 balls and place them 3 inches apart on a parchment-lined baking sheet. Bake in the center of the oven at 350 degrees for 25 to 30 minutes or until light golden brown. Cool on the baking sheet. Beat the whipping cream until stiff peaks form and sweeten with sugar. Split shortcakes horizontally. Divide Fresh Strawberry Sauce among 6 dessert plates. Layer a shortcake bottom, 1/4 cup sliced strawberries and 1/4 cup whipped cream over each plate of sauce. Cover with shortcake tops. Spoon the remaining strawberries and whipped cream over the shortcakes. Garnish with sprigs of mint.
Yield: 6 servings.

FRESH STRAWBERRY SAUCE

12 ounces California
    strawberries

Sugar to taste

Remove the stems and cut strawberries into halves. Place in a blender container and process until smooth. Sweeten with sugar. Cover until ready to use.

Photograph for this recipe is on the Cover.

❖ CREAM PUFF DESSERT

Be sure to use real butter.

1 cup water
1/2 cup (1 stick) butter
1 cup flour
4 eggs
8 ounces cream cheese,
    softened
3 1/2 cups cold milk
2 (4-ounce) packages
    chocolate instant
    pudding mix

8 ounces whipped
    topping
1/4 cup milk chocolate
    ice cream topping
1/4 cup caramel ice cream
    topping
1/3 cup chopped almonds

Combine the water and butter in a saucepan over medium heat and bring to a boil. Add the flour all at once; stir until a smooth ball forms. Remove from heat; let stand for 5 minutes. Add the eggs 1 at a time, beating well after each addition. Beat until smooth.

Spread in a greased 9×13-inch baking dish. Bake at 400 degrees for 30 to 35 minutes or until puffed and golden brown. Cool completely on a wire rack. Combine the cream cheese, milk and dry pudding mix in a mixing bowl and beat until smooth. Spread the cream cheese mixture over the puff. Chill, covered, for 20 minutes. Spread whipped topping over the cream cheese layer. Chill, covered, until ready to serve. Drizzle with chocolate and caramel toppings and sprinkle with almonds. Yield: 12 servings.

*Kimberly Mangels, Xi Tau
Havre, Montana*

MEMORIES

My fondest memory of the holidays is going to visit my paternal grandparents for Christmas. All my aunts, uncles, and cousins would be there. My grandpa would talk to each one of us sometime during the day. You could see the pride in his eyes. My grandma always made macaroni and cheese for the grandkids. She made the best! She put so much love in the food that you could just taste it. I am glad that my children got to see a couple of Christmases like this before my grandparents passed away. Family was very important to them.

*Becky Fazio, Xi Gamma
Pleasant Hill, Iowa*

RUSSIAN CREAM

2 cups heavy cream
1 cup sugar
1 tablespoon unflavored
    gelatin
2 teaspoons vanilla
    extract

1 teaspoon almond
    extract
2 cups sour cream
1 (16-ounce) package
    frozen raspberries,
    thawed

Combine the cream, sugar and gelatin in a heavy saucepan over low heat. Cook until sugar is dissolved, stirring constantly. Remove from heat and cool until slightly thickened. Pour into a mixing bowl. Beat at low speed until smooth while adding vanilla, almond extract and sour cream. Pour into individual custard dishes and chill. Spoon raspberries over the custard and serve. Yield: 4 servings.

*Tricia Carraway, Xi Epsilon Zeta
Sikeston, Missouri*

BAKLAVA

I won our chapter's cooking contest with this dessert. When "painting" the phyllo sheets with butter, try using a 2½-inch household brush instead of a pastry brush—the black bristles are easier to detect if they fall off! Baklava freezes beautifully before or after baking.

4 cups finely chopped walnuts	**½ teaspoon allspice**
1½ teaspoons ground cinnamon	**1 pound phyllo dough**
	2 cups (4 sticks) butter, melted
½ teaspoon ground cloves	**Whole cloves (optional)**
	Cinnamon Syrup

Combine the walnuts, ground cinnamon, ground cloves and allspice in a medium bowl and mix well. Layer 9 sheets of the phyllo dough in a buttered 11×15-inch baking dish, brushing each sheet with melted butter. Spread ⅓ of the walnut mixture over the top sheet. Repeat the procedure until all walnut mixture is used. Finish with about 6 to 8 phyllo sheets, again buttering each sheet. Cut the baklava all the way through with a very sharp knife to make diamond-shaped pieces and press a whole clove in the center of each. Baklava can be prepared up to this point and refrigerated, tightly wrapped, for a day or two. Sprinkle lightly with about a "handful" of water. Bake at 350 degrees for 1 hour. Reduce oven temperature to 300 degrees and bake for 15 minutes longer or until light golden brown. Let stand for about 10 minutes. Pour cooled Cinnamon Syrup evenly over the baklava. Let stand for 2 to 3 hours before cutting. Yield: 3 to 4 dozen.

CINNAMON SYRUP

1 cup water	**1 teaspoon lemon juice**
2½ cups sugar	**1 stick cinnamon**

Combine the water, sugar, lemon juice and cinnamon stick in a medium saucepan and bring to a boil. Reduce heat and simmer for 3 to 4 minutes. Remove from heat.

Jenny Lott, Kappa Beta
Douglas, Georgia

VANILLA ALMOND TORTE

1 frozen puff pastry sheet, thawed	**⅛ teaspoon almond extract**
½ cup whipping cream	**3 tablespoons sliced almonds**
4 ounces cream cheese, softened	**Cinnamon**
¼ cup sugar	
1 teaspoon vanilla extract	

Unfold the pastry sheet on a floured surface. Press together at folds and cut in half lengthwise. Place on a greased baking sheet. Bake at 350 degrees for 15 minutes. Let stand until cool. Slice cooled pastries in half horizontally. Whip the cream until stiff peaks form. Beat the cream cheese, sugar, vanilla and almond extract in a mixing bowl until light and fluffy. Fold in the whipped cream. Place a pastry layer on a serving plate and spread with ⅓ cup cream mixture. Repeat the layers 3 times to assemble a 4-layer torte. Sprinkle with almonds and cinnamon. Chill, covered, for 2 to 10 hours. Yield: 1 (9×4×2-inch) torte.

Charolett Dunkin, Xi Beta Epsilon
Woodward, Oklahoma

MEMORIES

When I bought my first car, my boyfriend convinced me to buy a Volkswagen Beetle. That was in 1960—a time when this car had to be ordered. It would take two months to get delivery on the car.

At work, others talked about the Volkswagen convertible. They said the convertible was only $200 more than the standard Beetle, and it was really cute. I went past the dealership on my way home from work and saw a convertible in the window. It was cute. I wanted to change my order. I called my boyfriend and told him that I needed to go back to the dealer and change my order. He agreed to go with me.

The dealership was closed when we arrived, but I learned the convertible I saw in the showroom was not a Volkswagen but a Porsche that was not just $200 more! My boyfriend told me I had better stick with my original order, and that he would get me the Porsche later. My boyfriend became my husband. I stayed with my original order and I am still waiting to get the Porsche convertible . . . and yes, I still have my original husband!

Synda Prisbrey, Alpha Delta Omicron
Bonne Terre, Missouri

PECAN ROLL

This is a recipe given to me by my maid of twenty years, who helped raise my children.

1 cup packed brown sugar	1/2 cup cream diluted with milk
1 cup granulated sugar	1 teaspoon vanilla extract
2 cups chopped pecans	
3 eggs, slightly beaten	Pinch of salt
1/4 cup (1/2 stick) butter, softened	Pastry Circles

Combine the brown sugar, granulated sugar, pecans, eggs, butter, cream mixture, vanilla and salt in a saucepan over medium-low heat. Cook until thickened, stirring frequently. Spread pecan filling over half of each pastry circle to within 1/2 inch of the edge. Fold each circle in half to enclose the filling and seal the edges. Place on greased baking sheets. Bake at 300 degrees for 30 minutes or until lightly browned. Yield: 3 rolls.

PASTRY CIRCLES

3 cups flour	1 teaspoon salt
1 teaspoon baking powder	3/4 cup milk
	3/4 cup shortening

Combine the flour, baking powder, salt, milk and shortening in a mixing bowl and beat until pliable but stiff enough to hold a filling. Roll into three 1/4-inch-thick circles on a floured surface.

Anne Williamson (55 years), Laureate Psi
Albany, Georgia

SUGARED CARROT FLUFF

2 pounds carrots, peeled, chopped	3 large eggs, room temperature
3/4 cup sugar	1/4 cup (1/2 stick) butter, softened
2 tablespoons flour	
1 1/2 teaspoons baking powder	1 1/2 tablespoons sugar
	Whipped cream (optional)
1 1/2 teaspoons vanilla extract	

Place the carrots in a saucepan over medium-high heat and add enough water to cover; bring to a boil. Reduce heat and simmer for 30 minutes or until very tender; drain. Combine the carrots, the 3/4 cup sugar, flour, baking powder and vanilla in a food processor container; process until smooth. Add the eggs 1 at a time, pulsing after each addition until blended. Butter a 1 1/2-quart soufflé dish and coat bottom and side with the 1 1/2 tablespoons sugar. Spoon the carrot mixture into the dish. Preheat oven to 350 degrees.

Bake for 45 minutes or until set in center. Serve with whipped cream. Yield: 10 servings.

Claire Stika (55 years), Gamma Master
Lafayette, Louisiana

CRUNCHY CANDIED YAM SOUFFLE

Kids love it!

4 eggs, separated	1/2 cup packed brown sugar
2 (18-ounce) cans candied yams (in syrup)	1 cup crushed cornflakes or other flake cereal
1/2 cup melted butter	2/3 cup chopped pecans

Beat the egg whites in a large bowl until stiff peaks form. Purée the candied yams in a blender; add 1/4 cup of the melted butter and the egg yolks and process until smooth. Pour the yam mixture over the egg whites, folding with a spatula until well combined. Spoon into a buttered casserole or straight-sided soufflé dish. Combine the brown sugar, cornflakes, pecans and the remaining 1/4 cup melted butter in a small bowl and mix well. Sprinkle over the top of the yam mixture. Bake at 350 degrees for 45 to 60 minutes or until puffed and firm. Yield: 8 servings.

Andria Wiltshire, Alpha Tau
Reno, Nevada

COLD SWEET POTATO CASSEROLE

1 cup flour	1 cup confectioners' sugar
1 cup (2 sticks) margarine, room temperature	3 cups mashed cooked sweet potatoes
1/2 cup chopped pecans	1 cup packed brown sugar
8 ounces whipped topping	
8 ounces cream cheese, softened	1 teaspoon vanilla extract

Mix together the flour, half the margarine and pecans and spread in a greased 9×13-inch baking dish. Bake at 350 degrees for 20 minutes. Let stand until cool. Combine the whipped topping, cream cheese and confectioners' sugar in a bowl and mix well; spread over the cooled pecan layer. Combine the sweet potatoes, brown sugar, the remaining 1/2 cup margarine and vanilla in a bowl and mix well. Spread over the cream cheese layer. Spread with additional whipped topping and sprinkle with additional chopped pecans if desired. Chill, covered, until ready to serve. Yield: 12 servings.

Louise P. Sledge, Xi Beta Kappa
Lexington, South Carolina

MEMORIES

My Grandma Leach is the one who taught me the most in the kitchen, from washing dishes by hand to making gravy, which I still cannot make the way she did. I remember standing on a chair so that I could reach the sink or the stove. Most foods were homegrown. We had fresh vegetables, fresh milk and fresh eggs. We would sit on the porch swing and take turns shaking cream in a jar to make butter. If anyone showed up at eating time, Grandma always had plenty of food to go around and you couldn't say no. I will treasure the times we shared in the kitchen. It was in her little kitchen where she taught me about life, love and, most of all, patience. Someday I hope to have the same impact on my grandchildren's lives that Grandma Leach had on mine.

Amy Machtolff, Nu Kappa
Guthrie, Oklahoma

AMY'S PHILIPPINE FLAN

This dessert was served at the first supper made by my new daughter-in-law in Canada after she escaped from the Philippines.

6 egg yolks	Grated zest of 1 lemon
2 eggs	1 teaspoon vanilla
1 (12-ounce) can	extract
evaporated milk	1 cup sugar
1 (14-ounce) can	
sweetened condensed	
milk	

Combine the egg yolks and eggs in a mixing bowl and beat well. Beat in the evaporated milk and condensed milk. Beat in the lemon zest and vanilla. Chill, covered, until serving time. Place the sugar in a heavy saucepan over medium heat. Cook until melted and light brown, stirring constantly. Pour the caramelized sugar into a loaf pan or ovenproof mold. Pour the chilled egg mixture over the sugar. Place the loaf pan in a larger baking pan. Add water to the larger pan to a depth of 1 inch. Bake at 300 degrees for 1 hour or until set. Yield: 8 or more servings.

Char Priebe, Preceptor Alpha Phi
Chilliwack, British Columbia, Canada

COFFEE MOCHA DESSERT

1 (11-ounce) package	40 marshmallows
chocolate wafer	1 cup strong coffee
cookies	12 ounces whipped
1/2 cup melted margarine	topping

Crush all but 13 of the chocolate wafers. Mix together the crushed wafers and the melted margarine. Press into a 10-inch springform pan. Edge with the 13 whole chocolate wafers. Combine the marshmallows and coffee in a heavy saucepan over low heat; cook until melted, stirring occasionally. Cool to room temperature. Fold in the whipped topping. Pour into the prepared springform pan. Chill, covered, until set. Sprinkle with grated chocolate if desired, and serve. Yield: 13 servings.

Paula Shields, Delta Sigma
Whitby, Ontario, Canada

FLOATING ISLANDS

This recipe has been in our family for over one hundred years. My aunt made this dessert for Sunday dinners when I was small.

2 cups heavy cream	1 tablespoon vanilla
4 egg yolks	extract
1/2 cup sugar	Meringue
Dash of salt	

Heat the cream in the top of a double boiler over direct heat until bubbles form. Combine the egg yolks, sugar and salt in a mixing bowl and blend well. Add a small amount of hot cream to the egg mixture and blend well. Add the remaining hot cream; blend well. Return the cream mixture to the double boiler and cook over boiling water for about 10 minutes, stirring constantly. Drop spoonfuls of Meringue into the hot custard; the heat from the custard will cook the egg whites. Serve in attractive individual bowls. Yield: 6 servings.

MERINGUE

4 egg whites	Dash of salt
1/4 teaspoon cream of	1/2 teaspoon vanilla
tartar	extract
1/2 cup sugar	

Beat the egg whites with the cream of tartar until foamy. Add the sugar gradually, beating constantly until stiff peaks form. Beat in the salt and vanilla.

Barbara J. Ross, Preceptor Iota Sigma
Carrollton, Texas

BLARNEY STONES

When I was in elementary school a classmate always brought these treats for her birthday. Years later I found the recipe in my mother's clippings. Now my grandchildren enjoy them.

2 cups flour	Confectioners' sugar
1 tablespoon baking	2 tablespoons milk
powder	1 teaspoon vanilla
Pinch of salt	extract
4 eggs	1 pound Spanish
2 cups sugar	peanuts, finely
1 cup hot water	ground
1/2 cup (1 stick) butter,	
softened	

Sift the flour, baking powder and salt together. Break the eggs into a mixing bowl and beat at medium speed for 5 minutes. Add the sugar and beat for 5 minutes longer. Beat in the hot water quickly. Fold in the flour mixture. Spread on a lightly greased rimmed baking sheet. Bake at 350 degrees for 45 minutes. Cool and cut into squares or bars. Place the butter in a mixing bowl and beat in enough confectioners' sugar to make a stiff frosting. Beat in the milk and vanilla. Frost all sides of the cake pieces and roll in the ground peanuts. Yield: 2 dozen.

Jan Snider, Xi Theta Zeta
Gilbert, Iowa

PAVLOVA

My mother and father always had lots of company, and this favorite dessert was made for Christmas, Easter, birthdays, and whenever guests were at our house. We lived in New Zealand, and we used real cream from the cow and grew our own gooseberries, strawberries, loganberries, and raspberries to decorate the Pavlova. We sometimes used kiwi fruit, or chopped fruit gelatin when fruit was out of season. This is a light dessert, very good after a heavy meal.

2 cups sugar	2 teaspoons vanilla
4 egg whites	extract
1/4 cup boiling water	1 cup whipped cream or
4 tablespoons	whipped topping
cornstarch	
2 teaspoons vinegar	

Preheat the oven to 425 degrees. Combine the sugar, egg whites, boiling water, cornstarch, vinegar and vanilla in a large mixing bowl and beat at medium speed for at least 15 minutes. Spread the mixture on a baking sheet lined with greased waxed paper, shaping into an 8- to 10-inch ring. Place in the 425-degree oven. Turn oven temperature to 250 degrees.

Bake for 1 hour. Turn off the oven and let the Pavlova remain in the oven until completely cool. Remove to a serving plate and decorate with whipped cream and fruit of choice. Yield: 8 to 10 servings.

Shirley K. Hudson (25 years), Laureate Alpha Delta
Roanoke, Virginia

CREAM CHEESE BAKE

When we moved into our home twenty-one years ago, a neighbor brought this over to welcome us to the neighborhood. We are still good friends after all these years.

1/4 cup (1/2 stick) butter,	2 (10-count) cans biscuits
melted	8 ounces cream cheese,
3/4 cup sugar	cut into 20 cubes
1 teaspoon cinnamon	

Spread the melted butter in a bundt pan. Mix together the sugar and cinnamon. Sprinkle 1/2 cup of the cinnamon mixture to cover the bottom of the pan. Flatten each biscuit and place a cream cheese cube and 1 teaspoon of the cinnamon mixture in the center of each. Shape into balls to enclose the filling and place seam side down in the bundt pan in 2 layers. Bake at 350 degrees for 25 minutes or until golden brown. Cool for 5 or 10 minutes and invert onto a serving plate. Yield: 16 servings.

Susan Laitner, Laureate Delta Epsilon
Independence, Missouri

HOT FUDGE SUNDAE DESSERT

24 chocolate sandwich	1 (14-ounce) can
cookies, crushed	sweetened condensed
1/4 cup melted butter	milk
1/2 gallon butter pecan	1/2 cup (1 stick) butter
ice cream, softened	8 ounces whipped
1 (16-ounce) can	topping
chocolate syrup	Chopped pecans

Combine the cookie crumbs and the 1/4 cup melted butter in a bowl and mix well. Press into a 9×13-inch baking dish and freeze for 30 minutes. Spread the ice cream over the frozen cookie layer and freeze for 30 minutes longer. Combine the chocolate syrup, condensed milk and the 1/2 cup butter in a saucepan. Bring to a boil; reduce heat and simmer for 5 minutes. Cool. Spread the cooled chocolate mixture over the ice cream layer and freeze for 30 minutes. Spread with whipped topping and sprinkle with pecans. Freeze until ready to serve. Yield: 3 dozen small servings.

Shirley Moorman (36 years), Laureate Zeta Alpha
Middleburg, Florida

ICE CREAM SANDWICH DESSERT

19 or 20 ice cream sandwiches	8 ounces whipped topping
1 (18-ounce) jar hot fudge sauce	1 (12-ounce) can Spanish peanuts with skins

Line an 11×13-inch baking dish with the ice cream sandwiches, placing 2 sandwiches parallel to the 11-inch side and the rest perpendicular to that side. Spread the entire jar of fudge sauce over the sandwiches. Cover with half the whipped topping and sprinkle with half the peanuts. Repeat layers of ice cream sandwiches, the remaining whipped topping and peanuts. Freeze. Yield: 1¹/₂ dozen servings.

Karen Maximuk, Xi Theta Psi
Overland Park, Kansas

CHEESE BLITZES

A good friend made these treats for my bridal shower twenty years ago, and everyone praised her for the effort she put into them. She shared her secret with me later—and this is one of the easiest recipes I have! You can freeze the blitzes weeks in advance and bake just before you serve them, making the house smell great.

1 loaf sliced white bread, crusts trimmed	³/₄ cup sugar
8 ounces cream cheese, softened	1 egg yolk
	1 teaspoon cinnamon
	¹/₂ cup melted butter

Roll each bread slice flat with a rolling pin. Combine the cream cheese, ¹/₄ cup of the sugar and egg yolk in a small bowl and mix until smooth. Spread the cream cheese mixture over the flattened bread slices and roll tightly as for a jelly roll. Mix the remaining ¹/₂ cup sugar and cinnamon in a shallow bowl. Dip each rolled blitz in melted butter and roll in cinnamon sugar to coat. Arrange on a cookie sheet and freeze, covered, for 2 to 10 hours. Thaw ¹/₂ hour before baking and cut each blitz in half. Bake at 350 degrees for 15 minutes. Yield: 2 dozen.

Marie Umbriac (30 years), Preceptor Alpha Upsilon
Tamaqua, Pennsylvania

CINNAMON BREAD ROLL-UPS

2 (24-ounce) loaves soft white sandwich bread, crusts trimmed	1 egg yolk
	1 teaspoon vanilla extract
16 ounces cream cheese, room temperature	Cinnamon to taste
2 cups sugar	1 cup (2 sticks) butter, melted

Roll bread slices flat with a rolling pin. Combine the cream cheese, ¹/₂ cup of the sugar, egg yolk and vanilla in a mixing bowl and beat until smooth. Mix together the remaining 1¹/₂ cups sugar and cinnamon in a small bowl. Place a teaspoon of the cream cheese mixture in the center of a bread slice and roll tightly from one corner to the opposite corner. Dip the rolled bread in melted butter, then roll in the cinnamon mixture. Place the roll-up on a nonstick cookie sheet. Repeat procedure until all bread slices have been used. Freeze the roll-ups, covered, for at least 20 minutes or up to a week. Bake at 350 degrees for 8 to 10 minutes or until hot and bubbly. Yield: 50 roll-ups.

Jackie Boos (36 years), Laureate Nu
Overland Park, Kansas

❖ MICROWAVE TIRAMISU

6 egg yolks	¹/₂ teaspoon plus ¹/₄ teaspoon vanilla extract
1 cup granulated sugar	
¹/₄ cup plus 3 teaspoons French Vanilla instant coffee powder	
	16 ounces cream cheese, softened
¹/₄ cup milk	1¹/₂ cups whipping cream
2 (8-ounce) packages ladyfingers	
1 tablespoon hot water	2 tablespoons confectioners' sugar
¹/₄ cup coffee liqueur	

Mix the egg yolks, sugar, the ¹/₄ cup coffee powder and milk in a medium microwave-safe bowl. Microwave on High for 3 to 4 minutes or until sugar is dissolved and mixture is slightly thickened, stirring once. Place the bowl in ice water for 15 minutes to cool. Line the bottom of a soufflé dish with ladyfingers placed split side up. Combine the hot water, 2 teaspoons of the coffee powder, coffee liqueur and ¹/₂ teaspoon of the vanilla in a bowl and mix well. Brush about 2 tablespoons of the coffee mixture over the ladyfingers. Beat the cream cheese until fluffy. Add the cooled egg mixture gradually, beating well after each addition. Whip 1 cup of the whipping cream in a small mixing bowl until stiff peaks form; fold into the cream cheese mixture. Spoon half the mixture over the ladyfingers layer. Repeat the ladyfingers, coffee mixture and cream cheese mixture layers. Press the remaining ladyfingers over the top. Brush with the remaining coffee mixture. Combine the remaining ¹/₂ cup whipping cream, confectioners' sugar, 1 teaspoon coffee powder and ¹/₄ teaspoon vanilla in a small mixing bowl; beat until stiff peaks form. Spread over the ladyfingers. Garnish with coffee powder. Chill, covered, for at least 2 hours before serving. Yield: 8 servings.

Karen Callaway (25 years), Xi Delta Nu
Covington, Louisiana

MEMORIES

I live over 2,000 miles away from my parents and two younger sisters, so we don't get to see each other very often—sometimes two or three years pass between visits.

Four years ago, I was given my best ever birthday present for my 40th birthday. My sisters called me a couple of days before my birthday and told me to be at the airport on a certain date. They had bought airplane tickets for themselves and me, and paid for a three-day weekend in Vail, Colorado, for just the three of us—no husbands or kids allowed. They even checked ahead of time with my husband to make sure he could handle everything in my kids' schedules for those days.

We have now made it an annual event. One long weekend each winter we pick a place fun to go, and spend the whole time just being sisters having fun.

Robin Bracewell, Xi Beta Rho
Stuttgart, Arkansas

CHOCOLATE CHIP CHEESE BALL

8 ounces cream cheese, softened	2 tablespoons brown sugar
1/2 cup (1 stick) butter (no substitute), softened	3/4 cup chocolate chips
1/4 teaspoon vanilla extract	3/4 cup finely chopped pecans or walnuts
3/4 cups confectioners' sugar	Graham crackers (cinnamon, honey or chocolate)
	Vanilla wafers

Combine the cream cheese, butter and vanilla in a mixing bowl and beat until fluffy. Add the confectioners' sugar and brown sugar gradually, beating just until blended. Stir in the chocolate chips. Chill, covered, for 2 hours. Place on a large piece of plastic wrap and shape into a ball. Chill, wrapped in plastic wrap, for at least 1 hour. Just before serving, roll the ball in chopped nuts. Serve with graham crackers, vanilla wafers or both. Yield: 1 cheese ball.

Joni Burd, Xi Xi
Phoenix, Arizona

ANGEL CAKE DESSERT

1 angel food cake	1 (10-ounce) jar maraschino cherries, drained, quartered
1 (3-ounce) package lemon gelatin	
1 (3-ounce) package lime gelatin	1 cup whipping cream, whipped, or 1 1/2 cups whipped topping
1/2 (10-ounce) package multicolor miniature marshmallows	

Break the angel food cake into marshmallow-size pieces. Combine the dry lemon and lime gelatin mixes and 2 cups boiling water in a bowl and stir well. Stir in 2 cups cold water. Let stand until the consistency of egg whites. Carefully fold in the cake pieces, marshmallows and cherries. Place in a greased tube pan. Chill, covered, for 6 to 8 hours. Invert onto a cake plate. Top with whipped cream and serve. Yield: 8 to 12 servings.

Colette Killebrew, Xi Delta Phi
Charleston, Tennessee

TIPSY PUDDING CAKE

This recipe is submitted in loving memory of our sister Pat Erb, who passed away three months ago. While recently thumbing through "Recipes to Survive on a 2-Burner Stove with No Oven" from a Staff NCO Wives Club in Japan, we were pleasantly surprised to find several recipes submitted by our sister Pat. She lived her life continuously weaving her web of friendship, and we know how happy she would be to share this recipe with her many sisters throughout the world.

Raspberry preserves	Whipped topping and sliced blanched almonds
12 thin slices pound cake, fresh or frozen	
Sweet sherry, or sweet orange juice	
1 (6-ounce) package vanilla instant pudding mix	

Spread raspberry preserves over 6 slices of the pound cake; cover with the remaining slices to make 6 sandwiches. Cut each sandwich in quarters and arrange in a 9×13-inch baking dish. Drizzle with just enough sherry to moisten. Prepare the pudding using the package directions and spoon over the cake sandwiches. Top with whipped topping and sprinkle with almonds. Yield: 8 to 12 servings.

Judy Bird (24 years) and Jackie Githens (28 years),
Laureate Psi
Havelock, North Carolina

ORANGE BAKED ALASKA

My kids loved this. My grownup friends called it a gourmet dessert!

1 pint vanilla ice cream	1/4 teaspoon cream of
3 large oranges	tartar
3 egg whites	6 tablespoons sugar

Scoop the ice cream into 6 balls; freeze for at least 5 hours. Cut the oranges horizontally in half. Cut a thin slice from the bottom of each half. Cut around the edges and membranes and remove fruit and membranes from the orange shells. Fill each orange shell with orange segments. Beat the egg whites with cream of tartar until foamy. Add the sugar 1 tablespoon at a time, beating until stiff glossy peaks form; do not underbeat. Place the filled orange shells on a baking sheet. Top each with a scoop of ice cream. Cover the ice cream with the meringue, sealing to the edge. Bake at 500 degrees for 2 to 3 minutes or until meringue is light brown. Serve immediately. Yield: 6 servings.

Judith K. Baker, Delta Mu Mu
Volcano, California

MEMORIES

T̄he only thing more fun for me than planning a party is the party itself. I love to think up and design a menu around a party theme. I have been known to take our programs very seriously and suggest recipes for our parties that take as long as ten days to prepare. One of my funniest and most treasured memories is helping one of my older sorority sisters do some spring cleaning. Ruthie knew that I loved cooking magazines and that I read cookbooks the way most people read novels. While cleaning, Ruthie very carefully placed a stack of magazines in my arms and, without so much as cracking a smile, ordered me to raise my right hand. Dumbfounded, I dutifully obeyed. She then said, "I do solemnly swear that I will never suggest, order or, in any manner, make any of my sisters cook anything from the contents of the magazines given to me this day. I swear, so help me God!"

Cecilia Welsh (29 years), Preceptor Lambda Theta
Blue Springs, Missouri

CROWN JEWEL DESSERT

I was a young Zeta Eta pledge looking for something to serve my sisters when I hosted my first sorority meeting. The year was 1969 and I found this recipe in our local newspaper. It was an instant hit with my sorority sisters, and they all asked for the recipe. I serve this easy, wonderful dessert with nuts or crackers and herbal tea or hot coffee.

1 (3-ounce) package lime	1/2 cup sugar
gelatin	1/2 cup cold water
1 (3-ounce) package	18 whole ladyfingers,
orange gelatin	split
1 (3-ounce) package	2 (4-ounce) packages
cherry gelatin	Dream Whip
3 cups boiling water	1 cup cold milk
1 1/2 cups cold water	1 teaspoon vanilla
1 cup pineapple juice	extract
1 (3-ounce) package	
lemon gelatin	

Prepare the lime, orange and cherry gelatin separately, using 1 cup boiling water and 1/2 cup cold water for each flavor. Pour into separate 8×8-inch glass dishes. Chill until firm. Cut into 1/2-inch cubes. Heat the pineapple juice in a saucepan; bring to the boiling point. Remove from heat. Add the dry lemon gelatin mix and sugar and stir until dissolved. Stir in the 1/2 cup cold water. Chill until syrupy. Line the bottom and side of a 9-inch springform pan with ladyfingers. Prepare the Dream Whip with milk and vanilla using the package directions. Fold into the syrupy lemon gelatin. Fold in the gelatin cubes. Pour into a 9-inch springform pan. Chill, covered, for 5 to 10 hours. Cut and serve. Yield: 16 servings.

I. Sue McMillan (33 years), Alpha Kappa Master
Mount Vernon, Ohio

ORANGE LIQUEUR TRIFLE

1 pound cake, cut into	Variety of fresh fruit
1-inch cubes	Whipped topping or
Liqueur, orange or other	whipped cream
flavor	Shredded coconut

Layer the pound cake cubes in a large glass bowl. Drizzle with liqueur. Add layers of fruit. Spread a thin layer of whipped topping over the fruit. Sprinkle with coconut. Repeat the layers of cake cubes, liqueur, fruit and whipped topping until the bowl is filled. Sprinkle the top layer of whipped topping with toasted shredded coconut. Decorate with fresh strawberries if desired. Yield: Variable.

Jean Poynor (39 years), Epsilon Master
Eureka Springs, Arkansas

STRAWBERRY BAVARIAN

My brother Walt began seventh grade well over six feet tall and everyone expected him to be a star basketball player, but this was not to be. That school year, however, he entered a cooking contest—the only male entrant. He made Strawberry Bavarian and ran away with top honors, grand prize, and a special commendation for being the only boy to participate. Forty years later, the memory still brings a broad smile to his face.

1 small angel food cake
1 (6-ounce) package
   strawberry gelatin
1½ cups hot water
2 (10-ounce) packages
   frozen strawberries,
   thawed

2 cups whipped topping
1 tablespoon cornstarch
Red food coloring
   (optional)

Tear the angel food cake into bite-size pieces. Prepare the gelatin with the 1½ cups hot water and allow to cool but not to set. Drain the strawberries, reserving the liquid. Stir the strawberries into the cooled gelatin. Fold in the whipped topping and cake pieces. Pour into a bundt or tube pan. Cover and place in the refrigerator until serving time. Before serving, make a glaze by adding the cornstarch to 1 cup of the reserved strawberry liquid in a saucepan over medium-low heat. Cook until thickened and transparent, stirring constantly. Remove from heat and cool slightly. Unmold the chilled gelatin onto a serving plate and drizzle with the glaze. Chill to set the glaze. Yield: 12 servings.

Marti Moehlau, Xi Delta
Silver Spring, Maryland

COCONUT ANGEL FOOD CAKE TRIFLE

1 envelope unflavored
   gelatin
½ cup cold water
4 egg yolks, beaten
2 tablespoons flour
¼ teaspoon salt
2 cups milk

4 egg whites
1 (4-ounce) package
   whipped topping mix
1 angel food cake
1 cup finely grated
   coconut

Soften the gelatin in the cold water. Combine the egg yolks and flour in a heavy saucepan and beat until smooth; beat in the salt. Place over low heat. Add the milk gradually, stirring constantly. Cook until custard just coats a metal spoon. Stir the gelatin mixture into the hot custard. Chill, covered, for 1 hour. Beat the egg whites in a medium bowl until stiff peaks form. Fold in the cooled custard. Prepare the whipped topping mix using the package directions.

Cut or tear the angel food cake into bite-size pieces. Line a 9×13-inch baking dish with half the cake pieces. Layer half the custard and half the coconut over the cake layer. Layer the remaining cake pieces and remaining custard over the coconut layer. Spread the Dream Whip over the custard layer and sprinkle with the remaining coconut. Chill, covered, for at least 1 hour before serving. Yield: 18 to 20 servings.

Betty Jo Flint, Alpha Rho
Madison, Indiana

SLIM SAVANNAH TRIFLE

Trifles are a favorite dessert in Savannah. I adapted this recipe to serve at chapter meetings because all of us are watching our calories. It's just as good (or better!) than the regular version.

1 (14-ounce) store-
   bought angel food
   cake
2 small packages
   vanilla sugar-free
   pudding mix

2 pints fresh
   strawberries, or
1 (20-ounce) package
   frozen whole berries
16 ounces fat-free
   whipped topping

Tear or cut the cake into ½-inch cubes. Prepare the pudding with skim milk using the package directions. Slice the strawberries. Layer the pudding, cake cubes, berries and whipped topping in a glass bowl, ½ at a time. Cover with plastic wrap and chill completely before serving. Yield: 10 to 12 servings.

Susan Parsley, Xi Eta Delta
Savannah, Georgia

❖ SWEETHEART TRIFLE

1 (2-layer) package
   chocolate cake mix
1 (10-ounce) package
   peanut butter chips
4¼ cups cold milk
½ cup heavy cream
¼ teaspoon vanilla
   extract

2 (4-ounce) packages
   chocolate instant
   pudding mix
12 ounces whipped
   topping
4 (2-ounce) Nestle
   Crunch candy bars,
   crumbled

Prepare the cake batter using the package directions. Pour into a greased 9×13-inch baking dish. Bake at 350 degrees for 30 to 35 minutes. Cool in the pan on a wire rack. Combine the peanut butter chips, ¼ cup of the milk and cream in a heavy saucepan over low heat. Cook until chips are melted and mixture is smooth, stirring frequently. Remove from heat. Stir in the vanilla. Cool to room temperature. Place the remaining 4 cups milk in a mixing bowl. Add the dry pudding mix and beat at low speed for 2 minutes. Crumble half the cake; place in a trifle bowl.

Layer half the peanut butter sauce, half the pudding, half the whipped topping and 2 of the candy bars over the cake layer. Repeat the cake, peanut butter sauce, pudding and candy bar layers. Chill, covered, until serving time. Yield: 12 to 15 servings.

Wendy Lee Boytim, Xi Epsilon Beta
Tyrone, Pennsylvania

NO-BAKE KAHLUA DESSERT

2 (7-ounce) packages
  Stella D'oro anisette
  toasts
3/4 cup Kahlúa
3/4 cup water
2 (4-ounce) packages
  vanilla cook-and-
  serve pudding

2 (4-ounce) packages
  chocolate cook-and-
  serve pudding
6 cups milk
8 ounces nondairy
  whipped topping
1/2 cup toasted almond
  slices

Line the bottom of a 10-inch springform pan with 15 of the anisette toasts, breaking them if necessary to fit. Combine the Kahlúa and water and blend. Pour half the Kahlúa mixture over the anisette toasts. Prepare the vanilla pudding using package directions with 3 cups of the milk. Pour the hot vanilla pudding over the toasts. Cool slightly. Add another layer of toasts. Pour the remaining Kahlúa mixture evenly over the toasts; let stand until absorbed. Prepare the chocolate pudding using package directions with the remaining 3 cups milk. Pour the hot chocolate pudding over the soaked toasts. Let stand until cool. Chill, covered, for 8 to 10 hours. Remove from the springform pan onto a serving plate. Spread whipped topping over the dessert and sprinkle with almonds. Cut into wedges and serve. Yield: 12 to 15 servings.

Donna Aven (30 years), Preceptor Alpha Alpha
Pearl River, New York

APPLE CRISP

7 large Granny Smith
  apples, peeled, cored
2 cups flour
2 cups sugar
2 teaspoons cinnamon

1/2 teaspoon pumpkin
  pie spice
1 cup (2 sticks)
  margarine
1 cup chopped walnuts

Slice the apples into a greased 9×13-inch baking dish. Mix the next 4 ingredients in a bowl. Cut in the margarine until the mixture resembles coarse crumbs. Layer the flour mixture over the apples. Sprinkle with chopped nuts. Bake at 350 degrees for 45 minutes or until apples are tender. Yield: 12 servings.

Mary Ann Northrup (38 years), Laureate Rho
Powell, Wyoming

BLUEBERRY GRUNT

When we were children it was a thrill to pick wild blueberries across the road during blueberry season. Mom would whip up this dessert from memory using her hands as measuring spoons. When we grew up, my brother insisted she stop to measure each ingredients so we could write down the recipe.

5 cups blueberries, fresh
  or frozen
1 1/4 cups sugar
1/2 cup water
1 teaspoon lemon juice
2 cups flour

1/2 teaspoon salt
2 teaspoons baking
  powder
2 tablespoons butter
1 cup milk

Combine the blueberries, 1 cup of the sugar, water and lemon juice in a large saucepan and bring to a boil. Simmer gently while preparing the topping. Measure the remaining 1/4 cup sugar, flour, salt and baking powder into a bowl; stir to blend. Cut in the butter. Add the milk and stir until moistened. Drop by spoonfuls over the simmering berry mixture. Simmer, covered, for at least 15 minutes longer. Serve with ice cream or whipped cream. Yield: 6 to 8 servings.

Tammy Watson, Theta Xi
Kamloops, British Columbia, Canada

RHUBARB CRUMBLE

We used to wait for the first tender rhubarb plants in spring so we could have this dessert. Now I make it with various fresh or frozen fruit.

1 cup flour
3/4 cup rolled oats
1 cup packed brown
  sugar
1 teaspoon salt
1 teaspoon cinnamon
1/2 cup melted butter

4 cups chopped rhubarb
1 cup sugar
1 tablespoon vanilla
  extract
1 tablespoon cornstarch
1 cup water

Combine the flour, oats, brown sugar, salt, cinnamon and melted butter in a bowl and mix well. Press half the flour mixture into an 8×8-inch baking pan. Spread the rhubarb evenly over the base. Combine the sugar, vanilla, cornstarch and water in a microwave-safe bowl. Microwave, loosely covered, on High until thickened, stirring occasionally. Pour evenly over the fruit layer. Sprinkle with the remaining flour mixture. Bake at 350 degrees for 1 hour. Serve with ice cream or whipped cream. Yield: 6 servings.

Larissa Hadley, Xi Epsilon Eta
Clearwater, British Columbia, Canada

FRESH YUMMY PLUM COBBLER

Yellow plums are best for this dessert.

1 pound sweet plums, pitted, quartered	1/4 cup sugar
2/3 cup packed brown sugar	1 egg, beaten
1/2 cup orange juice	1/2 cup milk
1 1/2 cups baking mix	2 tablespoons vegetable oil
1/4 teaspoon salt	1 teaspoon vanilla extract

Spread the plums in a buttered 8-inch-square or 1 1/2-quart baking dish. Sprinkle with the brown sugar. Pour the orange juice over the top. Combine the baking mix, salt and sugar in a large bowl and stir to mix. Combine the egg, milk, vegetable oil and vanilla in a separate bowl and blend. Add the milk mixture to the dry ingredients and stir just until moistened. Pour over the plum layer. Bake at 375 degrees for 45 minutes or until golden brown. Yield: 6 to 8 servings.

Crystal Livingstone, Theta Nu
Prince George, British Columbia, Canada

RASPBERRY PRETZEL DESSERT

My friends and family all enjoy this unique recipe.

2 cups broken pretzels	8 ounces cream cheese, softened
3 tablespoons melted margarine	1 tablespoon lemon juice
3 tablespoons confectioners' sugar	1 egg
2 cups boiling water	1 cup confectioners' sugar
1 (6-ounce) package raspberry gelatin	8 ounces whipped topping
1 (16-ounce) package frozen raspberries	

Combine the pretzels, margarine and the 3 tablespoons confectioners' sugar. Spread in a 9×13-inch baking dish, being sure to cover the bottom of the dish completely. Bake at 350 degrees for 10 minutes; let stand until cool. Combine the boiling water and the dry gelatin mix in a bowl, stirring until dissolved. Stir in the frozen raspberries; let stand until cool. Combine the cream cheese, lemon juice, egg and the 1 cup confectioners' sugar in a separate bowl and mix well. Fold in the whipped topping. Spread carefully over the top of the cooled pretzel mixture. Pour the semi-set gelatin mixture carefully over the cream cheese layer, being careful not to let the two layers mix. Chill until firm. Yield: 10 servings.

Dustie Beatty, Eta Delta
Toledo, Oregon

NANA'S GLOPP

This dessert has always been a special treat for our family. Nothing made my children happier than seeing Nana, their grandmother, coming to visit carrying a plate of Glopp. Nana passed away recently and her grown grandchildren now make this dessert themselves. It used to be called Glopp, but they now fondly refer to it as Nana's Glopp.

3 egg whites	1/2 cup chopped walnuts
1 cup sugar	1/2 teaspoon vanilla extract
1/2 teaspoon baking powder	Whipped cream and maraschino cherries
20 butter crackers, crushed	

Beat the egg whites in a medium bowl until stiff peaks form. Add the sugar and baking powder gradually, beating after each addition. Fold in the butter crackers, walnuts and vanilla. Spoon into a well-greased 7×11-inch baking dish. Bake at 350 degrees for 25 minutes. Cut into squares and serve each piece topped with whipped cream and a maraschino cherry. Serve warm or cold. Yield: 16 to 24 servings.

Pat Richardson (39 years), Epsilon Beta
Monticello, New York

MEMORIES

My years in Beta Sigma Phi started in the fall of 1976 in Erie, Pennsylvania. My neighbor (who, by the way, just completed 50 years in Beta Sigma Phi) submitted my name to a group of moms my age. This group of ladies, along with all the ladies I have met in many areas of the country in the past 25 years, have been heaven-sent to my family and me. Through good times and bad, my "sisters" have always been there for me. In 1992, my daughter joined our newly formed chapter in Texas; my two daughters-in-law joined us in 2001. My two granddaughters are Legacy members and are anxiously awaiting the day they too can be called "sisters." It is truly a family affair. Thank you, Beta Sigma Phi.

Cookie Danek (25 years), Xi Alpha Delta Eta
League City, Texas

BANANA SPLIT DESSERT

2 cups graham cracker crumbs	2 eggs
1/2 cup melted butter	3 bananas, sliced
2 cups confectioners' sugar	1 cup sliced strawberries
1 cup (2 sticks) butter, softened	1 (20-ounce) can crushed pineapple, drained
1 teaspoon vanilla extract	3 cups whipped cream
	1 cup crushed pecans or walnuts

Press a mixture of the graham cracker crumbs and melted butter in a 9×13-inch baking dish. Combine the confectioners' sugar, softened butter, vanilla and eggs in a mixing bowl and beat at medium speed for 2 minutes. Pour evenly over the graham cracker layer. Layer the bananas, strawberries and pineapple over the confectioners' sugar layer. Frost with whipped cream and top with crushed nuts. Chill, covered, for at least 12 hours. Serve with chocolate sauce and cherries if desired. Yield: 20 servings.

Diane L. Pruett, Preceptor Alpha Upsilon
Tamaqua, Pennsylvania

APPLE PIE QUESADILLA

2 (10-inch) flour tortillas	1 tablespoon butter or margarine, melted
1 (21-ounce) can apple pie filling	1 tablespoon sugar
1/2 cup finely shredded Cheddar cheese	1/2 teaspoon cinnamon

Place 1 tortilla on a baking sheet sprayed with non-stick cooking spray. Spread with apple pie filling to within 1/2 inch of the edge. Sprinkle with Cheddar cheese. Top with 1 tortilla. Spread the butter over the top with a spoon. Sprinkle a mixture of the sugar and cinnamon over the melted butter. Bake at 350 degrees for 8 to 10 minutes or until crisp and edges are just beginning to brown. Cut with a pizza cutter or sharp knife and serve at once. Yield: 4 servings.

Olga Clarke (38 years)
Satellite Beach, Florida

CHERRY CRUNCH

2 (21-ounce) cans cherry pie filling	1/2 cup chopped pecans or walnuts (optional)
1 teaspoon lemon juice	1/2 cup (1 stick) butter, melted
1 (2-layer) package white cake mix	

Spread the pie filling in the bottom of a buttered 9-inch-square baking dish. Sprinkle with lemon juice.

Combine the dry cake mix, chopped nuts and melted butter in a bowl and mix well; mixture will be crumbly. Sprinkle evenly over the pie filling. Bake at 350 degrees for 40 to 50 minutes or until golden brown. Yield: 9 to 12 servings.

Ann Barnhouse (26 years), Preceptor Alpha Nu
Oskaloosa, Iowa

LIGHT CHERRY DELIGHT

2 cups graham cracker crumbs	8 ounces light cream cheese, softened
1/2 cup (1 stick) margarine, melted	8 ounces whipped topping
1 1/4 cups confectioners' sugar	2 (21-ounce) cans light cherry pie filling

Combine the graham cracker crumbs, margarine and 1/4 cup of the confectioners' sugar in a bowl and mix well. Pat into a 9×13-inch baking dish. Bake at 350 degrees for 5 to 8 minutes. Let cool. Combine the cream cheese and the remaining 1 cup confectioners' sugar in a mixing bowl and beat until fluffy. Fold in the whipped topping. Chill, covered, for 1 hour. Spread over the cooled graham cracker crust. Spread the cherry pie filling over the cream cheese layer. Chill, covered, until ready to serve.
Yield: 15 servings.

Cynthia Worley, Xi Omicron Phi
Harlingen, Texas

CREAMY BLACK FOREST COBBLER

3 eggs	4 cups sifted confectioners' sugar
1 (2-layer) package chocolate cake mix	8 ounces cream cheese, softened
3/4 cup (1 1/2 sticks) butter, softened	1 (21-ounce) can cherry pie filling

Preheat the oven to 350 degrees. Place 1 of the eggs in a large bowl and beat slightly. Add the dry cake mix and butter; stir until well blended. Press the cake mixture into a greased and floured 9×13-inch baking dish. Combine the confectioners' sugar, cream cheese and the remaining 2 eggs in a medium bowl; mix well. Pour the cream cheese mixture evenly over the cake mixture. Spread the pie filling evenly over the cream cheese layer. Bake at 350 degrees for 30 to 40 minutes or until outer edges are lightly browned and center is almost set. Cool completely. Chill, covered, until about 1 hour before serving time. Serve at room temperature. Yield: 24 servings.

Cindy Layton, Xi Epsilon Nu
Cape Girardeau, Missouri

SCOTTISH "CLOOTIE" DUMPLING

"Clootie" Dumpling (Cloth Dumpling) was always made as part of a birthday celebration. Small trinkets, wrapped in waxed paper, were baked in the cake as gifts for the children. Sultanas are raisinlike dried fruits, fancy and delicious.

1 cup water	1 pound sultanas
3/4 cup sugar	1 tablespoon treacle
1 tablespoon (heaping)	(molasses)
mixed spice	2 cups flour or self-
1 tablespoon (heaping)	rising flour
cinnamon	1 teaspoon baking soda
1 cup (2 sticks)	2 eggs, beaten
margarine	

Combine the water, sugar, mixed spice, cinnamon, margarine, sultanas and treacle in a saucepan and bring to a boil. Simmer for 1 minute. Remove from heat. Mix in the flour, baking soda and egg. Line a medium microwave-safe bowl with plastic wrap, enough to go well over the edge. Pour the sultana mixture into the bowl. Microwave on medium for 9 minutes. Let cool. Invert onto a serving plate. Yield: 8 to 12 servings.

Sheila Stevenson, Xi Xi
St. Catharines, Ontario, Canada

CARAMEL DUMPLING PUDDING

1 cup water	1/2 teaspoon baking
3/4 cup packed brown	powder
sugar	Pinch of nutmeg
1 tablespoon butter or	Pinch of salt
margarine	1/4 cup evaporated milk
1 teaspoon vanilla	1/2 cup raisins
extract	1/4 cup chopped walnuts
1/2 cup flour	Ice cream

Bring the water and 1/4 cup of the brown sugar to a boil in a small saucepan over medium heat. Remove from heat. Add the butter and vanilla and stir until butter is melted. Pour into a greased 1-quart baking dish. Combine the flour, baking powder, nutmeg, salt and evaporated milk in a bowl and mix just until blended. Stir in the remaining 1/2 cup brown sugar. Fold in the raisins and walnuts. Drop by spoonfuls over the brown sugar mixture in the baking dish. Bake, uncovered, at 350 degrees for 30 minutes or until golden brown. Spoon into individual serving dishes. Top with ice cream. Yield: 2 servings.

 Louise Palmer (50 years), Preceptor Delta Nu
Amarillo, Texas

PERSIMMON PUDDING

This recipe belonged to my husband's grandma, who was born in 1900.

2 cups persimmons,	2 teaspoons cinnamon
rubbed through a	2 teaspoons baking
sieve	powder
1 cup sugar	3 cups flour, sifted
1 quart milk	

Combine the persimmons, sugar, half the milk, cinnamon, baking powder and flour in a large mixing bowl and mix well. Add the rest of the milk and beat well. Pour into a greased 9×13-inch baking dish. Bake at 350 degrees for about 1 hour or until firm and brown. Serve with plain or whipped cream, half-and-half or warmed milk. Yield: 12 servings.

Barbara Brock (26 years), Preceptor Alpha Eta
DuQuoin, Illinois

FANTASTIC BANANA PUDDING

My mother, a stay-at-home mom with eight children, made banana pudding from scratch for all family get-togethers. Since her death I have carried on the tradition, having altered the recipe somewhat! Everyone says it is not as good as Mom's—but it's the next-best thing!

2 (4-ounce) packages	8 ounces whipped
banana cream instant	topping
pudding mix	1 (12-ounce) package
3 1/2 cups milk	vanilla wafers
8 ounces sour cream	4 or 5 bananas, sliced

Combine the dry pudding mix with the milk and sour cream in a mixing bowl; beat until smooth. Add the whipped topping and beat until smooth and fluffy. Crumble 4 or 5 of the vanilla wafers and reserve for topping. Layer the remaining vanilla wafers, bananas and pudding mixture 1/2 at a time in a pretty crystal bowl. Repeat the layers. Sprinkle with the vanilla wafer crumbs. Chill, covered, for at least 4 hours. Yield: 10 to 12 servings.

Marsha Stevens, Xi Beta Epsilon
Rock View, West Virginia

Sharmaine Eastin, Kappa Chi, Ville Platte, Louisiana, prepares a delicious light blueberry bread pudding using skim milk, egg substitute and fresh or frozen blueberries. She serves this with **Super Easy Caramel Sauce**. Heat 14 vanilla caramels with 1/4 cup skim milk over low heat until smooth and creamy, stirring constantly.

STICKY DATE PUDDING

I first discovered this lovely dessert while on a trip to Scotland in the summer of 2001, then again on a trip to Australia in September of that year. When I returned home I searched through recipes and worked to perfect my new favorite dessert. At last this recipe came about.

8 ounces pitted dates (about ¹/₂ cup)	¹/₂ cup (1 stick) butter, room temperature
1 cup water	1 cup packed brown sugar
1³/₄ cups flour	4 large eggs
1¹/₂ teaspoons baking soda	1 tablespoon instant coffee granules
1 teaspoon baking powder	Toffee Sauce

Combine the dates and water in a saucepan and bring to a boil. Reduce heat and simmer for about 10 minutes or until dates are tender. Purée the date mixture or crush with a spoon. Sift together the flour, baking soda and baking powder. Cream the butter and brown sugar in a mixing bowl until light and fluffy. Add the eggs 1 at a time, beating well after each addition. Add the flour mixture in three parts, beating well after each addition. Stir in the puréed dates and instant coffee; batter will be stiff. Spread in a greased 9×13-inch baking dish. Bake at 350 degrees for 35 minutes or until cake is firm to the touch. Cool in the pan for 5 minutes. Remove to a work surface and slice in half horizontally with a serrated knife. Return the bottom half of the cake to the baking dish and drizzle with half the Toffee Sauce. Top with the second layer of the cake and drizzle with the remaining Toffee Sauce. Let stand, covered, at room temperature for up to 6 hours. Bake, uncovered, at 350 degrees for about 20 minutes or until hot and bubbly. Serve warm. Yield: 10 servings.

TOFFEE SAUCE

1³/₈ cups heavy cream	¹/₂ cup (1 stick) butter
1 cup packed brown sugar	

Combine the cream, brown sugar and butter in a saucepan over medium heat and bring to a boil. Boil gently until thickened, stirring constantly.

Joan Pacholko, Xi Kappa
Calgary, Alberta, Canada

MEMORIES

My G'ma was one of those good cooks who didn't use a recipe. The way that I got her Rice Pudding recipe was by handing her a cup or teaspoon of each ingredient. She would say that she either needed more or less of what I gave her. Now that G'ma is gone, it is a must at family gatherings.

Cricket Turley, Laureate Beta Xi
Dodge City, Kansas

Three years ago our town had an ice storm that knocked out the power for days. I am the chief of our local fire department auxiliary and our fire hall became a local shelter where we made 300 to 400 meals a day. To help us, a local prison sent us fifty pounds of cooked rice. Everyone was stumped with what to do with so much rice. I used half of it for Spanish rice and the other for rice pudding. The people who took shelter with us are still talking about the rice pudding. We now all have this common bond.

Bonnie McCormick, Xi Alpha Kappa
Brownville, New York

GLORIFIED RICE

Mother made this dessert to take to church dinners when I was growing up. I thought it was the prettiest and tastiest dish at every dinner! Use the cherry juice to make the dish pink for Valentine's Day.

2 cups cooked rice, cooled	1 (8-ounce) can crushed pineapple, drained
¹/₂ cup sugar	24 large marshmallows, or ¹/₂ (16-ounce) package miniature marshmallows
1 (10-ounce) jar maraschino cherries, drained, halved	
1 medium apple, peeled, diced	1 cup whipping cream, whipped

Combine the rice, sugar, maraschino cherries, apple, pineapple and marshmallows in a 2-quart bowl and mix well. Fold in the whipped cream. Chill, covered, until serving time. Yield: 10 to 12 servings.

Dorothea Nisbett (37 years), Laureate Theta Nu
San Antonio, Texas

NEW ORLEANS BREAD PUDDING

13 cups chopped bread	1¹/₂ cups chopped
5 cups milk	peaches
2 cups sugar	1 tablespoon vanilla
7 eggs, beaten	extract
1 tablespoon cinnamon	¹/₂ cup melted butter
¹/₂ cup raisins	Sweet Cinnamon Sauce

Combine the bread, milk, sugar, eggs, cinnamon, raisins, peaches, vanilla and butter in a large bowl and mix well. Spread in a 9×13-inch baking dish that has been sprayed with nonstick cooking spray. Bake at 350 degrees for 55 minutes. Serve with Sweet Cinnamon Sauce. Yield: 12 servings.

SWEET CINNAMON SAUCE

2 eggs, beaten	¹/₂ teaspoon vanilla
1 teaspoon cinnamon	extract
1 cup sugar	¹/₂ cup melted butter
¹/₂ cup milk	

Combine all the ingredients in a saucepan and whisk until smooth. Cook over low heat until thickened, stirring constantly.

Iris A. Sarvaunt (30 years), Xi Tau Upsilon
Shepherd, Texas

RHUBARB BREAD PUDDING

This was one of my grandmother's favorite rhubarb recipes. We grandchildren looked forward to her making it every spring with the first cuttings of rhubarb from her patch. We could hardly wait to bring in the pink stalks of rhubarb so Grandma could make this delicious bread pudding.

2 eggs, slightly beaten	4 slices day-old bread,
1¹/₂ cups milk, scalded	cubed
1 cup sliced rhubarb	1 cup sugar

Add the eggs slowly to the scalded milk, mixing well. Add the rhubarb, bread and sugar; mix well. Pour into a buttered 1¹/₂-quart baking dish. Bake at 350 degrees for 1 hour or until custard sets. Yield: 4 servings.

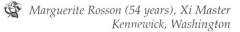 *Marguerite Rosson (54 years), Xi Master*
Kennewick, Washington

CHOCOLATE CHIP BREAD PUDDING

5 tablespoons butter	¹/₈ teaspoon salt
2 cups hot milk	2 cups cubed white
¹/₃ cup dark brown sugar	bread made from
1 teaspoon vanilla	slices with crusts
extract	trimmed
2 eggs	1 cup chocolate chips

Combine the butter, milk and brown sugar in a saucepan and heat until butter is melted, stirring frequently to blend. Remove from heat. Whisk in the vanilla, eggs and salt. Layer the bread cubes and chocolate chips in a greased 1-quart baking dish. Pour the egg mixture evenly over the bread and chips. Chill, covered with plastic wrap, for 5 hours. Place the baking dish in a larger baking pan. Add water to the larger pan to a depth of 1 inch. Bake, uncovered, at 350 degrees for 45 minutes or until browned. Yield: 6 servings.

Jeanne Caimano, Preceptor Gamma Xi
St. Petersburg, Florida

KAHLUA BREAD PUDDING

This was comfort food prepared by my grandmother when the family needed some cheering up. We lived on a ranch, and the smell coming from the kitchen during baking time was unforgettable, especially if we had been out in the cold weather.

6 slices Earth Grains	¹/₂ teaspoon salt
French bread	1 ounce Kahlúa
3 eggs	6 tablespoons butter,
3 cups milk	melted
¹/₃ cup sugar	

Cut or tear the bread into very small pieces about the size of croutons. Beat the eggs with a whisk in a medium bowl. Add the milk, sugar, salt, Kahlúa and butter; mix until color is uniform. Stir in the bread pieces and mix well. Let stand for about 10 minutes or until bread is fully saturated with liquid. Spread in a greased 8-inch-square baking dish. Bake at 325 to 350 degrees for 1 hour. Yield: 6 servings.

Mary Ellen Carey (48 years), Laureate Theta Omega
Sunnyvale, California

OLD-FASHIONED BREAD PUDDING

My four younger sisters and I grew up on a farm, and Mom always baked a lot of bread and cinnamon rolls. Getting off the bus after school to the smell of fresh bread is a wonderful memory.

4 cups small chunks of	¹/₄ teaspoon salt
white bread	¹/₂ teaspoon cinnamon
2 cups milk	¹/₂ teaspoon nutmeg
¹/₄ cup (¹/₂ stick) butter	¹/₂ cup seedless raisins
¹/₂ cup sugar	(optional)
2 eggs, slightly beaten	Lemon Sauce

Place the bread in a 1¹/₂-quart baking dish. Scald the milk with the butter and cool. Add the sugar, eggs, salt, cinnamon, nutmeg and raisins and mix well.

Pour the egg mixture evenly over the bread. Place the baking dish in a larger baking pan. Add water to the larger pan to a depth of 1 inch. Bake at 350 degrees for 40 to 45 minutes or until a silver knife inserted 1 inch from the edge comes out clean; don't overbake. Serve warm with Lemon Sauce. Yield: 6 to 8 servings.

LEMON SAUCE

1/2 cup sugar	1 tablespoon lemon
1 tablespoon cornstarch	juice
1 cup water	1 tablespoon grated
2 1/2 tablespoons butter	lemon zest

Combine the sugar and cornstarch in a saucepan over medium heat. Stir in the water gradually and bring to a boil. Boil for 1 minute, stirring constantly. Stir in the butter, lemon juice and lemon zest.

Marty Tharp (35 years), Preceptor Beta Sigma
Yukon, Oklahoma

LAYERED COOKIE DESSERT

1 (19-ounce) package chocolate sandwich cookies	2 (4-ounce) packages vanilla instant pudding mix
1/2 cup (1 stick) butter, softened	1 cup milk
8 ounces cream cheese, softened	8 ounces whipped topping

Crumble all but 12 of the cookies. Mix together the crumbled cookies and butter. Pat the cookie mixture into a greased 9×13-inch baking dish. Combine the cream cheese, dry pudding mix and milk in a mixing bowl; beat at medium speed for 2 minutes or until thickened. Spread evenly over the cookie layer. Spread whipped topping over the pudding layer. Crumble the remaining cookies and sprinkle over the whipped topping layer. Chill, covered, for at least 6 hours. Yield: 10 to 15 servings.

Jeanie Hammel, Preceptor Gamma
New Albany, Indiana

SNICKERS DESSERT

2 cups graham cracker crumbs	2 (4-ounce) packages vanilla instant pudding mix
3 tablespoons sugar	
1/2 cup (1 stick) margarine, softened	4 (8-ounce) containers whipped topping
1 (10-ounce) jar hot fudge sauce, heated	6 (2-ounce) Snickers Bars, chopped
1/2 cup milk	

Press a mixture of the graham cracker crumbs, sugar and margarine in a 9×13-inch baking dish. Pour the hot fudge evenly over the crumb layer; let cool. Combine the milk, dry pudding mix, whipped topping and chopped candy bars. Spread evenly over the fudge layer. Yield: 3 to 4 dozen servings.

Bronna Lyon, Laureate Delta Beta
Newtown, Missouri

RASPBERRY WINE DESSERT

I grew up in a family of big, hungry boys, and Mom prepared lots of stews, beans, and goulash. This was a very special dessert to go with the plain food.

1 (4-ounce) package vanilla cook-and-serve pudding mix	3/4 cup water
	1 (10-ounce) package frozen raspberries or strawberries
1/2 cup wine (burgundy, claret, or cabernet)	

Combine the dry pudding mix, wine, water and raspberries in a saucepan over medium heat. Bring to a boil, stirring constantly. Remove from heat and let stand for about 20 minutes. Pour into dessert glasses and top with whipped cream or whipped topping. Chill, covered, for 3 to 10 hours. Yield: 4 to 6 servings.

Sharon Hedden, Xi Beta
Harrah, Washington

PISTACHIO COCONUT DESSERT

1 cup flour	12 ounces whipped topping
1/2 cup (1 stick) butter, softened	
1/2 cup chopped walnuts or pistachios	1 (4-ounce) package pistachio instant pudding mix
8 ounces cream cheese, softened	1 (4-ounce) package coconut cream instant pudding mix
1 cup confectioners' sugar	3 cups milk

Combine the flour, butter and walnuts in a bowl and mix well. Press the mixture into a 9×13-inch baking dish. Bake at 350 degrees for 10 to 15 minutes or until beginning to brown. Cool completely. Cream the cream cheese and confectioners' sugar in a mixing bowl until light and fluffy. Fold in 1 cup of the whipped topping and spread over the cooled walnut crust. Prepare the pudding mixes, combined, with the milk using the directions on the packages. Pour evenly over the cream cheese layer. Spread with the remaining whipped topping. Chill and serve. Yield: 6 to 8 servings.

Margie A. Austin, Preceptor Xi
Devils Lake, North Dakota

MEMORIES

I will never forget my sisters from Xi Gamma Gamma in West Palm Beach, Florida. It was fall of 1984, and I went to Florida for the winter. I was a new pledge of one month, and I was told to contact a chapter there to visit with them and make up my meetings until I returned to my home chapter in Arkansas in early spring. Wow! Did I hit the jackpot—the gals quickly gathered me under their wings. They gave me my pledge training and sent me north in spring with a letter from them. Needless to say, the next winter months were like coming home to family. This chapter was the perfect example of what Beta Sigma Phi is all about: life, learning and friendship. P.S. We still stay in touch, too.

Sharon Jan Nolte Marler, Laureate Omicron
Crestview, Florida

CREAMY PISTACHIO DESSERT

This dessert travels well—make in advance for a potluck or other occasion.

1 cup flour	2 (4-ounce) packages
1/2 cup (1 stick) butter	pistachio instant
8 ounces cream cheese,	pudding mix
softened	3 cups milk
1 cup confectioners'	1 teaspoon vanilla
sugar	extract
2 to 3 cups whipped	
topping	

Place the flour in a bowl. Cut in the butter until mixture resembles coarse crumbs. Press in a 9×13-inch baking dish. Bake at 325 degrees for 10 minutes. Let stand until cool. Combine the cream cheese, confectioners' sugar and 1 cup of the whipped topping in a bowl and beat until light and fluffy; spread evenly over the cooled crust. Combine the dry pudding mix, milk and vanilla in a bowl and blend. Spread pudding mixture evenly over the cream cheese layer. Spread the remaining whipped topping over the pudding layer. Chill, covered, until firm.
Yield: 8 servings.

Lois Bennett (40 years), Laureate Omicron
Helena, Montana

PEANUTTY CHOCOLATE AND VANILLA WHIP

1 1/2 cups crushed	16 ounces whipped
peanuts	topping
3/4 cup (1 1/2 sticks)	1 (4-ounce) package
margarine	vanilla instant
1 1/2 cups flour	pudding mix
8 ounces cream cheese,	2 1/2 cups milk
softened	1 (4-ounce) package
1 cup confectioners'	chocolate instant
sugar	pudding mix

Combine 1 cup of the crushed peanuts, margarine and flour in a bowl and mix well. Press into a 9×13-inch baking dish; bake at 350 degrees for 10 minutes or until golden brown. Let cool. Combine 1/4 cup of the crushed peanuts, cream cheese and confectioners' sugar in a bowl and beat until well mixed. Stir in half the whipped topping and spread over the cooled peanut crust. Combine the vanilla pudding mix with 1 1/4 cups of the milk in a mixing bowl and beat until smooth. Spread evenly over the cream cheese layer. Combine the chocolate pudding mix with the remaining 1 1/4 cups milk and beat until smooth. Spread gently over the vanilla pudding layer. Top with the remaining whipped topping, additional crushed peanuts and shaved chocolate.
Yield: 24 servings.

Helen Walter, Preceptor Alpha Upsilon
Tamaqua, Pennsylvania

CHOCOLATE GRAHAM PUDDING

1 (16-ounce) package	3 cups milk
graham crackers	12 ounces whipped
2 (4-ounce) packages	topping
French vanilla	1 (16-ounce) can dark
instant pudding mix	chocolate frosting

Layer whole graham crackers in a buttered 9×13-inch baking dish. Combine the pudding mix and milk in a bowl and beat until smooth. Fold in the whipped topping. Layer half the pudding mixture, another layer of graham crackers, the remaining pudding mixture and a third layer of graham crackers over the first graham cracker layer. Chill, covered, for 3 hours or until set. Frost with the chocolate frosting and return to the refrigerator. Yield: 2 dozen servings.

Marlene Markey (36 years), Preceptor Epsilon Theta
St. Petersburg, Florida

GRAHAM CRACKER MARSHMALLOW PUDDING

My granny made it for us when we were children, and my mom made it after that. I made it for my children for all holidays, and now they make it for their children. It's wonderful.

³/₄ cup milk	Butter
2¹/₂ dozen marshmallows	Fine graham cracker
1 cup heavy cream	crumbs
1 teaspoon vanilla extract	

Scald the milk in the top of a double boiler over boiling water. Add the marshmallows and dissolve slowly, using a wooden spoon to turn and stir. Remove from heat and beat with an electric mixer until smooth. Fold in the cream and cool slightly. Stir in the vanilla. Cover the bottom of a generously greased 8-inch-square baking dish with graham cracker crumbs. Pour the marshmallow mixture gently over the graham cracker layer. Sprinkle with additional graham cracker crumbs. Chill, covered, for 8 to 10 hours. Yield: 6 to 8 servings.

Carol Workman, Beta Sigma Phi
Palm Bay, Florida

POOR MAN'S PUDDING

Years ago when I was a young girl in a family of nine children growing up in the province of Quebec, there were always beggars who would come at noon and ask for a hot meal. No one went away hungry. The dessert often served was called Pouding au Chômeur.

2 cups packed brown sugar	1 teaspoon vanilla extract
2 cups water	¹/₂ teaspoon salt
2 tablespoons butter	1¹/₂ cups flour
2 tablespoons shortening	2 teaspoons baking powder
¹/₂ cup granulated sugar	1 cup milk
1 egg	

Combine the brown sugar, water and butter in a saucepan over medium-high heat and bring to a boil. Boil for 3 minutes and remove from heat. Cream the shortening and sugar in a mixing bowl until light and fluffy. Beat in the egg. Beat in the vanilla and salt. Mix together the flour and baking powder on waxed paper. Add to the creamed mixture ¹/₃ at a time alternately with the milk, mixing well after each addition, beginning and ending with flour mixture. Pour into a greased 9-inch-square baking dish. Pour the brown sugar mixture evenly over the top; while baking, sauce will sink to the bottom. Bake at 350 degrees for 45 minutes or until a wooden pick inserted in the center comes out clean. Serve warm. Yield: 6 servings.

Colette M. Carrothers (50 years), Laureate Alpha Rho
Oakville, Ontario, Canada

HOT FUDGE PUDDING

1 cup sifted flour	2 tablespoons melted butter
2 teaspoons baking powder	1 cup chopped walnuts or pecans
¹/₂ teaspoon salt	1 cup packed brown sugar
³/₄ cup granulated sugar	
1¹/₂ tablespoons baking cocoa	¹/₄ cup baking cocoa
¹/₂ cup milk	1³/₄ cups water

Sift the flour, baking powder, salt, granulated sugar and the 1¹/₂ tablespoons baking cocoa into a bowl. Stir in the milk and butter and mix well. Stir in the chopped nuts. Pour into a greased 8-inch-square baking dish and sprinkle with a mixture of the brown sugar and the ¹/₄ cup baking cocoa. Pour the water evenly over the surface. Bake at 350 degrees for 45 minutes. Yield: 8 servings.

Donna Lichty, Xi Beta Zeta
Johnson City, Tennessee

BUTTER PECAN CHEESECAKE

1¹/₂ cups graham cracker crumbs	1¹/₂ cups sugar
	3 eggs
¹/₃ cup sugar	16 ounces sour cream
¹/₃ cup butter or margarine	1 teaspoon vanilla extract
¹/₂ cup chopped pecans	¹/₂ teaspoon butter flavoring
24 ounces cream cheese, softened	1 cup chopped pecans

Combine the graham cracker crumbs, ¹/₃ cup sugar, butter and ¹/₂ cup pecans in a bowl and mix well. Remove ¹/₃ cup of the mixture and set aside. Firmly press the remaining mixture in a greased 9-inch springform pan. Beat the cream cheese in a mixing bowl until light and fluffy. Add the 1¹/₂ cups sugar gradually, mixing well. Add the eggs 1 at a time, beating well after each addition. Mix in the sour cream, vanilla and butter flavoring. Stir in the 1 cup pecans. Spoon into the prepared springform pan and sprinkle with the reserved graham cracker crumb mixture. Bake at 475 degrees for 10 minutes. Reduce oven temperature to 300 degrees and bake for 50 minutes longer. Remove to a wire rack to cool. Chill, covered, until ready to serve. Yield: 12 servings.

Rose Ann Abernathy, Preceptor Delta
Centralia, Illinois

CHOCOLATE VELVET CREAM CHEESECAKE

My son loves this recipe. When he was two years old, he pulled the springform pan from the cabinet where it was stored and said, "Mommy, make the cake that goes in this pan." Thirty-four years later, it is still the cake I make every year for his birthday.

1 (11-ounce) package chocolate wafers, finely crushed	8 ounces cream cheese, softened
7 tablespoons melted margarine or butter	1 cup sugar
2 cups semisweet chocolate chips	2 teaspoons vanilla extract
4 eggs, separated	2 cups whipping cream, whipped
	3/4 cup chopped pecans

Combine the crushed wafers and margarine and mix well. Press into the bottom of a 9-inch springform pan. Bake at 325 degrees for 10 minutes. Melt the chocolate chips in the top of a double boiler over boiling water. Beat the egg yolks in a small bowl. Combine the cream cheese, 1/2 cup of the sugar and vanilla in a mixing bowl and beat until smooth and fluffy. Stir in the melted chocolate and the beaten egg yolks. Beat the egg whites in a small mixing bowl until soft peaks form. Add the remaining 1/2 cup sugar gradually, beating until stiff peaks form. Fold the egg white mixture into the chocolate mixture. Fold in the whipped cream and pecans. Pour evenly over the cooled chocolate wafer crust and freeze. Defrost in the refrigerator 45 minutes before serving. Decorate with whipped cream and serve. Yield: 12 servings.

Geri Hetterich (28 years), Preceptor Lambda Kappa
Dallas, Texas

EASY CHERRY CHEESECAKE

8 ounces cream cheese, softened	1 baked (9-inch) graham cracker shell
1/8 teaspoon salt	1 cup sour cream
2 eggs	2 tablespoons sugar
1 tablespoon lemon juice	1 tablespoon vanilla extract
1/2 cup sugar	1 (21-ounce) can cherry pie filling
1/2 teaspoon vanilla extract	

Combine the cream cheese, salt, eggs, lemon juice, the 1/2 cup sugar and the 1/2 teaspoon vanilla in a blender container; process until smooth. Pour into the cooled graham cracker crust. Bake at 325 degrees for 25 minutes. Combine the sour cream, the 2 tablespoons sugar and the 1 tablespoon vanilla in a bowl and mix well. Spread the sour cream mixture over the cream cheese mixture. Return to oven and bake for 5 minutes longer. Let stand until cool. Chill, covered, until ready to serve. Spoon cherry pie filling over individual pieces. Yield: 6 to 8 servings.

Rita K. Breid, Alpha Phi
Paris, Missouri

JUNIOR'S CHEESECAKE

When my mother took me shopping to May's and A&S in Brooklyn, the trip always included a stop at Junior's for lunch. My husband went to college in Brooklyn, and Junior's was a popular place for lunch for him too!

1/4 cup graham cracker crumbs	30 ounces cream cheese, softened
3/4 cup plus 2 tablespoons sugar	1 large egg
3 tablespoons sifted cornstarch	1/2 cup heavy cream
	3/4 teaspoon vanilla extract

Generously butter the bottom and side of an 8-inch springform pan. Sprinkle the graham cracker crumbs evenly in the bottom of the pan and refrigerate. Combine the sugar and cornstarch in a large mixing bowl. Beat in the cream cheese. Beat in the egg. Drizzle in the cream gradually, beating constantly. Add the vanilla and stir well. Pour into the prepared springform pan. Bake at 350 degrees for 40 to 45 minutes or until top is golden. Cool in the pan on a wire rack for 3 hours. Yield: 8 to 10 servings.

Mary A. Storey, Laureate Theta Nu
San Antonio, Texas

OREO CHEESECAKE

1 cup crushed Oreo cookies	1 cup sugar
1 tablespoon butter, melted	1 teaspoon vanilla extract
32 ounces cream cheese, softened	4 eggs
	20 Oreo cookies, quartered

Press a mixture of the crushed cookies and butter into a 9-inch springform pan. Bake at 325 degrees for 10 minutes. Beat the cream cheese, sugar and vanilla in a mixing bowl at medium speed until smooth. Beat in the eggs at low speed until blended. Gently stir in the quartered cookies. Pour the cookie mixture evenly over the cooled cookie crust. Bake at 325 degrees for 1 hour or until center is almost set. Loosen the cake from the side of the pan. Let cool before removing rim. Chill, covered, for 4 to 10 hours. Yield: 12 servings.

Kathy Foster, Xi Delta Upsilon
Great Bend, Kansas

MOM'S CHRISTMAS MINCEMEAT CHEESECAKE

1 1/2 cups vanilla wafer crumbs	24 ounces cream cheese, softened
3/8 cup melted margarine	2 teaspoons grated orange zest
1 3/4 cups mincemeat	1 cup whipping cream, whipped
4 cups miniature marshmallows	
1/3 cup orange juice	

Press a mixture of the wafer crumbs and margarine into a 9-inch springform pan. Bake at 350 degrees for 8 minutes. Chill. Spread the mincemeat over the chilled crust. Melt the marshmallows with the orange juice in the top of a double boiler over boiling water, stirring until smooth. Chill, covered, until thickened. Combine the cream cheese and orange zest in a mixing bowl and beat to blend. Beat in the marshmallow mixture. Fold in the whipped cream. Pour evenly over the mincemeat layer. Chill, covered, until firm. Yield: 10 to 12 servings.

*Anna Cameron (35 years), Alpha Master
Riverview, New Brunswick, Canada*

MOM'S LEMON CHEESECAKE

My grandmother "Mom" had this cheesecake in the refrigerator "ready and waiting" for me every time I went to visit her. She knew it was my favorite.

2 1/4 cups graham cracker crumbs	6 ounces cream cheese, softened
1/2 cup melted butter	1 cup sugar
2 tablespoons sugar	2 tablespoons lemon juice
1 (3-ounce) package lemon gelatin	1 cup finely chopped pecans (optional)
1 cup hot water	
1 (12-ounce) can evaporated milk, chilled	

Press a mixture of the graham cracker crumbs, butter and the 2 tablespoons sugar into a 9×13-inch baking dish, reserving 1/4 cup of the crumb mixture for the topping. Mix the gelatin mix and hot water and chill. Whip the evaporated milk in a mixing bowl until stiff peaks form. Cream the cream cheese with the 1 cup sugar and lemon juice in a mixing bowl until light and fluffy. Add the gelatin mixture gradually, beating until smooth. Fold in the whipped evaporated milk. Stir in the pecans. Pour slowly over the graham cracker layer. Sprinkle with the remaining crumb mixture. Chill, covered, for 8 to 10 hours. Yield: 16 servings.

*Debbie Harris, Alpha Zeta Theta
Richmond, Texas*

LEMON BISQUE

This dessert was a favorite in our house, and my brother always wanted it instead of a birthday cake. Mom passed away several years ago, but last summer I traveled home and surprised my brother with this dessert for his birthday. We cried awhile, then we ate it while talking of wonderful memories of our childhood and our departed mom.

1 (12-ounce) can evaporated milk	1/8 teaspoon salt
1 (3-ounce) package lemon gelatin	3 tablespoons lemon juice
1 1/2 cups boiling water	Grated zest of 1 lemon
1/3 cup honey	2 1/2 cups crushed vanilla wafers

Chill the can of evaporated milk for 8 to 10 hours. Dissolve the dry gelatin mix in the boiling water. Stir in the honey, salt, lemon juice and lemon zest. Let stand until slightly thickened. Beat the chilled evaporated milk in a mixing bowl until stiff peaks form. Beat in the partially thickened gelatin mixture. Spread half the wafer crumbs in a 9×13-inch baking dish. Pour the lemon mixture gently and evenly over the crumbs. Top with the remaining crumbs. Chill, covered, for about 3 hours. Serve plain or with whipped cream. Yield: 12 servings.

*Mary Lou Settle, Delta Theta
Hendersonville, Tennessee*

MEMORIES

We were a large family of eight and lived in a very small town in western Kansas. Our favorite dessert, no matter what the season, was homemade ice cream. Our neighbor had dug an icehouse so that we could always have ice. My mother would make the ice cream mix and my father would prepare the hand-crank 1 1/2-gallon freezer with icehouse ice and rock salt. We would take turns turning the handle and when it got really hard to turn, we knew that it was time to get our bowls and enjoy our delicious treat.

*Lucile Curtner, Laureate Theta Zeta
West Covina, California*

HOMEMADE ICE CREAM

I grew up on a dairy farm in southeast Kansas. We had an abundant supply of milk and cream, and always had rich homemade ice cream.

3 cups sugar
3 tablespoons flour
2 (15-ounce) cans lowfat
  evaporated milk
1 quart half-and-half
1 tablespoon vanilla
  extract
Milk

Mix together the sugar and flour in a large bowl. Add the evaporated milk, half-and-half and vanilla and mix well (I use a blender). Pour into an ice cream freezer container; add milk to the fill line. Freeze using manufacturer's directions. Yield: 1 gallon.

Pauline Huneycutt, Delta Theta
Neodesha, Kansas

CRUNCHY ICE CREAM

1/2 cup (1 stick)
  margarine, melted
3 cups crisp rice cereal
2 cups flaked coconut
1 1/2 cups chopped pecans
3/4 cup packed brown
  sugar
1/2 gallon New York
  Vanilla ice cream
1 (7-ounce) bottle Magic
  Shell chocolate
  topping

Combine the margarine, cereal, coconut and pecans in a large bowl and mix well. Spread in a 9×13-inch baking dish sprayed with nonstick cooking spray. Bake at 300 degrees for 30 minutes or until golden brown, stirring frequently. Return the cereal mixture to the bowl and mix in the brown sugar. Spread half the rice mixture evenly in the 9×13-inch baking dish. Slice the ice cream into 1/2-inch-thick slabs and fit in a single layer over the cereal layer. Spread the remaining cereal mixture over the ice cream. Press layers gently. Cover and freeze. Cut to serve; drizzle each serving with the topping. Yield: 8 to 10 servings.

Sally Toepfer, Preceptor Delta Mu
Apple River, Illinois

Rosella B. Jardine (40 years), Iota Master, San Juan Pueblo, New Mexico, grew up in the midst of fruit orchards. She says that the only fruit not edible right off the tree is the quince, so she shares **Baked Quince,** one of her mother's wonderful recipes. Peel, core and slice 6 small quince. Combine with 1/4 cup sugar, a pinch of salt and 1 1/3 cups hot water in a baking dish. Bake, tightly covered, at 325 degrees for 2 hours or until tender and deep red in color. Sprinkle with 1/4 cup sugar and bake, uncovered, until syrup is slightly thickened. Delicious hot or cold.

BANANA CHERRY NUT ICE CREAM

In the summers, which were long and hot in Oklahoma, we made ice cream at my grandmother's house on Sunday afternoons. For us children, cranking the crank and sitting on it to hold it down was considered Sunday afternoon fun.

4 ripe bananas, mashed
1/4 cup chopped
  maraschino cherries
1 (12-ounce) can
  evaporated milk
2 cups heavy cream
4 eggs, slightly beaten
1 1/2 cups sugar
1/2 cup chopped pecans
1/4 teaspoon salt
Milk

Combine the bananas, cherries, evaporated milk, cream, eggs, sugar, pecans and salt in a large bowl and mix well. Pour into a 1- to 1 1/2-gallon ice cream freezer container; add milk to the fill line. Freeze using manufacturer's directions.
Yield: 10 to 12 servings.

Charlotte Mathews, Xi Alpha Mu
Midland, Texas

LEMON ICE CREAM

My mother-in-law made this ice cream with raw eggs all her life. When we had to stop using raw eggs, her daughters created this recipe using sweetened condensed milk.

1 quart half-and-half
2 cups sugar
1 (14-ounce) can
  sweetened condensed
  milk
2 tablespoons lemon
  extract
1 teaspoon vanilla
  extract

Mix together the half-and-half, sugar, condensed milk, lemon extract and vanilla and pour into an ice cream freezer container. Freeze using manufacturer's directions. Yield: 1 1/2 quarts.

Karen Johnson (28 years), Zi Gamma Omicron
Clarksville, Arkansas

MAPLE FRANGO ICE CREAM

2 cups whipping cream
3 egg whites
3/4 cup confectioners'
  sugar
Pinch of salt
1 teaspoon maple
  flavoring
1/2 cup chopped pecans

Beat the whipping cream with chilled beaters in a chilled mixing bowl until stiff peaks form. Beat the egg whites in another mixing bowl until stiff peaks form. Fold the egg whites into the whipped cream. Stir in the confectioners' sugar, salt, maple flavoring and pecans. Pour into undivided ice cube trays.

Freeze until stiff peaks form. Remove from ice cube trays and slice. Garnish each slice with a dollop of whipped cream and a whole pecan. Yield: 6 to 8 servings.

Betsy Hall, Alpha Alpha
Ruidoso, New Mexico

"SIX THREES" ICE CREAM

My husband adapted this recipe from one given to him by an old army friend. It was a welcome change from our usual but wonderful homemade vanilla ice cream. He even won a hometown newspaper contest with the recipe.

Juice of 3 lemons	3 cups milk
Juice of 3 oranges	3 cups heavy cream
3 bananas, mashed	3 cups sugar

Place the lemon juice, orange juice and bananas in the freezer while beginning to make the ice cream. Combine the milk, cream and sugar in a large bowl; stir until sugar is dissolved. Pour into an ice cream freezer container. Freeze using manufacturer's directions until completely chilled and of mushy consistency. Add the fruit juices and bananas and continue freezing until ice cream is firm. Remove the dasher and pack in salt and ice for several hours or until you can wait no longer. Yield: 1 gallon.

Carol Bennett, Alpha Rho Zeta
Cross Plains, Texas

GRAPE JUICE SHERBET

1¼ teaspoons unflavored gelatin	1½ cups boiling water
½ cup cold water	2 cups grape juice
1 cup sugar	¼ cup lemon juice
	⅓ cup orange juice

Soften the gelatin in the cold water for 5 minutes. Combine the sugar and boiling water in a saucepan over medium-high heat; boil gently for 10 minutes. Stir in the gelatin mixture and pour into a large bowl. Let stand for 15 minutes. Add the grape juice, lemon juice and orange juice; mix well. Pour into a 1½-quart glass dish. Freeze. Yield: 12 to 15 servings.

Maxine Houser (28 years), Preceptor Eta Omicron
West Sacramento, California

SUMMERTIME FRUIT SHERBET

1 gallon pineapple sherbet, softened	2 (10-ounce) packages frozen raspberries, thawed
5 bananas, sliced	

Mix together the sherbet, bananas and raspberries. Freeze for 8 to 10 hours. Yield: 1½ gallons.

Lori Gilgen, Xi Theta
West Jordan, Utah

CHOCOLATE SAUCE FOR ICE CREAM

I remember the cast-iron saucepan my grandmother used to make this ice cream topping. Many family members have prepared the sauce, but it never seemed to be as good as Grandma's. Maybe it was the cast-iron saucepan.

3 tablespoons baking cocoa	⅓ cup light corn syrup
1½ cups sugar	⅔ cup evaporated milk
Dash of salt	2 teaspoons vanilla extract

Combine the cocoa, sugar and salt in a saucepan. Stir in the corn syrup and a few tablespoons of the evaporated milk to make a paste. Bring to a boil over medium-high heat, stirring constantly. Boil without stirring for 5 minutes. Remove from heat. Stir in the vanilla and the remaining evaporated milk. Cool. Chill, covered, until ready to use. Yield: 1 cup.

Beverly R. Taylor, Xi Eta
Newcastle, Wyoming

MEMORIES

What I remember and love most about my past is that it has been full of laughter and love. Our Christmas tradition is different from most. Four of us kids had four kids each, which would make for lots of gifts at Christmas. Instead, each household goes to the dollar store and spends twenty dollars on items. The items range from nice to hilarious. We put all of the items in garbage bags, and then the family gathers in a circle sitting on the ground. We pass it around, and each time you get the bag you reach in and pull out an item. Then we barter with each other until no one wants to wheel and deal anymore. We laugh, giggle and enjoy each other. This has been a family tradition since I was young, and our kids now enjoy it.

Saundra Johnson, Delta Iota
Meridian, Idaho

Metric Equivalents

A lthough the United States has opted to postpone converting to metric measurements, most other countries, including England and Canada, use the metric system. The following chart provides convenient approximate equivalents for allowing use of regular kitchen measures when cooking from foreign recipes.

Volume

These metric measures are approximate benchmarks for purposes of home food preparation.
1 milliliter = 1 cubic centimeter = 1 gram

Liquid	Dry
1 teaspoon = 5 milliliters	1 quart = 1 liter
1 tablespoon = 15 milliliters	1 ounce = 30 grams
1 fluid ounce = 30 milliliters	1 pound = 450 grams
1 cup = 250 milliliters	2.2 pounds = 1 kilogram
1 pint = 500 milliliters	

Weight	Length
1 ounce = 28 grams	1 inch = $2\frac{1}{2}$ centimeters
1 pound = 450 grams	$\frac{1}{16}$ inch = 1 millimeter

Formulas Using Conversion Factors

When approximate conversions are not accurate enough, use these formulas to convert measures from one system to another.

Measurements	Formulas
ounces to grams:	# ounces x 28.3 = # grams
grams to ounces:	# grams x 0.035 = # ounces
pounds to grams:	# pounds x 453.6 = # grams
pounds to kilograms	# pounds x 0.45 = # kilograms
ounces to milliliters:	# ounces x 30 = # milliliters
cups to liters:	# cups x 0.24 = # liters
inches to centimeters	# inches x 2.54 = # centimeters
centimeters to inches:	# centimeters x 0.39 = # inches

Approximate Weight to Volume

Some ingredients which we commonly measure by volume are measured by weight in foreign recipes. Here are a few examples for easy reference.

flour, all-purpose, unsifted	1 pound = 450 grams = 3 1/2 cups
flour, all-purpose, sifted	1 pound = 450 grams = 4 cups
sugar, granulated	1 pound = 450 grams = 2 cups
sugar, brown, packed	1 pound = 450 grams = 2 1/4 cups
sugar, confectioners'	1 pound = 450 grams = 4 cups
sugar, confectioners', sifted	1 pound = 450 grams = 4 1/2 cups
butter	1 pound = 450 grams = 2 cups

Temperature

Remember that foreign recipes frequently express temperatures in Centigrade rather than Fahrenheit.

Temperatures	Fahrenheit	Centigrade
room temperature	68°	20°
water boils	212°	100°
baking temperature	350°	177°
baking temperature	375°	190.5°
baking temperature	400°	204.4°
baking temperature	425°	218.3°
baking temperature	450°	232°

Use the following formulas when temperature conversions are necessary.

Centigrade degrees x 9/5 + 32 = Fahrenheit degrees
Fahrenheit degrees - 32 x 5/9 = Centigrade degrees

American Measurement Equivalents

1 tablespoon = 3 teaspoons	12 tablespoons = 3/4 cup
2 tablespoons = 1 ounce	16 tablespoons = 1 cup
4 tablespoons = 1/4 cup	1 cup = 8 ounces
5 tablespoons + 1 teaspoon = 1/3 cup	2 cups = 1 pint
8 tablespoons = 1/2 cup	4 cups = 1 quart
	4 quarts = 1 gallon

Merit Winners

MEMORIES
First Place
Golden, Naomi, page 19
Second Place
Alexander, Cheryl, page 37
Third Place
Buchanan, Marion, page 67
Heyden, Josephine, page 107
Moline, Sandee, page 91
Shell, Loise Evelyn, page 7
Weaver, Walda, page 129
Wicks, Frances, page 163
Wissler, Cheryl, page 189
Honorable Mention
Accordino, Barbara, page 183
Bravo, Mary, page 52
Connor, Sharron, page 100
Jeffords, Cynthia, page 135
Jensen, Dulci, page 109
LaCouvee, Noella, Page 18
Miles, Ann E., page 76
Persinger, Julie, page 116
Schwartz, Marilyn J., page 165
Welsh, Cecilia, page 197
Willcox, Anne, page 168

SNACKS AND BEVERAGES
First Place
Hill, Julie, page 14
Second Place
Camp, Margaret (Peggy) N.,
    page 14
Third Place
Walker, Janet, page 11
Honorable Mention
Bieber, Marilyn, page 18
Bradshaw, Rita K., page 15
Christiansen, Carrie, page 17
Doubravsky, Betty, page 17
Hild, Gretchen, page 11
Lukes, Lana, page 13
Mazurkiewicz, Riki, page 17
Rand, Kathy, page 14
Rector, Mary, page 9
Reed, Diana Attaway, page 15

Shugart, Amy, page 10
Watson, Becky, page 16

SOUPS AND SALADS
First Place
Ayres, Sandy, page 28
Second Place
Schwab, Breean, page 32
Third Place
Jemison, Anita, page 22
Honorable Mention
Allison, Shelly, page 26
Anderson, Sharon E., page 27
Buller, Becky A., page 20
Coates, Barbara T., page 22
Durrant, Nancy F., page 25
Friel, Dee, page 32
Gale, Dianne L., page 33
Goss, Frances, page 31
Lancaster, Diana, page 34
Sharp, Mildred, page 31
Theobald, Angela, page 34
Uhlir, Cindy, page 35
Watalla, Jo-Anne, page 24
Willems, Betty, page 23
Zeiss, Carol, page 32

MEAT AND MEATLESS DISHES
First Place
Stahl, Jonnie L., page 47
Second Place
Rice, Jane, page 42
Third Place
Colvin, Lynne, page 56
Honorable Mention
Arntz, Doris E., page 50
Barcelona, Miranda,
    page 38
Coe, Rita M., page 47
Davis, Joycee, page 66
Dittfurth, Lillie, page 60
Gaspari, Rose, page 65
Herbert, Jeri Lou, page 42
Jenkins, Sue, page 65

Kiger, Cheryl, page 59
Long, Louise, page 46
Luus, Donna, page 57
McCoy, Merline, page 66
Northern, Cheryl, page 63
Oleson, Shari, page 63
Preston, Kathie, page 62
Puntureri, Mary, page 49
Roberts, Judith, page 40
Schlotfeldt, Gayle, page 65
Shanafelt, Margie F., page 54
Stone, Louise H., page 58

POULTRY AND SEAFOOD DISHES
First Place
Cramer, Mary Ellen, page 86
Second Place
Higbee, Marilyn K., page 68
Third Place
Martin, Jacque L., page 68
Honorable Mention
Ackerman, Denise, page 73
Bogar, Fran, page 68
Brendon, Florence, page 83
Cannon, Sarah, page 75
Casson, Karen, page 78
Coffman, Bettie, page 74
Collins, Cora, page 79
Erickson, Shirley M.,
    page 79
Fassio, Barbara, page 74
Fobert, Beverley, page 79
Gatsos, Julia, page 85
Gorham, Denise, page 89
Hoffman, Leah, page 80
Jones, Maxine, page 88
Myers, Donna J., page 82
Owen, Norma, page 76
Rhodes, Suzanne, page 76
Shoults, Syble A., page 81
Sutherland, Anita, page 81
Tinsley, Mary, page 90
Van Stelten, Jean, page 87
Walker, Tami, page 73

Memory Contributors

Index

To order additional copies of

Memories of Home

call 1-800-251-1520

ACINI DI PEPE FRUIT SALAD

8 ounces acini di pepe
1 (15-ounce) can crushed
   pineapple
1 egg
1/2 cup sugar
1 tablespoon flour
1/4 teaspoon salt

1 (16-ounce) can fruit
   cocktail, drained
1 cup miniature
   marshmallows
1 cup whipping cream,
   whipped

Prepare the acini di pepe using the package directions. Drain the pineapple, reserving the juice. Place the egg in a heavy saucepan and beat with a wire whisk until foamy. Stir in the sugar, flour, salt and reserved pineapple juice. Cook over low heat until thickened and bubbly, stirring constantly. Combine the acini di pepe and egg mixture in a large bowl and mix well. Chill, covered, for about 1 hour. Stir in the pineapple, fruit cocktail and marshmallows. Fold in the whipped cream. Chill, covered, for about 1 hour or until completely chilled. Stir before serving. Yield: 8 servings.

Betty Schleicher, Xi Eta Epsilon
Sweet Springs, Missouri

SALMON PASTA SALAD

My sister and I are very close—although we live 900 miles apart! Whenever we are together we enjoy this dish, served with steamed broccoli.

8 ounces small to
   medium pasta shells
1 (15-ounce) can salmon,
   drained
1 green bell pepper,
   chopped
3/4 cup thinly sliced
   celery

1/2 cup chopped red
   onion
3/4 cup mayonnaise
1 tablespoon white wine
   vinegar
2 tablespoons chopped
   fresh dill, or
11/2 teaspoons dried

Cook pasta in boiling water for 10 minutes; drain. Rinse with cold water; drain again. Discard skin and bones of the salmon. Combine the pasta, salmon, green pepper, celery and red onion in a large bowl; mix well. Place the mayonnaise, vinegar and dill in a small bowl; whisk to combine. Add the mayonnaise mixture to the pasta mixture; mix well. Salt to taste. Chill, covered, for 24 hours before serving. Yield: 6 servings.

Dianne L. Gale, Laureate Kappa
West Palm Beach, Florida

MEMORIES

*W*hen I was growing up, I remember my family going to Grandma and Grandpa's house for Sunday dinners. Grandma would always fix an enormous meal of fried chicken, homemade noodles, green beans and rolls. One of my favorite dishes was her potato salad. No one else could make it as creamy as Grandma. Of course, she didn't use a recipe—just her great culinary skills! Both my grandparents are now gone, but I will always cherish the memories of those Sunday family dinners.

Kelle Pope, Theta Chi
Columbus, Indiana

GRILLED CHICKEN PASTA SALAD

2/3 cup olive oil
1/3 cup vinegar
1/2 cup torn basil leaves
4 boneless skinless
   chicken breasts
4 cups cooked bow-tie
   pasta

11/2 cups home-style
   seasoned croutons
1/2 cup drained
   marinated sun-dried
   tomatoes
1/2 cup coarsely chopped
   walnuts

Place the olive oil, vinegar and basil in a jar and shake vigorously. Reserve 2/3 cup of the basil mixture and use the remaining mixture to baste the chicken. Grill or broil the chicken for 15 minutes or until cooked through, brushing often with the basil mixture. Let chicken cool; slice into thin strips. Place the chicken, pasta, croutons, sun-dried tomatoes, walnuts and reserved 2/3 cup basil mixture in a bowl and toss to combine. Sprinkle with grated Parmesan cheese and serve immediately. Yield: 6 servings.

Cynthia Blaya, Laureate Beta
Henderson, Nevada

Mary Louise Reardon (58 years), Omicron Master, Maryville, Missouri, makes a delicious **Pineapple Buttermilk Salad** to serve as a sugar-free salad or dessert. She brings a 20-ounce can of unsweetened crushed pineapple to a boil in a heavy saucepan and stirs in a large package of any flavor of sugar-free gelatin until dissolved. Pour into a 9×13-inch dish, chill until slightly thickened and stir in 2 cups buttermilk. Chill until partially set and fold in 8 ounces light whipped topping. Chill until set.

CONFETTI POTATO SALAD

Serve with grilled hamburgers or barbecued ribs.

2¹/₂ pounds potatoes
1 cup chopped red bell
  pepper
1 cup sliced black olives
1 cup frozen green peas,
  thawed
¹/₄ cup chopped red
  onion
¹/₂ cup mayonnaise-type
  salad dressing
1 tablespoon prepared
  mustard
¹/₄ cup vinegar
¹/₂ teaspoon celery seed
¹/₂ teaspoon salt
1 teaspoon black pepper

Cook the unpeeled potatoes in boiling water for 20 minutes or until tender. Cool, peel and cut into bite-size pieces. Place the potatoes, red pepper, olives, green peas and red onion in a large bowl; toss to combine. Combine the mayonnaise-type salad dressing, mustard, vinegar, celery seed, salt and pepper in a small bowl and whisk until smooth. Add the dressing to the potato mixture and toss to combine. Chill, covered, for 2 hours before serving.
Yield: 8 servings.

Sharon Guiles, Preceptor Gamma Lambda
Burton, Michigan

ITALIAN POTATO SALAD

I got this recipe from my sister-in-law, who has been like a sister to me. It was handed down from her Italian grandmother. Serve with chicken, steak, or fish.

1¹/₂ pounds potatoes,
  unpeeled
8 ounces string beans,
  trimmed, halved
1 cucumber, peeled,
  diced
1 ripe tomato, diced
¹/₄ cup chopped red
  onion
¹/₄ cup olive oil
¹/₄ cup vinegar
¹/₂ teaspoon oregano

Combine the potatoes with enough water to cover in a saucepan. Bring to a boil. Boil for 20 minutes or until tender; drain. Let cool. Peel; cut into bite-size pieces. Cook the string beans in boiling water for 8 minutes or until tender-crisp; drain and cool. Combine the potatoes, string beans, cucumber, tomato, red onion, olive oil, vinegar and oregano in a large bowl; mix well. Season with salt and pepper to taste. Yield: 4 to 6 servings.

Angela Theobald (33 years), Laureate Epsilon Omega
Bradenton, Florida

HOT GERMAN POTATO SALAD

After I was married, Grandma Simon taught me how to make this delicious picnic potato salad. She told me the secret was to put the sugar, salt, and pepper on the potatoes just after slicing them. She suggested using small potatoes and preparing the salad several hours before serving.

3 pounds potatoes
¹/₂ cup sugar
1 teaspoon salt
¹/₂ teaspoon pepper
8 slices bacon
1 onion
2 tablespoons flour
¹/₂ cup vinegar
¹/₂ cup water

Wash the potatoes and cook them in boiling water for 20 minutes or until tender. Peel and slice when cool enough to handle. Place in a casserole or serving dish. Sprinkle the sugar, salt and pepper evenly over the potato slices. Cut bacon into small pieces and fry in a skillet until crisp. Remove bacon; drain. Add the onion, flour, vinegar and water to the bacon drippings in the skillet and bring to a boil, stirring constantly. Mixture will thicken; remove the onion. Sprinkle the bacon and drizzle the flour mixture over the potato slices. Keep warm. Yield: 8 to 12 servings.

Shirley Simon, Iota Master
Quincy, Illinois

CRAIG'S CURRIED CHICKEN SALAD

My son Craig, a chef in Houston, gave me this recipe after serving it at a family luncheon. Serve with crackers, mixed vegetables, fresh fruit, or all three. The servings are large.

³/₄ cup mayonnaise
1 tablespoon lemon
  juice
¹/₄ teaspoon salt
¹/₂ teaspoon (or more)
  curry powder
¹/₂ teaspoon tarragon
2 cups chopped cooked
  chicken
1 cup chopped celery
2 cups cooked brown
  rice
1 (4-ounce) can water
  chestnuts, drained
¹/₄ cup sliced green onion
Handful of seedless
  grapes, halved
¹/₄ cup toasted slivered
  almonds

Whisk the mayonnaise, lemon juice, salt, curry powder and tarragon in a small bowl until smooth. Combine the chicken, celery, rice, water chestnuts, green onion and grapes in a large bowl. Pour the mayonnaise dressing over the chicken mixture and mix well. Top with almonds. Chill, covered, for several hours before serving. Yield: 4 to 6 servings.

Diana Lancaster (40 years), Laureate Delta Tau
Amarillo, Texas

JAPANESE CHICKEN TOSS

To save time, use two bags of prewashed lettuce and two 5-ounce cans of chunk chicken.

1½ heads lettuce	1 cup sliced almonds
1 bunch scallions, thinly sliced	¼ cup sugar
	2 teaspoons salt
3 or 4 chicken breasts, cooked, chopped	1 tablespoon MSG
	½ teaspoon pepper
1 (12-ounce) bag chow mein noodles	¼ cup vinegar
	½ cup vegetable oil
¼ cup poppy seeds	

Wash lettuce and tear into bite-size pieces. Place the lettuce, scallions, chicken, chow mein noodles, poppy seeds and almonds in a large salad bowl; toss to combine. Place the sugar, salt, MSG, pepper, vinegar and vegetable oil in a jar and shake vigorously to combine. Pour the dressing over the salad just before serving. Toss and serve. Yield: 25 servings.

Donna O'Neill, Xi Zeta Rho
LeMars, Iowa

CILANTRO CHICKEN SALAD

3 pounds whole chicken breasts	¾ cup chopped walnuts
	¼ cup chopped scallions
Salt to taste	¾ cup chopped cilantro
¼ cup vegetable oil	1½ cups mayonnaise
1 cup chopped Vidalia onion	Freshly ground pepper to taste

Combine the chicken with enough water to cover in a saucepan. Bring to a boil. Boil for about 20 minutes or until tender; drain and cool. Remove and discard skin and bones. Shred chicken meat into a large bowl. Heat the vegetable oil in a skillet over medium-low heat. Sauté the onion in the hot oil for about 20 minutes or until golden brown. Add the onion to the chicken; cool to room temperature. Stir in the walnuts, scallions, cilantro, mayonnaise and pepper. Chill, covered, until ready to serve. Spread over croissants. Yield: 8 to 12 servings.

Lisa Mena, Xi Delta
Ponca City, Oklahoma

Virginia Fast (58 years), Kappa Master, Knoxville, Iowa, says that this **French Dressing** is the only salad dressing she makes. She combines 2 cups sugar, 2 cups olive oil, ⅔ cup ketchup, 1 small onion, minced and ½ teaspoon garlic salt in a large mixing bowl and beats at high speed for 15 minutes. Add a scant ⅔ cup vinegar and 1 teaspoon celery seed and beat for 5 minutes longer. Store in the refrigerator.

MEMORIES

I am the youngest from a family of five girls. We were all members of Beta Sigma Phi in Estevan. Some thirty years ago, we had our picture taken together at a Founder's Day Banquet. Believing that this had to be a noteworthy instance, we submitted a picture to International and it was published in Torch magazine. To my knowledge, this was and has been the one and only time that our small city in Saskatchewan had a picture published in our sorority magazine.

Beverley Dinsmore, Laureate Pi
Estevan, Saskatchewan, Canada

MARINATED ARTICHOKES AND SHRIMP IN CITRUS VINAIGRETTE

My friend is an excellent cook, so when I received rave reviews from her I knew this was a winner to be served over and over again. You can substitute fat-free mayonnaise for the regular mayonnaise if you like, and a 14-ounce can of artichoke hearts for the frozen ones.

1 large seedless orange, peeled, sectioned	2 teaspoons extra-virgin olive oil
3 tablespoons red wine vinegar	1 (9-ounce) package frozen artichoke hearts, thawed, drained
3 tablespoons mayonnaise	
	1 cup orange juice
1 teaspoon minced fresh thyme, or ¼ teaspoon dried	12 large shrimp, peeled, deveined, butterflied

Combine the orange, vinegar, mayonnaise, thyme and olive oil in a food processor container and process until smooth. Pour into a medium bowl and stir in the artichokes. Chill, covered, for 3 to 10 hours, stirring occasionally. Bring the orange juice to a boil in a medium saucepan. Add the shrimp; cook for 2 minutes or until pink and opaque. Arrange 2 or 3 artichoke hearts on each of six plates. Top with 2 or 3 shrimp. Drizzle with leftover vinaigrette from the artichoke marinade. Yield: 6 servings.

Cindy Uhlir, Preceptor Phi
Madison, Wisconsin

CATFISH SALAD

1/2 cup white wine	2 green onions, chopped
Worcestershire sauce to taste	1/2 cup pickle relish
5 catfish fillets	1/2 cup mayonnaise
2 hard-cooked eggs, chopped	1/2 cup chopped celery
	Salt and pepper to taste

Combine the wine and Worcestershire sauce in a bowl and whisk until smooth. Marinate the fillets in the wine mixture for about 15 minutes, turning occasionally. Grill over hot coals for 15 minutes, turning once; or bake at 350 degrees for 15 minutes or until fish flakes easily with a fork. Combine the fillets, hard-cooked eggs, green onions, pickle relish, mayonnaise and celery in the container of a food processor and process for 30 seconds. Season with salt and pepper and add more mayonnaise if desired. Serve over a lettuce leaf with crackers, or spoon into a fish mold and chill until firm. Yield: 8 servings.

Frances Reynolds, Delta Kappa
Ellisville, Mississippi

SWEET COOKED SALAD DRESSING

This recipe, a mayonnaise substitute over 100 years old, was my grandmother's. Instead of cooking in a double boiler, you can microwave the mixture until thick, stirring every three minutes.

9 eggs, beaten	1/2 teaspoon salt
2 1/4 cups sugar	1 cup vinegar
3/4 teaspoon dry mustard	

Combine the eggs, sugar, mustard and salt in the top of a double boiler and mix well. Stir in the vinegar. Cook over simmering water until thickened, stirring frequently. Yield: 1 quart.

Julie O'Brien, Delta Delta
Christina Lake, British Columbia, Canada

"THE RECIPE" SALAD DRESSING

My five sons named this salad dressing recipe "The Recipe" when they were young. The name came from The Waltons TV show, in which each sister had her special "Recipe." My sons loved this dressing so much that they asked Grandma to bring a jug of it with her every time she came to visit.

3 cups vinegar	2 large onions, finely chopped
2 cups water	
1 cup vegetable oil	2 large garlic cloves, minced
3 cups sugar	
1/4 cup salt	1 teaspoon celery seed

Combine the vinegar, water, vegetable oil, sugar, salt, onions, garlic and celery seed in a gallon jug and shake vigorously. Let stand, covered, in the refrigerator for 24 hours, shaking several times during the resting period and once again just before using. Yield: 2 quarts.

Dorothy Donay (30 years), Laureate Xi
Coldwater, Michigan

MEMORIES

My fondest memory is when all of us kids were at home. There were six of us, four girls and two boys. The boys never had a fighting chance at the bathroom, especially on a school morning. My stepfather was a Navy cook from Arkansas. He could cook better than my Mom, and we always wanted him to cook instead of her. With six children, it was guaranteed that there was plenty of laundry, cleaning and dishes to do. There was never a dull moment in our family.

Sheryl Fuller, Xi Beta Rho
Centerville, Iowa

SWEET-AND-SOUR SALAD DRESSING

1/2 cup sugar	1/2 cup vinegar
1 cup water	1 to 2 cups vegetable oil
1/2 cup lemon juice	1 cup ketchup
1/2 teaspoon salt	1 small onion, grated or finely chopped
2 teaspoons celery seed	
1/2 teaspoon pepper	

Combine the sugar and water in a heavy saucepan and bring to a boil. Boil for 10 minutes without stirring. Add the lemon juice and boil for 5 minutes longer. Remove from heat and let cool. Stir in the salt, celery seed, pepper and vinegar. Add the vegetable oil, ketchup and onion and beat until thick. Yield: 1 quart.

Romita Carol Cohee, Delta Theta
Neodesha, Kansas

Elise Allen, Zeta Upsilon, Bradenton, Florida, makes **Easy French Dressing** by combining a can of tomato soup, 3/4 cup vinegar, 1 cup vegetable oil, 1 tablespoon each salt and Worcestershire sauce and 1 teaspoon pepper in a jar and shaking vigorously. Store in the refrigerator.